STUDIES ON CH

A series of conference volumes sponsored
by the American Council of Learned Societies.

1. The Origins of Chinese Civilization, edited by *David N. Keightley*,
University of California Press, 1982.

2. Popular Chinese Literature and Performing Arts in the People's
Republic of China, 1949–1979, edited by *Bonnie S. McDougall*, University
of California Press, 1984.

3. Class and Social Stratification in Post-Revolution China,
edited by *James L. Watson*, Cambridge University Press, 1984.

4. Popular Culture in Late Imperial China, edited by *David Johnson*,
Andrew J. Nathan, and *Evelyn S. Rawski*, University of California Press, 1985.

5. Kinship Organization in Late Imperial China, 1000–1940, edited by
Patricia Buckley Ebrey and *James L. Watson*, University of California Press, 1986.

6. The Vitality of the Lyric Voice: Shih Poetry from the Late Han
to the T'ang, edited by *Shuen-fu Lin* and *Stephen Owen*,
Princeton University Press, 1986.

7. Policy Implementation in Post-Mao China,
edited by *David M. Lampton*, University of California Press, 1987.

8. Death Ritual in Late Imperial and Modern China, edited by
James L. Watson and *Evelyn S. Rawski*, University of California Press, 1988.

9. Neo-Confucian Education: The Formative Stage, edited by *William
Theodore de Bary* and *John W. Chaffee*, University of California Press, 1989.

10. Orthodoxy in Late Imperial China, edited by *Kwang-Ching Liu*,
University of California Press, 1990.

11. Chinese Local Elites and Patterns of Dominance, edited by *Joseph W.
Esherick* and *Mary Backus Rankin*, University of California Press, 1990.

12. Marriage and Inequality in Chinese Society, edited by *Rubie S. Watson*
and *Patricia Buckley Ebrey*, University of California Press, 1991.

13. Chinese History in Economic Perspective, edited by *Thomas G. Rawski*
and *Lillian M. Li*, University of California Press, 1991.

14. Bureaucracy, Politics, and Decision Making in Post-Mao China,
edited by *Kenneth G. Lieberthal* and *David M. Lampton*,
University of California Press, 1992.

15. Pilgrims and Sacred Sites in China, edited by *Susan Naquin*
and *Chün-fang Yü*, University of California Press, 1992.

16. Ordering the World: Approaches to State and Society in Sung
Dynasty China, edited by *Robert Hymes* and *Conrad Schirokauer*, University
of California Press, 1993.

17. Chinese Families in the Post-Mao Era, edited by *Deborah Davis* and *Stevan Harrell*, University of California Press, 1993.

18. Voices of the Song Lyric in China, edited by *Pauline Yu*, University of California Press, 1994.

19. Education and Society in Late Imperial China, 1600–1900, edited by *Benjamin A. Elman* and *Alexander Woodside*, University of California Press, 1994.

20. Chinese Historical Micro-Demography, edited by *Stevan Harrell*, University of California Press, 1994.

21. The Waning of the Communist State: Economic Origins of Political Decline in China and Hungary, edited by *Andrew G. Walder*, University of California Press, 1995.

22. The Consumer Revolution in Urban China, edited by *Deborah S. Davis*, University of California Press, 2000.

23. Becoming Chinese: Passages to Modernity and Beyond, edited by *Wen-hsin Yeh*, University of California Press, 1999.

24. Ways with Words: Writing about Reading Texts from Early China, edited by *Pauline Yu, Peter Bol, Stephen Owen,* and *Willard Peterson*, University of California Press, 2000.

Ways with Words

This volume and the conference from which it resulted were supported by the Joint Committee on Chinese Studies of the American Council of Learned Societies and the Social Science Research Council.

This book is a print-on-demand volume. It is manufactured using
toner in place of ink. Type and images may be less sharp than the
same material seen in traditionally printed University of California
Press editions.

University of California Press
Berkeley and Los Angeles, California

University of California Press, Ltd.
London, England

©2000 by the Regents of the University of California

Library of Congress Cataloging-in-Publication Data

Ways with words: writing about reading texts from early China / edited by Pauline Yu . . . [et al.].
    p. cm.—(Studies on China ; 24)
  Includes bibliographical references and index.
  ISBN 0-520-21605-9 (alk. paper)—ISBN 0-520-22466-3 (paper : alk. paper)
    1. Books and reading—China. 2. Books—China—Reviews. 3. Humanities—
China. I. Title: Writing about reading texts from early China. II. Yu, Pauline, 1949–
III. Series.
Z1003.5.C45 W39 2000
001.3'0951—dc21   99-059753
                                                                                      CIP

Manufactured in the United States of America

The paper used in this publication meets the minimum requirements of ANSI/NISO
Z39.48-1992 (R 1997) (Permanence of Paper). ♾

Ways with Words

Writing about Reading Texts from Early China

EDITED BY

Pauline Yu, Peter Bol, Stephen Owen, and Willard Peterson

UNIVERSITY OF CALIFORNIA PRESS

Berkeley   Los Angeles   London

CONTENTS

ABBREVIATIONS / *xiii*

ACKNOWLEDGMENTS / *ix*

Introduction: Reading Texts in the Chinese Humanities / *1*

CHAPTER 1. *Sheng min* (*Shi jing* [Classic of Poetry],
Mao 245: "Birth of the People")
Translations
Bernhard Karlgren / *11*
Stephen Owen / *12*

Questions about the Language of *Sheng min*
David R. Knechtges / *14*

Interpreting *Sheng min*
Stephen Owen / *25*

Reading *Sheng min*
Willard Peterson / *31*

Perspective on Readings of *Sheng min*
Pauline Yu / *34*

CHAPTER 2. *Mencius* 2A.2
Translation
D. C. Lau / *41*

Are You a Sage?
Willard Peterson / *45*

"There Has Never Been One Greater Than Confucius"
Peter Bol / *49*

Perspective on Readings of *Mencius* 2A.2
Stephen Owen / *54*

CHAPTER 3. *Qi wu lun* (*Zhuangzi:* "Seeing Things as Equal")
Translation: "The Sorting Which Evens Things Out"
A. C. Graham / *58*

Look at the Finger, Not Where It Is Pointing
Stephen H. West / *71*

Vision and Identity in *Qi wu lun*
Martin Powers / *78*

On Making Noise in *Qi wu lun*
Wai-yee Li / *93*

Perspective on Readings of *Qi wu lun:* I Am Not Dreaming This
Willard Peterson / *103*

CHAPTER 4. *Heart Sūtra* (*Xin jing*)
Translations
Stephen F. Teiser / *113*
Stephen H. West / *116*

The *Heart Sūtra*
Michael A. Fuller / *118*

Heart Sūtra
Stephen H. West / *121*

Perspective on Readings of the *Heart Sūtra:* The Perfection
of Wisdom and the Fear of Buddhism
Stephen F. Teiser / *130*

CHAPTER 5. *Zi jing fu Fengxian yong huai wu bai zi*
(Du Fu, "Going from the Capital to Fengxian")
Translation
Stephen Owen / *146*

What's in a Title? "Expressing My Feelings on Going from the Capital to Fengxian
Prefecture: Five Hundred Characters" by Du Fu
David R. Knechtges / *149*

Du Fu, "Song of My Cares en Route from the Capital to Fengxian"
Lynn Struve / *160*

The Crisis of Witnessing in Du Fu's "A Song of My Thoughts When Going
from the Capital to Fengxian: Five Hundred Words"
Wai-yee Li / *165*

Perspective on Readings of Du Fu, *Zi jing fu Fengxian yong huai wu bai zi*
Stephen Owen / *170*

CHAPTER 6. *Yingying zhuan* (Yuan Zhen, "Biography of Yingying")
Translation
Stephen Owen / *173*

The Story of Yingying
Pauline Yu / *182*

Mixture of Genres and Motives for Fiction in "Yingying's Story"
Wai-yee Li / *185*

On *Yingying zhuan,* by Yuan Zhen
Katherine Carlitz / *192*

Perspective on Readings of *Yingying zhuan*
Peter Bol / *198*

CHAPTER 7. *Bi fa ji* (Jing Hao, "Notes on the Method for the Brush")
Translation and Commentary
Stephen H. West / *202*

Bi fa ji
Stephen Owen / *213*

How To Read a Chinese Painting: Jing Hao's *Bi fa ji*
Martin Powers / *219*

Perspective on Readings of "The Record of the Method of the Brush"
Willard Peterson / *236*

GLOSSARY / *245*
CHINESE TEXTS / *261*
CONTRIBUTORS / *277*
INDEX / *279*

ABBREVIATIONS

BIHP	*Bulletin of the Institute of History and Philology*
BMFEA	*Bulletin of the Museum of Far Eastern Antiquities*
Sbby	*Si bu bei yao*
ZZ	*Zhuangzi*
ZZJS	*Zhuangzi jishi,* comp. Guo Qingfan, ed. Wang Xiaoyu (Beijing: Zhonghua shuju, 1982), 4 vols.
ZZZJ	*Zhuangzi zuanjian,* ed. Qian Mu (Hong Kong: Tongnan yinwu chubanshe,1951).

ACKNOWLEDGMENTS

The editors wish to express their profound gratitude to the Joint Committee on Chinese Studies of the American Council of Learned Societies and the Social Science Research Council for the grant in support of the workshop that took place in June of 1994, during which these essays were first presented and discussed. We would also like to acknowledge the insightful comments provided by the two anonymous readers for the University of California Press. Two graduate students at UCLA, Wang Chaohua and Wendy Swartz, provided invaluable assistance in the preparation of the manuscript, for which we are deeply grateful. Any errors or infelicities remain, of course, our collective responsibility. We thank our fellow participants for their contributions and hope that this selection of their essays will be as illuminating to other readers as it was to the twelve who first discussed them.

Introduction:
Reading Texts in the Chinese Humanities

This volume owes its inception to a conviction that reading is an essential art of the humanities, and one that students and scholars alike have great trouble with. It offers varying interpretations of seven texts produced in China during the first two of the three millennia of its intellectual and literary history. We believe that these readings and commentaries by twelve scholars of differing disciplinary training serve three purposes in the intellectual life of American education today.

First, we wish to encourage the reading and discussion of particular texts from disparate cultural traditions as a core experience in a humanistic education. By contributing a set of texts from traditions which are Chinese but also part of the shared legacy of East Asia, and which thus clearly fall into the admittedly problematic category of the non-Western, we seek to address what appears to be a continuing dominance, if not exclusivity, of Mediterranean humanistic concerns in Western academic institutions today. Curricula that take seriously the diversity of cultural traditions throughout the world should provide the opportunity to find something worth learning, and even something to be seduced by, in texts that have guided and troubled East Asia's humanists over the centuries.

Second, we hope that these readings will serve to challenge the presumption of a monolithic China that is all too often promoted by scholarship and popular culture alike, in both China and the West. Responding to Western political and economic domination of the world order, Chinese nationalism has stressed the ways in which China is possessed of an integrated, homogenous, state-centered culture (the same is true in Japan, Korea, and Vietnam), an at best unsubstantiated notion that European and American discourse has eagerly adopted and defined in opposition to modern "Western" values. This is a China to be transformed into something like us—democratic, scientific, capitalist, or socialist. The proponents of this image have regarded the intellectual and literary traditions in which our texts were transmitted only as camouflage for a despotic state, the self-justificatory instruments of unselfcritical elites. In seeking to resist this reductionism common to the study of non-Western areas, we would do well to recall the wisdom of our forebears, for among the first European intellectuals to travel to China and the first Chinese thinkers to take European traditions seriously— the Jesuits and the literati circles they encountered in seventeenth-century China—we do not find this grand opposition between East and West, or even between the Great Ming Kingdom and Italy, France, or England.

Third, we believe that a return to the particular texts that have constituted a cultural tradition can both illuminate the workings of that historical process and sharpen our understanding of interpretive practices that are all too easily taken for granted. As in the past, when we meet as scholars in the humanities today, distinctions in our basic commitments emerge, presenting us with choices that have consequences for the tasks of reading and writing. To what ends, for example, do we turn our attention to a specific text? Is the study of the particular justified by its contribution to the understanding of the whole of which it is constituent, or is the study of the whole important only as it contextualizes some particular? Although this may seem to be merely choosing sides in the hermeneutic circle, there is a more profound principle at stake here. In the first case we see the particular also as data for constructing knowledge of some larger event; we choose, for example, to read a poem or essay as a means of envisioning an author responding to questions in his times. In the second case we assume that the particular is always greater than any whole that may be said to contain it; that is, a particular text may be contextualized in many ways, but there is in that text a surplus that exceeds the aggregate of its contextualizations. Humanistic inquiry has room for both construing the larger picture and returning to reflect on the particular text, but our paths cross on the ground of the particular text as we proceed in different directions. The essays in this volume seek to chart these various trajectories.

The Chinese humanities have never constituted a single cultural entity. In these texts we are working mainly with two different traditions, one literary and the other intellectual historical. This is not simply a consequence of arbitrarily applying the distinction, familiar to Mediterranean civilization, between literature and philosophy or rhetoric and philosophy to the corpus of Chinese texts. There is no question that nineteenth- and twentieth-century Western ideas about literature and philosophy have colored how European and American scholars read Chinese texts. We should recognize, too, that they exerted considerable influence on twentieth-century Chinese scholars' own study of China's literary and intellectual traditions. Two well-known works by members of the "New Tide Society" from Peking University's first years, for example, were conceived under their influence and have profoundly shaped subsequent study: Fung Yu-lan's history of Chinese philosophy, which surveyed Chinese intellectual traditions in terms of categories such as rationalism and philosophy, and Guo Shaoyu's history of Chinese literary criticism, which reviewed ideas about literature and culture (wen) in terms of an imported notion of pure literature. And yet, for at least two millennia Chinese scholars, like their Western counterparts, differentiated between the study of literary traditions and that of intellectual historical traditions, and between literary and intellectual historical texts. (There is, however, one notable exception: in the opposition between philosophy and literature in China, the latter is not, as Plato contended, "fiction.")

While we are not suggesting that this distinction was fixed or constant, for present purposes it suffices to point out that at least from the Han dynasty on scholars worked with some version of these two categories. Literary works were separated from other categories within the written traditions of the bureaucratic elite almost from the beginning of the imperial era. The earliest bibliographic division, which Ban Gu then adopted for the "Treatise on Bibliography" in his *History of the Han Dynasty*, included the Classics, the various schools of thought, poems and rhapsodies, epigraphy, numerology, and the skillful arts (medicine, etc.). The fourfold division that later became standard simply was Classics, schools of thought, history, and belles-lettres. Beginning in the Han dynasty, historians also began to distinguish between those who made their mark through literary accomplishment and those known for their achievements in Confucian scholarship; for this reason they therefore grouped standard biographies in dynastic histories into *Wenyuan* ("literary garden") and *Rulin* ("scholarly grove") chapters. The modern word *wenxue* is translated as "literature," but as a term it dates back at least to the *Analects* of Confucius, and by Tang times could be understood as referring to two related but different kinds of activity: literary composition (wen) and writing concerned with moral values (xue). This seems quite congruent with a distinction between literature and philosophy.

As a consequence, within the modern university students of Chinese literature generally follow a somewhat different course of study from those working on Chinese intellectual history. Even when trained in the same department they are likely to have had different courses, to have read different books, to have mastered different styles of writing, to be schooled in different traditions of knowledge, and to be interested in different questions. For some these differences become less marked as learning broadens, but they persist nonetheless in the curricula and reading lists of the disciplines.

But the problem with adopting such distinctions in any rigidly consistent way in looking at the Chinese past, however familiar they may seem to us, is that doing so tends to universalize them, and it furthermore obscures shifts in the boundaries between the operative categories. That delineations between literary and historical studies were not, in fact, static is true both of the claims that might be made about texts as well as of those the texts themselves appear to make.

To illustrate this problem, consider two phrases attributed to Confucius. According to the first, "What is said without literary elaboration will not go far in practice" (*Zuo zhuan,* Xiang 25). Let us suppose that this is intended as a reminder that "how you say it" matters: to have influence one needs to say things in the right manner, with the understanding in this case that the right way has to do with embellishment, allusion, rules of expression, and elegance, which we now might suppose are of interest to scholars of literature. The second phrase is the straightforward statement that "Words are simply to get the point across" (*Lunyu,* 15.41). This emphasis on conveying meaning, we might expect, is more likely to appeal to philosophers, to those who regard speaking and writing as tools of communication, who employ technical vocabularies, and who wish that language could be simply transparent. Another classic formulation of this position is that of Zhuangzi: once we have the fish we can forget the fishtrap. By contrast, "What is said without literary elaboration will not go far in practice" ought to appeal to those literary figures who see that language mediates between people but also provides templates for perception and understanding, who understand that words have histories of usage, who insist that meaning is embedded in the manner of expression and thus irreducible to a propositional level, and who may imagine that language creates reality.

Both expressions attributed to Confucius contain arguable assumptions: that the manner in which something is said can determine how it is put into practice over the long term, and that it is possible simply to make a point without implying or revealing anything else and without requiring artful means to do it. The first expression was frequently cited in the introductions to literary biographies in the early seventh century, and yet it also signals the seventh-century approach to the exegesis of the Classics. The second phrase gained currency in the eleventh century—at times in contrast to the first—and although it well represented the practice of moral philosophers who began to eschew writing in literary genres as a teaching mode in favor of dialogue and lecture, it was used more commonly by scholars more "literary" than "philosophical."

Another way to frame this issue of differentiating texts is to focus on the relationship between the claims being made by a text itself and the means by which they can be validated. Consider, for example, a chronicle presented with the authorial assertion that no more than the simple facts are being recorded, as opposed to an analytic essay that purports to explain why it all happened. While any examination of this contrast also forces us to ask to what extent the meaning of either text can be taken apart from the form of representation, an even more salient question might be how we might test either claim. Any answer would clearly have to be sensitive to the case. Indeed, recalling our earlier discussion about the relative hermeneutic priority to be assigned to the individual text and some larger whole, we might think that if the particular example, this poem or that commentary, could be completely explained by any given articulation of context, then it would disappear. But how can this in fact happen? We must remember, after all, that context—while prior—is in practice always a retrospective construction to which we are led not only by the particularities of this text but of others as well. We are defining the questions to which this text is an answer, although we judge some definitions better than others. From this (what some would call) literary point of view, any text can be explained by many contexts, none of which, even in the aggregate, can fully account for the particular. Intellectual historians, whom some would associate with the use of the text as material for larger arguments about authors, audiences, and times, are from this perspective making choices about what information matters most. For them, a text cannot be read adequately without establishing the appropriate context.

Interestingly, the most enduring context in China is precisely what reveals the permeability of the borders between the literary and the intellectual historical—the state within whose frame we can see an important homology between the two fields. They were, from Han times on, the primary semi-autonomous arenas of cultural authority in an empire in which, from antiquity through Tang, the court had arrogated to itself the right to confer honor, wealth, justice, and power. In declaring that they—rather than the emperor and his minions—were ultimately responsible for defining good scholarship and good writing, writers and thinkers were also claiming a right to confer cultural prestige, independent of the court. Moreover, they placed a premium, however bittersweet, on achieving prestige through those activities rather than in public life. And, of course, they did so before the same elite public over which the state claimed a monopoly in granting such honor. An integrated intellectual and literary history of China, a history of the Chinese humanities, would include an account of attempts by the state to co-opt the literary and the intellectual and to make itself the source of all patronage, but it would also include accounts of figures who emerged from these fields and whom the state was later pushed to honor, despite their own lack of public success. From Confucius and Qu Yuan on, those who continued literary and intellectual traditions maintained a powerful mythology of socially acknowledged value that was unrecognized by political power, and perhaps necessarily so.

Literary and intellectual historical figures produced texts that spoke to their respective pasts, to the state, and to each other. They vied to compete with political authority, to represent the oppositional other in a world where the court was the acme of power, wealth, and cultural prestige. And yet in this homology we can see certain differences in assumptions, certain possibilities, that bear on the use of political power, the distribution of social prestige, and ultimately the reading of texts. These are assumptions about why we read, why on occasion we write, and how we choose to do either.

There is a third possible way to differentiate texts, one raised in an early discussion regarding the selection of texts for this volume. This is between "texts that do it" and "texts that talk about doing it": the question of performativity. At first glance this distinction appears to offer another means of distinguishing between the kinds of texts that have become central to literary studies and those of intellectual history. For example, a poem about being alone on a starry night can be read (and probably should be) as enacting the complex emotional response to that experience. The poem is "doing it" in that through language it creates an emotional event in the reading of the poem itself, without which we would not have the experience of that event. (Of course, some readers might remember here the famous remark from Auden's poem, "In Memory of W. B. Yeats": "poetry makes nothing happen.") A text that represents a persuader explaining to a feudal lord how he should govern his state is a text that "talks about doing it." The talking about governing does not enact the governing.

It is instructive to consider how this distinction breaks down, and here, in fact, we may espy something important about the relation of this volume of essays to the texts from early China our readers are writing about. At first— to give an account of our doubts—it seemed that differentiating between "texts that do it" and "texts that talk about doing it" was really an issue within contemporary literary studies, where it has been said that writing about literature (literary criticism, in other words) has become the most influential high literary form of our day. If "doing it" means "doing poems," then "talking about doing it" is "talking about doing poems," a step removed. Here, too, we can find a similar distinction in China, where a new bibliographic category was created in recognition of the popularity of notes evaluating and appreciating poetry (*shihua*) and where there was already a long tradition of theories about the composition and function of culture and literature. But if we turn to the intellectual historical side, can we assume that writing about thinking (or about how one does think but should not, and ought to think but does not) is already a step removed from thinking in action? Suppose we conceive of such writing as the practice of defining and justifying values; is it not "doing it" (where "doing it" is "thinking") as much as a poem about being alone on a starry night? At this point it seemed to us, depending on how we are defining the "it" some author is doing, that we could argue that the source-texts of intellectual history consist of writings that are indeed performing, in that they are the unfolding of thinking about values. Intellectual historians might argue that all "literary" works are in fact intellectual works in this sense, although on the face of it they remain more closely tied to the specific instance and particular occasion.

Are there then works that "talk about doing it" in intellectual history? One could argue that commentaries on philosophical texts, histories of philosophy, and histories of ideas and intellectuals all in fact are. Here too there is a long Chinese tradition. Consider the commentary on Laozi in the *Han Fei*, or the discussion of various schools in the "Tianxia" chapter of the *Zhuangzi*. We have distinguished between the Laozi text and the Han Fei talking about the Laozi text. But does this distinction still pertain if the "doing it" we have in mind is "thinking"? It cannot be maintained once we understand texts as representations of unfolding thought and affect. We could recognize that different kinds of texts were being produced and that in this case, for example, one text was providing the occasion for another text, but both texts are "doing it" in their own way. The distinction between literary and intellectual historical approaches thus does not have to be a function of different assumptions about language, or texts, or the nature of knowledge and reality. What matters is that we and the readers and writers of the last two thousand years in China have found it useful to keep making a distinction, even as we keep changing both its applications and our understanding of the extent to which it is fixed. And this is where we end up as scholars in America at the end of the twentieth century writing about these Chinese texts. We are adding another layer, using them as occasions for our own thinking. In writing about texts we are presenting our thinking, and we are also continuing a process of thinking through writing about texts that participates in the literary and intellectual historical traditions of China.

The texts we consider in this volume try to do different things, and the assumptions of two millennia ago are still evident. In accepting the mandate to illuminate the complexity of the Chinese humanities, we may find one important justification for the institutionalized distinction between literature and intellectual history: without it we would not be sure that different kinds of texts would be attended to. The majority of the scholars who have contributed to this volume have been trained in one of these two disciplines, and the works we chose by and large came from both as well. (We have done much less with two other kinds of texts—those from religious traditions and those of the fine arts.) In preparing these essays for the workshop that first brought us together, however, we agreed to adhere to the principle that all would read texts usually in the preserve of the other, and we asked that our writers reflect as explicitly as possible on the relevance of their disciplinary training to their approach to the work in question. As coeditors we have, with one exception, provided "Perspectives" on each set of readings as well. Reviewing the contributions to this volume the reader may find in fact that there are no radical extremes, that we dwell on the example at hand rather than the course of inquiry and training that led us to cross paths. Given the fact that in contemporary academic discourse more generally the lines have blurred, this should not surprise us: the new historicist reader of literature, for instance, is perhaps far more removed from the conservative center of literary studies than from history, just as the historian who has taken the "linguistic turn" may find more likely alliances with literary critics than with contextualizing intellectual historians. Even more striking is the degree to which both literary and intellectual historical possibilities emerged in all the texts, which, for the moment, themselves took precedence over our own scholarly programs and polemics.

We chose four texts that might be called monuments. We began with "Seeing Things as Equal" from the *Zhuangzi,* on the grounds that it has been fully assimilated by both literary and philosophical studies (a matter that perhaps ought to give us pause) and speaks to issues of language, meaning, and thought. "Seeing Things as Equal" deploys both playful language and a technical vocabulary; it profoundly doubts the possibilities for ultimate justification of any intellectual position yet is itself an example of rigorous disputation. We followed this with two texts we thought belonged unquestionably to the different fields. Du Fu's "Going from the Capital to Fengxian," from his "Meditation on History in One Hundred Rhymes," insists on being a Du Fu poem. Pious and moving, cultured and committed, it will be claimed by no one as philosophy. And yet as the discussion of this work unfolded it became clear that it was also possible to read "Going from the Capital to Fengxian" as both explicating and illustrating the poet's claim to authority over politics and his cultural grounds. Mencius's discussion of "cultivating the flood-like *qi*" (*Mencius* 2A.2) became one of the central philosophical statements of the Neo-Confucian tradition and is a much-debated piece in contemporary discussions of the text as a whole. Yet here, too, the dividing line was not all it was supposed to be, for the other half of Mencius's self-justification is his "insight into words" or "manners of speech." As a fourth "big" text, the *Heart Sūtra* was chosen to recognize a textual tradition that lies outside the standard categories of state bibliography and to introduce a seminal Buddhist text with the potential for a radical questioning of the value of intellectual culture. It was presumed to be the most difficult for any of us to assimilate into our own traditions. (Stephen Teiser's essay was solicited after the workshop itself and provides both a reading and a perspective on fellow contributions.)

The other texts supplemented these four and extended the range of our discussions. "Birth of the People," one of the oldest poems in the *Classic of Poetry,* is both an incantation and a justification for a sacrificial ceremony that reaches back to the origins of the Zhou people. The "Biography of Ying-ying" by the Tang poet and statesman Yuan Zhen is a famous example of the classical tale, one which is morally problematic in addition to being situated in the emerging culture of literati examination candidates. Jing Hao's "Notes on the Method for the [Painter's] Brush" aims to define "good" painting; it is also an example of what in the tenth century was "traditional" aesthetic theory.

Short texts like these allowed us to focus our attention. This did not make them easier to read. The written traditions of China may draw on the same body of characters and grammatical structures, but the perplexing differences in usage and reference over two millennia are legion. We acknowledge freely that translation is interpretation and that a command of the language of the original often requires great erudition; readers will note that references to and renditions of the Chinese texts in the various essays appear in as non-homogeneous a format as students are likely to encounter them in class. Need-less to say, editions of the original texts are equally heterogeneous. While we requested of participants essays of a length short enough to approximate what our students are usually expected to produce, we have not tried to simplify arguments or tone down scholarly excesses for the non-sinological audience. If we want the practice of the humanities to include many cultures and to cross boundaries between past and present, between ancient China and the United States today, and between history and literature, then we must learn to work around the occasional transliteration and the seemingly impenetra-ble scholarly reference. This is not the time to try to create a new canon of essential texts or imagine a new one-dimensional China for easy digestion.

Given the venerable tradition of literary and intellectual historical an-thologies in China, it has surprised us to find this a book without precedent. There is a place, we believe, for a volume that aims to show that the ways are various in which we as individuals—singly and in concert—can read and be puzzled by, can resist and be moved by, old Chinese texts. In presenting this series of short essays as material for reading, reflecting, and writing, we hope to restore the complexity of voice and diversity of interest both to the hu-manities of China and to Western humanistic inquiry as well. We ask only that humanists schooled in other areas be willing to look beyond the famil-iar and discover something of what is possible; thus encouraged, they will, we hope, gather their own teachers and friends in an effort to make Chinese traditions part of their own humanity.

ONE

Sheng min
Shi jing (Classic of Poetry),
Mao 245: "Birth of the People"

TRANSLATION OF SHENG MIN

Bernhard Karlgren

1. The one who first bore our [people =] tribe was [lady] Yüan of Kiang; how did she bear the [people =] tribe? She [was able =] understood well to bring yin and si sacrifices [in order to eliminate her having no child =] that she might no longer be childless; she trod on the big toe of God's footprint, she became elated, she was [increased =] enriched, she was blessed; and so she [was moved =] became pregnant, and [it was soon =] it came about quickly;[1] she bore, she bred: that was Hou Tsi ["Prince Millet"].—2. She fulfilled her months, and the first-born then came forth; there was no bursting, no rending, no injury, no harm, thus manifesting the divine nature of it;[2] did God on High not give her ease, did he not enjoy [her] sacrifices! [Quietly:] tranquilly she bore her son.—3. They laid him in a narrow lane, the oxen and sheep [at their legs =] between their legs nurtured him; they laid him in a forest of the plain, he [met with =] was found by those who cut the forest of the plain; they laid him on cold ice, birds covered and protected him; then the birds went away, and Hou Tsi wailed; it carried far, it was [great =] strong, his voice then became [great =] loud.—4. And then he crawled, [then] he was able to [straddle =] stride, to stand firmly; and so he sought food for his mouth; he planted it [sc. the soil] with large beans; the large beans were [streamer-like =] rankly-waving; the [culture of grain =] grain cultivated had plenty of ears, the hemp and wheat was [covering =] thick, the gourd stems bore ample fruit.—5. Hou Tsi's husbandry had the method of helping [the growth]; he cleared away

Reprinted with permission from B. Karlgren, *The Book of Odes* (Stockholm: Museum of Far Eastern Antiquities, 1971).

1. After the sacrifice to obtain child.
2. The miraculous conception.

the rank grass; he sowed it [sc. the ground] with the yellow riches; it was [regular =] of even growth and luxuriant; it was sown; it became tall, it grew, it flowered and set ears, it became firm and fine; it had ripe ears, it had solid kernels; and then he had his house in T'ai.—6. He sent down [to the people] the fine cereals; there was black millet, double-kernelled black millet, millet with red sprouts, with white sprouts; he extended over it [sc. the ground] the black millet and the double-kernelled, he reaped it, he [acred it =] took it by acres; he extended over it the millet with red sprouts and with white, he carried them on the shoulder, he carried them on the back; with them he went home and initiated a sacrifice.—7. Our sacrifice, what is it like? Some pound [the grain], some bale it out, some sift it, some tread it; we wash it so as to become soaked, we steam it so as to become steamed through; and then we lay plans, we think it over, we take southernwood, we sacrifice fat; we take a ram to sacrifice to the Spirits of the road; and then we roast, we broil, in order to start the following year.—8. We fill [food] in the *tou* vessels, in the *tou* and the *teng* vessels; as soon as the fragrance ascends, God on High [tranquilly =] placidly enjoys it; the far-reaching fragrance is truly [correct =] good; Hou Tsi initiated the sacrifice, and the [multitude:] people has given no offence nor cause for regret[3] unto the present day.

TRANSLATION OF *CLASSIC OF POETRY* CCXLV: "SHE BORE THE FOLK"

Stephen Owen

*She who first bore the folk—
Jiang it was, First Parent.

How was it she bore the folk?—
she knew the rite and sacrifice.
To rid herself of sonlessness

she trod the god's toeprint and she was glad.
She was made great, on her luck settled,
the seed stirred, it was quick.
She gave birth, she gave suck,
and this was Lord Millet.

3. By neglecting the sacrifice.

When her months had come to term,
her firstborn sprang up.
Not splitting, not rending,
working no hurt, no harm.
He showed his godhead glorious,
the high god was greatly soothed.
He took great joy in those rites
and easily she bore her son.

She set him in a narrow lane,
but sheep and cattle warded him
She set him in the wooded plain,
he met with those who logged the plain.
She set him on cold ice,
birds sheltered him with wings.
Then the birds left him
and Lord Millet wailed.
This was long and this was loud;
his voice was a mighty one.

And then he crept and crawled,
he stood upright, he stood straight.
He sought to feed his mouth,
and planted there the great beans.
The great beans' leaves were fluttering,
the rows of grain were bristling.
Hemp and barley dense and dark,
the melons, plump and round.

Lord Millet in his farming
had a way to help things grow:
He rid the land of thick grass,
he planted there a glorious growth.
It was in squares, it was leafy,
it was planted, it grew tall.
It came forth, it formed ears,
it was hard, it was good.
Its tassels bent, it was full,
he had his household there in Tai.

He passed us down these wondrous grains:
our black millets, of one and two kernels,
Millets whose leaves sprout red or white,

he spread the whole land with black millet,
And reaped it and counted the acres,
spread it with millet sprouting red or white,
hefted on shoulders, loaded on backs,
he took it home and began this rite.

And how goes this rite we have?—
at times we hull, at times we scoop,
at times we winnow, at times we stomp,
we hear it slosh as we wash it,
we hear it puff as we steam it.
Then we reckon, then we consider,
take artemisia, offer fat.

We take a ram for the flaying,
then we roast it, then we sear it,
to rouse up the following year.

We heap the wooden trenchers full,
wooden trenchers, earthenware platters.
And as the scent first rises
the high god is peaceful and glad.
This great odor is good indeed,
for Lord Millet began the rite,
and hopefully free from failing or fault,
it has lasted until now.

QUESTIONS ABOUT THE LANGUAGE OF *SHENG MIN*

David R. Knechtges

Mao shi 245, *Sheng min,* is a seminal poem in the early Chinese poetic tradition. First, the poem probably dates from the early Western Zhou, and thus it is one of the earliest extant Chinese poems. Second, it is a poem about a cultural hero, Hou Ji, commonly known in English as Lord Millet. Hou Ji was the reputed founder of the Zhou royal house, and this poem in praise of him provides valuable information about early Chinese cultural values. In order to read this poem, or any other poem in the *Shi jing,* one must attempt to resolve, or at least consider, a number of questions that long have tormented readers of this hallowed, ancient text. First, one must consider the question of the nature of the received version of the *Shi.* Although the *Shi* may have been put together in its present arrangement as early as the time of Confucius, the text that we now read was not established until the Han. The received text of the *Shi jing* is the *Mao shi* version. The *Mao shi* purports to represent a tradition of interpretation that originated with a man named Mao Heng, who lived in the second century B.C.E. He reputedly was a student of one of Xunzi's disciples and is known as the Elder Mao (Da Mao gong) to distinguish him from another member of this school, named Mao Chang (Xiao Mao gong).

The Mao School, which was a *guwen* school, claimed that the *Shi* originally contained 311 poems, but six were lost during the Warring States and Qin periods. The text of this school was not officially accepted until the end of the Former Han. The *Mao shi* contains a detailed commentary to the entire text. Exactly who wrote this commentary is disputed. The traditional belief is that it was written by Mao Heng. However, it is likely that the commentary was refined and elaborated on by subsequent generations of Mao School scholars, especially Mao Chang.

We do not have the Mao version of the *Shi* intact, for at the end of the Later Han dynasty the *Mao shi* was edited by the important classical exegete Zheng Xuan (127–200). His work is known under the title *Mao shi zhuan jian* (Commentary and Annotations to the Mao Version of the *Songs*). Zheng Xuan did not fully follow the Mao text, but adopted in a number of places readings and interpretations of the *Sanjia shi* of the Lu, Qi, and Han schools, which prevailed for much of the Former Han period. Although Zheng Xuan's text of the *Shi* inevitably suffered some corruption and alteration in the process of transmission, the received version of the *Mao shi zhuan jian* is the earliest known complete text of the *Shi*. Although one can find occasional variant readings among the fragments of the *Sanjia shi* and the Han Stone Classic version,[4] the *Mao shi zhuan jian* is the text on which scholars must rely, for the earliest "transcription" not only of the poems but of the Mao Commentary itself.

What this means is that the *Shi* text to which we have access is far removed from the time of the original composition of the songs themselves, some of which may date from the early Western Zhou. Furthermore, Zheng Xuan prepared his version of the *Shi* after the regularization of the script, which is clearly in evidence at the time of the compilation of the *Shuowen jiezi* in 100 C.E. The script and text of the received version of the *Shi* have been influenced by the ways in which the Han scholars wrote and pronounced the words of the songs. William R. Baxter, for example, has shown that the phonology of the *Shi jing* has been significantly influenced by Han dynasty

---

4. For a reconstruction of the *Sanjia shi* fragments see Chen Qiaocong, *Sanjia shi yishuo kao*, in *Huang Qing jingjie xubian;* and Wang Xianqian, *Shi sanjia yi jishu*, in *Shisi jing xinshu* (Taipei: Shijie shuju, 1956–61). There also are fragments of a Western Han manuscript of the *Shi* found in Fuyang, Anhui, in the mid-1970s. See Hu Pingsheng and Han Ziqiang, "Fuyang Hanjian *Shijing* jianlun," *Wenwu* (1984, no. 8): 13–21.

pronunciation and script. As Baxter aptly puts it, the *Shi* "as we now have it is a Zhōu text in Hàn clothing: both its script and, to some extent, its text have been influenced by post-*Shījīng* phonology, and are not always reliable guides to the phonology of Old Chinese."[5]

Baxter's caution about the unreliability of the received text of the *Shi* as a guide to Old Chinese phonology is important, for it tells us that the versions of the *Shi* poems that we read today are not the ancient Zhou versions, but late Han dynasty recensions of them. The Zhou versions were circulated primarily by means of oral transmission. In fact, according to Liu Xin (50 B.C.E.–C.E. 23), the reason that the *Shi* survived the Qin burning of the books intact is that it was recited as opposed to being transmitted in a written form.[6] Even if the *Shi* were written down in Zhou times, that written text undoubtedly would look different from the *Mao shi zhuan jian*. The script would not have been uniform, and if we were fortunate enough to have multiple versions of the *Shi*, there very likely would be variant ways of writing the same word.

Furthermore, each song had its own history before it was included in the *Shi*. We must remember that the *Shi jing* is after all an anthology, an anthology of songs selected and arranged by an unknown editor or editors who served at the Zhou court in the sixth century B.C.E. Many of these songs may have been part of a musical repertoire that extended back as far as the beginning of the Zhou (twelfth century B.C.E.). The lyrics to these songs undoubtedly were altered, either by faulty transmission or perhaps even deliberate revision to fit changing tastes. Thus, Fu Sinian has argued that the oldest pieces in the *Shi*, the "*Zhou Song*," suffered greatest damage in the process of transmission, and much of the damage occurred perhaps even before the songs were incorporated into the *Shi* anthology.[7]

I mention the problematic nature of the *Shi* text here, for I think it is important for us to understand what it is we are reading when we read a piece such as *Sheng min*. *Sheng min* belongs to one of the putatively older sections of the *Shi*, the "Ya" or "Elegantiae." The word *ya* (Old Chinese **ngrah*) was used in Zhou times interchangeably with *xia* (Old Chinese **grah*) to mean "Chinese" as distinct from non-Chinese. *Ya* also has the meaning of "correct" or "orthodox" (*zheng*) and perhaps indicates that these songs were the proper songs that were performed only at the Zhou court. *Ya* further has the sense of "elegant" and "dignified," and in this sense it may refer to the solemn and

5. See "Zhou and Han Phonology in the *Shījīng*," in William G. Boltz and Michael C. Shapiro, eds., *Studies in the Historical Phonology of Asian Languages* (Amsterdam and Philadelphia: John Benjamins Publishing Company, 1991), 30.

6. See *Han shu* (Beijing: Zhonghua shuju, 1962), 30.1708.

7. See Fu Sinian, "Zhou song shuo," *BIHP* 1 (1928): 95–117.

elegant setting in which the songs were performed—the Zhou court and ceremonial halls. Finally, it is possible that *ya* was used in a multiple sense: the *ya* songs are the orthodox, refined court songs of the royal Zhou domain (Xia).[8]

Whatever the precise meaning of *ya*, one can assume that the *Sheng min* was not only a product of the Zhou court, it was a song that played an important role in early Zhou court ritual. It was performed at court to music and probably involved ritual dance. Thus, in our reading of the piece, we must keep in mind its musical and ritual character.

Turning to the *Sheng min* song itself, we see that the received text consists of eight stanzas. The odd-numbered stanzas contain ten lines, and the even-numbered stanzas have eight lines. There does not seem to be any consistent rhyming pattern.

The text is filled with problematical readings, most of which have been argued and discussed by scholars from the time of the Mao Commentary and Zheng Xuan down to the twentieth century. The first stanza presents us with a host of enigmas and questions that long have baffled interpreters of the poem:

> She who first gave birth to the people,
> That was Jiang Yuan.
> How did she give birth to the people?
> She was able to perform the *yin*[a] and the *si*[a],
> In order to exorcise her childlessness.
> She trod on the big toe of the Lord of Heaven's footprint,
> And she was elated by what enlarged her, by what blessed her.
> She became pregnant, she was cautious.
> Then she gave birth and nourished [a child],
> This was Lord Millet.

The general sense of this first stanza is easy enough to understand: it tells of the miraculous conception of the first ancestor of the house of Zhou, Hou Ji. However, there is much in these lines that we do not understand. On the philological level there is the problem of how to construe lines five and six:

> "*Lü di wu min xin, you jie you zhi*"
> She trod on the big toe of the Lord of Heaven's footprint,
> And she was elated by what enlarged her, by what blessed her.

The punctuation here is not certain. The word *xin*[a] in all ancient texts is attached to *Lü di wu min*[a]. However, as Karlgren and Wang Li show, *min*[a] (*məh) rhymes with *zhi* group rhymes, and thus *xin*[a] / *hjəm must be separated from

---

8. See Sun Zuoyun, "Shuo ya," reprinted in *Shi jing yanjiu lunji*, ed. Lin Qingzhang (Taipei: Xuesheng shuju, 1983), 51–61.

it.[9] Indeed, this line as cited in the *Erya* does not contain *xin^a*.[10] If *xin^a* does not belong with this line, how should it be construed? It can be attached to *you jie you zhi*, as is done in some modern texts. One solution is to treat it as a single-syllable line.[11] It also may be an extra-metrical syllable that is a vestige of an early musical pattern.

These lines are also a good example of the obscurity of the language of the text and the difficulties involved in determining what word a particular graph was intended to represent. The graph *min^a*, for example, which the Mao Commentary glosses as *ji^a*, "quick," very likely is a loan for *mu^a*, "big toe," an explanation that Zheng Xuan gives. However, the equivalence of *min^a* and *mu^a* was already noted in the *Erya*, and Zheng Xuan very likely derived his explanation from it.[12] In fact, the Han Stone Classic version of this line reads another *mu^b* for *min^a*.

More problematic is the line *you jie you zhi*, which also occurs in *Mao shi* 211. Karlgren summarizes the various interpretations in Gloss #679. The Mao Commentary explains *jie/ *kriat* as *da* "big" and *zhi^a/ *tjəh* as *fu lu suo zhi^a* ("that on which the blessings settled"). Karlgren seems to understand *zhi^a* as *zhi^b* "blessing." He construes *you^a* as a "mark of the passive" (p. 142). Thus, he translates "she was [increased =] enriched, she was blessed." However, as Paul L-M Serruys has noted, Karlgren's explanation of *you^a* as a passive marker ignores its more common usage as a relative pronoun.[13] If *xin^a* is attached to *you jie you zhi*, the line could be translated "She was elated at what enriched her, at what blessed her." It is also possible that *you^a* may be a loan for some other word. For example, Gao Heng construes *you^a* as *nai* "and then."[14]

However, the meaning of *jie* is far from clear. Zheng Xuan interprets *jie* as *zuo you* or a "side-building" (literally "[buildings] on the left and right"). Although Karlgren remarks that "All this is obviously impossible," *jie* could mean something like "secluded" or "sequestered" in the sense of Lady Jiang's secluding herself after performing the ritual treading of Di's toeprint. C. H. Wang's "She lived in seclusion for a long time" is a very free rendering, but perhaps conveys the basic sense of *jie*.[15]

9. See Bernhard Karlgren, *Glosses on the Book of Odes* (Stockholm: Museum of Far Eastern Antiquities, 1964), Gloss #866; and Wang Li, *Shi jing yundu* (Shanghai: Shanghai guji chubanshe, 1980), 348.

10. See *Erya yishu, Sbby*, A3.16a.

11. See C. H. Wang, *The Bell and the Drum*, 38 n. 6.

12. See *Erya yishu, Sbby*, A3.16a.

13. See "Studies in the Language of the *Shih-ching:* I, the Final Particle *Yi*," *Early China* 16 (1991): 149 n. 73.

14. See *Shi jing jinzhu* (Shanghai: Shanghai guji chubanshe, 1980), 402 n. 6.

15. See *From Ritual to Allegory, Seven Essays in Early Chinese Poetry* (Hong Kong: The Chinese University Press, 1988), 77.

This is all admittedly very speculative and tentative, and I might add, not the last interpretation that has been made of this line. For example, following Zheng Xuan's gloss in *Mao shi* 211, Qu Wanli explains *jie* as *shexi* "to rest."[16] A similar interpretation is given by Yu Guanying, who says *jie* should be read *qie* "to rest." "After she performs her sacrifice, the lady rests."[17]

I am not sure where these divergent interpretations of this difficult line lead us other than to the conclusion that our reading of individual words and lines is based on highly shaky ground. Even the venerable Bernhard Karlgren's interpretations are not secure. They are certainly not the final word on the matter.

If we have trouble understanding the meaning of individual words, what can we make of the general sense of this stanza? The myth of Lady Jiang's becoming pregnant after treading in the toeprint of di^a is of course a compelling theme, and has parallels in many other world cultures. However, the treatment of it is so abbreviated that we cannot be sure exactly what is being said. Who, for example, is this di^a? Is it *shangdi* (Lord on High), or Di Ku of the Gaoxin clan? What is the significance of the *yin* and *si* sacrifices? Does Jiang Yuan's treading of Di's toeprint involve a particular type of ritual?

Commentators and scholars have not been reluctant to offer answers to these questions. The Mao Commentary identifies di^a as Gaoxin, a legendary ruler who reputedly preceded Yao.[18] Since Gaoxin is also known as Di Ku (Emperor Ku), this identification is theoretically possible. The Zhou in fact offered its di^b sacrifice to Di Ku, thus indicating it took Di Ku as its "remote ancestor." As Karlgren shows, this means that the Zhou must have considered Di Ku to be the father of Hou Ji.[19] Some sources do mention Di Ku as Jiang Yuan's husband, and thus there must have been an early tradition that identifies Hou Ji's father as Di Ku.[20] However, as Ma Ruichen and Karlgren argue, in the *Sheng min* poem di^a must be *shangdi* as already claimed by Zheng Xuan. Indeed, *Mao shi* 300 ("Bi gong"), which also tells of Hou Ji's miraculous birth, says it was *shangdi* who "made her fruitful."

Although Lady Jiang becomes pregnant by treading in the toeprint of Di, the song specifies that she was able to "eliminate" or "exorcise" (fu^a/ *$pjat$ = fu^b / *$pjat$) her childlessness by performing the yin^a and si^a rites. It is not

16. See *Shi jing tongshi* (Taipei: Lianjing chuban shiye gongsi, 1983), 484 n. 5.
17. See *Shi jing xuanzhu* (Hong Kong: Daguang chubanshe, 1966), 151 n. 6.
18. See *Mao shi zhushu*, 17A.2a.
19. "Legends and Cults in Ancient China," *BMFEA* 18 (1946): 216.
20. Sima Qian (*Shi ji* 4.111) says that Jiang Yuan was the primary consort of Di Ku. The *Shiben* (cited in *Yiwen leiju* 15.277) says that Di Ku had four consorts, and Jiang Yuan was his prime consort.

clear whether these terms are generic names, or whether they have a specific meaning. *Yin^a* can mean a purification rite, *jiesi*,[21] but we know virtually nothing about it. The word *si^a* is a generic word for "sacrifice." However, Chow Tse-tsung has argued that it originally meant a "sacrifice for fertility" or "to sacrifice in case of childlessness."[22]

The Han-time commentators, including Mao and Zheng Xuan, further associate the sacrifices that Lady Jiang performs here with another rite, the rite of the Jiao mei (Intermediary of the Suburb) or Gao mei (Supreme Intermediary). Mao says:

> To eliminate childlessness and to pray for children the ancients invariably instituted the Jiao mei. On the day of the arrival of the dark birds [= swallows] a Grand Victim offering [of an ox, goat, and pig] was made to the Jiao mei. The Son of Heaven personally attended the rites. The Queen Consort led the nine concubines and they were favored by him [i.e., had sexual relations with him]. Then obeisance was made to those whom the Son of Heaven had favored. Their girdles were hung with bow cases, and they were presented with bows and arrows in front of the Jiao mei.[23]

It turns out that Mao's description of this rite is drawn almost verbatim from the account in the "Yue ling" of the *Li ji* and the "Ji" section of the *Lüshi chunqiu* of the rite performed in the second month of spring to Gao mei.[24] The Gao mei or Jiao mei has been amply studied, and although there are many points of debate, such as the deity's sex and identity, there is general agreement that it was associated with a fertility cult.[25] Whether or not the *yin^a* and *si^a* rites mentioned here had anything to do with a Gao mei rite is impossible to say. I suspect that the Han-time commentators mention the Gao mei rite here mainly because it was the best known fertility rite mentioned in one of the canonical ritual texts. However, even though one cannot establish a certain connection between the rites mentioned in *Sheng min* and the Gao mei rite, the Han scholars had the correct instinct in understanding that they were part of a fertility ceremony.

21. See Ding Fubao, ed., *Shuowen jiezi gulin* (Taipei: Shangwu yinshuguan, 1959), 1A.44b–46a.

22. See "The Childbirth Myth and Ancient Chinese Medicine," in *Ancient China: Studies in Early Civilization*, ed. David T. Roy and Tsuen-hsuin Tsien (Hong Kong: The Chinese University Press, 1978), 63; and *Gu wuyi yu liushi kao* (Taipei: Lianjiang chuban shiye gongsi, 1986), 58–59.

23. See *Mao shi zhushu*, 17A.1b.

24. See *Li ji zhushu*, 15.4a–b; *Lüshi chunqiu, Sbby*, 2.1b.

25. See Wen Yiduo, "Gaotang shennü chuanshuo zhi fenxi," *Tsing Hua Journal of Chinese Studies* 10 (1935): 837–66; Chen Mengjia, "Gao mei jiao she zu miao kao," *Tsing Hua Journal of Chinese Studies* 12 (1937): 445–72; Kobayashi Taichirō, "Kōbai kō," *Shinagaku* (special issue,

Wen Yiduo has attributed special ritual significance to Lady Jiang's tread-ing in the toeprint of Di. He argues that a divine impersonator *shenshi* mimed the role of Di, and Jiang Yuan, dressed in the clothes of the divine imper-sonator,[26] danced in his footprints. She then rested (reading *you jie you zhi* as "then she rested, then she stopped") and had sexual relations with him.[27] Although this is a highly suggestive and original interpretation, it is possible that in seeking for the ritual that may lie behind this song we may be read-ing far too much into what simply is a naive retelling (or reenactment) of the marvelous birth of Hou Ji, the Zhou culture hero *par excellence*. Indeed, the ensuing stanzas portray Hou Ji's birth and life in a pattern that closely follows that of many heroic legends.[28]

Hou Ji's birth is described in the second stanza. The birth seems to be deemed unusual—but unusual in what way? The key line is *xian sheng ru da,* which has been variously explained. Zheng Xuan explains *da^a* as "lamb." *Da^a* (*that) possibly should be written *da^b* (*that), which means "newborn lamb." Karlgren (Gloss #868) rejects Zheng's reading on the grounds of no textual examples. Following the Mao Commentary "gloss" on *da^a* as *sheng* "to give birth," he takes *da^a* in the sense of "penetrate, burst through, come forth." Karlgren's reading requires construing *ru* as *er*. This is a possible usage for *ru*, but perhaps somewhat forced in this instance, in which *ru* seems to have its full sense of "like." Furthermore, as Kong Yingda pointed out already in the early Tang period, the Mao Commentary was not glossing *da^a* but ex-plaining the general sense of the line as referring "to giving birth."[29] What-ever the meaning of *da^a*, the unusual nature of the birth is its ease. Thus, it involved "no tearing, no rending / no hurt, no harm" *bu che bu pi, wu zai wu hai.* Indeed, the second line probably is a formula, for it occurs in *Mao shi* 300 also to describe the ease with which Lady Jiang gave birth to Hou Ji.

The description of Hou Ji's abandonment in Stanza 3 is similar to that found in stories of other culture heroes. Although Jiang Yuan's reason for

---

April 1942), 93–227; Derk Bodde, *Festivals in Classical China: New Year and Other Annual Obser-vances during the Han Dynasty 206 B.C.–A.D. 220* (Princeton: Princeton University Press, 1975), 243–61.

26. Wen bases this interpretation on a passage in the *Lun heng*, which says that Hou Ji's mother "dressed in the clothes of Di Ku, sat and rested in his place, and became pregnant." See *Lun heng, Sbby,* 2.15b.

27. See "Jiang Yuan lü daren ji kao," in *Shenhua yu shi* (Beijing: Zhonghua shuju, 1956), 73–80.

28. *Heroic Song and Heroic Legend,* trans. B. J. Timmer (London: Oxford University Press, 1963), 211–14.

29. See *Mao shi zhushu,* 17A.7a.

abandoning Hou Ji is not specified, the implication is that she exposed him because of the unusual nature of his birth. Like the heroes of other legends, the exposed Hou Ji is protected and fed by animals. Again, it is not the general idea of the song that is difficult to understand, it is the details. For example, consider the first four lines:

> "*Dan zhi zhi ai xiang, niu yang fei zi zhi. Dan zhi zhi ping lin, hui fa ping lin*"
> Then, she placed him in a narrow lane;
> Oxen and goats protected and suckled him.
> Then she placed him on a wooded plain;
> It happened that men came to cut the wooded plain.

The word *fei^a* literally means "leg." However, the Mao Commentary construes it as *bi^a*/ *pjiak*, "to avoid," "to shun." Zheng Xuan considers *fei^a* a loan for *bi^b*, which can either mean "to hide," "to cover," or "to protect" (as a loan for *bi^c*). Although Karlgren (see Gloss #432) claims these are not proper phonetic loans according to his reconstructions, in Li Fang-kuei's system, these are all quite possible loans: *fei^a* = *pjəd* and *bi^b*/ *bi^c* = *pjidx*.[30]

The word *zi* can mean *ru* "to suckle" or *yang* "to nourish."[31] A possible rendering of this line might be: "Oxen and goats covered and suckled him."

It would be tempting to read lines three and four as introducing the counterpart of the shepherds who rescue the infant hero. However, the subject of the line is not clear. It could be Jiang Yuan: upon meeting the woodcutters, she decided not to abandon her child on the wooded plain. Or it could be Hou Ji, who was found and cared for by the woodcutters.

In Stanza 4, the various feats of Hou Ji are recounted. At this point the life of the Zhou hero departs significantly from the pattern of the heroic life. Hou Ji does not acquire any invulnerability (e.g., no Achilles heel), he does not fight a monster, he does not go out to win the hand of a maiden, he does not journey to the underworld, he is not banished, and he does not die tragically. Rather, he distinguishes himself by planting crops:

> "*Dan shi pu fu, ke qi ke yi, yi jiu kou shi*"
> And then this one crept and crawled;
> He was able to rise up, he was able to stand
> In order to seek food for his mouth.

The second line is another example of a problematic Han-time reading. The Mao Commentary explains *qi^a*/ *kjai* as *zhi yi*, "to understand meaning," and *yi^a* / *ngjəh* as *shi*, "to know." The *Shuowen* cites this line as *ke qi ke*

---

30. See Serruys, "Studies in the Language of the *Shih-ching*: I," *Early China* 16 (1991): 151 n. 75.

31. For the meaning of "suckle" see *Shuowen jiezi gulin*, 15B.6601a–b.

yi. It glosses *yi*[b] as "a small child's having knowledge," which is similar to the meaning the Mao Commentary gives for *yi*[a]. Duan Yucai accepts the *Shuowen* reading as correct on the basis that the mountain radical was changed on analogy with *qi*[a].[32] Ma Ruichen thinks that Mao may have derived the meaning of *qi*[a] (**kjai*) from what he wrongly thought was similarity in sound to *zhi* (**trjœh*). He also argues that *qiyi* follows after *pufu*, "to crawl," and thus means "gradually being able to stand." Thus, he reads *qi*[a]/ **kjai* as *qi*[b]/ **kjiai* / *qi*[c]/ **khjiai* "to stand on one's toes." He construes *yi*[a] as *yi*[c], "to stand straight."[33] Although he acknowledges that the Mao-*Shuowen* reading is possible, Karlgren (Gloss #870) finally opts for an interpretation based on Waley and Ma Ruichen. (He follows Waley and construes *qi*[d] as *qi*[b] "to straddle" = "to stride."). Karlgren accepts Ma Ruichen's interpretation of *yi*[a] and thus translates "He was able to [straddle =] stride, to stand firmly."

The most problematical section of this poem appears in the following lines, which describe the various stages in the growth of grain:

"*Shi fang shi bao, shi zhong shi you, shi fa shi xiu, shi jian shi hao, shi ying shi li.*"
It sprouted, it formed pods,
It swelled, it grew long,
It formed stalks, it eared,
It became firm, it was well-formed,
It hung down, it ripened.

Ma Ruichen, who closely follows Cheng Yaotian, provides a detailed discussion of each word.[34] However, because of a lack of parallel usages in Zhou-time texts, even the learned explanations of Ma Ruichen seem more like guesses than definitive explanations. It is clear that the words *fang, bao, zhong, you*[b], and *li*[a] are technical terms, but their meaning seems to have been difficult to determine even for the Han-time commentators. Ma's method was to start with the Han-time gloss and move from there to find passages in other texts that contained the same or related words. Briefly summarized, his conclusions are: the word *fang* means "the beginning of sprouting" and *bao* is the gradual formation of the outer covering or pod. *Zhong*[a] could be read like *chong* in the *Zuo zhuan* line *yu fa ruci zhong zhong*, "my hair is short and thin as this,"[35] or possibly should be construed as a loan for *zhong*[b], "to swell."[36] The word *you*[b] is so rare there is very little textual evidence from which to determine its meaning. Cheng Yaotian glosses it as "the gradual

32. See *Shuowen jiezi gulin*, 2A.561a–b.
33. See *Mao shi zhuan jian tongshi*, 25.6a–b.
34. *Mao shi zhuan jian tongshi*, 25.9a–10a.
35. *Zuo zhuan*, the third year of Duke Zhao.
36. See *Shuowen jiezi gulin*, 7A.3076b, *Shuowen tongsheng dingsheng*.

growth of the sprouts." Zheng Xuan glosses *fa* as "the time of forming stalks," and Ma Ruichen expands on it by explaining that *fa* represents the formation of tall stalks, and *xiu*[a] the ears. The line *shi jian shi hao* is similar to a line in *Mao shi* 212: *ji jian ji hao*, which also describes grain. *Jian* presumably describes the firm kernels, and *hao* their well-formed shape. Ma Ruichen follows the Mao Commentary in explaining *ying* as the hanging ears. Finally, the difficult word *li*[a] that concludes the passage possibly means "ripe grain."

The explanations given by Ma Ruichen and Cheng Yaotian are basically reinterpretations of the Han-time commentaries, which in themselves may be flawed. I suspect that the received *Shi jing* text of these lines may not even adequately reflect the actual words that lie behind the script used to write them. However, it would be very difficult to go much beyond what Ma Ruichen and Cheng Yaotian have done with these words, and despite the highly speculative nature of their explanations, this is probably the best we can do. However, in following them, we should be aware of the highly tentative nature of our understanding.

The comments I have made about the "reading" of *Sheng min* are intended not so much to resolve questions as to raise them. Attempting to read *Sheng min* reminds me of a wonderful line in a *Sherlock Holmes* story: "You mentioned your name as if I should recognize it, but beyond the obvious facts that you are a bachelor, a solicitor, a Freemason, and an asthmatic, I know nothing whatsoever about you."[37] The same rule applies to the reading of *Sheng min*. Although we know a few facts, some important and some not so important, there is still much that we do not know, and perhaps will never know about the language and ritual context of these texts. We can speculate about the linguistic meaning, try to identify what words lie behind the Han-time transcription of them, and even decide which commentator to follow, but in the end, I fear that our reading often ends up being a choice between equally compelling, or even in some cases equally unsatisfactory, interpretations. Although this may seem like an overly pessimistic view about the possibility of understanding ancient Chinese texts, what I really wish to emphasize is that we should be aware of the limitations that any reader, ancient or modern, has in terms of linguistic knowledge about early Zhou dynasty Chinese. There is much that we simply do not know, and probably will never know. However, as long as we are aware of the philological traps into which one may fall in trying to read these ancient texts, we should continue to try to draw conclusions, however tentative, from them.

37. From "The Norwood Builder."

INTERPRETING *SHENG MIN*

Stephen Owen

Interpretation of the *Sheng min* is impossible to separate from thorny philological problems, many of which can never be solved with certainty. Before a general discussion let me offer two assumptions that touch both general interpretation and specifics of interpretation:

First, the *Sheng min* and the rest of the *Shi* probably existed as orally transmitted texts long before they were ever committed to writing, and even after their commitment to writing (when we cannot be sure, but I would guess late Chunqiu at the earliest), their primary mode of transmission was probably oral until (another guess) the late Warring States. Making this assumption, we should look at particular graphs as decisions shaped by later scribes, guided by already existing exegetical traditions. Thus the *Yuan* of Jiang Yuan is essentially the same "name" as the *Yuan* of Qu Yuan. Put this way, the issue goes far deeper than homophonic loan characters.

Second, the body of mythography that grew up around figures like Jiang Yuan and Hou Ji appears so much later that it cannot be relied upon to interpret the *Sheng min* (one of the most troubling aspects of the study of early literature is to dismiss historical distances of half a millennium or more on the vague premise that old traditions survive). Some of this later material is clearly euhemeristic; some of it seems primarily exegetical, with the particular points mentioned answering silences and problems of the *Sheng min* itself.[38] It seems likely that at least some of the mythographic material that survives in late Warring States and Han texts is very old—but we do not and cannot know precisely which elements are very old. Furthermore, we know from the much richer body of Greek mythography that there never was a single "myth" (until some authoritative mythographer like Ovid nailed a story down); rather there was a complex field of stories, sometimes contradictory, with strongly local ties, constantly being elaborated, plundering pieces of other stories, answering the demands of ideological change and the particular circumstances of the telling. Each teller is certain that there is only "one story," but each teller offers a different story. While we should always historically contextualize such pieces in principle, the nature of the material from the Western Zhou and the later material that purports to represent Western Zhou traditions does not meet even the minimal standards of interpretive validity. Here we are very much forced to focus our attention on the nature of representation in the *Sheng min* itself, and secondarily to look for

---

38. *Wenxue yichan* 1993 (6) has an article by Li Shaoyong on the Hou Ji legend ("Hou Ji shenhua tanyuan") examining such later sources, as well as references within the *Shi* itself.

corroborating usage elsewhere in the *Shi*. I say this not as an affirmation of literary formalism ("the text itself"), but to be critical about the historical appropriateness of materials that can be used to support the interpretation of such poems.

Finally, I would like to reaffirm Wang Ching-hsien's point that although the *Shi* texts exist within history, they do not come from any single moment in history. We do not know for certain, but judging from the early transmission of authoritative texts in other traditions (excluding the peculiar case of the *Rg Veda*, whose memorization techniques are, so far as I know, unique), texts grow, diverge, are reconciled, et cetera, in a very complex process of transmission that is neither oral reperformance in the Parry-Lord sense nor written-textual.

The first thing that should be said about the *Sheng min* is that it is not a narrative poem; it is a ritual poem, and the fragments of a narrative that it includes are determined by the needs of authorizing the rite. To us, as to later readers in the Chinese tradition, it might sound like elliptical narrative— hence the narrative given in the *Zhou benji* of the *Records of the Historian, Shi ji*, which is clearly exegetical, filling in missing pieces of the story—but the narrative fragments of *Sheng min* itself are chosen precisely for justifying the rite: thus for the needs of ritual argument it does not matter who abandoned Hou Ji or why, only that he passed these trials.

If the oral transmission of song and myth is local, various, and changing, there is a balancing need in ritual to assert an unchanging continuity with origins: "for Lord Millet began the rite, / and hopefully free from failing or fault, / it has lasted until now." The rite of the "one man" (the ancestor/ruler) becomes, without change or variation, the rite of the collective folk. That very desire for unchanging unity becomes a force that shapes the very idea of a "classic" ("continuity" being an important semantic component of *jing*), and the *Shi* as a "classic." But such explicit assertions of unity and continuity are signs of an anxiety about variation and change, which would result in "fault and cause for regret." If we understand cultural moments as questions rather than positions, I think we can see here one of the driving concerns of Western Zhou and Chunqiu culture. And insofar as the *Shi* represents the problematic assertion of the unity and continuity of Zhou culture, thinly spread in its feudal domination of North China with pressures for change from diverse regional cultures, such concern is understandable. In some of the *Daya* the ruler *seems to* speak as the ruler of all his subjects, but the "folk" (*min*) referred to in the *Sheng min* is clearly restricted to the original Zhou people.

This is a poem about the birth of the *min*, the Zhou "people." It is not the ancestry of the Zhou aristocracy nor of the human race, but of a particular tribe, unified by a putative common ancestry and thus subject to the "natural" authority hierarchies of the family. In contrast to the broader idea of *min*, I think that here, as suggested above, there is a non-Zhou "them," who are excluded from this family saga.

The derivation of the Zhou folk from a woman (though a woman of a different, if exceptionally distinguished, surname, the Jiang) is remarkable. Here it is hard not to contrast origin myths in Greece, where the mother is so often divinely raped. The question of "how" Jiang Yuan did it is answered by a statement of ritual mastery: "she knew the rite and sacrifice." There is no mistaking the *ke*'s here; she did it by will and by a technical skill. In the spirit of trying to notice the implications of the obvious, rather than identifying the particular rituals that she mastered, we should notice the homology between the kind of ritual lore she commands to carry out her will to bear a child and the ritual lore of the agrarian cycle that is supposed to be accurately reproduced at the end of the poem. If I may be forgiven an obvious and naive comparison, the issue of rape versus the control of "reproduction" is striking here. There is no terror in beginnings and the encounter with fertilizing divinity. The question is not rape but whether the woman does or does not have the ritual mastery, *ke*, to effect her will. The point of uncertainty addressed centers not on the eruption of the inexplicable but on the ability to master a technique. Again, braving naïveté, let me suggest that such technical mastery yielding results that can be reproduced is easily transferred to or derives from agrarian skills.

She treads on the god's toeprint. This is a "big toe," and whatever phallic metaphors are at work here, let us notice first of all that this is an act of will, preconditioned by ritual action, done to achieve a certain end in the instrumental *yi^d*. We do not know the circumstances under which she encountered the divine toe-print, but there is something more knowledgeable and purposeful implied here than the accidental discovery of the print in the *Shi ji* version and Jiang Yuan's almost whimsical decision to tread upon it ("Jiang Yuan went forth into the wilderness and saw the print of a huge man. Her heart was filled with delight and she wanted to step in it"). The "god," *di^a*, at the end of the poem is familiar, not fully embodied and enjoying the partially substantial emanations of the sacrifice; but this *di^a* in the first stanza is more troublesome—because he leaves toeprints.

However we interpret the following verbs, we know that we are describing a process of conception and birth. I won't here defend my interpretation of *zhi^a* as the god "settling" on the woman—an extension from Mao that Karlgren rejects as forced. It comes down to the same thing as Karlgren's *zhi^b*, "blessed," but conceptualizing blessing as something coming from the outside and staying on a person or a thing. Keeping in mind that the *Shi* is an oral/aural text, one hears the common word *zhi^a* in a specialized ritual context. This same phrase *you jie you zhi* is used in "Large Field," *Futian* (line

9), where it follows a line on the growing of millet and precedes a line on providing for men. The line should mean the same thing in both places, especially since in "Large Field" it is used in close conjunction with the term "millet," ji^b. Clearly in both cases it is blessing through growth and quickening, and unlike the more mammalian term for being made pregnant, $zhen^a$, it links what is happening to Jiang Yuan to a process of vegetative growth.

The poem names the phases of conception, pregnancy, and birth. There is a large question here. Why does the *Shi jing* always want to name "all" the variations and phases—of birth, of the kinds of grain, of the phases of grain-growth? If I may borrow (and somewhat twist) a phrase of Richard Halperin, this is the "poetics of primitive accumulation." It is a way of dealing with knowledge, as in a farmer's almanac, counting and enumerating phases and products—a ledger of the imagination. Without grasping the pleasure and beauty that must have attached to naming phases and varieties, it is hard to read these poems that seem to be among the earliest in the *Shi*. Such mnemonic taxonomies are, I would suggest, virtually indistinguishable from the taxonomy of phases in ritual action. It is a way of thinking about "sets," whether they are temporal phases, spatial, or taxonomic: if one says or does X and Y, Z is there. This is profoundly different from the epistemology of representation in much of the *Guofeng*, in which essentializing antitheses usually take the place of earlier taxonomic sets in asserting completeness.

At the risk of Germanic philosophizing, there does seem to be a difference between the order of events for a warrior aristocracy and for an agrarian aristocracy. For the warrior, events in time build to a single moment of decision (*Krisis*, crisis) that gives meaning to everything that went before and everything that follows. The agrarian aristocracy depends upon a sequence of phases in which each phase is just as important as any other; the omission of *any* phase is catastrophic; and the key moment lies between the completion of one cycle and the initiation of the next, which hopes for perfect repetition. Despite my distrust of the schematic antithesis implied here, I do find it useful to understand a basic distinction in representations and narratives.

Hou Ji is born and named. Let us be honest and say that Hou Ji is not just a name—it is literally "Lord Millet." Phonologically (in archaic Chinese) the Ji is far from the name Qi (the "Castoff," the "Sown"?) which he is later given. His attributes, though increasingly human, run a fine boundary between the vegetable and the human. Despite later euhemerization, the being described in *Sheng min* is something that shares attributes with plant and human.

To take an example: *xian sheng ru da*, translated as "her first-born sprang up." Commentators tell you often that the da^a is a lamb, even suggesting that Hou Ji was born surrounded by a placenta. They discount Mao's interpretation as "come forth." But if we look at one of the *Zhou Song*, "Mowing Grasses" *Zaishan*, we read *yiyi qi da*, "luxuriant the sprouting blades," with Zheng Xuan glossing *da*ᵃ as "breaking out of the soil." Hou Ji seems, in the words that describe him, far closer to John Barleycorn than to an ancient minister of agriculture, as he is presented in the *Shi ji*.

The account of the ease of parturition in the second stanza would, in this case, beautifully link the mythic with the agrarian, the sprouting without labor and pain.

The exposure stanza is particularly interesting. We may say that it refers to a myth with motives and agents known to the audience and thus not needing narration, or we may say that such narration is simply not essential to the ritual function of these moments. Hou Ji, babe or grain, is thrown into a narrow lane to be trampled by "cattle and sheep." It is hard not to notice that this first exposure involves animal-raising folk, as opposed to the agrarian identity of the Zhou people who "grow" from the gift of agriculture. The animals *feizi zhi:* again, looking at the words, the interpreter wants to think of the spread leg of animals, straddling and suckling or providing manure instead of trampling, thus avoiding the narrow lane that should ensure that the babe/sprout be crushed. Similarly, the encounter with the woodcutters in the forests suggests clearing spaces for planting. Unfortunately this set of agrarian issues breaks down with Hou Ji on the ice, protected by birds brooding on him (though again birds do play a role in the distribution of seed).

Surviving the three exposures, Hou Ji "wails," the voice that distinguishes him from mere plant. "He stood upright, he stood straight" spans the uprightness of the growing sprout and the uprightness of the human animal with legs spread. Hou Ji is, let me be clear, human; but these first phases of his growth have vegetative echoes.

Once he seeks to eat, he produces or reproduces the process of sowing: beans, grain, and gourds or melons. The itemization in this and the following stanzas reproduces, on a purely formal level, the naming of phases in growth. To "represent" something here seems to be to represent either its phases or variety with a quality appropriate to each phase or kind. The loving qualification of vegetables in the *Shi* is the rough counterpart of equally affectionate descriptions of armor and weaponry in Homer. There is a joy in naming a full complement.

To amplify the point raised earlier, itemization seems an essential principle in many of the *Daya* and *Zhou Song*. Itemization or "taking stock" works not only with categories of objects, but also with actions, narrative phases, and stages of process (sowing, weeding, reaping, etc.)—even in the hierarchical itemization of the landholder's family and workers in the *Zhou Song* "Mowing Grasses." Completeness seems clearly what is at stake: one names a full set of components to represent some whole, to guarantee its completeness. The negative counterpart is the possibility of error, omitting some element or allowing some part to change. Such errors in ritual are declared to have been avoided at the end of *Sheng min*. Such an abiding interest in complete sets and their reproduction seems to correspond to the mnemonics of the phases of an agrarian cycle and its counterpart in reproducible ritual.

"[He] had a way to help things grow": I am sure that some colleague will come up with some earlier usage, yet this seems to me one of the earliest usages of *Dao* in an abstract sense that I know of. If it is one of the very earliest usages of this powerful term, it is worth more reflection than it is normally given. *Dao* is here clearly "method," though a "method" that works with Nature rather than independent of Nature or identical to Nature left alone (later *Ziran*). It is *xiang^a*, "assisting," a relation to natural process that is usually elided in Western formulations of the "natural," but which is pragmatically obvious in the agrarian community. That *xiang^a* is a different way to think about what human beings do, a stance that is neither laissez-faire "natural" nor artificial. Without wishing to push beyond the scope of my text, I think this opens up a space that lets us understand the Sage. There is a profound history behind the peculiar importance that is placed on ministerial *xiang^a*: "assistance" is necessary in agrarian terms to the work of *Tian* (Heaven/Nature) just as "the assistant" *xiang^a* is necessary to the functioning of the "Son of Heaven."

In any case, this is what the farmer does, "working with" natural process in a systematic way, which is Hou Ji's lesson and legacy for the production of bounty.

After naming the phases of Hou Ji's planting and grain growth, "he had his household there in Tai." Settling and founding a family follow from the harvest. Insofar as agriculture is reproduction of a process, it can have the same site (and again, as with the dangerous cattle and sheep, one thinks of an alternative migratory way of life that has no home in a single place). And in the very next stanza the poem leaps to the (repeatable) present, the voice of the *min*, who *are* that family, still reenacting precisely Hou Ji's *Dao* of agriculture that was "passed down," *jiang*, to them. All the grains are here named, then taken back for the rite that Hou Ji initiated.

The speaker then rhetorically calls for a description of the rite, which itemizes actions of the participants just as the varieties of grain and the phases of growth were itemized. Before the sacrifice of the ram, there is an unobtrusive but perhaps significant line: "Then we reckon, then we consider." Deliberation, consultation, and thinking ahead are frequently brought up as central virtues in the *Daya* and *Zhou Song*. When Duke Liu conquers the land of Bin (in "Duke Liu") the care given to preparations for his folk-wandering is central; the conquest itself is virtually invisible. Again this is something that is striking in comparison to Homer's hot heroic tempers. But as with Jiang Yuan's planning her pregnancy, the ability to control events by technique and foresight is very much foregrounded in these poems.

The entire description of the sacrifice leads up to the line that concludes this stanza: "to rouse up the following year." The explicit mention of deliberation earlier in the stanza invites us to take yi^d in a strong sense as "in order to." The rite occupies the critical position in the agrarian cycle, between the completion of the harvest and the beginning of the next round. If this song is part of the ritual itself, it "reproduces" or represents the cycle, its origins, and the rite itself in words. This verbal "reproduction" of the process fills the only problematic moment within cyclical time. As the representation in *Sheng min* gives it, there is no hiatus: the harvest leads immediately to the rite, which initiates the next round.

The final stanza brings up to the moment of the rite, linking the world below and the di^a, the deified ancestors or single deity. The sacrificial vessels are filled; their aroma rises; and the *di* take pleasure, *xin*, in it. As in other cases, such as "Mowing Grasses," the ending asserts the perfection of the rite, with "perfection" here defined as unchanging continuity from origin to present.

READING *SHENG MIN*
Willard Peterson

Usually when I turn to the *Shi jing*, it is to try to understand the locus classicus of terms, phrases or lines that I encountered in some later text while pursuing my interests in early Chinese thought. With more or less the same motive, I also read in it with graduate students to try to enhance our understanding of earlier uses of words and ideas. Regardless of my motive, I normally end up trying to read the song/poem to tease out not just what the words might be saying, and what they might have meant, but also why such a set of words was put together, transmitted, and (I assume) in some sense used over an extended period. In short, I try to guess at what might be called the motive or intention historically embedded in that particular array of words preserved for us in any given song/poem.

Recognizing that no one today reads the *Shi jing* without help—lots of help—I find the song/poem I want to read in Qu Wanli's introductory *Shi jing yi yi* because I find his annotations synthesized from earlier commentaries present tradition-based, relatively unambiguous glosses or explanations rather than leaving me to choose from a range of earlier proposals; I am less inclined toward Gao Heng's *Shi jing jin zhu* because he tends to rationalize (in my intuitive judgment) the songs/poems for modern readers. As a non-expert, I am quite willing to be guided by the annotations but without feeling compelled to follow every gloss. (I know I always may have recourse to the Harvard-Yenching Index and to the collected commentaries when I need more examples or other suggestions.) I also find the song/poem in Karlgren so that I have reconstructed rhymes, if I want them, as well as a serviceable English translation of the entire text. I usually also turn to Waley's version of the poem because his is pleasant to read. With my three or four books opened to the appropriate pages, I then look at the Chinese text of the song/poem.

For present purposes, the song/poem is *Sheng min, Mao* 245.

Without taking much trouble (that is, without worrying over words and phrases I do not understand—the commentary will help me later), I read through *Sheng min* and agree with the apparent convention of dividing the text into eight sections. I notice there are seven lines (or more properly but awkwardly, breath segments) which have five zi but which are readily rationalized to my naive expectation of four zi per line. On inspection, the rhyme scheme is not obvious and does not seem to help my reading. I detect no reason not to accept that *Sheng min* is a written version of a song that was more or less in its present form by late Western Zhou, when it probably was being performed at the royal Zhou court. I infer that the last word (*jin,* the present or now) could refer to any occasion on which the song could be meaningfully performed at the court.

This last inference leads me to reread *Sheng min* and think about what is being said that would make it, in effect, continuously relevant to its early performers (I now distort the report on the process of my thinking to make my account more easily accessible to others.).

I quickly decide against my initial view, based on the imputed title, *Sheng min,* and the first two sections, about Jiang Yuan giving birth to Hou Ji, that this song/poem was primarily about the (mythic) origins of the Zhou ethnic group. (I also had been influenced by Gao Heng's remarks introducing *Sheng min* and Waley's placing it under his own created heading, "Dynastic Legends.") Clearly Hou Ji is the main character. He is named or present as the implied subject of verbs in all eight sections (except the seventh if we decide it is only referring to the moments *Sheng min* is currently being performed). Although *Sheng min* is a celebration of Hou Ji—his miraculous birth, survival, and legacies to his descendants—the thematic purpose of the song/poem seems to involve the si^a sacrifice associated with the rituals for the new year. This inference is reinforced (for me) by the question asked at the beginning of the seventh section: What about our si^a sacrifice (*wo si ru he*)? I notice that the word si^a occurs in sections 1, 2, 6, 7, and 8. I look again at the eight sections. The odd-numbered ones have ten lines, and the even-numbered ones have eight; perhaps they can be treated as paired. The first two sections give an account of Jiang Yuan using a si^a

sacrifice to induce a relationship with Di, who was pleased with the si^a sacrifice, and of her giving birth to Hou Ji. The next two sections tell of Hou Ji's survival as a baby and child with help from animals and by feeding himself with plant-derived foods. Sections 5 and 6 attest to Hou Ji's special achievements in raising food crops, particularly types of grain we conventionally presume to be like millet, and thus his meriting his name, Lord Millet; section 6 concludes with the harvest and with instituting the si^a sacrifice. Sections 7 and 8 describe the preparation of the millet and the sheep (the premier early Zhou sacrificial animal) to induce a prosperous new year by sending the aroma of the offering up to please Di on high. The *Sheng min* concludes with the affirmation that the participants are blamelessly (and therefore efficaciously?) continuing the si^a sacrifice instituted by their lineal ancestor, Lord Millet, and directed to his, and therefore their, ancestor deity, Di.

I have now persuaded myself that *Sheng min* represents an ideological claim made in answer to the rhetorical question, "what about our si^a sacrifice?" (*wo si ru he*), which subordinated the rhetorical question in section 1, "what about the coming into being of [our] people?" (*sheng min ru he*). In my imagination, the implied argument runs like this: We leaders of the Zhou people declare that the si^a sacrifices of grain and animals which we make at the new year are done in continuation of those done by Lord Millet, who is celebrated for giving our ancestors the techniques for growing and processing cereal crops, and who we all know was born to the childless Jiang Yuan by the intervention of the divine Di after a si^a sacrifice. (I go off on a tangent: Jiang Yuan was the first female parent from whom stemmed the male line which resulted in King Wen, King Wu, the Duke of Zhou, and the later kings of the Zhou polity. According to most readings, Jiang Yuan was also the female from whom stemmed the *min*, who therefore could be blood relatives of the Zhou kings. I am not aware of a definitive explanation that shows the boundary of kinship of *min* in, say, Western Zhou times. The possibilities seem to range from the narrowly construed elite group of recognized Zhou royal relatives [not necessarily all of them aristocrats] through all fully enfranchised descendants of those involved in the Zhou conquest of the Shang capital at Yin and its territories in the eleventh century B.C.E., to most broadly all of those regardless of status who claimed an ethnic affinity, not strictly a demonstrable kinship relation, to the Zhou rulers. Who constituted the *min* remains moot.)

Put in another way, the *Sheng min* tells us that si^a sacrifices link (1) those who now perform the sacrifices, (2) the cultural achievement of producing the animals and grains which not only are offered in the sacrifices but are also our primary sources of sustenance, (3) the ancestor honored both with bringing that cultural achievement to our benefit and instituting the sacrifices to ask that the productivity continue, (4) the mother from whom that ancestor sprang and who is the ultimate mother of our group, and (5) the deity on high who is pleased by the sacrifices, to which he (?) has in the past responded by, for example, enabling Jiang Yuan to give birth to a son who became our deified male ancestor, and by, for another example, enabling us to prosper in the new year.

My reading of the *Sheng min*—that the song was (intended to be) performed as an ideological act at the Zhou court's new year sacrificial ritual—demands that I consider something for which there is no direct evidence: what were the circumstances under which the song/poem came into being? I surmise that there was a song celebrating the divinity/ancestor Hou Ji in fertility rituals for both biological and agricultural productivity. "Si wen Hou Ji" (*Mao* 275) may be an example of this type of simpler song. The song was elaborated with sections on his birth and early tribulations. "Bi gong" (*Mao* 300) may represent a longer elaboration of the story by bringing Hou Ji's descent line explicitly down to the Duke of Zhou, who was ancestral to the lords of Lu, the objects of praise in the song/poem. I also surmise that at some time late in the Western Zhou period, the performers of the song or their sponsors became self conscious about the *si*[a] sacrifices and the concomitant performance of the song. The self-consciousness which is manifested in the last pair of sections has prompted me to read *Sheng min* as I have sketched here.

PERSPECTIVE ON READINGS OF *SHENG MIN*

Pauline Yu

As anyone familiar with the history of hermeneutics well knows, reading is an art whose methods and goals have been discussed and debated for as long as readers have encountered texts. Whether sacred or secular, texts confront us continually with issues of control and context, if we are only willing to acknowledge them: understanding of their syntax and lexicon, familiarity with generic conventions and other intertextual relations, concern with the impulses and motivations underlying their production, awareness of the purposes which they—and interpretations of them—might have served, reflection on the assumptions that generations of readers, including ourselves, have brought to the texts, and recognition of the ends to which we in turn might wish to direct them. We move constantly in circles—hermeneutical, political, emotional, philosophical, and more—chasing the tail of certainty that ever eludes us. Perhaps we suspect that an awareness and acceptance of the bases for that uncertainty may lend a curiously greater credibility to what we say, if we can but step back from our naturalized habits and strategies to bring to the fore and examine the nature of choices that are normally for various reasons unarticulated or simply taken for granted. Or perhaps we do not care if anyone listens. In any event, that elusiveness ought to ensure that there will always be something more to say.

Within the body of classical Chinese literature there are few texts that have become as difficult to read as the *Shi jing*, the Classic of Poetry. Its antiquity and its canonicity have combined forces to enshroud the poems in the anthology in formidable layers of meaning and interpretation that, not surprisingly, veil as effectively—perhaps even more so—as they reveal. The accretions of exegesis, gloss, and commentary, the debates among them, the intellectual and political grounds for such contentions, and the trajectories of such differences are well known to scholars in the field.[39] And the three readers of the poem selected for this volume, *Sheng min*, no. 245 in the Mao edition of the *Shi jing*, have chosen to confront what could be well-nigh impenetrable layers of obscurity in rather different, yet ultimately complementary, ways.

The title of David Knechtges's essay, "Questions about the Language of *Sheng min*," suggests immediately what his primary concern will be. A venerable philological tradition tracing its roots to European scholarship of centuries past has directed scholarly attention on ancient texts to the level of the word and its pedagogical energies on training students to capture and anchor the "linguistic remains" set adrift by its own insistence on their otherness and remoteness in time and space.[40] But whereas such training in some quarters can produce a narrowness of focus and a smug confidence that borders on hermeneutical hubris, Knechtges provides us with precisely the breadth of perspective and information that, to the contrary, enables the text to, as he puts it, "torment" us with the uncertain and unknowable.

Situating *Sheng min* within sediments of recension and commentary, Knechtges points out the principal disconcerting facts: first, the received text of the poem is that of the Mao school (second century B.C.E.), several centuries—and generations of oral transmissions—removed from its likely date of composition. Second, the Mao text itself as we have it incorporates variant readings and interpretations of poems from the schools of other contemporaneous exegetes of the Former Han, which were then collated and edited in the second century C.E. by the Later Han scholar Zheng Xuan (127–200). Third, we must assume that the text and script of the poem as

---

39. For an excellent account of this hermeneutical tradition, see Steven van Zoeren, *Poetry and Personality: Reading, Exegesis, and Hermeneutics in Traditional China* (Stanford, Calif.: Stanford University Press, 1991). See also C. P. Haun Saussy, *The Idea of a Chinese Aesthetic* (Stanford, Calif.: Stanford University Press, 1994), and Pauline Yu, *The Reading of Imagery in the Chinese Poetic Tradition* (Princeton, N.J.: Princeton University Press, 1987).

40. See Edward H. Schafer, "What and How Is Sinology?" *T'ang Studies* 8–9 (1990–91).

recorded in these editions reflect Han dynasty pronunciations and writing practices, rather than those of the Western Zhou, during which it first circulated, so that it can provide us with no reliable phonological information dating back to the era in which it was composed. Fourth, the individual histories of each song in the anthology are by no means uniform and thus contribute another dimension of variation and uncertainty to the collection as a whole. And fifth, it is not at all clear what the meaning of the rubric *ya,* under which *Sheng min* is classified in the collection, refers to, although it may allow us to assume that the work was linked to ritual performance at court, accompanied by music and perhaps dance as well.

The first third of Knechtges's essay thus quite effectively destabilizes the ground on which we will approach the song, and his progression through the piece itself continues to stress the "enigmas and questions that long have baffled interpreters of the poem." While the "general sense" of some stanzas is often "easy enough to understand," determining the meaning of individual graphs, or the subjects of certain lines, or the punctuation from line to line, tends not to be. If we can presume that the figure Hou Ji is to be taken as a cultural hero whose birth and life course follow patterns shared by those of other myths, we cannot, in Knechtges's view, decipher with any certainty the relationship between that biography and the long section of the poem that describes various stages in the growth of grain. Qing dynasty commentators have not gone far beyond the Han glosses of individual words, and Knechtges regards even this modest level of explanation as "highly speculative," one that raises as many questions as it may resolve.

Just as understanding an individual poem is often enriched by looking at others like it, so a method of reading is best illuminated through many examples. As other pieces in this volume and elsewhere demonstrate, reading in Knechtges's hands takes place on a fundament of erudition, a wealth of scholarly information about texts and transmission that he shares generously and in painstaking detail with his readers and students. His command of the apparatus is masterly and sure, but when the foundation—as in the case of the *Sheng min*—is as riddled with lacunae as he knows it to be, responsibility demands a recognition of limitation and an emphasis on the tentative and inconclusive. "Shaky" though he may consider this ground to be, it is, however, where we must start.

This is where Stephen Owen in his essay on *Sheng min* in fact begins: with an acknowledgment of the "thorny philological problems, many of which can never be solved with certainty" that beset a reading of a poem that went through centuries of oral transmission before being written down by scribes and that has become embedded in accretions of mythographic material whose specific historical provenance cannot be determined. That said, Owen then makes the declaration that sets the course for the rest of his essay: the *Sheng min* is a ritual poem whose narrative elements exist merely to justify the rite.

Whereas Knechtges is interested primarily in the language of the poem, Owen focuses scholarly concern on its story, or rather on the highly fragmentary nature of that story. It is one whose interstices and conclusions have been provided by commentaries occupying a different corner of the scholarly tradition from the one introduced by Knechtges. But however compelled later exegetes have felt to fill in those "missing pieces," for Owen those details that obsess them are ultimately inconsequential; what is important, rather, is the poem's ritual function within the culture. And it is not in fact the story itself, the "general sense" whose outlines, as Knechtges noted, are not difficult to discern, but its performative context and theoretical implications that matter.

The ritual purposes of the poem are manifold. First, as part of a sacrificial rite *Sheng min* in Owen's view asserts "an unchanging continuity with origins" and the center, an impulse that balances the aleatory and centrifugal tendencies of its oral transmission. Second, this assertion not only compensates for the anxiety that such variation can generate, it represents at the same time a larger claim for the unity and continuity of Zhou culture that Owen sees being waged in the *Shi jing* as a whole. And third, this unity is one of a particular "tribe," a people (*min*) to be distinguished from others by virtue of its lineage and descent from the woman, Jiang Yuan, whose impregnation opens the poem.

Owen's reading moves us consistently from attention to this poem in particular to consideration of other works in the *Shi jing* as well as those of other cultural traditions. Much of his commentary depends on adjudication among the conflicting philological options that torment Knechtges, decisions that must serve as the basis for the conclusions he is drawing about the text. Thus whereas Knechtges reserves judgment about the relationship between the human and agricultural dramas of the poem, Owen immediately points out the homology between the reproductive control Jiang Yuan exercises—the attention drawn to her mastery of the ritual that impregnates her—and the productive control of the agrarian cycle that is celebrated in the poem's second half. An admittedly contested interpretation of the usage of one word provides important support for the centrality of this homology, linking as it does "what is happening to Jiang Yuan to a process of vegetative growth." And indeed, as Owen points out later, in its painlessness her parturition resembles the ease of sprouting more closely than it does the agonies of animal birth, and there are distinct "vegetative echoes" in the description of her offspring's growth.

Focusing on the ritual function of the poem leads Owen to speculate further on other stylistic features of *Sheng min*. In its evident fondness for the naming of phases and products, shared with other works in the *Shi jing,* he sees a "poetics of primitive accumulation," an enumerative "ledger of the imagination" that both serves as an (agri)cultural mnemonic and also reflects an obsession with itemized completeness typical of agrarian society. Owen further, admittedly "at the risk of Germanic philosophizing," suggests that this structural patterning distinguishes an agrarian aristocratic culture from that of a warrior aristocracy, where events build up to a moment of crisis that overshadows and subsumes all others rather than constituting a sequence of equally important phases, none of which may be omitted, whether enumerated or executed.

Is the "risk" worth taking? Within the context of his discussion it is supported by further observations about other important contrasts between Homeric conventions and what we see in *Sheng min.* We need not dwell on the differences, and the speculations as to their bases, in order to accept the insights afforded into how the poem itself works. As Owen goes on to argue, the text both celebrates and enacts the rite that Jiang Yuan's offspring, Hou Ji, initiates, one for which the nature of his creation has prepared him. Ideals of completion are fulfilled on multiple levels, for just as the performance of the song identifies the origin and asserts the continuity from that past to the present, so too does it provide a crucial link within the cycle of agricultural production—expressing gratitude for a successful harvest and hope for renewed fertility in the future. The poem, then, mirrors itself: "If this song is part of the ritual itself, it 'reproduces' or represents the cycle, its origins, and the rite itself in words."[41]

Willard Peterson's "Reading *Sheng min*" similarly stresses this self-referential aspect of the poem, in an account that also meditates thoughtfully on his own motives and procedures in grappling with the text. The philological agonies that Knechtges explores Peterson sets aside: rather than dwelling on the uncertainties and insecurities that disagreements among multiple commentaries can produce, he accepts the syntheses and choices made by the twentieth-century scholar Qu Wanli—except, of course, when he chooses to reject them.

Peterson attributes what might be regarded as a rather complacent lack of concern with the "thorny philological problems," ones that Qu Wanli has resolved, into what are in his opinion "relatively unambiguous glosses or explanations," to his status as a "non-expert" in the field of classical Chinese literature, someone who is interested in texts like *Sheng min* principally because of the light they may shed on his own discipline of Chinese thought. Indeed, the first paragraph of his essay might lead one to expect yet another

---

41. That Owen, unlike Knechtges, refers to *Sheng min* as a "song" as often as he does a "poem" or "text" illuminates an important difference between the two readings.

reduction of a literary text to some document of historically contextualized intentionality.

To the contrary, Peterson is the consummate close reader, the only one of our three who systematically pays attention to the poem's stanzaic structure and rhyme scheme, and the balances within them, and to other aspects of its formal organization, such as the importance of the question asked at the beginning of the seventh section: "What about our si^a sacrifice?" As Peterson points out later, this is actually the second of the two questions that shape the course of the poem, the first being "What about the coming into being of [our] people?" And as we have seen, the responses to these two questions are provided in the song and clearly related to each other. Peterson concludes that ultimately the second subordinates the first. In his view, then, *Sheng min* is not primarily about the ethnic origins of the Zhou people; its main character, rather, is Hou Ji, who instituted the millet sacrifices that celebrate and guarantee the continuance of the dynastic line, and within which this song presumably plays a role.

As a reader interested in discerning a plausible motive or intention behind a literary work, Peterson has met with success. *Sheng min* "represents an ideological claim made in answer to the rhetorical question, 'what about our si^a sacrifice'" and was intended to be "performed as an ideological act at the Zhou court's new year sacrificial ritual," by linking the performers of the ritual with the cultural achievement of agricultural production, the ancestor who effected that achievement and instituted the ritual that perpetuates it, his progenitrix, and the deity who has made this all possible and whom the rites are designed to propitiate. The self-reflectiveness that Owen also calls to our attention has, Peterson concludes, prompted his reading of the song.

We have indeed come full circle. Jiang Yuan's initial infertility is eliminated by assiduous and efficacious performance of ritual, resulting in the miraculous birth of her son. Hou Ji, having survived a test of the elements, proceeds to master them as the quintessential farmer who cultivates and produces—after taming the excessive fertility of overgrown grasses (the inverse of his mother's original infertility, which also had to be tamed)—the millet that will play a central role in the sacrifices he institutes. These are the rites that will ensure the continuing fertility of the earth and the crucial timeliness of the harvest of which he, through sacrifice, is the analogous human product. And the song that is *Sheng min,* marked by a patterning within and between lines evocative of ritual performance and even perhaps some cosmic correspondence (so says Mao of the 10–8–8–10–10–8–10–8 pattern evident in the number of words per line), accompanies and enacts the ritual whose history it recounts. Its own efficacy is internally verified by the account of its origins that is its tale. The song seeks to effect that of which it speaks, the paradigm of endless continuity, by means of the measured cadences of its poetry, the echoes and symmetries that parallel the neatly planted rows of crops, and a multiplicity of rhythmic repetitions.

Both Owen and Peterson have made this point in their readings of *Sheng min*. Each of them chooses to focus on the performative function of the song as part of a sacrificial rite rather than to weave its elements together into a coherent narrative. Knechtges tells us rather of the frustrations traditional commentators have encountered in attempting to accomplish precisely that, to fill in the blanks behind and between individual graphs in the poem. More than one song in the *Shi jing* has been threatened with virtual collapse under the weight of such efforts. No responsible scholar can afford to ignore them, of course, but no inspired reader is likely to be daunted by them either. With Knechtges's wise caveats firmly in mind, we can, like Owen and Peterson, allow the poem to engage us as readers and to take its place in a larger cultural and international literary universe.

TWO

Mencius 2A.2

TRANSLATION

D. C. Lau

Kung-sun Ch'ou said, "If you, Master, were raised to a position above the Ministers in Ch'i and were able to put the Way into practice, it would be no surprise if through this you were able to make the King of Ch'i a leader of the feudal lords or even a true King. If this happened, would it cause any stirring in your heart?"

"No," said Mencius. "My heart has not been stirred since the age of forty."

"In that case you far surpass Meng Pin."

"That is not difficult. Kao Tzu succeeded in this at an even earlier age than I."

"Is there a way to develop a heart that cannot be stirred?"

"Yes, there is. The way Po-kung Yu cultivated his courage was by never showing submission on his face or letting anyone outstare him. For him, to yield the tiniest bit was as humiliating as to be cuffed in the market place. He would no more accept an insult from a prince with ten thousand chariots than from a common fellow coarsely clad. He would as soon run a sword through the prince as through the common fellow. He had no respect for persons, and always returned whatever harsh tones came his way.

"Meng Shih-she said this about the cultivation of his courage. 'I look upon defeat as victory. One who advances only after sizing up the enemy, and joins battle only after weighing the chances of victory, is simply showing cowardice in face of superior numbers. Of course I cannot be certain of victory. All I can do is to be without fear.'

"Meng Shih-she resembled Tseng Tzu while Po-kung Yu resembled Tzu-

From D. C. Lau, trans., *Mencius* (Harmondsworth: Penguin, 1976), 76–80. Reproduced by permission of Penguin Books Ltd. Notes are from the original.

hsia. It is hard to say which of the two was superior, but Meng Shih-she had a firm grasp of the essential.

"Tseng Tzu once said to Tzu-hsiang, 'Do you admire courage? I once heard about supreme courage from the Master.[1] If, on looking within, one finds oneself to be in the wrong, then even though one's adversary be only a common fellow coarsely clad one is bound to tremble with fear. But if one finds oneself in the right, one goes forward even against men in the thousands.' Meng Shih-she's firm hold on his *ch'i*[2] is inferior to Tseng Tzu's firm grasp of the essential."

"I wonder if you could tell me something about the heart that cannot be stirred, in your case and in Kao Tzu's case?"

"According to Kao Tzu, 'If you fail to understand words, do not worry about this in your heart; and if you fail to understand in your heart, do not seek satisfaction in your *ch'i*.' It is right that one should not seek satisfaction in one's *ch'i* when one fails to understand in one's heart. But it is wrong to say that one should not worry about it in one's heart when one fails to understand words.

"The will is commander over the *ch'i* while the *ch'i* is that which fills the body. The *ch'i* halts where the will arrives. Hence it is said, 'Take hold of your will and do not abuse your *ch'i*.'"

"As you have already said that the *ch'i* rests where the will arrives, what is the point of going on to say, 'Take hold of your will and do not abuse your *ch'i*'?"

"The will, when blocked, moves the *ch'i*. On the other hand, the *ch'i*, when blocked, also moves the will. Now stumbling and hurrying affect the *ch'i*,[3] yet in fact palpitations of the heart are produced."[4]

"May I ask what your strong points are?"

"I have an insight into words. I am good at cultivating my 'flood-like *ch'i*.'"

"May I ask what this 'flood-like *ch'i*' is?"

"It is difficult to explain. This is a *ch'i* which is, in the highest degree, vast and unyielding. Nourish it with integrity and place no obstacle in its path and it will fill the space between Heaven and Earth. It is a *ch'i* which unites rightness and the Way. Deprive it of these and it will collapse. It is born of accumulated rightness and cannot be appropriated by anyone through a sporadic show of rightness. Whenever one acts in a way that falls below the standard set in one's heart, it will collapse. Hence I said Kao Tzu never under-

---

1. I.e., Confucius.
2. For a discussion of this term see Introduction, p. 24ff [of D. C. Lau, trans., *Mencius* (Harmondsworth: Penguin, 1976)].
3. The *ch'i* here is the breath.
4. This seems to be the end of this passage, the rest of the section constituting a separate section.

stood rightness because he looked upon it as external.[5] You must work at it and never let it out of your mind. At the same time, while you must never let it out of your mind, you must not forcibly help it grow either. You must not be like the man from Sung.[6] There was a man from Sung who pulled at his rice plants because he was worried about their failure to grow. Having done so, he went on his way home, not realizing what he had done. 'I am worn out today,' said he to his family. 'I have been helping the rice plants to grow.' His son rushed out to take a look and there the plants were, all shrivelled up. There are few in the world who can resist the urge to help their rice plants grow. There are some who leave the plants unattended, thinking that nothing they can do will be of any use. They are the people who do not even bother to weed. There are others who help the plants grow. They are the people who pull at them. Not only do they fail to help them but they do the plants positive harm."

"What do you mean by 'an insight into words'?"

"From biased words I can see wherein the speaker is blind; from immoderate words, wherein he is ensnared; from heretical words, wherein he has strayed from the right path; from evasive words, wherein he is at his wits' end. What arises in the mind will interfere with policy, and what shows itself in policy will interfere with practice. Were a sage to rise again, he would surely agree with what I have said."[7]

"Tsai Wo and Tzu-kung excelled in rhetoric; Jan Niu, Min Tzu and Yen Hui excelled in the exposition of virtuous conduct.[8] Confucius excelled in both and yet he said, 'I am not versed in rhetoric.' In that case you, Master, must already be a sage."

"What an extraordinary thing for you to say of me! Tzu-kung once asked Confucius, 'Are you, Master, a sage?' Confucius replied, 'I have not succeeded in becoming a sage. I simply never tire of learning nor weary of teaching.' Tzu-kung said, 'Not to tire of learning is wisdom; not to weary of teaching is benevolence. You must be a sage to be both wise and benevolent.'[9] A sage is something even Confucius did not claim to be. What an extraordinary thing for you to say of me!"

"I have heard that Tzu-hsia, Tzu-yu and Tzu-chang each had one aspect of the Sage while Jan Niu, Min Tzu and Yen Hui were replicas of the Sage in miniature. Which would you rather be?"

5. Cf. VI.A.4.
6. In the writings of the Warring States period the man from Sung was a byword for stupidity.
7. The last part of this passage is found also in III.B.9.
8. Cf. the *Analects of Confucius*, XI.2.
9. Cf. ibid., VII.33. The version there seems less complete.

"Let us leave this question for the moment."

"How about Po Yi and Yi Yin?"

"They followed paths different from that of Confucius. Po Yi was such that he would only serve the right prince and rule over the right people, took office when order prevailed and relinquished it when there was disorder. Yi Yin was such that he would serve any prince and rule over any people, would take office whether order prevailed or not. Confucius was such that he would take office, or would remain in a state, would delay his departure or hasten it, all according to circumstances.[10] All three were sages of old. I have not been able to emulate any of them, but it is my hope and wish to follow the example of Confucius."

"Were Po Yi and Yi Yin as much an equal of Confucius as that?"

"No. Ever since man came into this world, there has never been another Confucius."

"Was there anything in common to all of them?"

"Yes. Were they to become ruler over a hundred *li* square, they would have been capable of winning the homage of the feudal lords and taking possession of the Empire; but had it been necessary to perpetrate one wrongful deed or to kill one innocent man in order to gain the Empire, none of them would have consented to it. In this they were alike."

"In what way were they different?"

"Tsai Wo, Tzu-kung and Yu Jo were intelligent enough to appreciate the Sage.[11] They would not have stooped so low as to show a bias in favour of the man they admired. Tsai Wo said, 'In my view, the Master surpassed greatly Yao and Shun.' Tzu-kung said, 'Through the rites of a state he could see its government; through its music, the moral quality of its ruler. Looking back over a hundred generations he was able to appraise all the kings, and no one has ever been able to show him to be wrong in a single instance. Ever since man came into this world, there has never been another like the Master.' Yu Jo said, 'It is true not only of men. The unicorn is the same in kind as other animals, the phoenix as other birds; Mount T'ai is the same as small mounds of earth; the Yellow River and the Sea are no different from water that runs in the gutter. The Sage, too, is the same in kind as other men.

Though one of their kind
He stands far above the crowd.

Ever since man came into this world, there has never been one greater than Confucius.'"

10. Cf. V.B.1.
11. I.e., Confucius.

ARE YOU A SAGE?

Willard Peterson

Mengzi 2A.2 ("Gongsun Chou") has stymied many readers. (I include myself and many of my students in this category.) It is long. There is no obvious theme or thread. The responses by Mengzi to Gongsun Chou's questions seem to go off in a direction not apparently implied by the question. Some of Gongsun Chou's questions pick up on a phrase or a point made by Mengzi, but others seem to lurch off into a new topic. The final, quoted sentence ("Since *min* have come into being, there never has been one grander than Kongzi") is not obviously sustained by the previous discussion, and does not seem to conclude anything. Many readers have chosen to focus on the implications to be discovered in the terms "unmoved heart" and *hao-ran zhi qi* and more or less disregard the rest of 2A.2. I propose that to follow the drift of the dialogue which we read in 2A.2, we might well keep our eyes on Gongsun Chou's questions.

We may presume that as a follower of Mengzi, Gongsun in his questions and comments is not challenging or contradicting his master, but is seeking to draw him out or receive clarification. (In 2A.1, Gongsun Chou refers to himself as a *dizi*, disciple, to Mengzi. If we were to regard Gongsun Chou as an adversary or critic of Mengzi, then my reading of 2A.2 could not be sustained.)

The passage begins with what is clearly a hypothetical situation put forward by Gongsun: Suppose Mengzi is placed in charge as a high minister of the government of the kingdom of *Qi*[a] (which was Gongsun's native place) and succeeds in implementing the Way (of the ancient sage kings), and in this he is no different from the famous minister Guan Zhong (whose achievements were discussed in 2A.1) who made his King of Qi into a *ba* (leader of the feudal lords and protector of the King of Zhou); if such a situation were to occur, Gongsun Chou asks Mengzi, would it move your heart? (Q1) Mengzi says no, and then, diverting Gongsun from his interest in implicit comparisons with Guan Zhong, Mengzi adds that his heart has not been moved since he was forty.

Reacting to his master's negative answer to the question trailing the hypothetical, Gongsun exclaims that if that is the case (if Mengzi has an unmoved heart), then Mengzi surpasses the fearless Meng Bin (don't you?). (Q2) Without denying the comparison, Mengzi brings in the example of Gaozi's also having an unmoved heart, which moves Gongsun's questioning away from Mengzi's person to a more general consideration.

Taking the bait, Gongsun asks if there is a way (or method) for having an unmoved heart (since there are at least two notable examples, Mengzi and Gaozi). (Q3) In his reply, Mengzi seems to go off on a tangent with examples of courage as an expression of an unmoved heart.

Trying to bring the topic back to Mengzi, Gongsun Chou formally asks (*gan wen*) to hear explicitly about his master's unmoved heart and Gaozi's. (Q4) Mengzi's explanation involves the terms heart (*xin*) and *qi*, which have both been part of the previous discussion of courage, and two terms not previously mentioned, words or oral expressions (*yan*) and will or intention (*zhi*); oral expressions are not unrelated to the heart, and the will is the commander of the person's *qi*. Elucidating the latter point, Mengzi offers a general proposition: "The will arrives, and *qi* is next," which implies that the movement of one's *qi* is dependent on the movement of his will, and which leads Mengzi to a further statement exhorting one to hold on to his will *and* not disturb his *qi* (i.e., to be cautious lest you agitate your *qi* independently of your will).

Gongsun Chou immediately sees the possibility that the second, exhortatory statement is redundant or else contradictory with the general proposition, and so he asks explicitly about the two in juxtaposition. (Q5) Mengzi clarifies the relation between the will and one's *qi* by allowing that each moves the other in some circumstances (i.e., the movement of one's *qi* is not simply dependent on one's will); he further adds that certain physical activities, which by definition involve one's *qi*, move his heart, contrary to what we might expect from the general proposition. (It is important to note here that Mengzi clearly allows what might be called the "physicality" of the functioning of the will and the heart.)

The next question posed by Gongsun troubles some readers because he seems to change the subject. He formally asks (*gan wen*) about his master's strengths (Q6), which has no context unless we recognize that they have been discussing what moves the heart and Gongsun's question returns to the matter of Mengzi's own unmoved heart. Mengzi's response declares his own strengths with regard to verbal expression (*yan*) and *qi*, the two terms linked to heart and will in his answer to the question (Q4) about the unmoved heart. The two-part response prompts the next two questions.

Gongsun formally asks (*gan wen*) what is meant by the term "flood-like *qi*." (Q7) (I adopt D. C. Lau's rendition of *hao-ran zhi qi*. I understand this to mean *qi* which is expansive and unimpeded, although commentators remain as uncertain as Gongsun Chou was.) Gongsun also asks what is meant by the phrase "know words" (*zhi yan*). (Q8) I leave aside (as does Gongsun Chou) Mengzi's explanation of what he means by "flood-like *qi*" which he is good at cultivating. Gongsun accepts his master's claim that he knows about a person's heart from his words, and that what is in his heart of course manifests itself in his political actions. (This again refers back to the answer to Q4.) Mengzi says, with reference to his knowing words, that "When a sagely person again appears, he shall inevitably be in accord with my words." (Note that Mengzi's sentence is not hypothetical or conditional. Note also that Mengzi is the one introducing the term "sagely person.")

Clever disputer that he is, Gongsun Chou seizes on what (I believe) he has been pressing for all along: a pregnant self-referential statement by his master. To set up his question, Gongsun cites the examples of five of Kongzi's disciples who had some partial achievements with regard to the use of verbal expressions (and who are regarded by some as sagely), and he also cites the example of Kongzi himself deprecating his own capacities in the use of powerfully laden verbal expressions. (We might now label these as performative utterances in governmental contexts.) Gongsun Chou's line of thought seems to be that if (a) Kongzi and his leading disciples are regarded as sagely but were less than perfected in their knowing words, and if (b) a sage of today would be in accord with Mengzi's words, then (c) Mengzi is superior to those predecessors and may be sagely. Thus Gongsun directly asks the big question: "If these [i.e., (a) and (b)] are so, then is not my master sagely?" (Q9) (In some versions of the text, the marker for the rhetorical question is dropped and the sentence is taken as an exclamation.) Mengzi, who declared that one of his strengths is that he "knows words," sputters "What talk is this!" and reminds Gongsun of two occasions on which Kongzi demurred when asked by a disciple if he were sagely. (One time the question was put in exactly the same words which Gongsun uses to pose his question [Q9].)

Disregarding the apparent disclaimer by Mengzi, Gongsun presses on by recalling that Kongzi's disciples were, in some respect or another, sages, and then he formally asks (gan wen), "Where do you stand?" (Q10) Mengzi simply brushes the question aside.

Gongsun Chou tries again by asking about other sages. "What about Bo Yi and Yi Yin?" (Q11) Mengzi accepts this question. He distinguishes between Bo Yi's, Yi Yin's, and Kongzi's ways of being involved in government, declares all three to have been sages of earlier times, and says he has not been able to implement their ways (of being involved in government [xing dao], which was premised in Gongsun's hypothetical situation leading to the first question). "But if this is about what I would want, then it is to learn to be Kongzi" (or, more accurately, to learn the way implemented by him). I infer that in this response Mengzi accepts Gongsun's initial premise: Mengzi conceivably could be in charge of the government of the kingdom of Qi and implement the way of sages. I also infer that therefore Mengzi is granting that he could be a sage, which is what Gongsun wants to hear all along. Mengzi adds that it is one particular sage—Kongzi himself—whom Mengzi would emulate, not the ones who were kings or who martyred themselves.

In response to this disclosure, Gongsun Chou asks for clarification about Kongzi's being a sage of a different sort than Bo Yi and Yi Yin. (Q12) Mengzi's response shifts the focus of the discussion from "sages" as a category to Kongzi as a particular exemplar (even though Mengzi has reminded Gongsun that Kongzi demurred when asked if he were sagely). "No, since *min* have come into being, there has not been [another] Kongzi."

Gongsun Chou asks for us: "If that is so, then are there commonalities [shared between Kongzi and others conventionally regarded as sages]?" (Q13) Mengzi's answer is bold if we take it as applicable to Gongsun's initial hypothetical situation: "The commonality is that when someone [with the qualities of a true king] succeeds as a ruler over a territory of a hundred *li* square [which is much smaller than the kingdom of Qi], he is able to have all-under-Heaven by being paid court by the aristocrats [of other states]." But, Mengzi stresses, he would not compromise his moral integrity to succeed to all-under-Heaven, which explains why Kongzi, and thus far Mengzi, were not ministers to a ruler who could be a true king. (It also explains what so many later rulers, whose position was secured directly or indirectly by killing at least one guiltless person, did not much like about Mengzi.) In my words, Mengzi is claiming that Kongzi was the same (except in result) as such sagely rulers as Yao, Shun, and King Wen, which is bold indeed considering that he wants to learn to be Kongzi.

This leads Gongsun Chou to ask formally (*gan wen*), How is Kongzi different? (Q14) Mengzi's answer is pure Mengzi. Remember that Gongsun Chou is Mengzi's disciple. Since the initial question, Gongsun has been asking, by various means, and Mengzi has been evading, the question, To whom is my master to be compared? To answer how Kongzi, who demurred when asked directly if he were a sage, was a sage different from other sages (who were in the role they were in initially because of birth, marriage or conquest), Mengzi quotes (or perhaps appears to quote, as the statements are not attested elsewhere) three disciples of Kongzi. The three disciples each say Kongzi was a sage. ("Far more accomplished than Yao and Shun." "Since *min* came into being, there has not been [another like] my master." "Sages in relation to *min* are of the same category. . . . Since *min* have come into being, there has never been one grander than Kongzi.") Simply on the basis of this response, Gongsun Chou is expected to believe that Kongzi was a sage because his disciples said so. Gongsun Chou wants to know if his master, who has declined to rank himself among the disciples (see his refusal of Q10), is a sage. Well, . . .

I surmise that in 2A.2 Mengzi is tacitly proposing a bargain: given that the sagely Kongzi had some disciples who are regarded as sagely, if Mengzi is said by his disciples to be a sage, then Gongsun Chou might . . . (hmmm).

The astounding thing about this passage is that some admirers of Mengzi at least since the twelfth century have sought to pursue his wish of learning to be a sage.

"THERE HAS NEVER BEEN ONE GREATER THAN CONFUCIUS"

Peter Bol

What are we facing in this passage? Is it an exposition constructed in service of an argument—a whole whose parts are intended to move the reader along a well-plotted course—or is it a dialogue that begins somewhere but soon takes leave of the main line as Mencius and a student move laterally to explore related subjects? How can the beginning, on the question of whether great political success (but also morally responsible success) would stir Mencius's heart, be integrally connected to the concluding claim that Confucius is the most significant human being to have walked the face of the earth? I do not know how I could prove that this is a sustained argument and that the beginning and ending are connected in a necessary fashion. I have decided to assume that the ending connects to the beginning. The reading that follows results from asking how a heart not stirred is relevant to understanding why Confucius is the greatest man in history and how Mencius's understanding of Confucius's greatness bears on the problem of the unstirred heart.

THE UNSTIRRED HEART

The issue with Mencius's "heart that is not stirred" (*bu dong xin*) is the sensation of self-interest awakened by external reward and punishment. Mencius's claim for himself is that even the ultimate social rewards he might expect would not move him. But how can one attain such a state? Initial answers to these questions emerge from the three examples of courage. Courage in the face of danger is more obvious, perhaps, but it refers to the same problem as courage in the face of reward: the ability to hold one's own course and counsel. The three examples are levels of attainment. Bogong You is willing to maintain his dignity—his sense of his own worth—at whatever the cost in whatever the context. Meng Shishe had a sense of duty. Meng did not ask what would be advantageous to himself, he did what he was supposed to do without calculation. It is not, Mencius tells us, that one is better than the other but that Meng, with his "firm grasp of the essential," brings us closer to the crux of the matter: doing what is right. This is where the third example fits in. Zengzi has the firmest grasp of all, for he holds to Confucius's teaching that the source of courage is a conviction that one is in the right. Attaining this conviction depends on *zifan*. For the translator *zifan* is "looking within" but I prefer to take it more literally as "self-reflection" or "turning [something] back on oneself." Zengzi, for example, turns Confucius's words back on himself to determine what is right in thinking about courage.

These three cases of courage introduce a complex that will reappear in the discussion that follows. Courage is about fear out of self-interest, an emotional state that can be experienced with excruciating intensity—it is *qi* in tumult—and yet our first two characters are able to suppress fear with determination or will-power. In other words, they are evidence that the will is more powerful than *qi*. Mencius insists on showing that a moral question is, in some basic sense, (also) a physical question: control over the body's instinctive reactions. However, Zengzi's Confucius does not aim to suppress fear; he will (and should) experience fear when he is going against the right. He is more complete in many ways: he accepts emotions rather than suppressing them, he is more self-conscious rather than less, and he makes distinctions according to the situation rather than absolutely. In a sense he combines Bogong's sense of self with Meng's sense of duty.

THE MEDIATING HEART

The heart is in the middle, between the external situation and the physiological realities of one's internal states (*qi*). It makes the connection between the perception of deeds and words and the experience of particular emotions. As the commentators have found, Gaozi's words are ambiguous. The translator's "If you fail to understand words, do not worry about this in your heart; and if you fail to understand in your heart, do not seek satisfaction in your *qi*"[12] provides more certainty about whose words, heart, and *qi* are at issue than the original allows. In fact, I do not think it matters whether Gaozi is not seeking to understand the heart of the other, the one that led to the words, or not seeking in his own heart; in either case he is not seeking. The issue for Mencius is that Gaozi, who represents a different kind of unstirred heart, refuses to make the connections between external and internal. When language doesn't work leave it be, says Gaozi, when you don't understand don't get yourself stirred up. Perhaps this is sound advice for equanimity in withdrawal, from a man who appears to think that the physical state is the basis for thought and expression. Although Mencius has a serious dispute with Gaozi over human nature and the status of ethical principles and refers to the last matter here, he does not seem particularly concerned with whatever Gaozi intended—by accepting half of the statement and rejecting the other he avoids the issue—but he clearly opts for the centrality of the heart as the source for the words and as that which can guide the *qi*.

The centrality of the heart gives it a mediating role between the individ-

---

12. D. C. Lau, trans., *Mencius* (Harmondsworth: Penguin, 1976), 77. Alternative readings are discussed in *Mengzi zhengyi* 6.194–97.

ual's perceptions of the world and the feelings that initiate his responses to it. But this also means that both language and *qi* can indicate something about the heart. At this moment, however, Mencius is compelled to acknowledge part of Gaozi's position: that the *qi* can influence the heart. To put the heart in command, to make it central, is an effort rather than an inevitable consequence of one's being. "Take hold of your will," he proclaims, and "do not expose your *qi* [to extremes]."[13] In short, Mencius calls for focusing the heart's attention and a regimen of restraint for the body.

SENSING ONE'S OWN HEART

Mencius's claim for himself against Gaozi is that he is good at cultivating his flood-like *qi* and has insight into words. In the context of his exposition, however, we can read his discussion of cultivating the flood-like *qi* as an answer to the question of how someone trying to cultivate an unstirred heart can know the moral state of his heart. Mencius's answer to this question brings him to the difficult problem of explaining how someone who takes his own heart as a guide can know that he is doing the right thing.

As I read him Mencius promises that one can learn to maintain a state of moral correctness and that one can tell in a physical way whether one is in that state or not. Taking the physical pulse is taking the moral pulse at the same time. Conducting oneself morally is cultivating one's flood-like *qi* as the sensation of all-embracing inclusiveness and ultimate toughness. The physical state is cultivated by a continuous process of doing good. Here Mencius's difference with the handy adversary Gaozi allows us to see an important point. Gaozi's mistake in making righteousness external meant that particular acts were seen as good and could thus lead to the conclusion that "sporadic" attempts to do the right thing had some moral payoff. Not so. By insisting that moral conduct be connected to a physical sensation Mencius can separate rightness from rule. That is, he can say that what is right depends on the actor's understanding of the situation he confronts and that the correctness of the response will be physically apparent. One will need no rule-book, no ledger that gives points per good or bad deed; one will maintain the moral state by doing what one knows and feels is right. The promise has its escape clause: the foolish and impatient do not realize this is a long and gradual process.

13. Lau translates *bao*[a] as "abuse" (do not abuse your *qi*), but in Mencius *bao*[a] is otherwise used consistently for exposing something to the sun and air. I take the point here to be that one must avoid exposing oneself to situations which, like the stumbling and hurrying of one who is so ill-timed that he must run, upset the *qi* sufficiently for it to overpower the will.

KNOWING THE HEARTS OF OTHERS

At this point readers might grant that were it clear what was in the heart and where its standards came from then cultivating flood-like *qi* might work well as a guide to action. Now is the moment for Mencius to claim, as he does elsewhere, that all hearts instinctively tend to prefer the good, just as the palate likes sweetness, or that all men possess hearts with the beginning of virtues. In short, Mencius ought to conclude by telling us that our hearts are innately capable of guiding us. But he does not. Instead the discussion turns to "insight into words." This topic fits with his account of the mediating role of the heart, and it is one of the two ways in which Mencius thinks his own cultivation of the unstirred heart is better than Gaozi's approach. I would suggest that it is also the beginning of Mencius's answer to the question of where the heart's standards come from and why Confucius is the best of humanity.

"Insight into words" takes us most immediately to the claim that the way someone speaks (or writes) reflects accurately the state of the speaker's heart and mind. Mencius is willing to extend this. The failings that come into being in the heart and become the personality traits of speech also interfere with service in government. One's interaction with the outside world (speech and action) thus reflects qualities of the heart. At this point Mencius's interlocutor begins politely to question the value of "insight into words." The issue is the status of virtuous conduct relative to the three other activities the citation of Confucius's disciples alludes to: rhetoric, cultural studies, and governance.[14] Is Mencius claiming to be better than Confucius, a sage thus, since the latter was unwilling to accept a reputation for rhetoric (i.e., "insight into words")? Is it not the case that those who behave virtuously are complete "replicas of the Sage in miniature" while those good at other things replicate only one aspect of the Sage? In other words, why this concern with rhetoric, government, and culture, Mencius is asked, when you ought to know that virtuous conduct alone is more than adequate? It is a problem, in fact, for Mencius sidesteps in such an obvious manner that he seems to be calling attention to his maneuvers: even Confucius did not claim to be a sage, how should I? Let us not ask these questions for the moment.

And too suddenly we are with Bo Yi, Yi Yin, and Confucius. But I do not think Mencius has changed the subject. Rather, I suspect he is finding a way to counter the view that virtuous conduct is adequate in itself.

14. In *Analects* 11.3 disciples of Confucius are grouped into these four categories. This is brought up first by the contrast with Zai Wo and Zigong, both known for rhetoric, and then by the contrasting of Zixia and Ziyou (cultural studies) with Zizhang (who in *Analects* 20.2 is concerned with governance).

"THERE HAS NEVER BEEN ONE GREATER THAN CONFUCIUS"

Bo Yi and Yi Yin represent opposing dogmas yet they are equally sages. Both rely on dogmas to know what is right—that is, one will serve anyone and the other would serve only the right ruler—yet had they been given the chance both would have brought moral order to the world and neither would have harmed a single innocent in order to serve the common good. They are parallels to the two men of courage, Bogong You who would always defend his honor and Meng Shishe who would always sacrifice himself. They live by rules that tell them what is virtuous and what is not. Confucius, however, was no less a sage but had no such rule. Confucius was different because, as was the case with his idea of courage, he acted according to his own sense of what was appropriate.

This brings us to the point of "insight into words." For the person whose judgment of what is right depends upon his assessment of the situation, there can be no easy dogmas. The problem with a narrow conception of virtuous behavior—one that separates it from rhetoric, culture, and government—is that it does not need to take the situation into account; instead of teaching one how to be effective it tells him he can be satisfied with being courageous. Insight into words is the ability to know what other men are capable of; without assessing the other people who compose the situation, it is not possible to assess the possibilities for effective action. Knowing when good can be accomplished ought to be an essential part of doing good. There is more. Confucius was wiser than Yao and Shun—an extraordinary claim—because (I submit) Mencius sees that Confucius had the ability to assess the kings of the past. He could tell from their culture (rites and music) the quality of policy and rulership and, Mencius tells us, Confucius reviewed all of history and evaluated all the rulers.

I want to return to the question of where the mind gets its guides, for the ability to take the mind as a guide when the effectiveness of moral action depends on the situation makes this a pressing issue. It is usually held that Mencius supposed that all are born with the same moral propensities (the doctrine of the "four beginnings"). Here, however, we are given a very different possibility: the man who "reflects" by using knowledge of the past and thereby creates a heart for himself. Confucius was committed to learning for himself and to teaching others what the connections were between the heart and social consequences through a review of history. He thus gave himself something to look at when, confronting a situation that demanded a choice, he needed to "reflect" and see whether his course of action was right. Confucius was a man among men, but he was the first Mencius had ever heard of who realized that one could learn to take one's own heart and mind as the standard of true morality. Confucius developed this through his judgment of the past, where what men with power had in mind and the consequences could be plainly seen. Mencius understood how he had done it. But this is not a package that can be acquired with a single effort, as the man of Song discovered. What can be learned is the theory that lies behind the process and some key aspects of cultivation. These are universal (the Sage reborn would not change Mencius's words) but it remains for each individual to do it on his own, by creating the means of self-reflection through learning: by using history as a means of understanding the connection between the possible inclinations of the heart and their consequences and by using Confucius as an example of seeing that one can decide how to act according to one's evaluation of the situation.

PERSPECTIVE ON READINGS OF *MENCIUS* 2A.2

Stephen Owen

Let us begin by recognizing that these readings by two intellectual historians, themselves related as teacher and student, are very much alike in some ways. Both are internal readings, not attempting to place the text in a historical context or an intertextual context. Neither offers sustained reflection on what is meant by particular words, combining historical philology and philosophy. Both interpretations trace the text from beginning to end, clarifying its coherence. The value, however, of such procedural agreement is that it permits us to see some profound differences that are often concealed by the simpler and more obvious differences of approach mentioned above.

The shared attention to the coherence of this passage, whose very textual unity has been suspected, highlights the question Peter Bol raises at the beginning of his discussion: is this dialogue or argument? What is the relation of the end to the complex parts (note that both readers choose their titles from the end)? Clearly the main body of the passage is neither proof nor formal demonstration of the end, in which case the main body would be necessary only to sustain the validity of the conclusion. But the question of coherence permits us to ask how ideas work in the *Mencius*.

Let me here interject an assumption: *Mencius* 2A.2 is *not* a dialogue in the oral sense, or even the accurate transcription of such a dialogue; it is the imitation of a dialogue or, at most, the re-creation of a dialogue that actually occurred. Its moves are mediated by the writer's sense of how dialogues with Mencius worked and how ideas were developed; they are not the actual contingencies of a particular oral dialogue. Like many of the written dialogues of Plato, this text uses signatures of oral dialogue; for example, Mencius dismisses a question by Gongsun Chou by saying "Let's set that aside for now" (without ever returning to it). Such things happen in the contingency of oral dialogue. Either such signatures of oral dialogue in writing are purely formal (that is, they are included only for dialogic verisimilitude) or they are significant. And if they are significant, it is important to account for how.

Both Bol and Peterson run up against this problem in different ways. After articulating the central question of whether this text is "an exposition constructed in service of an argument" or a dialogue that "soon takes leave of the main line" to "move laterally to explore related subjects," Bol decides to treat the text as an argument; that is, the end follows from the beginning and the parts are related in a necessary sequence. Bol does a remarkably persuasive job of this, but his initial assumption, however forthright, permits him to avoid addressing why the text takes the form it does—the obvious problem that led to his initial statement of the question. At moments, however, the movement of the text forces Bol to take a passage differently. When Mencius evades Gongsun Chou's questions whether he is himself a sage, and, if not, which of Confucius's disciples he would rather be, Bol writes: "It is a problem, in fact, for Mencius sidesteps in such an obvious manner that he seems to be calling attention to his maneuvers: even Confucius did not claim to be a sage, how should I? Let us not ask these questions for the moment."

Framed by Bol's sustained drive toward argument, this moment of interpretation is not taking the text as pure argument, but as something else. Here the dialogic form is neither overlooked nor treated as accident; it is apparently significant.

Willard Peterson, in contrast, takes the text as a true dialogue which has a "drift," guided by Gongsun Chou's questions. This reproduces the epistemological theater of early Confucianism: "meaning" already exists complete in the master, and it emerges into words only as it is elicited by the disciple or questioner. The coherence of the text, then, lies in the ability of the questioner to trace clues, make connections, and pose problems. But Peterson takes the radical alternative to argument, that this is more or less authentic *unmediated* dialogue. Thus Peterson is willing to dismiss the early section on examples of courage as a "tangent" where the line of questioning has apparently gone adrift (Bol, in fact, gives a strong reading of this passage and shows that is a necessary stage in his linear reading). In the section referred to above, in which Bol hints that Mencius's dismissal of a question is purposive, Peterson comments, "Mengzi simply brushes the question aside."

I offer this comparison to suggest the value of reflection on the form of textual representation, that it is neither the inert container of an argument nor the unmediated recording of an event. "What Mencius had to say" cannot be separated from the way in which knowledge can appear. Peterson's account, following Gongsun Chou's questions, is, in this way, immensely compelling because he accepts the drama of knowledge: that is, a notion of the completeness of meaning already existing within a wise person, some of whose essential features can be mapped by the questioner's skillful handling of contingent response. And indeed Peterson's conclusion confirms the necessity of the disciple-questioner as the means by which a sage can "appear."

Peterson's superb instincts for following the theater of eliciting knowledge sometimes seduce him into taking that theater as life, whose contingencies are truly unforeseen and sometimes irrelevant. I am not arguing here for a self-consciously "literary" writing of these dialogues; rather I am suggesting that the writing is shaped by a sense of how such a dialogue "should have" or "must have" occurred, a sense which presumes not quite linear argument but a necessity that can only "appear" in the guise of contingency. As Bol's exposition shows, a number of the dialogue's apparently wrong turns are actually leading in the right direction. There is a complex determination behind the apparent liberty of dialogue.

Bol's conclusion that Confucius was the greatest sage by his knowledge of the past and his ability to reflect on it is wonderfully persuasive; it carries Bol's refusal to acknowledge the dialogue (which is "words," *yan*) right up to the very end of his reading. Going back to the three examples of courage toward the beginning, in which, as Bol says, "Zengzi has the firmest grasp of all, for he holds to Confucius's teaching that the source of courage is a conviction that one is in the right," Zengzi's understanding of courage is distinguished from the two preceding examples by something else besides its content, something that may, in fact, be intimately related to the capacity for *zifan*, "self-reflection." Zengzi's understanding of courage is mediated by words, what he *learned* from what someone else said. It may be that the disjunction of knowledge in words, as opposed to instinctive courage, is necessary for *zifan* in its several senses, including Bol's suggestive "turning [something] back on oneself." Verbal transmission from the past is *almost* central to the Confucian project (Mencius's unease that it seems central but somehow *should not* be is how I would account for Mencius's explicit rejection of the necessity of verbal mediation in the passage immediately following—he does not reject verbal mediation, only its necessity). The *yan* that keeps recurring in the dialogue is not simply eloquence or the immediate psychological manifestation of oral words (though these are part of *yan*); *yan* is also what was said in the past and transmitted, the very medium of learning. And if Confucius is superior to Yao and Shun by his knowledge of the past, he knows the past through the mediation of transmitted words, as Mencius himself knows Confucius, and as any potential sage will know the rightness of Mencius's own words (as Mencius claims).

This brings us back to the question of dialogue. The idea of an "argument" presumes that its particular articulation is merely incidental; that is, the "same" argument can be presented in many verbal forms. Clearly Mencius believes that there is a moral lesson, a "something" to be articulated that exists independent of articulation; but that does not answer the question of whether articulation is incidental. A bad person, an uneasy person, a hesitant and inarticulate person can all make the same "argument" about the good; and the argument will remain equally valid. By this standard Mencius cannot accept the validity of an "argument" in and of itself; as Bol reminds us, a moral sense of the right has its truly physical counterpart in an unperturbed *qi*, and is manifested in words, which is apparent to one who "understands words," *zhi yan*, the condition from which the words were uttered. Hence the validity of a moral utterance cannot be dissociated from its circumstantial articulation; and circumstantial articulation is essentially dialogic.

As I said, however, this is not the true transcript of dialogue but its representation—which is, in fact, also the way all words get handed down in the tradition. It restages the scene of learning, shaping the account by what was learned. But perhaps I am wrong in insisting that we pay attention to the mediation of writing; perhaps the ultimate validation of the text can only be seen in Peterson's mode of reading, by forgetting the purposive mediation that we know is present and "hearing" the text as if it were the immediate exchange between Mencius and Gongsun Chou.

THREE

Qi wu lun
Zhuangzi: "Seeing Things as Equal"

TRANSLATION
"The Sorting Which Evens Things Out"
A. C. Graham

The last word in the title *Ch'i wu lun* is sometimes understood as "discourse" ("The discourse on evening things out"), sometimes in its more basic sense of "sort out (in coherent discourse)." Comparison with the three-word titles of the other *Inner chapters* favours the latter alternative. *Lun,* "sorting out," is the one kind of thinking always mentioned with approval in *Chuang-tzŭ.* Outside Taoism it suggests grading in superior and inferior categories, but Chuang-tzŭ detaches it from valuation, turns it into "the sorting which evens things out."

The theme of the chapter is the defense of a synthesising vision against Confucians, Mohists and Sophists, who analyze, distinguish alternatives and debate which is right or wrong. It contains the most philosophically acute passages in the *Inner chapters,* obscure, fragmented, but pervaded by the sensation, rare in ancient literatures, of a man jotting the living thought at the moment of its inception. It is a pity that the Syncretist who assembled the chapter seems to have been out of sympathy with these intellectual subtleties designed to discredit the intellect, for he has relegated a number of closely related passages to the *Mixed chapters* (pp. 101–8, 110f [in Graham, *Chuang-tzŭ: The Seven Inner Chapters*]).

Tzŭ-ch'i of Nan-kuo reclined elbow on armrest, looked up at the sky and exhaled, in a trance as though he had lost the counterpart of himself. Yen-ch'eng Tzŭ-yu stood in waiting before him.

Reprinted from A. C. Graham, *Chuang-tzŭ: The Seven Inner Chapters and Other Writings from the Book* Chuang-tzŭ (London: Allen & Unwin, 1981), 48–61.

"What is this?" he said. "Can the frame really be made to be like withered wood, the heart like dead ashes? The reclining man here now is not the reclining man of yesterday."

"You do well to ask that, Tzǔ-yu! This time I had lost my own self, did you know it? You hear the pipes of men, don't you, but not yet the pipes of earth, the pipes of earth but not yet the pipes of Heaven?"

"I venture to ask the secret of it."

"That hugest of clumps of soil blows out breath, by name the 'wind.' Better if it were never to start up, for whenever it does ten thousand hollow places burst out howling, and don't tell me you have never heard how the hubbub swells! The recesses in mountain forests, the hollows that pit great trees a hundred spans round, are like nostrils, like mouths, like ears, like sockets, like bowls, like mortars, like pools, like puddles. Hooting, hissing, sniffing, sucking, mumbling, moaning, whistling, wailing, the winds ahead sing out AAAH!, the winds behind answer EEEH!, breezes strike up a tiny chorus, the whirlwind a mighty chorus. When the gale has passed, all the hollows empty, and don't tell me you have never seen how the quivering slows and settles!"

"The pipes of earth, these are the various hollows; the pipes of men, these are rows of tubes. Let me ask about the pipes of Heaven."

"Who is it that puffs out the myriads which are never the same, who in their self-ending is sealing them up, in their self-choosing is impelling the force into them?

"Heaven turns circles, yes!
Earth sits firm, yes!
Sun and moon vie for a place, yes!
Whose is the bow that shoots them?
Whose is the net that holds them?
Who is it sits with nothing to do and gives them the push that sends
    them?

"Shall we suppose, yes, that something triggers them off, then seals
    them away, and they have no choice?
Or suppose, yes, that wheeling in their circuits they cannot stop
    themselves?
Do the clouds make the rain?
Or the rain the clouds?
Whose bounty bestows them?
Who is it sits with nothing to do as in ecstasy he urges them?

The winds rise in the north,
Blow west, blow east,
And now again whirl high above.

Who breathes them out, who breathes them in?
Who is it sits with nothing to do and sweeps between and over them?"[1]

•   •   •

"Great wit is effortless,
Petty wit picks holes.
Great speech is flavorless,
Petty speech strings words.

"While it sleeps, the paths of souls cross:
When it wakes, the body opens.
Whatever we sense entangles it:
Each day we use that heart of ours for strife."

The calm ones, the deep ones, the subtle ones.

"Petty fears intimidate,
The supreme fear calms.
It shoots like the trigger releasing the string on the notch,"

referring to its manipulation of "That's it, that's not."

"It ties us down as though by oath, by treaty,"

referring to its commitment to the winning alternative.

"Its decline is like autumn and winter,"

speaking off its daily deterioration. As it sinks, that which is the source of its deeds cannot be made to renew them.

"It clogs as though it were being sealed up,"

speaking of its drying up in old age. As the heart nears death, nothing can make it revert to the Yang.

---

1. Chuang-tzŭ's parable of the wind compares the conflicting utterances of philosophers to the different notes blown by the same breath in the long and short tubes of the pan-pipes, and the noises made by the wind in hollows of different shapes. It is natural for differently constituted persons to think differently; don't try to decide between their opinions, listen to Heaven who breathes through them.

The trance of Tzŭ-ch'i reappears in a *Mixed chapter* fragment (p. 105 [in Graham, *Chuang-tzŭ: The Inner Chapters*]), where he speaks of a progressive objectivisation of successive selves from which he detaches himself. Here he has finally broken out of the dichotomy, losing both "the counterpart of himself" and "his own self."

"That hugest of clumps of soil," a phrase peculiar to the *Inner chapters* (pp. 86–8 [in Graham, *Chuang-tzŭ*]), seems to conjure up an image of the universe so far in the distance that it is no bigger than a clod you could hold in your hand.

The poem which we identify as the conclusion of the dialogue survives only in one of the *Outer chapters*, the "Circuits of Heaven" (chapter 14). But the Buddhist *Chih-kuan fu-hsing ch'uan-hung*

Pleasure in things and anger against them, sadness and joy, forethought and regret, change and immobility, idle influences that initiate our gestures—music coming out of emptiness, vapour condensing into mushrooms—alternate before it day and night and no one knows from what soil they spring. Enough! The source from which it has these morning and evening, is it not that from which it was born?[2]

• • •

"Without an Other there is no Self, without Self no choosing one thing rather than another."

This is somewhere near it, but we do not know in whose service they are being employed. It seems that there is something genuinely in command, and that the only trouble is we cannot find a sign of it. That as "Way" it can be walked is true enough, but we do not see its shape; it has identity but no shape. Of the hundred joints, nine openings, six viscera all present and complete, which should I recognize as more kin to me than another? Are you people pleased with them all? Rather, you have a favourite organ among them. On your assumption, does it have the rest of them as its vassals and concubines? Are its vassals and concubines inadequate to rule each other? Isn't it rather that they take turns as each other's lord and vassals? Or rather than that, they have a genuine lord present in them. If we seek without success to grasp what its identity might be, that never either adds to nor detracts from its genuineness.[3]

• • •

Once we have received the completed body we are aware of it all the time we await extinction. Is it not sad how we and other things go on stroking or jostling each other, in a race ahead like a gallop which nothing can stop? How can we fail to regret that we labour all our lives without seeing success, wear ourselves out with toil in ignorance of where we shall end? What use is it for man to say that he will not die, since when the body dissolves the

chüeh (preface dated A.D. 766) cites it from the *Inner chapters* (*Taishó Tripitaka* No. 1912, p. 440C), from which it would have been excised when *Chuang-tzŭ* was abridged, to avoid duplication. The fit is so neat that it can be located here with some confidence.

2. Chuang-tzŭ might be either the author or the annotator of these verses about the heart, the organ of thought. The "supreme fear" which calms would be the fear of death, reconciliation with which is Chuang-tzŭ's central concern.

3. Chuang-tzŭ starts from a quotation or a provisional formulation of his own. His theme is again the heart, the organ of thought. Should it be allowed to take charge of our lives? Isn't it merely one of many organs each with its own functions within an order which comes from beyond us, from the Way?

heart dissolves with it? How can we not call this our supreme regret? Is man's life really as stupid as this? Or is it that I am the only stupid one, and there are others not so stupid? But if you go by the completed heart and take it as your authority, who is without such an authority? Why should it be only the man who knows how things alternate and whose heart approves its own judgements who has such an authority? The fool has one just as he has. For there to be "That's it, that's not" before they are formed in the heart would be to "go to Yüeh today and have arrived yesterday." This would be crediting with existence what has no existence, and if you do that even the daemonic Yü could not understand you, and how can you expect to be understood by me?[4]

• • •

Saying is not blowing breath, saying says something; the only trouble is that what it says is never fixed. Do we really say something? Or have we never said anything? If you think it different from the twitter of fledgelings, is there proof of the distinction? Or isn't there any proof? By what is the Way hidden, that there should be a genuine or a false? By what is saying darkened, that sometimes "That's it" and sometimes "That's not"? Wherever we walk how can the Way be absent? Whatever the standpoint how can saying be unallowable? The Way is hidden by formation of the lesser, saying is darkened by its foliage and flowers. And so we have the "That's it, that's not" of Confucians and Mohists, by which what is *it* for one of them for the other is not, what is *not* for one of them for the other is. If you wish to affirm what they deny and deny what they affirm, the best means is Illumination.

No thing is not "other," no thing is not "it." If you treat yourself too as "other" they do not appear, if you know of yourself you know of them. Hence it is said:

"'Other' comes out from 'it,' 'it' likewise goes by 'other,'"

the opinion that "it" and "other" are born simultaneously. However,

"Simultaneously with being alive one dies."

and simultaneously with dying one is alive, simultaneously with being allowable something becomes unallowable and simultaneously with being unallowable it becomes allowable. If going by circumstance that's it then going by circumstance that's not, if going by circumstance that's not then going

4. "I go to Yüeh today but came yesterday" is a paradox of the Sophist Hui Shih (p. 283 [in Graham, *Chuang-tzŭ*]), here mentioned only for its absurdity.

by circumstance that's it. This is why the sage does not take this course, but opens things up to the light of Heaven; his too is a "That's it" which goes by circumstance.[5]

•   •   •

What is It is also Other, what is Other is also It. There they say "That's it, that's not" from one point of view, here we say "That's it, that's not" from another point of view. Are there really It and Other? Or really no It and Other? Where neither It nor Other finds its opposite is called the axis of the Way. When once the axis is found at the centre of the circle there is no limit to responding with either, on the one hand no limit to what is *it*, on the other no limit to what is not. Therefore I say: "The best means is Illumination." Rather than use the meaning to show that

"The meaning is not the meaning,"

use what is *not* the meaning. Rather than use a horse to show that

"A horse is not a horse"

use what is *not* a horse. Heaven and earth are the one meaning, the myriad things are the one horse.[6]

•   •   •

Allowable?—allowable. Unallowable?—unallowable. The Way comes about as we walk it; as for a thing, call it something and that's so. Why so? By being so. Why not so? By not being so. It is inherent in a thing that from some-

5. In disputation if an object fits the name "ox" one affirms with the demonstrative word *shih*, "(That) is it"; if it is something other than an ox one denies with a *fei*, "(That) is not." Here Chuang-tzŭ tries to discredit disputation by the objection that at any moment of change both alternatives will be admissible. He appeals to a paradox of Hui Shih, "The sun is simultaneously at noon and declining, a thing is simultaneously alive and dead." (p. 283 [in Graham, *Chuang-tzŭ*]), and generalizes to the conclusion that any statement will remain inadmissible in the moment when it has just become admissible. It was also recognized in current disputation (as we find it in the Mohist *Canons*) that one can say both "Y is long" (in relation to X) and "Y is short" (in relation to Z), and that even with words such as "black" and "white" which are not comparative one has to decide whether to "go by" (*yin*) the black parts or the white when deeming someone a "black man." Chuang-tzŭ sees it as the lesson of disputation that one is entitled to affirm or deny anything of anything. He thinks of Confucians and Mohists who stick rigidly to their affirmations and denials as lighting up little areas of life and leaving the rest in darkness; the Illumination of the sage is a vision which brings everything to light.

6. There are extant essays by the Sophist Kung-sun Lung arguing that "A white horse is not a horse" and "When no thing is not the meaning the meaning is not the meaning." Chuang-tzŭ thinks he was wasting his time; since all disputation starts from arbitrary acts of naming, he

where that's so of it, from somewhere that's allowable of it; of no thing is it
not so, of no thing is it unallowable. Therefore when a "That's it" which deems
picks out a stalk from a pillar, a bag from beautiful Hsi Shih, things however
peculiar or incongruous, the Way interchanges them and deems them one.
Their dividing is formation, their formation is dissolution; all things whether
forming or dissolving in reverting interchange and are deemed to be one.
Only the man who sees right through knows how to interchange and deem
them one; the "That's it" which deems he does not use, but finds for them
lodging-places in the usual. The "usual" is the usable, the "usable" is the interchangeable, to see as "interchangeable" is to grasp; and once you grasp
them you are almost there. The "That's it" which goes by circumstance comes
to an end; and when it is at an end, that of which you do not know what is
so of it you call the "Way."

To wear out the daemonic-and-illumined in you deeming them to be one
without knowing that they are the same I call "Three every morning." What
do I mean by "Three every morning"? A monkey keeper handing out nuts
said, "Three every morning and four every evening." The monkeys were all
in a rage. "All right then," he said, "four every morning and three every
evening." The monkeys were all delighted. Without anything being missed
out either in name or in substance, their pleasure and anger were put to use;
his too was the "That's it" which goes by circumstance. This is why the sage
smoothes things out with his "That's it, that's not," and stays at the point of
rest on the potter's wheel of Heaven. It is this that is called "Letting both alternatives proceed."[7]

•   •   •

The men of old, their knowledge had arrived at something: at what had it
arrived? There were some who thought there had not yet begun to be
things—the utmost, the exhaustive, there is no more to add. The next
thought there were things but there had not yet begun to be borders. The
next thought there were borders to them but there had not yet begun to be
"That's it, that's not." The lighting up of "That's it, that's not" is the reason

---

had only to pick something else as the meaning of the word, name something else "horse," and
then for him what the rest of us call a horse would not be a horse.

7. "The 'that's it' which deems" (*wei shih*): in disputation over whether an object fits the
name "ox," the object is "deemed" (*wei*) an ox by the judgement "That's it" (*shih*). Chuang-tzŭ
allows the flexible "'That's it' which goes by circumstance" (*yin shih*), but rejects absolutely the
rigid "'That's it' which deems."

"Letting both alternatives proceed": in disputation a decision to call an object "X" "proceeds"
(*hsing*) to all objects of the same kind. But for Chuang-tzŭ one never loses the right to shift
from one alternative to the other and allow either to "proceed" from the instance to the kind.

why the Way is flawed. The reason why the Way is flawed is the reason why love becomes complete. Is anything really complete or flawed? Or is nothing really complete or flawed? To recognise as complete or flawed is to have as model the Chao when they play the zither; to recognise as neither complete nor flawed is to have as model the Chao when they don't play the zither. Chao Wen strumming on the zither, Music-master K'uang propped on his stick, Hui Shih leaning on the sterculia, had the three men's knowledge much farther to go? They were all men in whom it reached a culmination, and therefore was carried on to too late a time. It was only in being preferred by them that what they knew about differed from an Other; because they preferred it they wished to illumine it, but they illumined it without the Other being illumined, and so the end of it all was the darkness of chop logic: and his own son too ended with only Chao Wen's zither string, and to the end of his life his musicianship was never completed. May men like this be said to be complete? Then so am I. Or may they not be said to be complete? Then neither am I, nor is anything else.

Therefore the glitter of glib implausibilities is despised by the sage. The "That's it" which deems he does not use, but finds for things lodging places in the usual. It is this that is meant by "using Illumination."[8]

• • •

"Now suppose that I speak of something, and do not know whether it is of a kind with the 'it' in question or not of a kind. If what is of a kind and what is not are deemed of a kind with one another, there is no longer any difference from an 'other.'"

However, let's try to say it.

- There is "beginning," there is "not yet having begun having a beginning."
- There is "there not yet having begun to be that 'not yet having begun having a beginning.'"
- There is "something," there is "nothing."
- There is "not yet having begun being without something."
- There is "there not yet having begun to be that 'not yet having begun being without something.'"

All of a sudden "*there is* nothing," and we do not yet know of something and nothing really which there is and which there is not. Now for my part I

8. Systems of knowledge are partial and temporary like styles on the zither, which in forming sacrifice some of the potentialities of music, and by their very excellence make schools fossilise in decline. Take as model Chao Wen *not* playing the zither, not yet committed, with all his potentialities intact.

have already referred to something, but do not yet know whether my reference really referred to something or really did not refer to anything.[9]

• • •

"Nothing in the world is bigger than the tip of an autumn hair, and Mount T'ai is small; no one lives longer than a doomed child, and P'eng-tsu died young; heaven and earth were born together with me, and the myriad things and I are one."

Now that we are one, can I still say something? Already having called us one, did I succeed in not saying something? One and the saying makes two, two and one make three. Proceeding from here even an expert calculator cannot get to the end of it, much less a plain man. Therefore if we take the step from nothing to something we arrive at three, and how much worse if

9. In this and the next passage Chuang-tzǔ criticises two supposed examples of describing in words the whole out of which things divide. He thinks that analysis always leaves an overlooked remainder, and that the whole cannot be recovered by putting the parts together again. According to the current logic, an object either is an ox or is not, so that having distinguished the alternatives we ought to be able to recover the totality by adding non-oxen to oxen. Chuang-tzǔ's refutation of this assumption is highly elliptical, and it is possible that he intends his effect of making the mind fly off in a new direction at every rereading. But in Chinese as in other philosophy a gap in the argument which hinders understanding (as distinct from a flaw in an argument which we do understand) can generally be filled by exploring implicit questions and presuppositions in the background. Here Chuang-tzǔ is picking out points in common between oxen and non-oxen which distinguish them both from a still remaining Other. In the first place both have a beginning, which excludes from them whatever preceded the beginning of things. Can we continue, by negating and adding, to incorporate this remainder into the totality? What preceded things is that in which they "had not yet begun to have a beginning." But in saying this retrospectively we speak as though things were somehow present before they began; we are driven to a further negation, "There had not yet begun to be that 'not yet having begun having a beginning.'"

It is also common to oxen and non-oxen that they are "something," what there is, in contrast with "nothing," what there is not. As empty space nothingness is a measurable part of the cosmos; but can we not arrive at the totality by adding Nothing to Something? Here Chuang-tzǔ assumes a position far from obvious to a modern reader but implicit throughout early Taoist literature. There can be Nothing only when there is Something, a void only when there are objects with intervals between them, and both divide out from a whole which is neither one nor the other. Each thing has limited properties, is "without something," but the whole out of which it differentiates is both "without anything," since things have not yet emerged, and "without nothing," since everything emerges from it. Then having added Nothing to Something, I have still to add a remainder which "has not yet begun to be without something." But again we are speaking retrospectively as though there were already things to be present or absent, and again we have to negate: "There had not yet begun to be that 'not yet having begun to be without something.'" Both Chuang-tzǔ's sequences are no doubt intended to lead to an infinite regress.

He concludes with the simpler point that as soon as we introduce Nothing as the remainder we contradict ourselves by saying "There is" even of what there is not, Nothing.

we take the step from something to something! Take no step at all, and the "That's it" which goes by circumstance will come to an end.[10]

• • •

The Way has never had borders, saying has never had norms. It is by a "That's it" which deems that a boundary is marked. Let me say something about the marking of boundaries. You can locate as there and enclose by a line, sort out and assess, divide up and discriminate between alternatives, compete over and fight over: these I call our Eight Powers. What is outside the cosmos the sage locates as there but does not sort out. What is within the cosmos the sage sorts out but does not assess. The records of the former kings in the successive reigns in the Annals the sage assesses, but he does not argue over alternatives.

To "divide," then, is to leave something undivided; to "discriminate between alternatives" is to leave something which is neither alternative. "What?" you ask. The sage keeps it in his breast, common men argue over alternatives to show it to each other. Hence I say: "To 'discriminate between alternatives' is to fail to see something."

> The greatest Way is not cited as an authority,
> The greatest discrimination is unspoken,
> The greatest goodwill is cruel,
> The greatest honesty does not make itself awkward,
> The greatest courage does not spoil for a light.
>
> When the Way is lit it does not guide,
> When speech discriminates it fails to get there,
> Goodwill too constant is at someone's expense,
> Honesty too clean is not to be trusted,
> Courage that spoils for a light is immature.

These five in having their corners rounded off come close to pointing the direction. Hence to know how to stay within the sphere of our ignorance is to attain the highest. Who knows an unspoken discrimination, an untold Way? It is this, if any is able to know it, which is called the Treasury of Heaven. Pour into it and it does not fill, bale out from it and it is not drained, and

---

10. Hui Shih had said that "Heaven and earth are one unit" (p. 284 [in Graham, *Chuang-tzŭ*]). At first sight one might expect Chuang-tzŭ to agree with that at least. But to refuse to distinguish alternatives is to refuse to affirm even "Everything is one" against "Things are many." He observes that in saying it the statement itself is additional to the One which it is about, so that already there are two (Plato makes a similar point about the One and its name in *The Sophist*). It may be noticed that Chuang-tzŭ never does say that everything is one (except as one side of a paradox [p. 77 in Graham, *Chuang-tzŭ*]), always speaks subjectively of the sage treating as one.

you do not know from what source it comes. It is this that is called our Benet-nash Star.[11]

• • •

Therefore formerly Yao asked Shun

"I wish to smite Tsung, K'uai and Hsü-ao. Why is it that I am not at ease on the south-facing throne?"

"Why be uneasy," said Shun, "if these three still survive among the weeds? Formerly ten suns rose side by side and the myriad things were all illumined, and how much more by a man in whom the Power is brighter than the sun!"[12]

• • •

Gaptooth put a question to Wang Ni.

"Would you *know* something of which all things agreed 'That's it'?'"

"How would I know that?"

"Would you know what you did not know?"

"How would I know that?"

"Then does no thing know anything?"

"How would I know that? However, let me try to say it—'How do I know that what I call knowing is not ignorance? How do I know that what I call ignorance is not knowing?'

"Moreover, let me try a question on you. When a human sleeps in the damp his waist hurts and he gets stiff in the joints; is that so of the loach? When he sits in a tree he shivers and shakes; is that so of the ape? Which of these three knows the right place to live? Humans eat the flesh of hay-fed and grain-fed beasts, deer eat the grass, centipedes relish snakes, owls and crows crave mice, which of the four has a proper sense of taste? Gibbons are sought by baboons as mates, elaphures like the company of deer, loaches play with fish. Mao-ch'iang and Lady Li were beautiful in the eyes of men; but when the fish saw them they plunged deep, when the birds saw them they flew high, when the deer saw them they broke into a run. Which of these four knows what is truly beautiful in the world? In my judgement the principles of Goodwill and Duty, the paths of 'That's it, that's not,' are inextricably confused; how could I know how to discriminate between them?"

11. "Benetnash Star": The standard text has the obscure *Pao kuang* ("Shaded light"[?]), but there is a plausible variant, *Yao-kuang*, "Benetnash," the star at the far end of the handle of the Dipper. The Dipper by turning its handle up, down, east and west, marks the progress of the four seasons (cf. Joseph Needham, *Science and Civilization in China*, 3/250). As a metaphor for the prime mover of things Chuang-tzŭ chooses not the stationary North Star but the circumpolar star which initiates the cyclic motions.

12. This story seems out of place. Perhaps it was intended as an illustration of "This is why the sage does not take this course but opens things up to the light of Heaven" (above).

"If you do not know benefit from harm, would you deny that the utmost man knows benefit from harm?"

"The utmost man is daemonic. When the wide woodlands blaze they cannot sear him, when the Yellow River and the Han freeze they cannot chill him, when swift thunderbolts smash the mountains and whirlwinds shake the seas they cannot startle him. A man like that yokes the clouds to his chariot, rides the sun and moon and roams beyond the four seas; death and life alter nothing in himself, still less the principles of benefit and harm!"[13]

● ● ●

Ch'ü-ch'üeh-tzû asked Ch'ang-wu-tzû

"I heard this from the Master: 'The sage does not work for any goal, does not lean towards benefit or shun harm, does not delight in seeking, does not fix a route by a Way, in saying nothing says something and in saying something says nothing, and roams beyond the dust and grime.' The Master thought of the saying as a flight of fancy, but to me it seemed the walking of the most esoteric Way. How does it seem to you?"

"This is a saying which would have puzzled the Yellow Emperor, and what would old Confucius know about it? Moreover you for your part are counting your winnings much too soon; at the sight of the egg you expect the cockcrow, at the sight of the bow you expect a roasted owl. Suppose I put it to you in abandoned words, and you listen with the same abandon:

'Go side by side with the sun and moon,
Do the rounds of Space and Time.
Act out their neat conjunctions,
Stay aloof from their convulsions.
Dependents each on each, let us honour one another.
Common people fuss and fret,
The sage is a dullard and a sluggard.
Be aligned along a myriad years, in oneness, wholeness, simplicity.
All the myriad things are as they are,
And as what they are make up totality.'

How do I know that to take pleasure in life is not a delusion? How do I know that we who hate death are not exiles since childhood who have forgotten the way home? Lady Li was the daughter of a frontier guard at Ai. When the kingdom of Chin first took her the tears stained her dress; only when she

---

13. In the opening exchange Gaptooth is pressing for an admission that there must be something which is knowable: (1) Would you know something which everyone agrees on? Wang Ni denies it, perhaps because there could be no independent viewpoint from which to judge a universally shared opinion. (2) Then at least one knows what one does not know. But that is a contradiction, or so Chuang-tzǔ thinks (like Meno in Plato's dialogue); the Mohist *Canon*

came to the palace and shared the King's square couch and ate the flesh of hay-fed and grain-fed beasts did she begin to regret her tears. How do I know that the dead do not regret that ever they had an urge to life? Who banquets in a dream at dawn wails and weeps, who wails and weeps in a dream at dawn goes out to hunt. While we dream we do not know that we are dreaming, and in the middle of a dream interpret a dream within it; not until we wake do we know that we were dreaming. Only at the ultimate awakening shall we know that this is the ultimate dream. Yet fools think they are awake, so confident that they know what they are, princes, herdsmen, incorrigible! You and Confucius are both dreams, and I who call you a dream am also a dream. This saying of his, the name for it is 'a flight into the extraordinary'; if it happens once in ten thousand ages that a great sage knows its explanation it will have happened as though between morning and evening."

You and I having been made to argue over alternatives, if it is you not I that wins, is it really you who are on to it, I who am not? If it is I not you that wins, is it really I who am on to it, you who are not? Is one of us on to it and the other of us not? Or are both of us on to it and both of us not? If you and I are unable to know where we stand, others will surely be in the dark because of us. Whom shall I call in to decide it? If I get someone of your party to decide it, being already of your party how can he decide it? If I get someone of my party to decide it, being already of my party how can he decide it? If I get someone of a party different from either of us to decide it, being already of a party different from either of us how can he decide it? If I get someone of the same party as both of us to decide it, being already of the same party as both of us how can he decide it? Consequently you and I and he are all unable to know where we stand, and shall we find someone else to depend on?

It makes no difference whether the voices in their transformations have each other to depend on or not. Smooth them out on the whetstone of Heaven, use them to go by and let the stream find its own channels; this is the way to live out your years. Forget the years, forget duty, be shaken into motion by the limitless, and so find things their lodging places in the limitless.

What is meant by "Smooth them out on the whetstone of Heaven"? Treat as "it" even what is not, treat as "so" even what is not. If the "it" is really it, there is no longer a difference for disputation from what is not it; if the "so" is really so, there is no longer a difference for disputation from what is not so.[14]

B 48 discusses this problem, and points out that one can know something by name without knowing what objects fit the name. (3) Then one knows that no one knows anything—another contradiction.

14. Since anything may at one time or another be picked out as "it," if it were really the name of something (in Western grammatical term, if it were not a pronoun but a noun) it would

• • •

The penumbra asked the shadow:

"Just then you were walking, now you stop; just then you were sitting, now you stand. Why don't you make up your mind to do one thing or the other?"

"Is it that there is something on which I depend to be so? And does what I depend on too depend on something else to be so? Would it be that I depend on snake's scales, cicada's wings? How would I recognise why it is so, how would I recognise why it is not so?

Last night Chuang Chou dreamed he was a butterfly, spirits soaring he was a butterfly (is it that in showing what he was he suited his own fancy?), and did not know about Chou. When all of a sudden he awoke, he was Chou with all his wits about him. He does not know whether he is Chou who dreams he is a butterfly or a butterfly who dreams he is Chou. Between Chou and the butterfly there was necessarily a dividing; just this is what is meant by the transformations of things.[15]

LOOK AT THE FINGER, NOT WHERE IT IS POINTING
Stephen H. West

O body swayed to music, O brightening glance,
How can we know the dancer from the dance?
YEATS, "AMONG SCHOOL CHILDREN"

Several of the texts read in our sessions—the *Heart Sūtra,* the *Mencius* 2A.2, and the *Qi wu lun*—all have at their core a message about language, appearance, and reality.[16] But these texts are also part of a literary canon, in which

---

be the name of everything. Chuang-tzŭ likes the thought that instead of selecting and approving something as "it" one may use the word to embrace and approve everything, to say "Yes!" to the universe; we find him doing so in p. 102 [in Graham, *Chuang-tzŭ*].

15. "Showing what he was" seems to connect with the earlier reference to "showing" that a horse is not a horse (above). If so, the point is that the Taoist does not permanently deem himself a man or a butterfly but moves spontaneously from fitting one name to fitting another. Cf. "At one moment he deemed himself the logician's 'horse,' at another his 'ox'" (p. 94 [in Graham, *Chuang-tzŭ*]).

16. I would like to thank Ting Pang-hsin for his help with phonological reconstructions and William Boltz for his comments on this paper.

meaning and semantic understanding yield to such things as implicit structure, tone, imagery, irony, symbol, or any of the various other literary devices that create an artistic work, that turn word and message into something worth contemplating or savoring as a constructed artifact in itself. These texts have as much literary and artistic force as they do literal philosophical force; in fact, their language is often unyielding to the kind of specificity that those who would construct logical and organic representations of meaning desire. In *Zhuangzi*, in particular, whatever "message" there is to apprehend is, in my eyes, outshone by the performance of the text itself. *Zhuangzi* is the relentless rocker of the boat who rescues himself endlessly from self-created trouble, playing with words and phrases that dazzle like fire juggled in the night. Mockery, irony, self-indulgence, and play mark the *Qi wu lun,* a virtuoso performance that demonstrates better than any other early text how the language of classification can be destabilized by that of experience. *Zhuangzi* leads us toward no single definition of meaning, a "this" or "that," or to intellectual closure; but to an open-ended experience of *how* something means, to the difference between a proposition—"love stinks, but I'm obsessed"—and its expression in a singular artistic moment that possesses a kind of demonic power—"I have sworn thee fair and thought thee bright /
Who are as black as hell, as dark as night."

The language of the *Zhuangzi* is as complicated as the world it purports to describe, developing ever richer possibilities that verge on the profound only to be undermined by a radical sense of humor, shifting in seemingly endless directions of affirmation and then rejection. While A. C. Graham may have believed that this chapter was a wonderful example of a sage musing out loud, thereby describing the text as a kind of loose amalgam of random thoughts, it is the very precision of the language and the sureness of its control that leads us into Zhuangzi's planned labyrinth of confusion. It is not surprising that by limiting his search to meaning and to the language of classification Graham, like those before him, has been forced to search for meaning in silence.[17] But that search ignores the rich language of experience of the text, in which, overwhelmed by phonological repetitions and grammatical ambiguities, we are led into a world of indistinguishable and confusing sound and sense. I would like here to look at the opening

17. A. C. Graham, *Chuang-tzŭ: The Seven Inner Chapters and Other Writings from the Book* Chuang-tzŭ (London: Allen and Unwin, 1981), 55 n.: "Chuang-Tzŭ's . . . assumption is highly elliptical, and it is possible that he intends his effect of making the mind fly off in a new direction at every re-reading. But in Chinese as in other philosophy a gap in the argument which hinders understanding (as distinct from a flaw in an argument which we do understand) can generally be filled by exploring implicit questions and presuppositions in the background."

of the passage in an attempt to show how Zhuangzi destabilizes sense through irony and a phonological manipulation that creates an ambiguous space of interpretation.[18]

> Ziqi of Nanguo was sitting, leaning on his armrest, gazing upward at the heavens and breathing softly, absent-minded as though his "lodging" was lost.

The passage begins by setting the stage for a performance by two characters, a master and disciple, an ironist and the butt of his irony. Ziqi is "breathing softly" in harmony with the resonance of Heaven only to be interrupted by his disciple. The usual rendering of this character (xu^a) as "exhale" or "sighing" will not do. Here it must, by virtue of the phonetic series to which it belongs, mean something close to "emptiness." The *Shuowen* defines it as "to puff," but a fragment from the *Shenglei*, a Wei dynasty text on finals or rhymes, gives the following definition: "To exhale strongly is called 'puff'; to exhale softly is called 'empty breathing.'" This use is attested much later, for instance, in the minimal pair in Liu Yuxi's lines, "Breathing emptily produces rain and dew, breathing strongly produces the wind and thunder." Since Ziqi is going to pun on this word below, we should read it probably as the quiet, shallow, barely perceptible breathing, as of a trance.

> absent-minded as though his "lodging" was lost.

This phrase has been variously interpreted as an experience in which the spirit ($shen^a$) leaves the body ($shen^b$). Graham, who has produced what is now the standard translation ("in a trance as though he has lost the counterpart of himself"), chooses to follow Guo Xiang's commentary and read $ngugx^a$[19] as a phonemic loan for the character $ngugx^b$, "mate, counterpart, duplicate": "A person who joins Heaven equalizes 'that' and 'me'; therefore there is nothing exterior [to the self?] in which to join in harmony. So, trance-like, one releases from form,[20] as though it had lost its matched duplicate." Other com-

---

18. I am using the *Zhuangzi jishi*, ed. Wang Xianqian, comm. Guo Xiang, subcomm. Cheng Xuanying, *Xinbian zhuzi jicheng*, vol. 1 (Beijing: Zhonghua shuju, 1961), 43–48. See also Harold Roth, "Chuang-tzu," in *Early Chinese Texts: A Bibliographical Guide*, ed. Michael Loewe (Berkeley: Society for the Study of Early China and the Institute of East Asian Studies, 1993), 56–67.

19. Li Fanggui, "Studies in Archaic Chinese Phonology," *Tsing Hua Journal of Chinese Studies*, n.s. 9 (1971): 1–60; final letter of each reconstruction: *ping* = -ø; *shang* = -x; *qu* = h; *ru^a* = -p, -t, -k, -k^w, r.

20. This term, *jieti*, is also used for death, when the *hun* and *po* souls leave the physical body behind. There is a logical connection with "dead ashes" and "withered trees"—in that it indicates a difference between a living organic entity constituted of both spirit and physical self and a husk of corporeal matter left behind either by death or by release of the soul through an out-of-body mental experience.

mentators quibble over the exact meaning of $ngugx^a$, Yu Yue for instance, who considers it a phonological borrowing for "lodge" ($ngjugx$):

> "Lost his $ngugx^a$": exactly what it says below in "I lost me." Guo Xiang's commentary, "As though he had lost his match," does not accord with the meaning of "losing me." Sima Biao says that $ngugx^a$ means "body" and his theory gets the point. But to say that "body and spirit combine to make $ngugx^a$" is wrong. $Ngugx^a$ should be read $ngjugx$, which means "to lodge." The spirit is lodged in the body, so the body is called "lodge."

His criticism of Sima Biao, who had stated that body and spirit combine to make $ngugx^a$, may seem a semantic or phonetic quibble over a particular word, but Sima Biao may actually have touched on a difficult issue he sensed in the original. All commentators prior to him were inclined to consider a person to be constituted of a combination of "body" and "spirit" or, as Yu Yue does, to see the body only as a repository for spirit. In either case, it is to see a person as a sum of two separate entities. Sima Biao, on the other hand, seems to take $ngugx^a$ to mean something like a process that results in a state of being in which these two elements are combined. This would lead us in the direction of understanding the line, therefore, as "he lost the process by which spirit and body were constituted as a matched pair." That is, Ziqi had transcended all distinction, including that between form of body and spirit. This seems to be clearly how Cheng Xuanying, the Tang commentator, understood the passage:

> $Ngugx^a$: is duplicate/match. That is to say that body and spirit are a pair, and "thing" and the "self" are a duplicate match. Ziqi was leaning on his armrest in a state of "sitting and forgetting," had concentrated his spirit, was far off in his thoughts, so he raised up his head to heaven and sighed. Becoming aware in all subtlety of *ziran*, he had separated from his form and distanced himself from discriminatory knowledge. Trance-like, he let his physical form fall away and both body and mind were together left behind, and other and self were both forgotten. Therefore, it was as if he had forgotten both match and duplicate.

This seems a particularly good example of how lexical ambiguity, the possibility of punning, and the use of the precise terminology of meditation create deeper ambiguity within the text. The words $ngugx^b$ (mate, match), $ngjugx$ (lodge), and $ngugx^a$ are all near homophones and we must at least consider the fact that Zhuangzi was aware of the possibilities of interpretative play when the passage was written. That is, rather than this being a question of the "right word" it may be more a question of how freely interpretative process can move between alternative readings.

"Wherein is it that / What state must one be in so that

Form can indeed be made to be like withered wood,"

Ju is frequently used as the second part of binomial interrogatives (ct. *shui ju* and *he ju*), but Cheng Xuanying's subcommentary here glosses it as "to reside at peace [*an chu*]" and explains:

> He had just desired to request to learn more, so he rose and stood in
> attendance, [saying], "How can one reside in peace—with spirit focused
> and perception quieted, suddenly transform what was before (?), and con-
> sequently cause the form to soon be withered wood and without difference,
> the heart to be the same as dead ashes and without differentiation? There
> has to be some kind of subtle art, the source of which I request you to reveal."

Guo Xiang's commentary at this point suggests that the practice of "leaning on an armrest" is a particular form of meditation practice: "Ziyou had seen 'those leaning on the armrest' before, but had yet to see one like Ziqi." The subcommentary picks up on this to reinforce its interpretation of the disci- ple's motives: "Ziyou had previously observed 'sitting in meditation' but had yet to exhaust the abstruse mystery of it. Now encountering 'leaning on the armrest,' this is different than [the practice] of olden times. He felt that this quieted at-rest without inner-emotion was strange and so expressed this pur- port of startled doubt." To follow this reading subtly changes the focus of the text from person to practice: "The [practice] of 'leaning on the armrest' now is not the same as that of former times."

> Ziqi spoke, "Is it not wonderful, that you asked about it? Right now 'I' had
> lost 'me.' Did you know it? You have heard the pipes of humans and have yet
> to hear the pipes of earth; you have heard the pipes of earth but have yet to
> hear the pipes of heaven, right?"

The irony of this reply is generally understated in translation. Notice that the grammar defines the act of asking—not the question itself—as "good." There can be little doubt here about the sarcastic attitude of the master whose meditation has just been interrupted by the eager student. Guo Xiang's com- ments are directed toward the trance-state of Ziqi: "'I' lost 'me'; so it turns out 'me' has forgotten itself. If 'me' has forgotten [even] itself, then can there be any thing worth perceiving under heaven? Therefore: losing outer and inner in each case—only after that can one transcend and obtain both si- multaneously." Cheng Xuanying, however, has caught on to the level of irony and situated the story from the viewpoint of the disciple. While he ac- knowledges that the master allows the question, he goes on to point out the dullness of the student: "Ziqi had forgotten both outer scene and [inner] knowing; 'things' and 'me' were both suspended. Ziyou did not get it and was alarmed and doubtful, so [Ziqi] demonstrated the capabilities of 'leaning on the armrest.'" By shifting the emphasis from person to practice, from Ziqi to the technical aspects of "leaning on the armrest," it allows the student to ask if he can learn the "secret trick," the "method" of the meditation exercise, thereby focusing on technique and practice rather than "forgetting." Cheng Xuanying's wonderful last line, "to show him the capabilities of the practice," leads into the irony of the following passage.

> Ziqi spoke, "Now, the pent-up breathing of that Great Clod—its name is said to be 'wind.' This is the case only when it is not activated; if activated then the myriad apertures angrily howl [*nagh-gag*^{w}]. And have you alone not heard it whistle and whine [*liəg*^{w}*-liəg*^{w}]?
>
> In mountain forests' lofty peaking [*·jədh-tjiəd*]
> In apertures and holes in grand trees a hundred armspans around,
> Like noses [*rjəg-bjiədh*],
> Like mouths [*rjəg-khugx*],
> Like ears [*rjəg-njəgx*],
> Like a socket [*rjəg-kid*],
> Like a pen/bowl, [*rjəg-guanx*],
> Like a mortar [*rjəg-gjeg*^{w}*x*],
> Like something that's a deep pool [*rjəg--rig-tjiagx*],
> Like something that's a grimy pit [*rjəg--ag-tjiegx*]—
> Water splashing [*kiak*^{w}*-tjiagx*],
> Arrow releasing [*hak*^{w}*-tjiagx*],
> Cursing [*thjit-tjiagx*],
> Breathing [*-hiəp-tjiagx*],
> Shouting [*kiag*^{w}*h-tjiagx*],
> Sobbing [*gag*^{w}*-tjiagx*],
> Deepening [*·iag*^{w}*-tjiagx*],
> Lamenting [*krag*^{w}*-tjiagx*].
> The one in front moans [*gjwag*]—
> And the one following sings out [*ngjwung*]—
> In light winds, small harmony,
> In heavy, great harmony.
>
> Harsh winds cease and then the multitude of apertures become empty. And can it be you alone who has not seen its shivering and shaking, quivering and quaking?"
>   Ziyou spoke, "Earth's pipes—the multitude of apertures are these for sure; human pipes—the tubes laid side-by-side are these for sure. Dare I ask what heaven's pipes are?" Ziqi spoke, "Puffing—different in a myriad ways, but making each be what is unique to itself. It binds together that seized upon by each thing—and who is it that stirs them up?"

The meaning of this passage has been well-worked over by Graham, who follows the standard understanding of this passage: it is about the speech act.

Ziqi invites his disciple to look behind the words of various philosophers—speech, the thing that comes out through the human aperture—to something else. What I would like to draw attention to here is the deep irony of the section. This is not simply an explanation of how "heaven" or "self-thusness" is a nothingness that takes on shape, sound, and activity through whichever phenomenon it is manifested, but also a wonderful critique of the student. The master's response is in the mode of performance; he simply turns into one of the apertures that he describes (i.e., demonstrates its capability), puffing out his own theory, thereby creating the same problems of shi[a] and fei and of confusion he intends to dismiss. If we remember the description of the master in the beginning, "Ziqi of Nanguo was sitting, leaning on his armrest, gazing upward at the heavens and breathing softly, absent-minded as though his 'lodging' was lost," we can read the line above, "Harsh winds cease and then the multitude of apertures become empty," in at least one other possible way. Ziqi is not just telling his disciple *about* great winds that are stirred up, but is actually in the process itself. Two important phonological principles come into play at this point, the first being the paronomasia of xu^u and xu, the second a play on the fact that in early texts *feng* can mean both "wind" and "to instruct." We can read this passage, then, as an ironic jab at the student: "Look, you dolt, you didn't recognize the breath of heaven that was coming out of me. Who was it who stirred me out of this trance? You, because you wanted words, you wanted me to name it. Well, words are nothing but puffs, and after I get done with all these words, these puffs of mine, then I will return to a state of quiescence, the wind will be gone (and this harsh criticism of you will be over)."

The structure and phonology of this passage echo the sense almost perfectly. The varied line-lengths and the repetition, particularly, of the comparative *rjəg* and the nominative particle *tjiagx* propel the central part of the passage. The waxing of the wind is generated by increasing phonological harmony: *rjəg-X* binds the first part of his description, in which he is describing the various apertures, functioning in one sense like head rhyme. Then, as he moves from physical apertures to sounds of the wind, he switches to the nominalized adjectives (*X-tjiagx*). He also accomplishes a phonological bridge from one structure to another by using both the comparative and the nominalized adjectives in two lines (*rjəg-X-tjiagx*). As the wind grows more intense, the rhymes become closer together and more stable:

Shouting [$kiag^wh$-$tjiagx$],
Sobbing [gag^w-$tjiagx$],
Deepening [$\cdot iag^w$-$tjiagx$],
Lamenting [$krag^w$-$tjiagx$].
The one in front moans [$gjwag$]—

This generated motion is then caught athwart at the end of the passage first by changing rhyme (*ngjwung*—at exactly the point the wind in front ceases) and then by the length of the lines in the final question. The grammar here returns to the more logical structure inhering in prose and the phonology falls flat—the pipes of heaven are neither open to discussion (since language has to denote them as "something") nor perceivable as sound—no attributes can be assigned.

This disjuncture, this countermotion, also demonstrates the difference between the language of experience and classification. The central part of the passage is as close to pure poetry as prose can come—it precisely defines the *attributes* of sound, capturing one essential quality about the wind, about the pipes of the earth, without ever describing *it* as substance. The repetitive use of attributes, in fact, while giving the illusion of defining the substance of earth's pipes, ends up destabilizing that definition by positing a proliferation of traits and qualities that run the gamut from the human body, to trees, to pens of animals, to cups, to puddles of water—suggesting an infinite explosion of characteristics that essentially defeats any attempt at classifying or identifying.

While I have treated only the opening of this section, my intent was to show that there are ways of reading such texts that allow for a wider and perhaps intentional ambiguity. I hoped to demonstrate that commentary, while a necessary adjunct to the text itself, is created with its own set of structures. This is of course nothing new to the reader. But it is worthwhile remembering that much commentary is concerned with something singular—a borrowing that can be identified as one word, a way to read one passage. But at the same time it unnecessarily limits the ambiguous space a playful writer like Zhuangzi creates; one in which he can both argue for a position or positions and simultaneously destabilize the philosophical ground from which he argues. In this case, it serves to create a certain irony, carried out in the mode of performance. The audience, like the young disciple, is indirectly taunted by that ironic performance, left to flounder in a confused world of sound and sense. We can, like the commentator, make decisions that force the text into a singular discourse, or we can appreciate it for its play, its ambiguity, and its perfect demonstration that nothing in the world that is perceivable is fixed in definable form, except as we give up possibility after possibility to come to our own sense of closure.

VISION AND IDENTITY IN *QI WU LUN*

Martin Powers

Early in *Qi wu lun* Zhuangzi addresses the problem of identity—how do we know the difference between one thing and another? This issue has special significance for students of visual representation, because it is a question all pictorial artists must answer in some unique way. Zhuangzi puts the matter this way:

Fei bi wu wo, fei wo wu suo qu. (line 14)

These lines suggest a translation like: "If there were not that other, there would be no 'me'; if there were no 'me,' there would be no ground upon which to choose." The text suggests a dependent relationship between "that other" and "me." But the issue being addressed here is not ontological, as it might at first seem. The scholarship of A. C. Graham and Chad Hansen has shown that the "other" and "me" refer to different positions within an on-going debate. Without your point of view, mine would have no significance. Any two sets of views, pro and con, are mutually generating. Graham early on established this by pointing out Zhuangzi's use of demonstratives, for this shows that Zhuangzi is speaking of assertions made from a particular stand-point.[21] Hansen developed this idea, stressing the perspectival nature of statements in Zhuangzi's philosophy.[22] Bearing this in mind, the passage cited above might better be translated as: "If there were not that other's [point of view], I should not have mine; if I did not have my [point of view], then there would be no basis for taking a stand."

Zhuangzi's awareness of the interdependent relationship between rival points of view reveals itself at more than one level. At the literal level, the text says that the position from which or for which one argues has no absolute status, but is relative to some other contrasting point of view. But Zhuangzi also seems to take his relativity seriously at the level of prose style. In his article on *Qi wu lun*, A. C. Graham noted that Zhuangzi gives the reader "the sensation of a man thinking aloud, jotting the living thought at the moment of its inception." Such a prose style eschews any claim to an omniscient perspective, preferring instead to draw the reader into the text as an equal participant. Hansen goes further, suggesting that Zhuangzi's unusual literary style is in fact a narrative device enabling him to discuss philosophy without contradicting his most essential insights about the interdependence of meaning: "Zhuangzi's style signals his status as the premier philosopher of perspective. His staging of fantasy dialogues releases him from trying to make any transperspectival conclusions and yet allows him to philosophize freely."[23] As Hansen points out, Zhuangzi's awareness of the relativity of perspective

---

21. A. C. Graham, "Chuang-Tzu's Essay on Seeing Things as Equal," *History of Religions* 9.2–3 (1969–1970), 142–43; Chad Hansen, *A Daoist Theory of Chinese Thought: A Philosophical Interpretation* (Oxford: Oxford University Press, 1992), 265.

22. Hansen, *Daoist Theory*, 282–84.

23. Hansen, *Daoist Theory*, 266.

is inherently pluralistic. This is why his narrative strategy rejects any appeal to external authority. No one, not even the author, can escape the condition of interdependency.

Hansen's point about the perspectival nature of the proposition shows that Zhuangzi's concern is not ontological—"I exist only because you do"—but rather epistemological: "My interpretation becomes meaningful only in contrast to yours." If we assume, for the moment, that a person's identity is determined by the position s/he takes on important issues, then Zhuangzi's remarks address the issue of identity, not existence.[24] Such an assertion challenges the normal assumption that your picture of the world, or mine, possesses an inviolable integrity, like a closed figure on a blank ground. It suggests, instead, that your view and mine "figure" one another, like a counterchange design in which each "figure" serves as the other's "ground."

To a historian of art, this situation parallels the problem of epistemology in pictorial art, for every strategy of representation rests upon choices about the nature of identity: "How do I know what this depicted object is?" If the Third Duke of Windsor wants a painting of a flower pot, the artist must first decide how to make the pot recognizable. In vision this boils down to a question of figure and ground—to what extent can the pot's features be integrated with its surroundings without losing its identity.[25]

It will come as no surprise that, historically speaking, a majority of pictorial traditions are based upon a fairly firm distinction between figure and ground. Objects are most often assumed to possess some integrity: the contours of a vase do not interpenetrate those of a book nearby. This corresponds to the notion that ordinary objects have distinct and permanent identities. We call a book a book because it is not a vase; pre-modern artists painted it the same way. But Zhuangzi's assertion suggests the world is not so simple. His argument resembles more closely a pictorial system in which figure and ground are roughly equal in status; a system in which the identity of any object could coalesce with its surroundings, like some fawn dissolving among dappled, sunlit reeds.

Zhuangzi is not known for overt discussion of political theories, yet this epistemology entails political consequences, for it rejects all appeals to an ultimate authority. This position is perhaps most evident in his attitude toward the problem which Aristotle conceived in terms of a "prime mover,"

24. I will argue that this is a standard assumption of bureaucratic theory later in this essay.

25. Of course, in practice, the artist does not personally "decide" what criteria must be met before audiences will recognize his painted marks as a flower pot. As a member of a particular culture and linguistic community, the artist knows the extent to which the audience regards an object's identity as independent of adjacent objects. Rudolf Arnheim explored the relationship between visual identification and thought in *Visual Thinking* (Berkeley: University of California Press, 1971), 32ff.

that cosmic correlate of earthly rulers in the European tradition.[26] In a line of reasoning reminiscent of Aristotle, Zhuangzi asks if there might not be someone ultimately in charge. His conclusions are not those of Aristotle: "We do not know what it is that causes all this. It is as if there were something genuinely in control, but it is notable that we cannot find any trace of it. I can accept [the idea] that it can carry out [its operations], but we do not see its form. We encounter the circumstances [of its operation], but it has no [fixed, substantial] form."

Reality resides in activity, not substance. For this reason, a prime mover has little to contribute to the system. Zhuangzi follows this passage with a remark that, even if something were in charge, it would make no difference anyway, from our perspective.

There is a good reason why Aristotle needed a prime mover. For Aristotle, substance is real, a solid presence maintaining its integrity against the "ground" of the world. Motion is not real for, by definition, it is not permanent. If substance moves, ultimately there must be something permanent and real that makes it move—hence, the need for a prime mover. Such a view contrasts with Zhuangzi's epistemology of interdependent views. In Zhuangzi's world, where figure and ground are mutually generating, the identities of objects would change depending upon context, but would be no less real for that. If this interpretation sounds surprising, it is consistent with the commentary on the passage just cited: "Of all the creatures and situations of the world, each is distinct in its inclination and position, as if some ruler had caused them to be that way. But if we search for some trace of this ruler, in the end there is none to be found. This shows that all things are as they are by virtue of themselves [naturally—*ziran*]; no one causes them to be as they are." The last statement is critical. In the end, we find no trace of a transcendental arbiter. Distinctions, identities, arise as a consequence of perspective. But because no supposition is made equating permanence and reality, there is no need to assume that contingent identities—the phenomena in the flux—are unreal. Let us reconsider these two points: (1) identities arise because of perspective, and (2) permanence is not a necessary attribute of the "real." If we accept these two points, then the phenomenon in its context is *necessarily* self-so, since nothing transcendental causes it to be as it is—all phenomena are *ziran*.[27] In this scheme, an object's reality does not derive from its relationship to a transcendent power—figure on ground—

26. Stephen Toulmin, *Cosmopolis: The Hidden Agenda of Modernity* (New York: Free Press, 1990), 125–29.

27. Of course the term *ziran* does not occur in the first two chapters of the *Zhuangzi*, but it does occur in two of the *Inner chapters* with the meaning "natural" as opposed to artificial. See Wang Shishun and Han Mujun, eds., *Laozhuang cidian* (Jinan: Shandong jiaoyu, 1993), 781.

but only from a particular, local constellation of interacting perspectives. Without this understanding the concept of *ziran* might have seemed arbitrary. But once we comprehend the perspectival nature of Zhuangzi's epistemology, *ziran* becomes a necessity. It proceeds necessarily from the idea that non-permanent events are nonetheless real.[28]

Was this brilliant thesis a chance product of Zhuangzi's poetic intellect, or did it have a broader basis in his society and time? While Zhuangzi's ideas are characteristically original, most of his images are drawn from a broad body of lore shared with contemporaries. When Zhuangzi and his students describe the wind, the clouds, immortals or dragons, the context invariably makes it clear that, while the point of the parable may be novel, the image rests upon shared knowledge. Was there anything in the common culture of the Warring States period akin to the epistemology of interdependent identities? Is it possible that anyone ever visualized natural phenomena in a fashion consistent with Zhuangzi's epistemology?

Here the visual record may offer some help, for epistemology is not the sole prerogative of philosophers. Everyone makes assumptions about identity, and artists have to apply theirs in practical ways. Most artists in literate cultures have assumed that objects have distinct and stable identities. If one looks at late Warring States material culture, however, it is apparent that some artists of that period could conceive of objects with two or more possible identities, depending upon the viewer's perspective. The work of these artists may provide our best model for those collective cultural assumptions to which Zhuangzi appeals.

Historians are familiar with various kinds of counterchange designs in the art of early China, especially in mid-Warring States bronzes, where one finds dragon heads disposed as if in an Escher engraving. In this early period, the dragon design appears to have been associated with the nobility, serving as an insignia of rank. By the late Warring States period, however, dragons occur frequently on mirrors, items of personal adornment (fig. 3.1). These mirrors could be attached to the belt and thus would be seen by fellow officials or courtiers. Because noble birth was not a necessary qualification for official rank in Warring States China, the dragon emblem could not have been restricted to a hereditary elite. This helps to explain why, in Warring States literature, the dragon can be employed as a metaphor for men of talent. It is no longer so closely associated with the nobility as before. Bearing this in mind, it will be worthwhile to consider how the Warring States dragon was rendered.

On mirrors of the third century B.C.E., the dragon shares many features of contour, orientation and structure with its surroundings. In such cases it is not that the figure and ground shape one another equally; it is rather that

---

28. It follows, as Hansen notes, not that reality is one, but that it is many.

Figure 3.1. Bronze mirror, late Warring States period, third century B.C.E. Freer Gallery of Art, Smithsonian Institution, Washington, D.C. Acc. No. 35.14. Photograph courtesy of the Freer Gallery of Art.

the figure is easily assimilated to its surroundings. It shares with its surroundings a common path of flow and a common set of structures; consequently, its "identity" is easily changed. These flows and structures do not transcend the figures—as would a neutral ground—but are inherent in all of them. As a consequence, the object's identity becomes dependent upon the viewer's perspective. Viewed at a distance, a design on a Warring States mirror might be "seen" as a cloud design, but up close it resolves itself into

Fig. 3.2. Bronze mirror, detail of fig. 1. Photograph courtesy of the Freer Gallery of Art.

a dragon (fig. 3.2). Even at close quarters, it is possible to read it as either cloud or dragon, but not both at the same time.

The shapes of cloud designs are difficult to "read," difficult to execute and difficult to conceive. Could artists have fashioned this multivalent creature/process if they were unable to conceive of variable or contingent identities? Could they have designed a dragon which denied their very concept of identity? One suspects the communities they served must have felt comfortable with such a notion. This would not require of either artist or patron any understanding of Zhuangzi's philosophy; it would merely require familiarity with Chinese traditions about dragons and *qi.* Our best evidence for such traditions lies in late Warring States texts where the dragon image occurs purely as a metaphor, not as an object of belief. Such metaphorical uses presuppose general knowledge of the dragon's characteristic features.

Depending upon whose dates one accepts, the *Zhou yi* may be one of the earliest texts to use the dragon as a metaphor for a man of affairs.[29] The use

29. Regarding the *Zhou yi,* see Willard J. Peterson, "Making Connections: 'Commentary on the Attached Verbalisations' of the Book of Change," *Harvard Journal of Asiatic Studies* 42, no. 1 (1982): 67–116.

of this metaphor takes for granted the notion that dragons can fly and adapt their form to circumstances. By late Warring States times the metaphor appears to have become widespread. Han Feizi, for instance, cites a passage from Shenzi comparing the man of affairs to a dragon. In its familiar surroundings of mists and clouds, the dragon can exercise its wondrous powers; severed from this environment, however, it loses them. In just this way, Shenzi argues, a man's capacity to exercise his talents is contingent upon circumstances (shi^b).[30]

Han Feizi does not specify what kinds of powers the dragon could exercise, but the same metaphor occurs in the *Yanzi*. There the author reveals the kinds of suppositions readers would make regarding the dragon's powers: "Now the dragon is a creature with spiritual powers. With the advantage of but a foot of cloud, it is able to hide its body and carry out its transformations [*hua*] far and wide. Otherwise women and children could catch it and play with it. This is the necessary result of the force of circumstances [shi^b]."[31]

In these passages the dragon is a metaphor for a man of talent. Talent alone cannot ensure a brilliant career; only when circumstances are right can a great man carry out his "transformations," like a dragon who hides its presence or transforms its identity. In *Zhuangzi*, also, we find a long passage comparing talented men to dragons in their ability to transform according to circumstances.[32] Clearly these authors were not introducing new theories about dragons. On the contrary, they made use of a well-known image to make a philosophical point more easily understood. Everyone in Warring States China "knew" that the dragon in the clouds could alter its perceived identity. Bearing this in mind, perhaps the ambiguity of the Warring States dragon design is no accident. Perhaps, from the viewpoint of a Warring States artist, intrinsic mutability was an essential feature of the dragon's generic condition.

The art historical community employs a number of terms to isolate meaningful elements in a visual image, terms such as "attribute," "icon" or "emblem." "Generic condition" is a term I would suggest using to designate those qualities of an image that carry epistemological implications. In post-Renaissance Europe, for example, substantiality (volume, weight and texture) was part of the generic condition of all things, sometimes even the haloes of saints. Likewise, a Ramboesque physique was part of the generic condition of able-bodied adult males. Those who have seen reproductions of the *Raft of the Medusa* will recall that even the bodies of men who have "starved" to death would make most men over forty envious. Every artist in a given com-

30. Chen Qiyou, ed., *Han Feizi jishi* (Beijing: Zhonghua, 1959), 17.886–89.
31. *Yanzi chunqiu jishi* (Beijing: Zhonghua, 1961), *fulu*, 596–97.
32. Guo Qingfan, ed., *Zhuangzi jishi*, 4 vols. (Beijing: Zhonghua, 1961), 20.668.

munity must be able to portray the generic condition of an object in order for it to be recognized as a proper picture. Consequently the generic condition imposes constraints upon style, not merely attributes. Artists must find a pictorial strategy adequate to render the required generic conditions. I shall not argue the point extensively here, but since textual descriptions of clouds, spirits and dragons typically emphasize their transformations and little else, it seems likely that mutability of identity was part of the generic condition of clouds, spirits and dragons in late Warring States and early Han China.

Insofar as Warring States designs illustrate the dragon's mutability they could, conceivably, serve as graphic models for the kind of perspectival system Zhuangzi advocates. I must confess, however, that I was not the first to get this idea. One of Zhuangzi's followers apparently saw the connection first. In *Tian yun* we find a passage in which Confucius compares Laozi to the ever-mutable dragon: "[Having just visited Laozi] Confucius said: 'Today I have seen a dragon: Gathering together, he assumes form; dispersing, he completes his designs. He rides [*cheng*] on the clouds and *qi*, nourished by the Yin and Yang. I stood there with my mouth open and was unable to shut it. How should I have ventured to correct him?'"[33]

Hayashi Minao was the first to notice that this passage suggests a knowledge of contemporaneous dragon designs.[34] In fact, considering that the author could not have seen a "real" dragon (assuming they do not exist), he must have been referring to the current generic concept of dragon, the same concept that would inform dragon designs. Hayashi did not, however, analyze the implications of the dragon paradigm for the thought of the period. Let us consider more closely just how it is that visual structure and metaphorical content interpenetrate in this passage.

It is possible to read the passage as one complex metaphor in which spatial relations convey ideas. Note that, while Laozi's talents are figured in the form of a dragon, the latter's powers are expressed as a spectrum of relations between figure and ground, that is, dispersion and condensation. Just as condensation presupposes a legible form on a ground, so does dispersion correspond to a pattern-like condition in which the contour of the figure dissolves into the ground. When a form unifies into a whole with distinct contours, it assumes a recognizable form (*cheng ti*). As the form disperses, so does its current role, but not its identity, for now it forms a design (*cheng zhang*). The action of condensing and dispersal implicitly associates Laozi with

33. *Zhuangzi jishi*, 14.525. Compare James Legge, trans., *The Texts of Taoism*, 2 vols., The Sacred Books of the East series, ed. Max Müller, vols. 39–40, reprint ed. (New York: Dover, 1962), I:358.

34. Hayashi Minao, "Chugoku kodai no ibutsu ni omotte wasareta ki no tozo teki hyoken," *Toho Gakuho* 61 (March 1989): 16.

the dragon's transforming power because that is the way "transformation" in dragons is expressed. The constriction and dilation of dragons and spirits in mid–Warring States ornament may likewise be construed as an expression of this same generic condition. The author skillfully exploits the reader's knowledge of such designs to create a rich conceptual resonance here. Because the geometry of the image is as it is, Warring States writers could utilize it to express the notion of foregrounding oneself politically, or disappearing among the masses. This, of course, is the key feature of the dragon metaphor as we find it in the *Zhou yi*. Gathering and dispersion thus illustrate, structurally, the mutability of role and identity which is Laozi's strength. The dragon image was an ideal vehicle for issues of role and identity.

In my translation, the English phrase "completes his designs" (*cheng zhang*) is intended to capture something of the polysemous character of the original. In the *Shu jing*, the *Guoyu* and the *Zuo zhuan, zhang*, "designs," is often treated as the visual correlate of *de*, "virtue," "power." It is an emblematic design on clothing or vessels corresponding to that virtue which justifies a man's allocation of resources. In this usage *zhang* is not just a design. It is a design that reveals some characteristic quality of the bearer. Here, Laozi's *zhang* is likewise the artificial design that expresses his ability to transform. It is the very structure of his mutability.

This excursion into the visual culture of the Warring States period might strike some as a digression, but it has implications for the interpretation of Zhuangzi and other writers. It is apparent from the use of dragon/cloud imagery in both the art and literature of the period that the concept of mutable identities was not confined to an elite club of ancient linguistic philosophers but was available in Warring States culture generally. The dragon trope was in fact part of a much larger discourse of indeterminate form which functioned as a model for the negotiation of authority. Significantly, the spatial structure underlying this discourse was not the center-periphery model so appealing to European monarchs during their period of bureaucratic development, but a complex configuration of monarchical authority in relation to functionaries. The discourses of which I speak survive in such texts as *Guanzi, Lü shi chunqiu, Jingfa* and *Huainanzi* and include in their lexicon a variety of terms derived from a dynamic model of political exchange, terms such as *dao, xun, yin,* or *wuxing*. Time does not permit a thorough analysis of these terms and their roles in fluid models of authority. Nonetheless, it is clear that these discourses share with the dragon image the metaphor of determinate and indeterminate form as a structure for constructions of sovereignty. Consider the following passage from the *Jingfa*:

> He who wields the Dao can mount on heaven's alternating [currents] and can penetrate the distinction between ruler and minister. He can examine

in detail [*fu mi cha*][35] the causes of all things and yet avoid [personally] causing anything to be. He can achieve simplicity and tranquility, [riding] in the vast universe without form, and thereafter can deal with the world correctly.[36]

In this passage the monarch's autonomy is figured in the same manner as that of a talented man in Warring States literature, namely, in the image of a dragon riding heaven's undulating currents. In both cases, freedom corresponds to a state of indeterminate form. Thanks to recent scholarship by Karen Turner, R. P. Peerenboom, Wang Xiaobo, Huo Cunfu and others we now know that, in bureaucratic theory, determinate "form" (*xing*[a]) can be a technical term referring to bureaucratic performance.[37] It can signify a recognizable set of dispositions and abilities, or what one might call an authorizing identity. In the passage just cited, like many others, the monarch is advised not to reveal his own form, so that his ministers cannot second-guess his intentions. Instead, while the monarch mounts on heaven's currents, riding in the universe of indeterminate form—a condition which signals his autonomy—the men in his bureaucracy are able to assume their own form. This is why the *Jingfa* continues in this passage to argue that:

> He who grasps the Dao in viewing the world has no fixed opinion, no fixed position, no intervention [*wuwei*][38] and no private interest.[39]

35. The editor's note suggests that *fu* here is a mistake and should be omitted. Its meaning, however, is similar to the *mi* which follows. Both mean "richly," "densely."

36. The Mawangdui Silk Texts Compilation Committee, ed., *Jingfa*, (Beijing: Zhonghua, 1976), 3.

37. The nature and role of bureaucratic theory terms has been discussed mainly in the growing body of literature on so-called "Huanglao" thought, a term with which no one seems quite pleased (on this problem see Tu Wei-ming, "The Thought of Huang-lao: A Reflection on the Lao Tzu and Huang Ti Texts in the Silk Manuscripts of Ma-wang-tui," *Journal of Asian Studies* 39, no. 1 (November 1979): 95–110. This area of research has grown explosively in recent years and shows no sign of tapering off. Here I can recommend only a few sources. Karen Turner, "The Theory of Law in the Ching-Fa," *Early China* 14 (1989): 58–60, provides a good review of the English, Chinese and Japanese literature on Huanglao theory up to 1989. Liu Weihua and Miao Runtian in "Huanglao sixiang yuanliu," *Wenshizhe* (1986, no. 1): 24–33, trace the development of this tradition in stages. Wang Xiaobo, "Han chudi huanglao zhi zhi yu fajia sixiang," *Shihuo yuekan* 11, no. 10 (1982): 7–30, provides an excellent review of the historiography of interpretation of key Huanglao concepts in this century. Huo Cunfu and Li Jing, "Huanglao di falü sixiang yu wenjing zhi zhi," *Jilin daxue shehui kexue xuebao* 4 (1985): 15–21, provide a particularly good analysis of the socio-historical dimension of this school's activity and in doing so demonstrate how many terms once regarded as mystical actually had very pragmatic applications.

38. For a discussion of *wuwei* as non-interference, see R. P. Peerenboom, "Natural Law in the Huang-lao Boshu," *Philosophy East and West* 40, no. 3 (1990): 309–30, esp. 321.

39. *Jingfa*, 2.

Now this might sound like a strange construction of sovereignty. Why should a sovereign monarch not hold to his opinion? Why should he avoid intervening in administration? The text goes on to explain:

> For this reason, in government, each person will determine his own form [$xing^a$], title, sounds and distinguishing signs. When the form [performance] and name [job description] are established, and when sounds and signs are determined, then nothing will escape your knowledge [and, therefore everything can be governed].[40]

The author of the *Jingfa* essay was not the first to make this argument. He was writing in a tradition of political theory which received its first detailed exposition in the writings of Han Feizi:

> Now every thing has an appropriate [place], and every material has its use. Each assumes its position [role] as is appropriate. That is why relations between superior and subordinate [in government] do not require intervention [*wuwei*] [from the monarch]. Let the cock take charge of the night; let the fox take charge of the mice. Each has its own competency, so the monarch has nothing to be concerned with. If the monarch advocates his own view [lit., is "long" on something], affairs will not appear square ["true"].[41]

Wuwei requires discussion. Writing about early Han texts such as the *Jingfa*, Ssu Hsiu-wu understands it to mean "not interfering" with the people's activities.[42] In reference to Han Feizi's thought, R. P. Peerenboom recognizes *wuwei* as implying "hands-off management by the ruler, who assigns the details of daily operations of the government to his ministers." He also relates *wuwei* to other aspects of bureaucratic theory, including the notion that "appointments are made on the basis of ability, duties are clear and do not overlap, one person responsible for one post, nature is impersonal" and so on.[43]

I am inclined to agree with Peerenboom on all these points. As Han Feizi explains in the passage just cited, deliberate action by the monarch is not necessary or even desirable if the right man can be matched to the right job. Why should the king run about chasing mice if the fox does it well? Once this is understood, the key to good government becomes the objective as-

40. *Jingfa*, 1–2. See also Karen Turner's insightful analysis of the implications of this idea for natural law in "The Theory of Law in the Ching-Fa," esp. 60–61.

41. Chen Qiyou, *Han Feizi*, 8:121. See also this author's discussion of this material in "The Many Meanderings of the Meander in Early China," in *World Art: Proceedings of the XXVI International Congress for the History of Art* (University Park: Pennsylvania State University Press, 1990), 171–80.

42. Ssu Hsiu-wu, *Huanglao xueshuo yu hanchu zhengzhi pingyi* (The Huanglao tradition of thought and early Han political criticism) (Taipei: Taiwan Xuesheng, 1992), 12.

43. R. P. Peerenboom, "Natural Law in the Huang-lao Boshu," *Philosophy East and West* 40, no. 3 (1990), 309–30, esp. 321, 313.

sessment of the fox's ability. This cannot be accomplished if the monarch
has preconceived views. As soon as he shows himself to be "long" on one view,
the situation can no longer be perceived "squarely."

Han Feizi sees the threat to objectivity as twofold. If the monarch has pre-
conceptions, such as the notion that noblemen are better than commoners,
this will skew his assessment of "things." This is why Han insists that "[Un-
der the law] punishments never fail to reach to the highest officers; rewards
never discount the commonest man."[44] Following the same reasoning Han
worries that, should the monarch reveal his own preferences, his men are
likely to "shape" themselves to fit his prejudices, thus making a true assessment of the situation impossible:

> Therefore it is said: "A monarch should never reveal his own preferences."
> If he reveals his preferences, his officers will naturally [zi] shape [lit.,
> "carve and polish"] themselves [to suit his fancy]. A monarch should never
> reveal his intentions. If he reveals his intentions, his officers will naturally
> [zi] exaggerate their special abilities. Therefore it is said: "If you eliminate
> [evidence of] your preferences, your officers will naturally [zi] [reveal them-
> selves] plainly. If you eliminate [evidence of] knowledge and erudition,[45]
> then your officers will naturally [zi] put things in order." Therefore, though
> you will [in fact] have knowledge, it will not be because you take a position.
> Rather you will allow[46] everything to realize its own position [so you will
> have knowledge of your men's true abilities]. Although you will [in fact]
> take action, this will not be because you display your own sagacity. Rather
> you will observe the [circumstances upon which] your officers' [actions]
> depend [yin]. Although you will [in fact] be brave, this will not be because
> you show your rage. Rather you will allow all your officers to completely
> exercise their martial abilities.[47]

The monarch assumes the role of observer. His detachment is not a function of royal virtue, but is effected by his refusal to interfere. He accomplishes this by keeping his own form and position indeterminate. An
officer facing a task is allowed to produce his own claim, a hypothesis, his
response. The monarch need not intervene. His "emptiness" and "quietude"

44. Xue He and Xu Keqian, *Xianqin faxue sixiang ziliao shizhu* [Exegesis of materials for the study of legal thought in pre-Qin China] (Jiangsu: Jiangsu guji, 1990), 80.

45. Basically I follow Wang Niansun here, taking *jiu* to refer to "skill," but I believe that the reference is to the kind of knowledge and skill discussed in the *Zhuangzi* passages in chapter 3. There is a suggestion of "craft," but also a reference to the kind of bookish learning and rhetor-ical sophistry associated with Confucianism in late Warring States writings.

46. The term *shi* here is deliberately and wonderfully ambiguous. It usually implies "cause," but it can also mean "to allow." Here it means that the monarch, in one sense, "controls" things, but not directly. He does so by allowing others to exercise their abilities.

47. Chen Qiyou, *Han Feizi*, 67.

signal his detachment from the details of administration. All the monarch need do is to judge a man's competence. He will assess a man's "form," not against an absolute standard, but against the claim which the candidate himself generated:

> The monarch promotes them according to the title assigned. If he does not know the appropriate title to assign, he seeks the answer by reviewing the man's form [performance] again. When the form [performance] and the name [title] match, then [the monarch] puts the product to use.[48]

This model presumes that the men who *potentially* serve as officials—men who do not yet boast official status—possess abilities of their own. These abilities cannot be predicted from family origin but must be determined by experiment. Human worth is not inherited, nor is it imposed from above. It is generated by the self (*zi*). Such a conclusion is required by arguments in Han Feizi, but is stated explicitly in an essay on the "procedure" (*dao*) of rulership in the *Huainanzi*, an essay recognized as closely allied in thought to the *Jingfa*:[49]

> Although there may be executions in the nation, it is not because of
> the monarch's wrath; although there may be promotions at court, it is
> not because the monarch grants them. If criminals are executed, they do
> not resent the monarch because their punishment is the consequence of
> their own crime; if men are promoted, they do not feel they owe it to the
> monarch because this is the consequence of their own accomplishments.
> [In this way] the people [*min*] will know the [true] source of profit and
> punishment; they will know that it all depends upon their bodily selves.[50]

Although the symbolic source of authority remains the monarch, the monarch does not personally shape his men, for that would distort their true nature, making their forms difficult to define, thereby threatening the efficiency of the state bureaucracy. Rather he allows them to display their own talents so that they end up defining themselves. This, in turn, allows an objective assessment of their performance. The ultimate responsibility for the promotion lies with the individual who gets it or loses it, not with the monarch. The bureaucrat's position and identity are self-determined.

48. Chen Qiyou, *Han Feizi*, 121. Translation consulted W. K. Liao, trans., *The Complete Works of Han Fei Tzu*, 2 vols. (1939; reprint, London: A. Probsthain, 1959), I:53–56.

49. The appendix supplied with the 1976 edition of the *Jingfa* lists close parallels between essays in the *Jingfa* and other Classical period texts. The *Huainanzi* appears frequently, with the largest number of parallels coming from the "Procedures of Rulership" chapter and the "Source of the Course" chapter. *Jingfa*, 167–88. See also Roger T. Ames, "'The Art of Rulership' Chapter of the Huai Nan Tzu: A Practicable Taoism," *Journal of Chinese Philosophy* 8 (1981): 225–44; Wang Zanyuan, "Huainanzi yu fajia di falun bijiao" (Comparing Huainanzi's legal theories with those of the legalist school), *Guowen xuebao* 14 (1985): 69–91.

50. *Huainan honglie jijie*, 2 vols. (Beijing: Zhonghua, 1989), 9.282.

Early bureaucratic theory made practical use of an epistemology whose implications Zhuangzi was among the first to articulate. But it may well be that Zhuangzi was not the inventor of this epistemological orientation, for we find much the same logic in both literary and pictorial descriptions of dragons. Perhaps the use of the dragon image in discussions of the nature of identity is no accident. Lacking mathematical structures for abstract thought, Warring States writers, like their Greek contemporaries, may have utilized visual imagery as a framework for thought.[51]

Let us apply this spatial model to a specific problem in *Qi wu lun*. In his reading of that chapter, Graham maintains that Zhuangzi understood how any division (*bian^a*) leads to contradictions. Since division leads to contradictions, Graham concluded that "we should . . . avoid contradiction by refusing to make this distinction." The article in which Graham proposed this was relatively early in date and it seems unlikely to me that any of us would have developed our current understandings of Zhuangzi without the profusion of insights Graham provided in that article. Still, on this point Graham may have erred. Hansen proposes instead that Zhuangzi attributes ontological status, not to one view, but to all possible perspectival views. This idea comes only with difficulty to Western scholars, judging from traditional portrayals of Zhuangzi as a glaze-eyed mystic.[52]

Could a Warring States mirror cast any light on the problem of distinctions in Zhuangzi? Let us try. It is evident that, from one point of view, the design on the mirror is a dragon; from another point of view, however, it is a cloud. Since you cannot comprehend it as cloud and dragon at the same moment, it follows that making distinctions is unavoidable. Therefore, one could legitimately say: *fei bi wu wo, fei wo wu suo qu* (line 14).

So far, Hansen and Graham could agree. It does not follow, however, that contradictions arise as soon as distinctions are made. Clearly they arise only if we attribute privileged ontological status to the dragon as opposed to the cloud (or vice versa). But this need not be the case and, indeed, would not normally be the case were we looking at the mirror. Who would fight over whether the design was "really" a dragon or a cloud? Should circumstances require it to be a dragon, the dragon is there; should we need to view it as cloud, it is easy to switch. Our choice will be based, not on ontological considerations (the Truth), but on practical considerations: "What consequences

51. For craft metaphors in Greek thought see John Onians, "Idea and Product: Potter and Philosopher in Classical Athens," *Journal of Design History* 4, no. 2 (1991): esp. 66–67. For a thoughtful review of the use of craft metaphors in Warring States thought, see David Keightley, "Craft and Culture: Metaphors of Governance in Early China," *Proceedings of the Second International Conference on Sinology, Academia Sinica* (Taipei: Academia Sinica, 1989), 31–70.

52. See Hansen, *Daoist Theory,* 269.

ensue if I take it to be a dragon?" In this sense, all perspectival views are admissible, but not at the same time and not under all circumstances.

To my knowledge little work has been done in the China field on the issue of identity in pictorial art and its relationship to epistemology, but a review of Zhuangzi's *Qi wu lun* helps to highlight ways in which vision and thought may contribute to a single mode of argument.

ON MAKING NOISE IN *QI WU LUN*

Wai-yee Li

Qi wu lun contains one of the most remarkable descriptions of noise in early Chinese literature. Nanguo Ziqi dwells on the piping of humans (*renlai*), piping of earth (*dilai*), and piping of heaven (*tianlai*). The piping of earth, the myriad noises made by wind blowing through bends, holes, and hollows of various shapes and sizes, is described with such sound and fury that we sometimes forget the supposed detachment of the speaker, Nanguo Ziqi. He is privy to such music because he has "lost his self" (*sangwo*): his body is like withered wood, his heart like dead ashes. Even as music comes out of emptiness (rows of tubes, the myriad hollows, apertures of the human heart and head), Nanguo Ziqi can listen because he is emptied of his "self" and has attained a higher level of perception-consciousness. Listening in this instance is not merely passive reception of the sensual immediacy of sounds but also active engagement in philosophical understanding. The extended description of the piping of earth is followed by a cryptic definition of the piping of heaven: "For that which blows the ten thousand different voices makes each come into its own, as each of itself takes from it [according to its nature]. This animator—who is it?" (ZZ, 3.8–9). There are at least three ways of interpreting the piping of heaven: as the spontaneous self-generation and self-functioning of the piping of earth and of men (Guo Xiang, Cheng Xuanying, ZZJS, 50); the generative force or principle that fashions the piping of earth and of men (Graham, 150);[53] or the balance between "self-engendering" (*ziji*) and the actualizing energy, between "self-choosing" (*ziqu*) and the impelling force. In all three cases the listener plays a transformative role. In the words of Yao Nai: "To him who has lost himself, the myriad hollows and rows of tubes are all piping of heaven" (ZZZJ, 2.9).

Nanguo Ziqi "lost his self." In "Free and Easy Wandering" ("Xiaoyao you"), "the supreme being has no self" (*zhiren wuji*) (ZZZJ, 1.4). Related formulations include "abstinence of the mind" (*xinzhai*) in "The Human World" ("Renjian shi," ZZZJ, 3.30), and "forgetting" (*wang*) in "The Sign of Virtue

---

53. A. C. Graham, "Chuang-Tzu's Essay on Seeing Things as Equal," *History of Religions* 9.2–3 (1969–70): 137–59.

Complete" ("De chong fu") and "The Great Ancestral Teacher" ("Da Zong-shi," *ZZZJ*, 5.45, 6.59–60). Transcendence is conceived in terms of nega-tivity and absence. The proposition that "loss of self" heightens perception-consciousness is a paradox that brings out other paradoxes in the *Zhuangzi*. Expression and creation depend as much on the procreative void as on acts of choice, transformation, and interpretation. "Loss of self" is dramatized through performance in front of an audience. Nanguo Ziqi, for all his obliv-ion, indifference, and self-forgetfulness, is quick to respond to his inter-locutor Yancheng Ziyou. His state of being is quietistic, but his language is elliptical, dramatic, performative, provocative. He can treat the myriad voices as equal because all partake of, or are translatable into, the piping of heaven, but in order to see things as equal he has to rise above them by ap-pealing to the category of the piping of heaven. In other words, among things seen as equal he cannot count himself. The idea of "loss of self" is in part a response to this contradiction. But it also coexists with the sense of higher consciousness. All noises can be seen as equal, but Nanguo Ziqi's own voice deliberating the nature of, and relationship between, piping of men, earth, and heaven carries more authority.

In this beginning passage of Nanguo Ziqi's loud ruminations, the self is absent yet vocal, words are contingent yet necessary, formation or creation is self-generated yet determined. In the *Qi wu lun* as a whole, the double lives of words such as noise (*sheng*[a]), words (*yan*), knowledge (*zhi*[c]), judgment (*bian*[a]), argument (*lun*[a], *yi*[e]), transformation (*hua*), and self (*wo*) issue in two parallel arguments. One establishes all knowledge, judgment, and argument as relative. The other differentiates the argument at hand from other argu-ments by exploring the possibility of a new philosophical language. These two positions are in turn augmented by two notions of the self: one demol-ished as inconstant and arbitrary, the other exalted as transcendent; and two modes of reasoning and expression, one emphasizing division and frag-mentation, the other, unity and flux.

Let us first consider the perspective of division. In order to undermine the self, the source of competing arguments, Zhuangzi breaks it up into composite, competing parts. Here Zhuangzi uses again the metaphor of "music coming out emptiness" (*yue chu xu*) (*ZZ*, 4.13), not to celebrate spontaneous generation, but to demonstrate the unaccountable, capricious transformations of the human heart. "Without them [mental states] there is no I, without me they have nothing to draw from" (*fei bi wu wo, fei wo wu suo qu*) (*ZZ*, 4.14–15). This is a reverberation of the motif of the piping of earth and heaven: who makes the music, the hollows or the wind? What is the music, the piping of earth or the piping of heaven? Whereas the an-swer to these questions can easily be "both" with no necessary implications of tension, here the mutual dependence of self and other (*bi*, i.e., mental states) undermines the integrity of both. It is not certain that the self is prior to ever-changing mental states. The self has no center, because it cannot be established which organ or faculty should be held more dearly, which should be regarded as the "true lord" (*zhenjun*) or "true controller" (*zhenzai*). Its sources are not known. Its inevitable fate is unfreedom, death, and degeneration.

The self thus understood issues in utterances based on the authority of contrived, arbitrary judgments (*chengxin*). Zhuangzi ponders this kind of language: "For words are not blowing breath. Words say something, but what is said is not fixed. Are words really spoken? Or have words never been spoken? For those who regard words as being different from the twitter of fledglings—is there a distinction? Or is there no distinction?" (*ZZ*, 4.23–24). Words are both more and less than blowing breath. Unlike blowing breath, speaking words is a referential act and thus purports to signify in a specific way. Also unlike blowing breath, speaking words cannot claim free, spontaneous signification or connection with the piping of heaven. Given the arbitrary and conventional nature of linguistic reference, are words really distinct from the twitter of fledglings? The more insistent the significatory intent, the more serious the danger of lopsidedness and partial illumination ("To illuminate what cannot be illuminated [for the other]," *ZZ*, 5.45). The true function of words is obscured by demonstrative and counter-demonstrative statements (*shifei*), as shown in the mutual negation of the Confucians and the Mohists. Zhuangzi claims to see as equal all utterances that resort to fine distinctions and vain disputations.

In response to the instability of reference ("what is said is not fixed"), the Mohists aspires to the ideal of an austere, functional, transparent language; the Confucians emphasize the need for the rectification of names, for the proper correspondence of things and names supposedly sustain moral-political order; the logicians expound paradoxes that claim internal, self-referential, analytic coherence. Zhuangzi makes a virtue of necessity and celebrates unstable reference as play and polysemy. Language is not measured against an Ineffable Reality. Instead, as a dynamically changing field of meaning, language matches the flux of experience and phenomena. We recall the description of Zhuangzi's style in the final chapter, "All Under Heaven" ("Tianxia"):

> Absent, boundless, formless, ever-transforming, inconstant. Is this death
> or life? Does it stand together with heaven and earth? Does spiritual illumi-
> nation come along? Faint and indistinct, where does it go? In a trice where
> does it turn? The myriad things are all encompassed, none is worth return-
> ing to. Among the ancients there are those whose way and art lies therein.
> Zhuang Zhou heard of their ways and delighted in them. He used absurd,
> far-fetched formulations, fantastic words, phrases without limits and bound-

aries. Ever so often unrestrained, he did not use direct, forthright language, because he did not see things from one side. He considered the world beclouded—it was impossible to use sober language to communicate with it. He used "goblet words" to be boundless and ever-changing, "repeated words" to convey truths, "lodged words" to create breadth. Alone he came and went with the spirit of heaven and earth, and did not view the myriad things arrogantly. . . . Above he wandered with the Maker of Things, below he befriended those who treat life and death as externalities and are without beginnings and endings. (*ZZZJ*, 33.277–78)

According to Cheng Xuanying, "goblet words" (*zhiyan*) are indeterminate (*buding*): "For the goblet, when overflowing, leans to one side, when empty, stands upright. That is why the vessel of goblet is used as comparison for supreme language" (*ZZJS*, 33.1100). In this sense "repeated words" (*chongyan*) and "lodged words" (*yuyan*) are but subcategories of "goblet words," for correspondences and range of reference also function to augment "everchanging boundlessness" (*manyan*). Adeptness in this language is concomitant with the most-praised activity in Zhuangzi: roaming, and wandering, or playing (*you*).

In *Qi wu lun* also parallel formulations juxtapose words and Daoist transcendence.

"The Dao has never had boundaries; words have never had constancy" (*ZZ*, 5.55). Both boundaries and immutable meanings are functions of statements that demarcate differences. Words are celebrated for lacking norms of reference: inconstancy defies vain distinctions and parallels the boundlessness of the Dao. The recurrent parallel drawn between words and the Dao points to a new ideal philosophical language. "By what is the Dao hidden that truth and falsehood exist? By what are words hidden that demonstrative and counter-demonstrative statements come to be? The Dao is hidden by small achievements; words are hidden by superficial brilliance [literally, foliage and flowers]" (*ZZ*, 4.24–26). "The Way comes to be as one walks it; things come to be thus as one calls it thus" (*ZZ*, 4.33). Even as the Way transcends truth and falsehood, words have a function higher than that of demonstrative and counter-demonstrative statements, once they are freed from clever disputations and glib rhetoric.

Language establishes difference. Etymologically, *lun*[a] (discourse, discuss, theorize) is linked to *lun*[b] (sort out), and *bian*[a] (discriminate, differentiate) to *bian*[b] (debate, argue). Hence the praise of silence in *Qi wu lun*. "Great disputation does not speak" (*ZZ*, 5.59). "There is forming and flawing when Zhaoshi plays the *qin;* there is no forming and flawing when Zhaoshi does not play the *qin*" (*ZZ*, 5.43). "Separation is formation, formation is destruction" (*ZZ*, 4.35). Even the music of the master *qin*-player Zhaoshi is a sacrifice of the musical possibilities that are potential in silence. Ideally, language should be inconstant, paradoxical, all-encompassing, effacing boundaries and distinctions, so as to approximate silence. However, language can only be transcended through language. Again and again sages break their silence with a rather comfortable "however" (*suiran*).

Zhuangzi attempts to develop a new style of philosophical language that allows him to discourse on all utterances as equal. He uses provisional and hypothetical statements that leave room for prolepsis: "Now suppose I make a statement here. I do not know whether it belongs to the category of demonstrative and counter-demonstrative statements, or whether it does not belong to that category. However, not being in a category is also a kind of category—in that sense it is not different" (*ZZ*, 5.47–49). He thus dismantles in advance his own claim of making statements different from all other statements (Wang Fuzhi, *ZZZJ*, 16). Having accepted the basic premise that his own statement cannot claim to be sui generis or to escape all categories, he nevertheless cheerfully continues. The phrase "however, let me find words for it" appears twice in the chapter (*ZZ*, 5.49, 6.65 66). It confirms verbal expression as the art of the possible.

Zhuangzi then tries words and conceptions that establish outermost limits, aspire to infinite division, and play on infinite regress. "There is a beginning. There is a not yet beginning to be a beginning. There is a not yet beginning to be a not yet beginning to be a beginning" (*ZZ*, 5.49). The two antecedent stages to "there is a beginning" can only be imagined verbally. Words acquire a new kind of independence from reference. The same exercise is repeated with different emphasis in the case of the paired opposites "being" and "non-being." "There is being. There is non-being. There is not yet having begun to be non-being. There is not yet having begun to not yet having begun to be non-being. Suddenly there is non-being, and I do not know whether 'there is non-being' actually means 'there being' or 'there not being.' I have referred to something, and I do not know whether what I have referred to actually refers to something or does not refer to anything" (*ZZ*, 5.49–51). What begins as meditation on the idea of infinite past which undermines all notions of origins turns into a sudden confrontation with a logical contradiction and ends in a statement on skepticism. "Suddenly there is non-being": this is the language of immediate experience and half-involuntary mental engagement; the mind cannot cope with infinite regress, and has to seize on something as a provisional starting point. But the statement "there is non-being" balances uncertainly between "there being" and "there not being." Hence the final note of skepticism on the possibility of reference in language. Skepticism, however, does not undermine the authority of Zhuangzi's own words but paradoxically augments it, because it confirms his readiness to doubt and challenge his own premises.

The passage on beginnings, being, and non-being shares with the logicians the delight in making infinite divisions. But infinite proliferation of distinctions is arrested by the urgency of the statement "suddenly, there is non-being," which in turn raises questions on the possibility of resolving contradictions and the viability of linguistic reference. The idea of oneness responds to these questions. By translating the idea of "seeing things as equal" into the most striking metaphors, Zhuangzi apparently reconciles opposites, abolishes differences, and redefines linguistic reference. "Heaven and earth exist along with me, the myriad things and I are one." A. C. Graham points out rightly that this statement, which has often been singled out as summarizing one essential aspect of Zhuangzi's thought, actually functions as one reference point in an argumentative process. For Zhuangzi follows the proclamation of oneness by undermining its validity. "Since oneness is achieved, shouldn't there be words for it? Since oneness has been called such, how can there be no words for it? Oneness and the word makes two, two and one makes three." The idea of oneness depends on language, yet language inevitably destroys it. Instead of simply asserting oneness, Zhuangzi emphasizes the need to see differences in oneness, and oneness in differences, in the spirit of the "adaptive 'that's it'" (*yinshi*, Graham's translation).

The "adaptive 'that's it'" transcends the logic of either-or. Other metaphors used to the same effect in *Qi wu lun* include the treasury of heaven (*tianfu*), the potter's wheel of heaven (*tianjun*), the whetstone of heaven (*tianni*), "proceeding on two alternatives (or walking two roads)" (*liangheng*), the axis of the Dao (*Daoshu*), illumination (*ming*). The treasury of heaven is knowledge of "the wordless disputation, the untold way" and thus transcends the opposition of language and silence. Both the potter's wheel of heaven and the whetstone of heaven are images for harmonizing and mediating competing versions of truth. The axis of the Dao is located where no position can find its opposite. All are metaphors of flux, inclusiveness, and mediation. Translated into stylistic terms, metaphors transcending either-or become premises constantly revised, extended, overturned; statements that cast sidelong glances at their opposites, incorporate, play with, and argue against them. In this sense Zhuangzi is always dialogic, even when he is speaking in his own voice. He is always responding to an imaginary interlocutor. Hence his frequent choice of the dialogue form, by which he can encompass different voices and challenge his own conceptions. The context of interlocution also establishes speech as a playful concession, silence being presumably preferred.

The exchange between Nie Que and Wang Ni is a good example. Nie Que's questions echo major issues in the chapter. "Do you know whether it is true that all things are equal?" "Do you know what you do not know?" "Does anything know anything?" (ZZ, 6.64–65). The first question harks back to the idea of seeing things as equal. The second one repeats in question form an assertion made earlier in the chapter, "thus knowing how to stop at what is not known is supreme knowledge" (ZZ, 5.60). The third question hints at the impossibility of knowledge. Wang Ni's answer to all three questions is "how would I know that?" His disclaimer theoretically undermines the premises of the chapter. Absolute skepticism has no place for words beyond the statement that knowledge is impossible. But Wang Ni is not content with silence: "However, let me try to find words for it. How would I know that what I call knowledge is not ignorance? How would I know that what I call ignorance is not knowledge?" (ZZ, 6.66). From the position of skepticism, which enjoins silence, he proceeds to discuss authoritatively the relativity of judgment. The determination of proper abode, proper taste, and proper form depends on one's nature. He then turns to his own judgment (zi wo guan zhi), according to which humanity and righteousness, affirmation and negation, are just so much confusion and impossible to distinguish from one another. This implicit elevation of his own judgment merges with the mythical image of the sage's (zhiren) power and grandeur with which he concludes his speech (ZZ, 6.71–73). Here skepticism cannot be debilitating because it subtly celebrates a new sense of self.

The dialogic mode functions as a bracketing device and allows Zhuangzi to transcend the logic of either-or. The presentation of dreaming and waking states as infinite regress, which may be arrested only with the Great Awakening (dajue), takes place within a dialogue.

> Qu Quezi asked Chang Wuzi, "I have heard from the Master, 'The sage does not apply himself to any affairs. He neither hankers after profit nor avoids harm. He takes no pleasure in acquisition and follows no path. Not saying anything, he says something; saying something, he does not say anything, and he roams beyond dust and grime.' The Master regarded these as wild words, but I consider them the Working of the Subtle Way." Chang Wuzi said, "This is what would confound even the Yellow Emperor, why would Qiu [Confucius] understand it? But you too are calculating too far in advance. You see the egg and seek the rooster, you see the slingshot and seek the roasted bird. I shall speak for you reckless words, you should listen recklessly. How about that? . . . "

Contexts of quotation and interlocution here establish a kind of competition. Qu Quezi claims to be quoting Confucius, while at the same time he congratulates himself on having surpassed Confucius, who does not seem to appreciate or understand his own description of the Daoist sage. What obtains is a rather tame summary of Daoist attributes, although for Confucius these are already "wild words" (*menglang zhi yan*). Chang Wuzi claims that Qu Quezi anticipates conclusions too readily, and in doing so turns Daoist transcendence into final, conclusive stasis. By contrast, Chang Wuzi dramatizes the transcendence of opposites as Daoist thought process, with all its pathos, anguish, and playfulness. He begins with an invitation to hypothesis: "I shall speak for you reckless words, you should listen recklessly. How about that?"

Chang Wuzi's "reckless words" move from declamatory splendor to profound skepticism. He gives his version of the Daoist sage: "Going by the side of the sun and the moon, holding under his arms space and time, merging with all things, leaving aside all uncertainties, respecting the common run of humanity. The crowd is toiling and anxious, the sage is foolish and oblivious, sees through the ten thousand ages to form One Purity, affirms the myriad things and let them enfold each other." But this authoritative account is immediately followed by unresolvable questions premised on the certainty of death and the impossibility of knowledge. He seeks to treat life and death, waking and dreaming states, as reversible doubles, but prefaces his comparisons with "How would I know. . . . "

> How would I know that to love life is not a delusion? How would I know that to hate death is not like someone who, having lost his home as a youth, knows not the way of return? . . . How would I know that the dead one does not regret his initial longing for life? Those who dream of drinking wine cry and weep in the morning; those who dream of crying and weeping go hunting in the morning. While we are dreaming we do not know that we are dreaming. In our dreams we try to use divination to interpret our dreams [within dreams]. Only upon waking do we know that we have been dreaming. And it is upon the Great Awakening that we know this is our Great Dream. Yet the foolish ones think of themselves as awake, furtively certain of their knowing. Ruler? Herdsman? How limited! Confucius and you are both dreaming. I who call you dreaming am also dreaming. As for these words, their name is Supreme Paradox. If after ten thousand ages there is one meeting with the Great Sage who knows how to explain this, it would have been like waiting between morning and evening. (*ZZ*, 2.21)

There is such urgency in confronting mortality and the uncertainty of knowledge that Chang Wuzi can only appeal to an Archimedean point ("the Great Awakening," the meeting with the Great Sage) and an infinitely precious and precarious language ("the Supreme Paradox," *diaogui*)—all within the framework of "reckless words listened to recklessly."

The movement between the first and second sections of Chang Wuzi's speech (i.e., the initial account of the Daoist Sage and the series of questions on life and death, dreaming and waking) enacts the dialogic process postulated earlier. A declamatory statement with an aura of finality, often itself radical and akin to what we think of as "Daoist," is bracketed and (implicitly) questioned. This is a recurrent ploy in the *Zhuangzi*. As noted earlier, this is how he posits the statement "Heaven and earth exist along with me, the myriad things and I are one": he follows the proclamation of oneness by questioning its viability.

Chang Wuzi's questions on dreaming and waking states, life and death, thus dramatize the flux and tensions of processes of thought and expression. The reversibility of these opposites is not the "message" to be distilled. But this commitment to process and striving to go beyond the outermost limits is deeply unsettling: we can in fact never be certain that we are not dreaming. The same logic and pathos characterize Zhuangzi's earlier discussions of beginnings and being. Like the statement "suddenly there is non-being," the references to Great Awakening and the meeting with the all-comprehending Great Sage in Chang Wuzi's speech function to arrest infinite regress. They represent a logical and psychological necessity. Conversely, the reversibility of dreaming and waking states and the hypothetical impossibility of going beyond dreams create and challenge this necessity. By calling the language referring to such matters "Supreme Paradox" Zhuangzi is again claiming for himself a new philosophical language that celebrates play and polysemy. The frame of "reckless words listened to recklessly" heightens the tension between what can be said and what cannot be said and establishes the movement toward the "space" between word and world, the mediation that makes the relationship between them possible. It is Zhuangzi's version of "proceeding on two alternatives."

The view of language as flux encompassing opposites, always straining to transcend itself, has its counterpart in a comparable idea of the self, which is why the butterfly dream is a fitting conclusion to a chapter that begins with the myriad voices. In other words, the new philosophical language unfolding in *Qi wu lun* is a mode of being in the world. Language must be playful, paradoxical, transforming, and transformative so that one may achieve reconciliation with the ultimate transformation, death. The language transcending life and death, dreaming and waking states allows the "letting loose of the bonds" (*xuanjie, ZZZJ*, 6.55) and the "removal of fetters and shackles" (*jie qi zhigao, ZZZJ*, 5.42). The butterfly dream does not simply assert the sameness of life and death, waking and dreaming states, or the relativity of judgment. The tone modulates between freedom for the spirit ("joyous and carefree in being a butterfly" [*ZZ*, 7.95]) and the anguish of skepticism and mortality ("He did not know about [Zhuang] Zhou"). The idea that the dreamer may be dreamed by another ("He did not know whether he was Zhuang Zhou dreaming of being a butterfly, or a butterfly dreaming of being Zhuang Zhou" [ZZ, 7.95–96]) mocks knowledge and the sense of freedom as illusory.

In Zhuangzi the idea of transformation is burdened with the certainty of death ("His shape is transformed, and his mind is destroyed along with it. Is this not a great sorrow?" [*ZZZJ*, 2.11]) and the impossibility of knowledge ("For knowledge has to depend on something in order to be appropriate, and that which it depends on is never fixed" [*ZZZJ*, 6.47]). The idea of transformation may be divested of its negative echoes through active participation in the process of transformation. In "The Great Ancestral Teacher," the metamorphosis of even the human body is accepted and celebrated: "Now if one regards heaven and earth as a great foundry, and the maker of transformations as the great smith, where would I go and not agree? Suddenly asleep, in a trice I wake up" (*ZZZJ*, 6.55). In the butterfly dream, mastery of the process of transformation is achieved through the act of naming.

There is then a symmetry to the beginning and ending of the chapter. Even as Nanguo Ziqi embarks on performative ruminations after his moment of oblivion and self-forgetfulness, Zhuangzi, after experiencing "loss of self" as butterfly in the dream, ponders and gives a name to the transition between dreaming and waking states: the Transformation of Things (*wuhua*). The apparent moral of the butterfly dream is that Zhuangzi and the butterfly, self-consciousness and its negation, are equally valid manifestations of the Dao. By the same token, the moment a lucid intelligence expounds on the Transformation of Things is no less transcendent than the moment of undifferentiation and intuitive union of the Dao. Again, the key term is mediation, as realized by the spirit and the voice moving between the dreaming and waking states. Nevertheless, there is a certain asymmetry between the two states of being in the parable. The butterfly is completely at one with itself; it does not ask whether it is Zhuangzi dreaming of being a butterfly or a butterfly dreaming of being Zhuangzi. It is upon waking that Zhuangzi poses the question, affirms the difference between the two states of being, and asserts that the difference defines two poles of a process of transformation, itself part of the great flux of all things. Zhuangzi is keenly aware of the irony implicit in this asymmetry. Transcendence is a form of forgetting, but philosophical reflection and language are rooted in remembering. The telling of the butterfly dream is thus also a mode of "proceeding on two alternatives," a playful acceptance of the differentiating edge of philosophy and language. The idea that the world may be dreamed can lead to anguish and skepticism, Zhuangzi confronts it with a new philosophical language and a new conception of subjectivity, turning it into a token of human freedom, marked not only by sublime self-forgetfulness of dream—Zhuangzi is "joyous and carefree in being a butterfly"—but also by reflection and linguistic act, the naming of the "Transformation of Things" that enacts mediatory movement between dreaming and waking, life and death, language and silence.

PERSPECTIVE ON READINGS OF *QI WU LUN*

I Am Not Dreaming This

Willard Peterson

A few nights ago I dreamed I was in Serb-controlled territory, somewhere near Macedonia. Someone held what he said was a gun to the back of my head. I could not see it, but I did not doubt its existence. I was pushed into a shadowy room and told I must answer some questions put by Sextus Empiricus. I knew of his name as the physician who authored *Outlines of Pyrrhonism,* and there he was, seated across an old wooden table from me. I was nervous, with the famous skeptic in front of me and an unseen gun behind me. As if to reassure me, he gently said he wanted to ask me about skepticism in the Land of Silk. I must have looked bewildered, but he went on about how at the time Pyrrho appears to have distinguished himself for living in accord with the Skeptical persuasion, there was someone far away called Master Zhuang, wasn't there? I nodded in assent only because the chronology seemed about right. And didn't this Zhuang write that we find it difficult to affirm as true any particular argument or belief when each always has an opposite that may seem equally true? And that such competing claims are undecidable? And that by suspending judgment about conflicts over true or not true, right or wrong, real or unreal, affirmable or not, and the like, one achieves tranquility of mind? I wanted to scratch my chin but sensed the gun and thought I should not raise my hand from the table. I was thinking that what Sextus Empiricus had said was vaguely familiar, maybe the *Qi wu lun* chapter, so I mumbled that it could be so. Well then, he went on, this Zhuang fellow was a skeptic who lived his skepticism, wasn't he? I swallowed and started to stammer that I needed time to think about the question, when there was a loud noise behind me—an explosion—and I was lying on my bed.

I reflected on my dream. (I do not wish to burden you with the task of interpreting my interpretation.) I decided I would enlist the help of the papers by West, Powers, and Li to gain some perspective for answering the question put by Sextus Empiricus. Of course the question is generated from a Greek (or at least a Greek language) philosophical tradition and would impose foreign criteria on a text produced in Chinese, but I decided since I was already doing some such violence by thinking and writing at the end of the twentieth century and in English, I would not be deterred. After all, Sextus Empiricus could not maintain that only Greek is proper language and all else is bar-bar. I also thought that since we know next to nothing about how Sextus Empiricus lived his life in the second century somewhere in the eastern Mediterranean world, and since he disavows knowing how Pyrrho, the eponymous skeptic of later accounts, lived his life in the fourth century before the common era, I should leave aside the part of the question about how Zhuang Zhou lived. We have little certainty about anything that might pass for a fact about Zhuang Zhou, however eager readers over the centuries have been to make inferences and draw conclusions. Also disputable is any determination (by reference to tradition, modern scholarly consensus, philosophical intuition, linguistic analysis or whatever) of where in the text we readers can surely locate Zhuangzi's ideas.[54] As a reader I am intrigued and frustrated by the text we know as the *Zhuangzi,* whether the thirty-three chapter standard version or a smaller, presumptively core set such as the seven "Inner" chapters. I am frustrated because even when with the aid of commentators I can say the words of a passage of the text and accept that there is an agreed meaning for obscure and otherwise unknown words and phrases, every attempt to settle on what a passage "means" tends to end up being subverted by other passages in the *Zhuangzi.* How the text succeeds in subverting itself and frustrating readers intrigues me. Since I do not know who Zhuang Zhou was—that is, the facts of his life—and I do not know which were his ideas among the compilation we know as the *Zhuangzi,* I expediently recast the question put to me by Sextus Empiricus to be: are the meanings conveyed by the words of the *Qi wu lun* chapter, regardless of who authored them, consonant with "skepticism" as expounded by the words in the *Outlines of Pyrrhonism?*

What is meant here by skepticism? I do not mean "vulgar skepticism," the notion that a skeptic is one who habitually doubts everything and who, by making claims to know that we cannot know anything, is self-refuting and life-denying. Pointing out that skepticism as a philosophical stand can be distinguished from the vulgar characterization, the translator of Sextus Empiricus's *Outlines of Pyrrhonism* for the Loeb series, R. G. Bury, made the point this way:

> A "sceptic," in the original sense of the Greek term, is simply an "inquirer" or investigator. But inquiry often leads to an *impasse,* and ends in incredulity or despair of a solution, so that "inquirer" becomes a "doubter" or a "disbeliever," and Scepticism receives it usual [vulgar] connotation. . . . When Scepticism was revived and reorganized under the name of "Pyrrhonism," its main task was to challenge this assumption and to maintain, if not the

54. See the discussion at the beginning of Liu Xiaogan, *Classifying the Zhuangzi Chapters* (Ann Arbor: Center for Chinese Studies, University of Michigan, 1994), esp. 1–3. Liu also considers the available early evidence about the life of Zhuang Zhou.

impossibility of knowledge, at least the impossibility of positively affirming its possibility. Its watchword was "Suspend judgement."[55]

The Skeptic refutes any "dogma," which is defined as "assent to a non-evident proposition," and any set of dogmas which are claimed to be "dependent both on one another and on appearances."[56] But it does not follow that a Skeptic knows nothing. Sextus Empiricus sought to make a critical distinction.

> When we say that the sceptic does not dogmatize, we are not using "dogma" in the more general sense in which some say it is dogma to accept anything (for the sceptic does assent to the experiences he cannot help having in virtue of this impression or that: for example, he would not say, when warmed or cooled, "I seem not to be warmed or cooled"). Rather, when we say he does not dogmatize, we mean "dogma" in the sense in which some say that dogma is assent to any of the non-evident matters investigated by the sciences. For the Pyrrhonian assents to nothing that is non-evident.[57]

Sextus Empiricus maintains that Skepticism is not merely negative in intent or effect. "Scepticism is an ability, or mental attitude, which opposes appearances to judgements in any way whatsoever, with the result that, owing to the equipollence of the objects and reasons thus opposed, we are brought firstly to a state of mental suspense and next to a state of 'unperturbedness' or quietude."[58] According to Sextus Empiricus, skeptics "follow a line of reasoning which, in accordance with appearances, points us to a life conformable to the customs of our country and its laws and institutions, and to our own instinctive feelings."[59] This seems a long way from the disparaging stories about Pyrrho acting on his "not knowing anything" to the extreme of not stopping himself from walking off a cliff unless saved by the intervention of friends. Showing that he knew something, Sextus Empiricus wrote three books' worth of discussion of Pyrrhonism to set forth his view of (to borrow Michael Frede's title) the Skeptic's beliefs.

55. R. G. Bury, trans., *Outlines of Pyrrhonism*, by Sextus Empiricus (1933; Cambridge, Mass.: Harvard University Press, 1990), Introduction, xxix. I prefer the spelling "skeptic" and its derivatives, but in quotations I shall follow each author's preference. For another, more systematic account of the skepticism of Sextus Empiricus and its bearing on our understanding of parts of the *Zhuangzi* that is largely congruent with mine, see Paul Kjellberg, "Sextus Empiricus, Zhuangzi, and Xunzi on 'Why Be Skeptical?'" in *Essays on Skepticism, Relativism, and Ethics in the Zhuangzi*, ed. P. Kjellberg and P. J. Ivanhoe (Albany: SUNY Press, 1996), 1–25.

56. *Outlines* I.16, trans. Bury, 13.

57. *Outlines* I.13. The translation is by M. F. Burnyeat, in his "The Sceptic in His Place and Time," in *Philosophy in History: Essays on the Historiography of Philosophy*, ed. Richard Rorty, J. B. Schneewind, and Quentin Skinner (Cambridge: Cambridge University Press, 1984), 229. Compare Bury, 9–11.

58. *Outlines* I.8, trans. Bury, 7.

59. *Outlines* I.17, trans. Bury, 13.

Finding much of philosophical interest in Greek Skepticism, Michael Frede puts the saving distinction in somewhat different terms. He proposes the label "dogmatic skepticism" for "the view that nothing is, or can be, known for certain,"[60] the position that critics of skepticism traditionally ascribe to it. Frede explicates what he calls "classical skepticism," as a view that involves withholding assent without claiming one ought to withhold assent (205), that involves denying the common assumption that knowledge and truth are necessarily correlated (210), that involves not holding reason in contempt while also not expecting that any certainty derives from reasoning (200), and that involves being content to accept what seems evident without making claims about its truth or reality (194). (I apologize to Frede for radically reducing and oversimplifying his explication. You should read him for yourself.)

How do West, Powers and Li help me to answer Sextus Empiricus's question about the consonance between Pyrrhonism or "classical Skepticism" and the views in the *Qi wu lun* chapter?

Steve West's reading of the opening segment of the *Qi wu lun* chapter emphasizes literary qualities over any "message" or "philosophical force." For West, the text itself (as a set of inscriptions on a page rendered as formed sounds over a bounded period of time?) performs spectacularly, "like fire juggled in the night." The performance involves a process we might call "experiencing language" (or West's "language of experience"), which not incidentally destabilizes the process of "classifying language" (or West's "language of classification"). West presents a compelling account of reading and hearing the text making air "whistle and whine" as it moves through things and is moved by things. The passage plays with words, plays on words, and plays with Ziyou's expectations about words. There is nothing like this performance in Sextus Empiricus's *Outlines of Pyrrhonism.*

The common understanding of the opening passage, according to West, is that by his performance "Ziqi invites his disciple to look *behind* [emphasis added] the words of various philosophers . . . to something else." If this is taken to mean that there is a truth (or reality or Heaven or Way or Self-thusness or Nothing) behind Ziyou's and our experiencing the performance of the words and that Nanguo Ziqi expects Ziyou and us to apprehend that something else and to assent to the primacy of that non-evident truth over our direct experience, then the "common understanding" would be dogmatic and suspect from a skeptical position. In his own imagined paraphrase, West puts Nanguo Ziqi's point rather differently: "Look, you dolt, you didn't recognize the breath of heaven that was coming out of me." And the meaning even of that

60. Michael Frede, "The Skeptic's Two Kinds of Assent and the Question of the Possibility of Knowledge," in *Essays in Ancient Philosophy* (Minneapolis: University of Minnesota Press, 1987), 201.

paraphrase must be elusive; as West says, "the pipes of heaven are neither open to discussion (since [classifying] language has to denote them as 'something') nor perceivable as sound—no attributes can be assigned." West concludes that Nanguo Ziqi's playful, ambiguous, destabilizing performance is a "perfect demonstration that nothing in the world that is perceivable is fixed in definable form," a demonstration which we can appreciate only "as we give up possibility after possibility to come to our own sense of closure." West's reading is that, after being disturbed from a state of tranquility, Nanguo Ziqi's "wind" reminds us that perceptions, words, and meanings are all in flux and indeterminate. By implication, we might construe the performance as conveying a message, something like, "suspend judgment."

Someone might claim that the segment of text West examines goes further than undermining a correlation between words and certainty; it is a dogmatic denial of any possibility of (genuine) knowledge. But such a claim would be vitiated if we recognize that the whistling, whining, puffing and breathing softly are constituent parts of what is presented to us readers as an exchange of words between Ziyou and Nanguo Ziqi. Later in the *Qi wu lun*, we read that "Saying [words] is not puffing [breath]" (line 23). There the point is further developed that what saying says is indeterminate, and even that must be said. This is not a nihilistic approach to words. I could contemplate trying to argue to Sextus Empiricus that he might consider Nanguo Ziqi's noisy message as a contribution to opposing judgments "in any way whatsoever."

As an art historian, Marty Powers finds issues of identity and point of view latent in the first few sentences of another segment of *Qi wu lun* (lines 14–18). His suggested translation reads:

If there were not that other's [point of view], I should not have mine; if I did not have my [point of view], then there would be no need to take a stand. . . . We do not know what it is that causes all this. It is as if there were something genuinely in control, but in the end we find no trace of it. I can accept [the idea] that it can function, but we do not see its form. It has effects on us [thoughts, feeling, responses], but it has no [fixed, substantial] form.

Powers takes Zhuangzi to be speaking for himself in this passage and embeds him in assumptions represented in the conventions of visual imagery of his society in his time. He has Zhuangzi making non-evident assertions that endorse a kind of relativism (or "perspectival system") in which all assertions are valid. This interpretation would not be much help if I were to prepare a positive response to the question put by Sextus Empiricus. For Sextus Empiricus's sake, the *Qi wu lun* segment (lines 14–18) can be read, at the risk of over-interpretation, as an argument undermining an unevidenced presumption that there is no causal agent which commands that which occurs in our universe. This is my version of the segment:

[Someone might say,] By not other-ing, there is no me-ing, and by not me-ing, there is no that-which-picks [as so or not so; that is, the claim is being made that there *is* no agent which makes things what they are because my *not* differentiating self and other precludes an assumption or knowledge of such an agent].

This is somewhat close, but one [who asserts this still] does not know that by which they may be caused. [That is, does he know if undistinguishable entities or processes, not to mention distinguishable ones, are caused by the Way to be as they are, or if each is so-of-itself, as Guo Xiang centuries later argued, or if there is some other non-evident explanation of that by which "they" are caused?]

[Now consider arguments *for* the presumption that there is that by which things are caused. Some say,] It is as if there is a genuine commander [which causes things to be as they are], but it is just that we do not apprehend its [self-revealing] signs. [They say,] In that [its commands] can be implemented, we trust [the commander is causing things], even though we do not perceive its physical form. [They say,] It has particulars, but has no physical form.

[Now pretend for the moment that it has a physical form like a human body, as if] The hundred joints, nine apertures and six organs are contained .and present in it. With which [particular part] am I to be as kin? Are you pleased with all of you [i.e., all parts of your body]? Say you have a personal preference among them. If you did, are all [the other parts] to act as the subordinates and minions [of the preferred part]? Are these subordinates and minions inadequate to govern conjointly? [i.e., does your body, or any organism, require a single controller to give commands?] Or are they to take turns in the roles of ruler and subordinate? Say they have a genuine ruler present among them [which has no physical form]. One may succeed in apprehending its particulars or not succeed, but [neither outcome] would enhance or detract from its being genuine [if it did genuinely exist, so we still cannot do more than dogmatically affirm that we know or do not know that-by-which-they-are-caused.]

We still do not know whether there is a genuine commander or causal agent. If we do not know whether a microcosm, the human body, has a constituent part which commands the other parts to function as they do, or if in spite of appearances it does have a ruler, then by analogy we also might remain skeptical about whether or not the macrocosm has that by which things internal to it are caused. Either assertion is untenable from a skeptical point of view. Although Powers's chosen passage does not seem to support the point, at the end of his discussion he proposes what might seem to be a relativistic way of "seeing." (We should notice the contrast between West's emphasis on hearing and Powers's on seeing.) Powers's example is seeing a cloud or a dragon in a design on a human artifact. The point is equally well made if we were to refer to a certain place in the sky at a certain moment as a cloud or a dragon. Powers asks, "Who would fight over whether the design was 're-ally' a dragon or cloud?" Maybe not designs, but Sextus Empiricus might answer that dogmatic philosophers have been fighting over what is "really so" for thousands of years. That's their big problem. Powers goes on, "Should circumstances require it to be a dragon, the dragon is there; should we need to view it as cloud, it is easy to switch. Our choice will be based, not on ontological considerations (the Truth), but on practical considerations. . . . In this sense, all perspectival views are admissible, but not all at the same time." Taking "practical considerations" as the main criteria for seeing (or hearing or knowing?) is more an appeal to a weak version of pragmatism than a call to suspend judgment. Powers's stress on points of view may not involve affirming one's belief in (as he puts it) the Truth of what one sees, but in any given instance what he sees or hears or reads or otherwise apprehends is exclusively so. "I know the dragon is there" is not an assertion to which Sextus Empiricus could assent, even if someone maintained it were so for only five minutes. From my perspective, Powers subordinates the *Qi wu lun* to his own "perspectival system" and thus obviates a reading which is skeptical.

In her reading of *Qi wu lun*, Wai-yee Li wants to spare the author from the damnation of skepticism. She cites and comments on most of the passages I thought one might use to respond to Sextus Empiricus. The lines beginning with "Saying [words] is not puffing [breath]; saying says something, but what is said is indeterminate" (lines 23–24) have the effect of demolishing certainty, which might go toward satisfying Sextus Empiricus's comment that "scepticism is an ability, or mental attitude, which opposes appearances to judgements in any way whatsoever."[61] In *Qi wu lun*, the back and forth about "it" and "other" might not be just relativism. The example of Confucians and Mohists confidently, and contradictorily, asserting "that's it, that's not" (line 26) suggests that the author is not condoning all points of view as valid. Opposition to any sort of affirmation leads us to suspension of judgment. Do you believe our world has a beginning (The Beginning)? Do you believe you can maintain the simple assertion, "There is something"? Do you believe the claim, "There is Unity (or Oneness)"? The author of *Qi wu lun* shows all of these and more are not tenable assertions (lines 49–51; 53). He shows that arguing over alternatives cannot be certainly resolved (lines 84–90). He also offers an escape from conflicts that are inevitable in arguing. "What is meant by 'Even them [arguments] out on the whetstone of Heaven'? [What it means is] Affirming a 'not affirmed' and saying it is so to a 'not so.' [I am presuming the passage is about you and me arguing.] Since your affirmation is as if there is a resulting affirmation, then there is

61. *Outlines*, I.8, trans. Bury, 7.

no disputing the difference of affirming it with not affirming it" (lines 90–91). That is, when you say it is not a dragon, I say, yes, you say it is so, and consequently there is no argument as I have affirmed your "not affirmed" and you cannot say "not affirmed" to my "affirmed.") The result of this strategy of "evening out arguments" for setting aside disputation may be a sort of bliss: "Forget the years, forget duty, be stirred [only] by the limitless, and consequently lodge it all in the limitless." (line 92)

Another expression that is akin to classical skepticism is in the passage that begins "Allowable? Allowable. Unallowable? Unallowable" (line 33) and insinuates the notion that things are just so (of themselves, without our needing to affirm them as so). The ugliness of one woman and the beauty of another may be so, but the distinctions are dissolved in the fancy verbiage about knowing about oneness (or ultimate unity), which in turn is ridiculed as another case of the phenomenon known as "Three in the morning." It appears that the author of *Qi wu lun* is hinting that we are making monkeys of ourselves when we believe in the validity of all of these big assertions about transcending differences with subtle ideas (lines 33–40).

The skeptical perspective is put quite neatly by a character named Wang Ni. He responds, "How would I know that?" to assertions about knowing proposed by Gaptooth (lines 64–65). ("Know" here means something like "know to be true" or "believe to be true," and not merely "aware that Gaptooth has made an assertion in the form of a question.") Wang Ni declines to affirm Gaptooth's formulation of the dogma of vulgar skepticism: "If it is so [that you deny knowing the two previous assertions about knowing, one positive and one negative], then [are you affirming that] animate things have no knowing?" (line 65). Instead, Wang Ni offers to try to express a skeptical view of knowing: "How do I know that what I call 'knowing something' is not 'not-knowing'; how do I know that what I call 'not knowing something' is not 'knowing'?" (You and Gaptooth can work out the logic here, I trust.) Wang Ni then proceeds, by asking questions rather than making (refutable) assertions, to imply that animate things (including humans) choose their abodes, choose their foods, and choose their company, apparently according to the evidence of their experience. When it comes to our imputing values to these choices, Wang Ni has recourse to his question, "How would I be able to know their discriminating [is based on such values]?" But Gaptooth is a slow learner and seeks to have Wang Ni assent to another assertion about which there is no evidence. Gaptooth says, "If you do not know [even discriminating] benefit from harm [as you have just said animate things do], then is it that a perfected man inherently does not know [discriminating] benefit from harm?" (line 71). We should recall that this was the charge made against Pyrrho in the later stories about his declining to check himself from walking into harm's way. Wang Ni does not respond with doubt; instead, he appears to affirm what is not evident and puts the perfected man out of our phenomenal world. Is Wang Ni being facetious? Ironic? Affirming a higher level of transcendent being? As he might say, "How would I know that?"

Wai-yee Li's strategy for dealing with the possibility of reading skepticism in the passages she cites from *Qi wu lun* is to see the problem as one of words and language rather than knowing and believing. She asserts, "Skepticism, however, does not undermine the authority of Zhuangzi's own words but paradoxically augments it, because it confirms his readiness to doubt and challenge his own premises." If he is a thinker with premises and paradoxically augmented words, Zhuangzi would not be much of a candidate for skepticism. Wai-yee Li implies she means "skepticism" in the vulgar sense when she says that "Absolute skepticism has no place for words beyond the statement that knowledge is impossible." Since Zhuangzi (or whoever authored *Qi wu lun*) is enmeshed with words, and meanings, and arguments (and maybe, if I am on track, with issues about "knowing"), he or she obviously is not a skeptic in the vulgar sense. To block a skeptical reading of *Qi wu lun*, Li finds its words have "double lives" forming "two parallel arguments." She reads *Qi wu lun* as offering us a sense of language, self and expression which transcends "the anguish of skepticism and mortality" and opens out "freedom for the spirit" even while mediating difference and distinction. Thus in the final passage, the dreamed butterfly is "joyous and carefree," an appropriate figure for Zhuangzi's higher line of argument.

In contrast, I read the account involving the dreamed butterfly (lines 94–96) as taking another crack at those who assert they know something for sure. We all might be tempted to affirm that we know that in the dream the butterfly does not know (has no awareness of) the person in whose head occurs the process called dreaming (as a sequence of biochemical processes). We all might be tempted also to affirm that we know that when the dreamer wakes, he conceivably might think (for a moment, or as a philosopher's ploy) that he could be being dreamed by the butterfly, although we know that the awakened dreamer is a person and he would not have self-awareness of being dreamed (just as we suppose the dreamed butterfly does not) if he were indeed in a dream. This is more or less the standard interpretation of what is apparently meant by the passage after, "Suddenly, he awakes." It does not upset what we all might be tempted to affirm here, and it does not lead us to skepticism. However, presuming on the absence of clearly stated subjects of the verbs, I suggest another reading. I suggest that we are being told that the dreamed butterfly suddenly becomes aware (still inside its dream) that it is a Zhuangzi in a new dream. We are being told that Zhuangzi dreams "being a butterfly": the dreamed butterfly is aware (in its own dream) of "being a Zhuangzi." Now we cannot say of this latter state that it is exclusively

Zhuangzi's dreaming or that it is butterfly's dreaming, can we? We do not know how to affirm one to the exclusion of the other, even though in the previous case we thought we could affirm that it is Zhuangzi dreaming a butterfly dream. Am I moved to suspend judgment?

Could I convince Sextus Empiricus that the author of *Qi wu lun* was a skeptic? My impression is that what the author was trying to express could be consonant with Michael Frede's words of explanation. "On the whole, though, the skeptic will mostly believe what experience suggests to him. What fundamentally distinguishes the skeptic from other people are not the beliefs he has but his attitude toward them. He no longer has the more or less naive and partially dogmatic attitude of the 'ordinary' man; his relation to his beliefs is permeated by the awareness that things are quite possibly different in reality, but this possibility no longer worries him."[62]

I remember I was sitting in my chair slowly rereading Frede's essay, "The Skeptic's Beliefs." I am dozy. Suddenly I am aware that Steve, Marty and Wai-yee are in the room with me, but how did they get in? Their mouths are moving and I hear sounds. I understand they are saying no, no, I have misrepresented their ideas, I have it all wrong, where do I get off claiming to say what they are thinking. I realize behind them, in the shadows, is a short old man wearing a long grey gown. His mouth is moving and I know he is slyly saying something about being on the bank of the Hao river.

62. Frede, *Essays*, 199.

FOUR

Heart Sūtra
Xin jing

TRANSLATION OF THE *HEART SŪTRA*
Stephen F. Teiser

THE SCRIPTURE ON THE HEART OF *PRAJÑĀPĀRAMITĀ*

[Part One.] When the Bodhisattva Observer of the Self-Existent was practicing the deep *prajñāpāramitā*, he had an illuminating vision that all five heaps are empty, and he delivered all from suffering.

[Part Two.] "Śāriputra, form is not different from emptiness, and emptiness is not different from form. Form is identical to emptiness, and emptiness is identical to form. Sensation, concept, action, and consciousness are also like this."

[Part Three.] "Śāriputra, all of these constituent elements of existence are marked by emptiness: they are not produced and not extinguished, not defiled and not pure, not increasing and not diminishing."

[Part Four.] "Therefore in emptiness there is no form, nor is there any sensation, concept, action, or consciousness. There is no eye, ear, nose, tongue, body, or mind. There is no form, sound, smell, taste, contact, or [mental] element. There is neither realm of sight, nor [any of the others] up to the realm of mental consciousness. There is neither ignorance nor the end of ignorance, neither [any of the others] up to old age and death nor the end of old age and death. There is no suffering, accumulation, extinction, or path. There is neither wisdom nor attainment."

[Part Five.] "Because there is nothing to be attained, by relying on *prajñāpāramitā*, the Bodhisattva's mind has no obstructions. By having no obstructions, he has no fears, he distances himself from backwardness and delu-

Figure 4.1. Stein manuscript no. 4406. The text of the *Heart Sūtra,* including a copyist's note. By permission of the British Library. The accompanying translation by Stephen Teiser is based on this manuscript, which was written on paper and bound as a scroll, and which was unearthed from the caves at Dunhuang (modern-day Gansu province). It was probably copied in the ninth century in one of the sixteen major temples in Dunhuang. (For the dating of this manuscript, see Ikeda On, *Chūgoku kodai shahon shikigo shūroku,* Tōyō bunka kenkyūjo sōkan no. 11 [Tokyo: Tōkyō daigaku tōyō bunka kenkyūjo, 1990], no. 2058.) This copy was taken by Sir Aurel Stein (1862–1943) to England, where it is now housed in the British Library. It contains an unsigned appendix extolling the benefits of chanting the text. The appendix is unusual but by no means unique. At least two other copies of the *Heart Sūtra* discovered at Dunhuang contain nearly identical colophons. (See the appendix to the manuscript held in Saint Petersburg, Dkh 292, described in Lev N. Men'shikov, et al., *Opisanie Kitaiskikh Rukopisei,* 2 vols., Dun'-khuanskogo Fonda Instituta Narodov Azii, Akademiya nauk SSSR [Moscow: Izdatel'stvo Vostochnoi Literatury, 1963, 1967], 1:130–31, no. 320; and the preface to the manuscript held in the National Library in Beijing, catalogued as no. 4466 [62], reproduced in Huang Yongwu, ed. *Dunhuang baozang,* 140 vols. [Taibei: Xinwenfeng chubanshe, 1981–1986], 83:302a–03a.)

Figure 4.2. *(opposite)* Pelliot manuscript no. 2168. The text of the *Heart Sūtra.* Photograph courtesy of the Bibliothèque Nationale de France, Paris. This manuscript of the *Heart Sūtra,* also found at Dunhuang, lays out the words of the text in recursive format. It is structured in the form of a pagoda, with a drawing of Avalokiteśvara at the base. The dotted lines (written in red in the original, in contrast to the text, which is written in black), show the order in which the text is read. After the title at the top, the text begins under Avalokiteśvara and moves down diagonally to the left. At least a few other copies written in this format survive from Dunhuang; other manuscripts with the same format include Stein no. 4289 (reproduced in Huang Yongwu, ed., *Dunhuang baozang,* 35:187); Stein no. 5410 (reproduced in ibid., 42:410); and Pelliot no. 2731 (reproduced in ibid., 123:515b–16a).

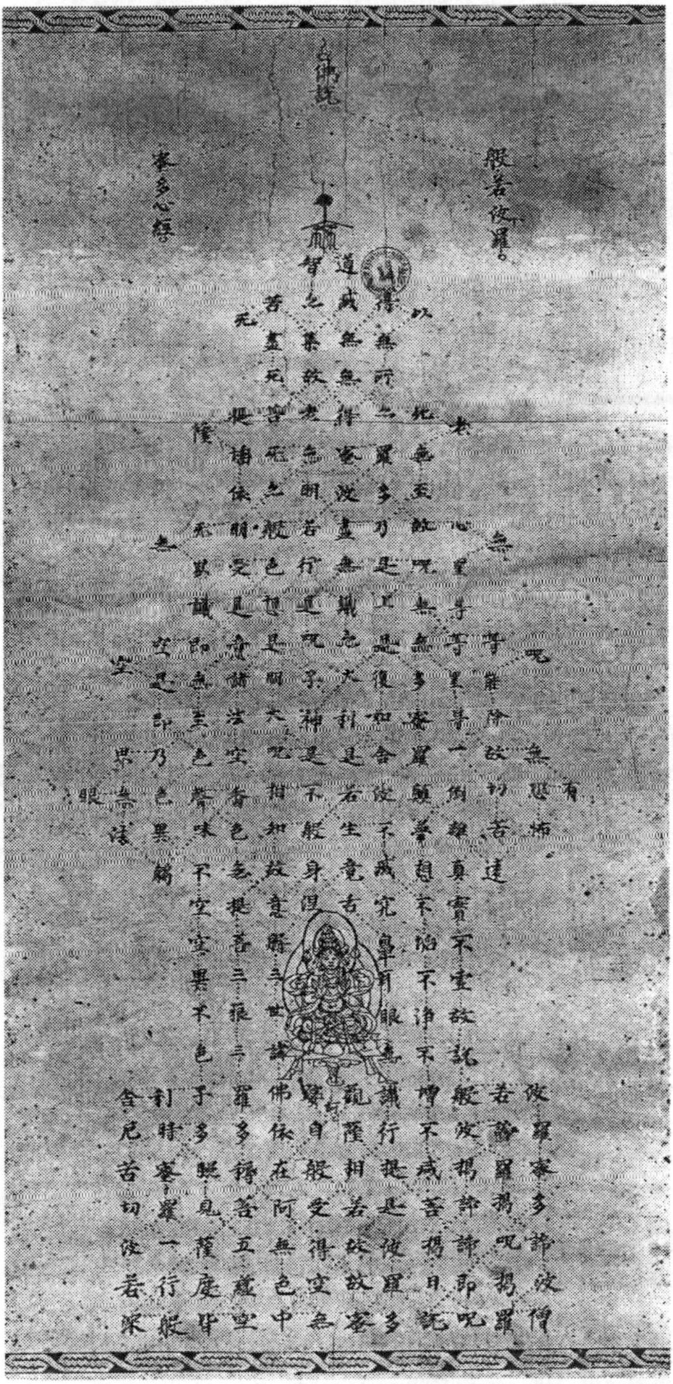

Figure 4.2.

sions, and lodges ultimately in *nirvāṇa*. By relying on *prajñāpāramitā*, all Buddhas of the three ages attain *anuttarasamyaksaṃbodhi*."

[Part Six.] "Therefore it should be known that *prajñāpāramitā*—this great spell, this great illuminating spell, this great unsurpassed spell, this great unequalled spell—can do away with all suffering. Because it is real and not vacuous, we say the spell of *prajñāpāramitā*. Now we say the spell: *Gate gate pāragate pārasaṃgate bodhi svāhā*."

THE SCRIPTURE ON THE HEART OF *PRAJÑĀPĀRAMITĀ*

[Copyist's note:] Reciting this scripture will destroy the ten abominations, the five heinous acts, and the ninety-five evil ways. If you want to repay the kindness of all the Buddhas of the ten directions, then recite the *prajñā* of the Observer of the Self-Existent one hundred or one thousand times. It extinguishes sins without fail. Recite it constantly day and night, and there will be no prayer left ungranted.

TRANSLATION: THE *HEART SŪTRA*
Stephen H. West

I have hazarded a translation of how I think the text would appear to a middlebrow Chinese consumer of vernacular literature who knew neither Buddhist doctrine nor Sanskrit. All Buddhist terms that are translations into Chinese have been left in Chinese; all transliterated Buddhist terms have been reproduced in middle Chinese sounds. I have chosen to follow Li Zhi's paraphrase of the sūtra as a guide to translation and the translation, therefore, varies from that done by Hurvitz.[1]

HEART SŪTRA OF WISDOM TRANSCENDENT

1. The Absolutely Free bǝk-sat—
2. Moving in deepest puɑt-ʈa-puɑ-la-mǐĕt-ta,
3. Shining upon and making manifest that all five stored accumulations are empty,
4. Delivering all from suffering and obstruction.
5. Çiai-lǐǝp-tsǐǝ
6. Form is no different than emptiness,
7. Emptiness is no different than form,

---

1. Hurvitz, Leon. "Hsuan-tsang (602–664) and the *Heart Scripture*," in *Prajñāpāramitā and Related Systems: Studies in Honor of Edward Conze*, ed. Lewis Lanchaster, Berkeley Buddhist Studies Series (Berkeley: University of California, 1977), 103–22.

8. Form is simply emptiness,
9. Emptiness is simply form.
10. Sensation, thinking, function, and perception are all like this.
11. Çiai-lĭəp-tsĭə
12. These various laws are but images of nothing,
13. Unborn, undying,
14. Not filthy, not purely clean,
15. Not increasing, not diminishing.
16. For this reason in emptiness,
17. There is no form,
18. No sensation, thinking, function, or perception.
19. No eye, ear, nose, tongue, body, or consciousness,
20. No shape, sound, taste, flavor, feel, or law.
21. From no-eye realm,
22. Clear to a no-consciousness-realm.
23. There is no ignorance,
24. And in addition, no end of ignorance.
25. Even to the point there is no old-age or death,
26. And in addition, no end to old age and death.
27. No suffering, accumulation, extinction (of suffering), or way
    (out of it).
28. No knowledge and in addition no attainment.
29. And because there is no attainment,
30. Bək-diei-sat-tua
31. Because they rely on puɑt-ʈa-puɑ-la-mĭĕt-ta
32. Their heart/mind is without preoccupation or obstruction,
33. And being without preoccupation or obstruction,
34. They are without terror and fear,
35. And have departed from dream thoughts that turn everything
    upside-down,
36. And gone to the limit of niet-puɑn.
37. All bək-sat of the three worlds,
38. Because they rely on puɑt-ʈa-puɑ-la-mĭĕt-ta
39. Have attained a-nuok-ta-la-sam-mɔk-sam-bək-diei.
40. Therefore it can be known that puɑt-ʈa-puɑ-la-mĭĕt-ta
41. This great incantation / is a great incantation,
42. This great, illumined incantation, this unequalled incantation
    / is a great, illumined incantation, is an unequalled incantation
43. This peerless incantation. / Is a peerless incantation.
44. Because it can root out all suffering
45. Is authentically real and not empty.
46. Speak the incantation of puɑt-ʈa-puɑ-la-mĭĕt-ta.

47. Speak now the incantation, saying,
48. kĭɛt-tiei, kĭɛt-tiei
49. puɑt-la kĭɛt-tiei, puɑt-la kĭɛt-tiei
50. puɑt-la sǝŋ kĭɛt-tiei
51. puɑt-la sǝŋ sa-χɑ

THE *HEART SŪTRA*

Michael A. Fuller

This essay is not so much a reading of the *Heart Sūtra* as a report on the process of reading. My central concern is not to elucidate the *Heart Sūtra*—there are many other much better sources—but to trace one particular engagement where a literary scholar ventures into the *terra incognita* of the religious. The alien quality I find in the *Heart Sūtra* is not a matter of lore: no student of Chinese literature can be entirely ignorant of Buddhism, its fundamental tenets, its vocabulary, and its history. Genuinely engaged reading, however, demands more: a willingness to consider that a text might be true. When I approach Chinese poetry, I attempt to honor the commitments within which the texts were written. The mainstream of the Chinese poetic tradition, however, is profoundly humanistic: poems were written to other men about pressing personal, social, political, and moral concerns. While worlds of meaning beyond human experience—both Daoist and Buddhist—surrounded poets as they wrote, these other worlds rarely intruded. (Hanshan is, of course, conspicuous because he is the exception.) I am at home in the world of classical Chinese poetry, but religious, otherworldly commitments mystify me.

So, for me, a text like the *Heart Sūtra* is a mystery within a mystery, *xuan zhi you xuan*. Trained in the hermeneutics of the literary tradition, I am unsure how I am to honor my commitment to read the *Heart Sūtra* seriously, that is, as more than merely a document. What beliefs, what conventions of reading should I bring to it? Students of Buddhism surely know these answers, but I do not. Indeed, the point of this exercise is precisely to see the costs of specialization, what training gives and where it fails. For example, consider the title: the puɑt-ńĭĕ-puɑla-mi-ta Heart Sūtra. How are we to understand the transliteration? Are we to see the characters yet *hear* Sanskrit? Or is the "word" naturalized? Is it "Chinese?" Even as "Chinese," does it not stand as an otherness of meaning, an emptying out of signifiers, a pointing elsewhere? Is this the linguistic embodiment of mystery? And do religious texts not *need* such self-denial of the language of the text? I don't know. I don't even know if I am supposed to know, or if even asking such a question is a mark of alienation so complete as to preclude meaningful engagement with the text. My reading thus is framed with doubt, but I proceed.

I begin the text itself with much concern and little to reassure me. The first word of Xuanzang's (602–664) translation is *guan*, to observe, meditate, visualize. Are we to contemplate an unbounded bodhisattva, taking *Zizai pusa* as the object of the verb? Eventually, by comparing the various versions of the text, I realize that *Guanzizai pusa* is in fact Avalokiteśvara, more commonly known as *Guan shi yin* (shortened to *Guan yin* to avoid Tang Taizong's name). This sort of confusion is endemic to all transcultural reading, so at least Buddhist and literary texts share *some* problems of reading. The next sentence is perhaps of the same order: is "puat-ńiĕ-puala-mi-ta" the *direct* object or the *locative* object of *xing*? That is, does one enact the perfection of wisdom or travel in it? The analysis of the Sanskrit suggests the metaphor of a river. What does it signify that Xuanzang elides such metaphorical usage, or is it implicit in *shen*, "deep [water]"? Should I know it? Is it in fact stale convention? Just opening rhetoric? All traditions have their own lore. Without the echoes to which I have grown accustomed in reading literary prose, I acutely feel the silences, the knowledge I do *not* bring to the Buddhist tradition. Indeed, in the next sentence, I encounter a metaphor when it would have been simpler to *not* have one: why *zhao*? What is the lore here? Does the wisdom emit light? That is, is such wisdom an active use of the mind that engages the phenomena of the world, or is it simply receptive? Or am I bringing literary habits to the reading of a text not meant for such reading? Unsure, I go on.

The *Sūtra* quickly gets to the heart of the matter, as it were, the famous assertion, *se bu yi kong, kong bu yi se, se ji shi kong, kong ji shi se*. It seems to be a universal statement, but why is it addressed to Śāriputra? Would the Bodhisattva have said something different to someone else? Surely he would. Is this statement then only an expedient means? Are we to cling to it and see only the finger, not the moon? How are we to understand the text? How do we apply it? As a student and teacher of classical literature, I have often read and taught Zhuangzi's attack on classificatory language in the *Qi wu lun*. When I then read a sentence like "Appearance does not differ from emptiness, emptiness does not differ from appearance," I cannot but expect an ironizing reflection on how the statement, if true, makes its own utterance suspect. Yet I find nothing of the sort, only earnest explication. The text proceeds to list the categories of Buddhist psychology and concludes that they are "like this," *ru shi*. The *Sūtra*'s comparative analysis of the emptiness of categories seems to leave us still fixated on the activity of the comparing mind. Even the plainest of texts cannot escape the problem of the commitments made by its language.

I bracket the issue of the language and plunge on: how will the text substantiate its thesis? We find—not unexpectedly—the dissolution of categories of binary opposition in the description of the indescribableness of emptiness. Next the text moves on to the inapplicability of phenomenal human modes of perception in grasping emptiness. Then for a moment I am lost. When I read the statement *wu wu ming yi wu wu ming jin*, it seems ill-formed by the usual rules of classical syntax. I parse it as

$$[wu_{\text{ verb}} + [wu\ ming\ ]_{\text{object}}]_{\text{subject}} + jin_{\text{ verb}}$$
"The state of non-enlightenment not existing ends."

Or perhaps

$$wu_{\text{ verb}} + [wu_{\text{ verb}} + [ming_{\text{ subject}} + jin_{\text{ verb}}]_{\text{object}}]_{\text{object}}$$
"There is no state of an extinguishing of enlightenment not existing."

Neither makes much sense. Only after looking at the account of the Sanskrit does it become clear that the syntax is:

$$wu_{\text{ verb}} + [[wu_{\text{ verb}} + ming_{\text{object}}]_{\text{subject}} + jin_{\text{ verb}}]_{\text{object}}$$
"There is no state of an extinguishing of non-enlightenment."

The language here strikes me as highly marked as "Buddhist," that is, as the language of the specialist requiring technical expertise in its interpretation. Or is it perhaps simply language that forces one to *call* for a specialist, one more mark of the otherness of meaning in the text? I stress the resisting quality of the language of the *Sūtra:* it does not have the ease and direct plainness of the preface written by Huizhong (fl. 730). Consider the phrase *wu ku ji mie dao.* My first reading was, "There is no accumulation of suffering that extinguishes the Way." This again clearly cannot work. The only way to know that "suffering," "accumulation," "extinguishing," and "the Way" are coordinate is to read the Sanskrit text or seek clarification elsewhere. Indeed, in the line *yi ban-ruo-bo-luo-mi-duo gu de a-nou-duo-luo-san-miao-san-puti* (lines 38–39 in West's translation), that is, "Relying on *prajñāpāramitā* [they] obtain *anuttara samyaksambodhi*," one might as well be reading the Sanskrit. Xuanzang surely could have written other than as he did.

The *Heart Sūtra* seems to encode the argument that meaning must be elsewhere. But what is at stake? Why does this pointing elsewhere matter? Does it imply that individuated subjectivity cannot be trusted by itself, that it must always be guided? Or is the notion of incompleteness, the radical inadequacy of individuated subjectivity, perhaps the very ground for religion and its discourse? Does poetry touch on these issues? We can see corollary pointings beyond the text in allusions both to the poetic tradition itself and to the larger corpus of historical and textual references. Moreover, it is precisely these contexts that ground the possibility of poetry remaining meaningful beyond its moment of production. Still, there is no encoding of the need for a master exegete. Poetry, I think, pushes in the other direction: its formal structuring holds out a promise of at least a moment of completeness for the individual. To *bu tian*, "mend Heaven," is to fit all the pieces—the historical, contingent, dying self, *this* place, *these* people, these many factors, *this* moment—into a coherent whole.

It is only in light of this distinction between the poetic and the religious that I can make sense of the *Sūtra*'s conclusion. How is the recitation of a *mantra* not a form of clinging? Does the fact that it is a Sanskrit transliteration point one upward, so that mastery of the *mantra* in the end is the self-overcoming of language? The *mantra* begins as completely opaque: the words are meaningless, empty placeholders for a meaning to be discovered in the Sanskrit. Once understood, the *mantra* has done its job and led one into a world in which the words, already cut adrift from their written signifiers, can be discarded altogether, except now "discarding" itself is meaningless. There is nothing to discard, there is no one to discard, there is no discarding. This new world is foreign to me. The *Heart Sūtra* is perhaps its road map, but it is written in a language I cannot read. Or is it simply a language that I, in my pride, *will* not read? I do not know and look for guidance.[2]

HEART SUTRA
Stephen H. West

I am not a Buddhologist, yet I have a keen awareness of the importance of this text in Chinese language, culture, and tradition. My lack of Buddhist knowledge has both advantages and disadvantages; the disadvantage, of course, is that I am not equipped to read the *Sūtra* as a doctrinal text, a specific document of a specific sect. But it is also an advantage. We are too eager, generally, to allow a text like the *Heart Sūtra* to become swallowed up by its own tradition, to be surrounded and walled off by impregnable commentaries, or held captive by esoteric doctrinal debate. Too often, the understanding and the use of such texts outside of the religious tradition itself is relegated to a minor, neglected role, except as it might relate to an understanding of how a particular text highlights, debates, or otherwise foregrounds religion in some other context. By the Tang, the *Heart Sūtra* was certainly an essential textual element of Chinese civilization, although the way it was understood at any particular point in time reflects the experiences, predilections, and limitations of any particular cultural or subcultural community that appropriated it.[3]

To suggest what I mean in another way, I would like to offer the follow-

2. I have found Donald S. Lopez, Jr.'s *The Heart Sūtra Explained* (Albany: SUNY Press, 1988) useful in preparing this essay since it deals specifically with the Indian and Tibetan commentary.

3. I would like to thank Robert Gimello for comments on an earlier version of this paper. I have adopted some of the changes he suggested.

ing passage from a late Yuan text that should strongly suggest another potential contextualization of religious tracts or works that, from the point of view of purely Chinese language and culture, seem obscure or involuted:

> [A singer of ballads, fighting with her madam, sings]
> I would never have thought that these moon halls and breeze kiosks,
> These bamboo streams and flowered paths,
> Would turn into such a dismal sight!
> I make my livelihood by putting up a good front every day,
> And my mother seeks to struggle through in "all keys and modes."
> Everything she says on her part runs down what I do,
> She runs off so much at the mouth that even the household gods are unable
>   to rest.
> I play four or five rounds of "iron cavalry" at the theater,
> Only to find six or seven scenes of warfare waiting at home.
> What I sing is "Chronicles of the Three Kingdoms," preceded by ten Great
>   Songs,
> But my mother [bests me] with the "History of the Five Epochs," with the
>   "Eight-Yang Classic" stuck on for good measure.
>
>   Just look!
>
> Compare it to the singing and shouting of a regular performance,
> And you have to get up even more spirit,
> Have to begin and end it with even more liveliness,
> Manipulate it all around with even more smooth familiarity!
> But there's none of those "lips sweet or lines beautiful,"
> Just a whole territory of rare and dangerous troubles
> Where she slaps me around,
> And answers with a stubborn reply
> That squeezes out my marrow,
> Thumps my skull,
> Flays my skin
> And pierces my legs with an awl![4]

While the *Heart Sūtra* does not occur in her list of textual sources for oral combat, that the convolutions and intricacies of Daoist canons and secular historical classics are incorporated as concrete metaphors for the unending and complex nagging of a money-grubbing madam means that such texts are absorbed into the consciousness at quite a different level than in scholarly or religious debate. They are assimilated because of sound or for their immediate lack of understandable sense. I would presume this would

4. Shi Junbao, *Zhugongdiao fengyue ziyunting zaju*, in *Yuankan zaju sanshizhong xinjiao*, vol. 1, ed. Ning Xiyuan, *Lanzhou daxue guji zhengli congshu* (Lanzhou: Lanzhou daxue chubanshe, 1988), 195.

even be more so for the *Heart Sūtra*, which in one sense is a stylistically stilted piece of writing, and in another one whose own teachings are contravened by semantics.

At the higher end of the spectrum of appropriation, the educated Chinese of the Tang, one who was neither a practicing Buddhist nor a scholiast of the tradition, would read this text against others in his own culture, the most logical being the Five Classics, the Hundred Schools, the histories, and poetry. And while by the Tang the parameters of literary Chinese that had been based on pre-Han and Han texts had been stretched by Buddhist texts and other vernacular forms,[5] a contemporaneous reading would, I suspect, still be completely different than any we give it today. Being able to contextualize the Tang Chinese text among other Buddhist scriptures—Tibetan, Khotanese, and Sanskrit, for instance—and living in a world of numerous translations and an abundance of textual material, we have the luxury of playing a kind of gamesmanship, reading into the Chinese text a freight of meaning that it cannot support as a lone document. For instance, when we see the words *se shou xiang xing shi*, we know that they are translations of the Five Aggregates (*wu yun, Pañcaskandha*): *rūpa* (form), *vedanā* (feeling), *samjñā* (perception), *samskāra* (impulses), and *vijñāna* (consciousness). In the Chinese tradition these five terms would first of all suggest: *se,* how things appear in form, color, or texture; *shou,* what a person receives or suffers as sensation, fate, circumstance, or lot; *xiang*[b], what a person thinks, in the sense of forming mental images rather than reflection or forethought; *xing*[c], what a person does or how a person acts in terms of deportment, morality, or simple deeds; and *shi,* the act of recognition or discrimination. Outside of the context of Buddhism, the semantic fields of these words broadens into a larger cultural arena and, except for *xing*[c], none of them are heavily invested with moral implications.

However, an educated reader would at least recognize some of these terms—the "five heaps," "form," "consciousness"—as belonging to a "basic [Buddhist] catechism, along with karma and rebirth."[6] We could draw a parallel here, perhaps, with an educated non-Christian of late antiquity who would recognize that the word *logos* had something to do with "the second person of the Trinity" or "with Platonic notions of rational order in the cosmos."[7] In fact, the importation of Buddhist language may account for new

5. Jerry Norman, *Chinese,* Cambridge Language Survey (Cambridge, England: Cambridge University Press, 1988), 111; see also Jiang Shaoyu, "Ru Tang qiufa xunli xingji zhongde kouyu ci," in *Jindai Hanyu yanjiu,* ed. Hu Zhu'an, Jiang Shouyu, Yang Naien (Beijing: Shangwu yinshu guan, 1992), 94–111.

6. Robert Gimello, private communication, 19 May 1994.

7. Ibid.

possibilities in the native tongue, for example, the ability to pair *se* and *kong* in a way that suggests the uselessness of venery or the futility of sexual gratification in a way that it could not have been expressed before.[8] It certainly powered some important critical terminology, as in *bense*, "basic form," one of the important aesthetic registers of drama.

But the vernacular language of the *Heart Sūtra* would also have posed certain problems for the Chinese reader of early times. For instance, the following lines, an attempt at substance identification, result in a rather interesting equation, subverted to an extent by the semantic fields underlying the propositions:

6. *Se bu yi kong*
7. *Kong bu yi se*
8. *Se ji shi kong*
9. *Kong ji shi se*

The last two lines, in particular, like the modern Mandarin, *zhege jiu shi nage*, tie together two fields that are understood to be distinct and separate, that is, the underlying semantic notion is that "this" is not really "that" until they are linguistically joined. This, I presume, is what led Li Zhi to rewrite this passage in classical Chinese and comment on it thusly: "Shelizi, do not consider what I speak of as 'emptiness' to be 'emptiness.' If I speak of appearance, it is no different than emptiness, if I speak of emptiness it is no different than appearance. But to simply say that they do not differ is to say that there is something about these two entities which is in opposition. And even if you combine them into one, there still exists [an entity] of oneness."[9]

The message of the *Sūtra* is typically Indo-European in the sense that it is involved with both substance (as in its relationship to the illusory) and causation. The first element, substance, is self-apparent in the text through the obsession with defining what things are and are not. This grammatical structure invites comparison with similar attempts to identify abstract entities in the native tradition. If we look, for instance, at how *ren* ("co-humanity," "humaneness," "human-heartedness," etc.) is defined in traditional Confucian texts, one will find that classical Chinese does not draw substantive identities, but rather analogical parallels through a topic-comment structure, in which the comment can only be a partial description of the topic, never a complete identity:

8. For instance, the closing lines of "The White Maiden Locked Forever Beneath the Thunderpeak Pagoda," cited below, n. 18.
9. Li Zhi, "*Xinjing* tigang," in *Fenshu* (Beijing: Zhonghua shuju, 1975), 3:100.

ren zhe ren ye	The humane one—human.
ren zhe bu you	The humane one—unanxious.
ren zhe wu di	The humane one—lacks enemies.
ren zhe yi qi suo ai ji qi suo bu ai	The humane one—extends that which he loves to that which he does not.
ren zhe bi you yong	The humane one—inevitably possesses physical bravery.
ren zhe le shan	The humane one—delights in the mountains.
ren zhe ai ren	The humane one—loves humanity.
ren zhe wu bu ai	The humane one—loves everything.
ren zhe jing	The humane one—is quiet.

This kind of relational, analogical structure also implies an inductive or inferential process rather than one of direct causation or paratactic substance-identity. This can be partially ascribed to the lack of subordination in classical language (although I would not carry this argument as far as others). But it is interesting to note that the structures in the *Heart Sūtra* that use the particle *gu* seem to be attempts to replicate a determinate or causative structure:

16. *shi gu kong zhong*
29. *yi wu suo de gu*
31. *yi ban ruo bo luo mi duo gu*
33. *wu gua ai gu*
38. *yi ban ruo bo luo mi duo gu*
45. *zhen shi bu xu gu*

According to the Harvard-Yenching indices for the Thirteen Classics, while the structures *yǐ . . . gu* or *yī . . . gu* are used with some frequency in the *Zuo zhuan*, they seldom occur, for instance, in the *Mencius* or the *Analects*. Even in the *Zuo zhuan* they are not the preferred form of expressing logical causation; rather they appear to be event-related.[10] The traditional *yi shi* or *gu* as a head phrase in a second coordinate clause are still favored ways of expressing consequent events.

Secondly, we must consider the plethora of transliterated Buddhist terms in the *Sūtra*, which I have rendered into middle Chinese (following Wang Li's transcriptions):

bək-sat	Bo[dhi]sat[tva]
puɑt-ʈa-puɑ-la-mĭĕt-ta	prajñāpāramitā

10. I realize, of course, that this begs the question of events as inherently logical structures that may be reflected semantically or grammatically in any text.

çiai-lǐəp-tsǐə	Sāriputrā
bək-diei-sat-tua	Bodhisattva
niet-puɑn	Nirvāṇa
a-nuok-ta-la-sam-mɔksam-bək-diei	anuttarasaṃyaksaṃbodhi
kǐɛt-tiei, kǐɛt-tiei	gate, gate
puɑt-la kǐɛt-tiei,	
puɑt-la kǐɛt-tiei	pāragate, pāragate
puɑt-la səŋ-kǐɛt-tiei	pārasaṃgate
puɑt-la səŋ sɑ-χɑ	pārasaṃsvāhā

While it is true that neologisms percolate at a regular rate into any language, I would argue that these words either retain their essential foreignness in early Chinese or have been assimilated in ways that utilize sound rather than meaning. They would have been appealing sounds, to be sure—the consonantal and vowel alliterations resonate with traditional Chinese word usage, both in classical—as in *shuangsheng dieyun*—and in vernacular, in such echoics as *po-suomosuo* (feeling, patting, feeling up [adverbial form]) or *qiliuqulü* (crooked, twisting; panting hard). Yet they would have remained unique and distinguished as something apart from "normal" words, especially given the lengthy syllable count of some nouns. This lends a certain instability to the text as an understandable document. By way of comparison, consider this Khotanese commentary on the *Heart Sūtra* translated by Sir H. W. Bailey:

> The *deva Buddha* was pleased to expound the *dharma* of the *Mahā-para-jñāpāramitā*. The *prajñā-pāramitā* is *samyak*, great *bodhi*, *vijñā-paryāya*, the one *dharma* of *skandhas*. Now what *is vijñāna?* That is unpolluted by *svabhāva* in all the *sarvadharmas*. This is called *dharma-kāya*, dominant in *samādhāna*. The *bodhisattva* has the same *svabhāva*.[11]

The point here is that this is recognizably a paragraph of English, but to the non-initiated it is also completely opaque.

And there are two ways of dealing with that opaqueness. One is to attempt to understand what it says by entering into the text as a religious document, possessing its terminology, and by virtue of that possession gaining passage into a more transparent world of doctrine. The other, and more closely associated with a non-elite level of culture, is to seize upon sound, a mantra of vocalized syllables by which an individual acquires some kind of magical, unformulated, power through simple incantation.

There is evidence that the *Heart Sūtra* was first understood in China as a mantra, a ritual linguistic talisman rather than as a pristine summary of the

---

11. H. W. Bailey, "Mahā Prajñāpā ramitā-sū tra," in *Prajñāpāramitā and Related Systems: Studies in Honor of Edward Conze*, ed. Lewis Lancaster, Berkeley Buddhist Studies Series (Berkeley: University of California Press, 1977), 154.

doctrine of emptiness.[12] The text (lines 44, 45) suggests this in its description of the efficacy of the actual mantra, which it describes as "genuinely real and not negative." The meaning of the text is bound up with simply saying it—in this it is much like the rosary in Catholicism or perhaps the Gloria from the Catholic missal. Whatever meaning the words, terms, and phrases may have, it is the repeated invocation that finally carries the power; the sacramental use of the mantra substantiates the value of the text in a way that exegesis cannot. We should remember, too, that this sūtra was often written on the body, written in blood, burned and eaten, or chanted over and over. Performance of the text (or its use as a prop in performance) gave it meaning—a good example of how something that is essentially meaningless or "empty" can be consequential.

Another point worth considering is that the structure of the *Sūtra* invites one to isolate binary opposites in an attempt to privilege "substantive authenticity." This may be a clever, hyperbolic grammatical device to underscore one of the major points of the *Sūtra*, which is that one cannot separate the truth (or lack of truth) of "emptiness" from that which obtains for "form." Since neither really exists, to make a distinguishable binary pair is therefore to render both false. This point, that neither form (*se*) nor emptiness (*kong*) exists, was also made by Li Zhi in his rewrite of the *Sūtra* during the Ming, when he chided: "This being so, the difficulty of speaking about 'empty' has long been a problem. Those who speak about 'appearance' get mired down in 'appearance,' those who speak of 'emptiness' get mired down in 'emptiness. . . . '"[13] *Journey to the West* aside, the *Heart Sūtra* appears to be appropriated into Chinese literature both as ideology and as mantra, and generally split along classical-vernacular lines.[14] Its influence in Chinese poetry and poetic criticism can be seen, perhaps, in the work of such writers as Su Shi. For instance, Huang Tingjian thought that Su Shi's famous quatrain "Inscribing Westwood Wall" from his Lushan excursion exemplified the interplay of appearance and illusion.

> Looked at athwart it turns into a range; by side view it turns into a peak,
> Distant, close, high, low—each different.
> Unable to recognize the authentic face of Lushan,
> All because my body is in *this* mountain!

12. John R. McRae, "Ch'an Commentaries on the *Heart Sutra:* Preliminary Inferences on the Permutation of Chinese Buddhism," *Journal of the International Association of Buddhist Studies* 11 (1988), 89, citing Fukui Fumimasu.
13. Ibid.
14. A wonderful irony is that the words *mandarin* (as in Mandarin Chinese) and *mantra* both stem from the same Sanskrit root. Small comfort for first-year language students!

Huang's comment:

    a. This is a seasoned man ranging in discourse through the *prajñāpāramitā*, yet having not a single excess word. If it weren't the tip of his pen, could such an untransmittable wonder as this be spat out?[15]

    b. This is a seasoned man ranging in discourse through the *prajñāpāramitā*, yet having not a single excess word. If there were not a tongue at the end of his pen, how could he have spat out such an untransmittable wonder as this?[16]

This is not the only Buddhist interpretation of the piece, of course. Shi Yuanzhi's commentary also cited the following passage from the *Huayan jing* in reference to this work: "In a single mote of dust the multiple differences between worlds great and small are as great as the number of dust motes. Level, high, low, each different. The Buddhas all go there, where each turns a prayer wheel." These readings did not go uncontested, however, and Wang Wengao, in his commentary to the poem, rebutted the necessity of a Buddhist reading, arguing that sentences forged out of learned Buddhist lore would be forced, and lack the "native sensibility," the sensitive response of the refined nature, that was characteristic of good verse: "Poems like this generally are a product of a moment's refined sensibility. If we demand that they be forged out of some Buddhist allusion that has first to be internalized, then their sense and flavor would be forced. . . . If 'Shi's Commentary' has to substantiate this line by reference to the *Huayan jing,* then all poetry is transformed into dregs. This is what I deem paying attention to the notes instead of to the poem."[17] On the one hand, however we interpret this poem (and it is so marvelously open to interpretation!), it is certainly not necessary to resort to such texts as the *prajñāpāramitā sūtra* to elicit a reading. On the other, Su Shi knew a lot about the *prajñāpāramitā* tradition, and even if it did not provide the outright philosophical basis for this poem it had probably filtered into his poetic vision of the world. It is probably in this later sense, as a subtle yet penetrative influence, that the *Sūtra* opened up a discursive space in Chinese poetics by introducing a complex relationship between form and illusion.

    But if we may return to the passage that I opened this discussion with,

---

15. This variant found in Huihong, *Lengzhai yehua* (*Biiji xiaoshuo daguan,* ed.), 7.1a.

16. This variant found in Hu Zi, *Tiaoxi yuyin conghua,* vol. 1, ed. Liao Deming (Hong Kong: Zhonghua shuju, 1976), 39.169.

17. Su Shi, *Su Shi shiji,* vol. 4, ed. and annot. Wang Wengao, punct. and coll. Kong Fanli, *Zhongguo gudian wenxue jiben congshu* (Beijing: Zhonghua shuju, 1979), 23.1219. Wang's arguments stem, of course, from contemporary debates about poetics in the Qing.

I think we can see another possibility and a potentially wider arena for the *Heart Sūtra*. That is as a mantra, an amulet, an incantation. This is certainly the way it was appropriated into vernacular texts. For instance, the term *kǐet-tiei*, from the incantation (which, I am told, in Sanskrit means "go") is transformed in Chinese vernacular to a spirit general, a guardian of the law, and is clearly conceived as having the same kind of form as Jin'gang, as these passages from *Shuihu zhuan* and "The White Maiden Locked Forever Beneath Thunderpeak Pagoda," from the *Jingshi tongyan*, show:

> Even if one were a *kǐet-tiei*, one could not stand up to him; even if one were a Jin'gang, one would have pay obeisance in his honor.[18]

> He had the appearance of a *kǐet-tiei* and the features of a Jin'gang.[19]

> The Chan master grew enraged, grumbled over and over and then shouted, "Where is *kǐet-tiei*? Go, fetch that anomaly of the Green Fish here and have it change back to its original form with the White Snake and then hear my judgment!"[20]

The mantric quality of the *Sūtra* is also bolstered by the intense repetition of key terms: *se* and *kong*, for instance, and the preponderance of negatives, all of which make for a confusing, perhaps half-understood, text *at the level at which vernacular literature circulated*.

To sum up, then, from the Chinese perspective, this text can be read in two basic ways. The first is as a distillation of the school of perfect wisdom, a small but powerful treatise on form and emptiness that is approachable (and, because of the language, intriguing). The *Sūtra* represents elements of the *prajñāpāramitā* school that were exploited by traditional poetics and offered, at most, an alternative and, at least, a slight twist on native concepts of phenomena and illusion so well worked out in such texts as *Zhuangzi*. In vernacular literature, it forms a part of a vocabulary adopted from Buddhism either for its incantatory power[21] or for a form of number magic (cf. the oft-used pair in drama of *wu yun liu gen*, "the five aggregates and the six roots" in a series of numbers) that is such a feature of arias in Yuan drama and in other forms of performing literature.

18. Shi Nai'an and Luo Guanzhong, *Shuihu quanzhuan*, ann. Li Quan (Chengdu: Sichuan wenyi chubanshe, 1990), ch. 4, 1:74.

19. Ibid., ch. 74, 2:1101.

20. Feng Menglong, *Jingshi tongyan*, ann. Yan Dunyi (Beijing: Renmin wenxue chubansshe, 1990), 2:496.

21. For instance, the incantations recited by the abbot and acolytes in the mass for the dead staged in Act One of *The Monk of the Bright Moon Leads Halcyon Liu to the Other Side (Yue ming heshang du Liu cui)*.

PERSPECTIVE ON READINGS OF THE *HEART SŪTRA*

The Perfection of Wisdom and the Fear of Buddhism

Stephen F. Teiser

The readings of the *Heart Sūtra* by Fuller and West are remarkable both for what they do and for what they claim (somewhat disingenuously, I think) not to do. What they do is to offer interesting, erudite, and complex readings of a medieval Chinese text. In this essay I want to explore just what those readings amount to—their moves, their strategies, their presuppositions— by also considering what it is they try to avoid. Both authors go out of their way to announce, "I am not a Buddhologist," the confession with which West begins his reading.

What does it mean to begin a reading with a disavowal? Is it simply another gesture toward academic modesty, such as when an authority in the field prefaces a book with the claim, "I am not an authority in the field"? Not exactly, for in this case the disavowal amounts to more than the trope of the humble scholar. Fuller and West have fairly clear ideas about Buddhology. For Fuller, it seems that Buddhologists have the peculiar ability to interpret Buddhist language in an unusual way. Language marked as "Buddhist" is, for Fuller, "the language of the specialist requiring technical expertise in its interpretation." In this view, the language of the text itself makes a demand— clear to specialist (the Buddhologist) and nonspecialist (Fuller) alike—that it be interpreted *as* unusual language and *by* a specialist. The exercise of technical expertise, however, hardly seems to distinguish the Buddhologist from other scholars. It is easily argued that the reader of Chinese poetry or philosophical prose perpetrates the same crime as does the Buddhologist. How, for instance, does one make sense of the word "sunflower" in a poem by Du Fu, or a reference to the "Great Clod" in an essay of Zhuangzi? Usually one needs to have been schooled in a tradition of poetry or intellectual history, and if not, one seeks out the dictionaries, handbooks, or commentaries on which scholars depend. One needs, in short, to be a specialist in a specific literary tradition with the ability to use the tools of the trade.

In West's opinion, Buddhology is distinguished from other scholarship by a style of exegesis that is doctrinal and esoteric. Buddhologists tend "to read the *Sūtra* as a doctrinal text, a specific document of a specific sect." They divide Buddhism into exclusive schools of thought and assign distinctive beliefs to each sect. As interpreted by Buddhologists, a text tends to "become swallowed up by its own tradition, to be surrounded and walled off by impregnable commentaries, or held captive by esoteric doctrinal debate." Against this portrait it is fair to ask whether the non-Buddhist texts discussed in this volume have in fact been treated any differently. Have categories like

"Confucianism," "Daoism," "Aesthetics," or "Poetics" not been invoked, either in the specific readings or in the decisions made by the editors about which texts to include in the first place? Have the various readings included here been written without recourse to the commentaries and sediments of recension in which traditional Chinese texts come so intricately wrapped? What makes the Buddhist packaging "esoteric" and the non-Buddhist commentaries more accessible?

If textual expertise and doctrinal esotericism are not unique to Buddhology, why are Fuller and West so intent on denying that they are Buddhologists? To answer that question we need to have before us a counterexample of "Buddhological" discourse. Thus, I will offer a "Buddhological" reading of the *Heart Sūtra*. I will then examine how the three readings by Fuller, West, and Teiser deal with several specific issues. Privileged by occupying the position of both partisan reader and distanced author of a "perspective," I will conclude with a discussion of the differences, real and imagined, between the three readings.

The self-disclosure with which I begin my reading is that I am a Buddhologist, of sorts. My reading of the *Heart Sūtra* is based on acquaintance with the history of Buddhist thought,[22] Chinese versions of the text and commentaries,[23]

22. A general introduction to the Mahāyāna background to the *Heart Sūtra* is available in Paul Williams, *Mahāyāna Buddhism: The Doctrinal Foundations* (London and New York: Routledge, 1989). On the Prajñāpāramitā literature more specifically, see Edward Conze, *The Prajñāpāramitā Literature*, Indo-Iranian Monographs, vol. 6 (The Hague: Mouton, 1960).

23. The version of the *Heart Sūtra* that Fuller, West, and I focus on is attributed to Xuanzang (602–664), the Buddhist monk, pilgrim, and translator. It is entitled *Boruo boluomiduo xin jing*, which corresponds to the Sanskrit *Prajñāpāramitā-hṛdaya-sūtra*. In addition to the two manuscript versions reproduced as figures 4.1 and 4.2, I have used the recension printed in the standard modern scholarly canon compiled in Japan, *Taishō shinshū daizōkyō* (abbreviated as *T*), ed. Takakusu Junjirō, Watanabe Kaigyoku, and Ono Gemmyō, 100 vols. (Tokyo: Taishō issaikyō kankōkai, 1924–1935). It is *T* no. 251, appearing in columns a–c of page 848 in vol. 8 (denoted as *T* no. 251, 8:848a–c). Over the centuries many other versions have existed, only some of which are still extant. For a complete historical study, see Fukui Fumimasa, *"Hannya shingyō" no rekishiteki kenkyū* (Tokyo: Shunjusha, 1987).

Surviving versions of the same (or similar) text as Xuanzang's include a translation, *Mohe boruo boluomi damingzhou jing*, attributed to Kumārajīva (Chinese name: Jiumoluoshi, 350–409), *T* no. 250; and a complete transliteration of the Sanskrit text in Chinese sounds, *Tang fan fandui ziyin boruo boluomiduo xin jing*, anonymous, *T* no. 256. Another, longer version of the *Heart Sūtra* exists in five separate translations. They are: *Pubian zhizang boruo boluomiduo xin jing*, Fayue (653–743), *T* no. 252; *Boruo boluomiduo xin jing*, Prajñā (Boruo, 744–ca. 810), *T* no. 253; *Boruo boluomiduo xin jing*, Prajñācakra (Zhihuilun, fl. 847–882), *T* no. 254; *Boruo boluomiduo xin jing*, translated from the Tibetan by Chos Grub (Facheng, fl. 832–865), *T* no. 255; and *Shengfomu boruo boluomiduo jing*, Dānapāla (Shihu, fl. 980–1017), *T* no. 257.

Chinese commentaries on Xuanzang's version include: *Boruo boluomiduo xin jing youzan*, Kuiji (632–682), *T* no. 1710; *Boruo boluomiduo xin jing zan*, Uŏnč'ŏk (Yuance, 613–696), *T* no. 1711; and *Boruo boluomiduo xin jing lüeshu*, Fazang (643–712), *T* no. 1712. Studies and trans-

and the work of modern Buddhologists in Europe, America, and East Asia.[24]

The version of the *Heart Sūtra* attributed to Xuanzang occupies an anomalous position in Chinese Buddhism. As many Chinese commentators point out, the sūtra is unusual because it omits the lines with which most Buddhist sūtras begin. They are the words attributed to Ānanda, the closest disciple of the historical Buddha, who shortly after the Buddha's death recited all of the sermons the Buddha had preached, thus fixing in oral form the earliest canon. Most sūtras begin with the words, "Thus have I heard. Once, when the Buddha resided at. . . . " The linguistic omission means that the scripture lacks a framing narrative; unlike most sūtras, it reads more like philosophical discourse and less like story. Most later Chinese versions of the *Heart Sūtra,* in fact, remedy the deficiency, adding a properly sūtra-style opening. Another anomaly is apparent in the first word of the text. Xuanzang uses what in the Tang-dynasty context is an unusual rendering of the name of the bodhisattva Avalokiteśvara, Guanzizai. Prior to Xuanzang, the commonly accepted rendering of the bodhisattva's name was Guanyin (or Guanshiyin), based on a reading (or misreading) of the Sanskrit as Avalokita-svara, literally "Observer of Sounds (of the World)." Instead, Xuanzang parses the Sanskrit as Avalokita-iśvara (Guanzizai, literally "Self-Existent Who Observes" or "Observing Lord"), an opinion which was, like many of Xuanzang's choices in translation, simultaneously accepted as authoritative and ignored by the vast majority of Chinese Buddhists, who persisted in using the incorrect but more popular form.[25]

Most commentators make an effort to explain the significance of the two characters named in the text, the bodhisattva Avalokiteśvara and the disci-

---

lations focusing on the Sanskrit versions of the *Heart Sūtra* include: Edward Conze, *Buddhist Wisdom Books, Containing the Diamond Sūtra and the Heart Sūtra* (London: George Allen and Unwin, 1958); and idem, "The *Prajñāpāramitā-hṛdaya-sūtra,*" in Conze, *Thirty Years of Buddhist Studies* (London: Bruno Cassirer, 1967), 148–67.

24. Important studies of the *Heart Sūtra* in its Chinese context include: Francis H. Cook, "Fa-tsang's Brief Commentary on the *Prajñāpāramitā-hṛdaya-sūtra,*" in *Mahāyāna Buddhist Meditation: Theory and Practice,* ed. Minoru Kiyota (Honolulu: University of Hawaii Press, 1978), 167–206; Fukui, *"Hannya shingyō" no rekishiteki kenkyū;* Leon Hurvitz, "Hsüan-tsang (602–664) and the *Heart Scripture,*" in *Prajñāpāramitā and Related Systems: Studies in Honor of Edward Conze,* ed. Lewis Lancaster, Berkeley Buddhist Studies Series no. 1 (Berkeley: University of California Press, 1977), 103–21; John R. McRae, "Ch'an Commentaries on the *Heart Sūtra:* Preliminary Inferences on the Permutation of Chinese Buddhism," *Journal of the International Association of Buddhist Studies* 11, no. 2 (1988): 87–115; and Jan Nattier, "The *Heart Sūtra:* A Chinese Apocryphal Text?" *Journal of the International Association of Buddhist Studies* 15, no. 2 (1992): 153–223.

25. See *Datang xiyu ji,* Xuanzang, *T* no. 2087, 51:883b; and *Fanyi mingyi ji,* Fayun (1088–1158), *T* no. 2131, 54:1061c–62a. My English translation ("Observer of the Self-Existent")

ple of the Buddha most advanced in wisdom, Śāriputra. They also devote a significant amount of space to explaining what *prajñāpāramitā* ("perfection of wisdom") means; in the title the sūtra claims to be the essence of it, and Avalokiteśvara practices it, but nothing else is predicated of it. In this case my own interpretive instincts are historical: I understand "the perfection of wisdom" as marking an important development in early Mahāyāna Buddhism. While earlier forms of Indian Buddhism did not ignore wisdom, the forms of Mahāyāna that grew up in southwestern India beginning about 100 B.C.E. stressed a new model for the religious life, summarized by the doctrine of six perfections (*pāramitā; boluomiduo* in transliteration; usually *du^a* in translation). The first and most fundamental virtue is charity (*dāna*, derived from the same Proto-Indo-European root as the word "donor"; *bushi* in Chinese), a practice in which lay people excel but which is open to all. The sixth perfection is that of *prajñā*, translated into Chinese as *zhi^d* (or *zhi-hui*) and transliterated as *boruo*, "wisdom." In the context of early Mahāyāna Buddhism, bringing one's wisdom to perfection entails a complex, dialectical movement. This particular kind of wisdom is not based on everyday knowledge or on sagacity, nor is it achieved by developing an ability inherent at birth. Rather, it is produced through a process of transcendence, in which the usual terms of knowledge are first stated and elaborated, then emptied of all meaning, and then, as if from a higher plane, filled with a new significance.

In my reading, the *Heart Sūtra* both argues for and enacts the dialectical transformation of knowledge signified by the term "perfection of wisdom." What I have marked as Part One in my translation establishes the basic terms of analysis: in the view of Avalokiteśvara, the five heaps are empty. To understand the five "heaps" (or "accumulations," Sanskrit *skandha*) we need to know in the first place that when Buddhists deny the permanence of the spirit or soul, they break down the constituents of human life into these five functions, which Buddhologists typically render as "form," "sensation," "concept," "action," and "consciousness." It is also important to recognize that the five heaps are simply one template among many that can be used to analyze the world, taking apart experience by dividing it into categories, events, or entities. What is true of the five heaps will *mutatis mutandis* be true of all discrete things one assumes to exist in the world. The text moves from the former (heaps) to the latter (the broadest possible class of things, "all *dharmas*" (*zhufa*) in the sense of "all the constituents of existence") in Part Three. In

---

reflects the interpretation of a "typical" Tang-dynasty reader, who would not be aware that the case-markers in Sanskrit contradict the customary word order in Chinese, which is Verb-Object.

Part One the quality predicated of the elements of individual existence is emptiness (Skt. *śūnyatā*, Ch. *kong*). Here too I would suggest we begin to unravel the meaning of emptiness not by referring to early Chinese philosophical traditions, etymologies in Chinese lexicons, or the word's associations in the Chinese poetic tradition, but by looking to the history of the term in Buddhism. As a Buddhist concept, emptiness means not simply "hollow" or "lacking everything," but rather "empty" (in the adjectival sense) of a very particular thing, what the Buddhists call "own-being" (Skt. *svabhāva*, Ch. *zixing*). Own-being is a kind of identity; it not only makes a thing what it is, as an essence it also exists independently of all other essences and endures forever. If any one of the five heaps—consciousness, say—were not empty of own-being, then consciousness as an element in the world would be eternal, and it would exist regardless of whether it was supported by other factors of life like form or sensation. What Avalokiteśvara sees is that all of the constituents of life lack permanence or independence.

With the principal subject and predicate stated in Part One, Avalokiteśvara proceeds in Parts Two and Three to explicate the basic proposition at greater length. Using the first of the five heaps (form), Avalokiteśvara begins by explaining the manner in which subject and predicate are related. They are not different from each other, and they are identical. These two propositions are stated in doublets. Then, he says, the other four heaps "are also like this."

In Part Three Avalokiteśvara develops the original claim first by expanding the range of the subject. Whereas before he spoke of the five heaps, now he makes "all the constituent elements of existence" the topic. Secondly, he complicates the predicate, answering the question of what it means to be marked by emptiness. We might take a moment to consider what the text is arguing against here. If an element were not marked by emptiness, we could (in the world of early Indian Buddhist scholasticism, which I adopt momentarily as one interpretive horizon) claim with certainty that it originated at a particular time or ceased to exist at a particular time, or that it was inherently pure or impure, or that it was perfect or imperfect. The assumption—which from the standpoint of later Buddhist thought is wrong—that grounds these claims has to do with the subject; it is the presupposition that each element of existence is permanent and permanently distinguishable from other elements by virtue of its own-being. Once own-being is denied, which is tautological to saying that once emptiness is established, then all of the predicates attaching to own-being (concerning production, purity, and perfection) must be denied as well.

Part Four turns the tables: it seems to be saying just the opposite of what was advanced in Parts One, Two, and Three. Against the earlier assertion that the constituents of existence "are empty," "are marked by emptiness," and "are emptiness," Part Four begins with the assertion that "in emptiness

there is no form" or any of the other elements. And, as if to sharpen the contradiction, the sentence begins with the logical shocker "therefore" (*shi gu*,
"for this reason"). We can, of course, read Part Four simply as a contradiction and leave it at that. On this reading, the *Sūtra* is at worst confused and
illogical, at best staking out a sophist's position that views all predication as
inherently self-contradictory. But we could also ask if what the text is *doing
with knowledge* might not be related to what it is *saying about knowledge*. We
need to allow for the possibility that the text is making a comment about the
very grounds of naming. The latter reading, it seems to me, accords best with
what is going on in Parts Four and Five of the text and with the particular
phase of Buddhist philosophy in which scholars locate the *Sūtra*.

The specific qualities said to be lacking in emptiness in Part Four com-
prise an interesting set, composed of several numerical lists. The first list (beginning with form and ending with consciousness) names the five heaps, of
course, and any reader patient enough to have come this far could hardly
avoid being turned around by this contradiction of the opening formulation. The second list is composed of the eighteen sense elements of existence,
made up of three sublists of six members each. The first six are the sense organs (eye, ear, nose, tongue, body, and mind), the second six are the sense-
objects those organs perceive (sights, sounds, smells, tastes, contacts or objects of touch, and *dharmas* or objects of mind), and the third are the realms
of experience, the fields defined by the six vectors, as it were, marked out
by the organs and their objects (from the realm of sight to the realm of consciousness). The third list is the twelvefold chain of dependent origination,
to which the *Heart Sūtra* refers elliptically by noting only its first element (ignorance) and its last ones (old age and death). The fourth list is the four noble truths, phrased in a way which, as Fuller demonstrates in his reading, is
difficult to make out in Chinese unless one is already clued in—through prior
acquaintance with Buddhism, possession of specialist's knowledge, or academic suspicion fueled by access to reference tools. The last two elements
named are wisdom and attainment, the first often glossed as the superior
form of knowledge touted in the title, the latter as the achieving of medita-
tive powers, of stages leading to enlightenment, or of enlightenment itself.
From a historical perspective this section of the *Heart Sūtra* is interesting because it presents a relatively new concept, that of emptiness, in contradis-
tinction to the hitherto unquestioned categories used by Buddhist philosophers in analyzing existence. What does it mean to say that none of those
things is to be found in emptiness?

Even in the earlier forms of Buddhism to which the Mahāyāna schools in
general and the perfection of wisdom texts in particular were reacting, the
analysis of existence was an exercise which, according to its authors, aimed
at liberation from suffering. If that soteriological project is relevant to un-

derstanding Part Four, then it is possible to interpret the long statement of what is not found in emptiness as the perception of one who is established in or working towards the perfection of wisdom and enlightenment. Indeed, almost from the beginning the scripture itself makes such a distinction. The *Heart Sūtra* begins with third-person narration of what Avalokiteśvara is doing and what he knows. Then it shifts—albeit suddenly, without explicit quotation markers like "he said"—to reporting Avalokiteśvara's direct speech. In the narrative context, Avalokiteśvara is addressing Śāriputra; in the context of the scripture, that direct speech is the wisdom of one who has perfected wisdom. In this reading, the assertions of Part Four represent the approach to existence of one who practices the perfection of wisdom. To one who truly understands that all things are marked by emptiness, such things as form and consciousness, the senses and their objects, the four noble truths, even wisdom and enlightenment have ceased to exist as permanent, independent entities. They might exist temporarily—and in a Buddhist worldview, "temporary" can amount to many lifetimes—but their existence is devoid of own-being. It is not that they lack any existence at all (the assertion of Part Four according to a nihilistic reading), but that they lack an essence. A change has occurred—in the perspective of the ideal reader, and in the understanding of the constituents of existence—between Parts One and Four.

Part Five of the *Heart Sūtra* explains what people who have made that change can now accomplish. Bodhisattvas are free of the doubts and delusions that cloud the untrained mind. Their destination is *nirvāṇa*, though we should note that *nirvāṇa* is only a penultimate goal, since the sūtra goes on to valorize the achieving of *anuttarasamyaksambodhi* (supreme, perfect enlightenment) by buddhas, who are even farther advanced than bodhisattvas. Although both *nirvāṇa* and *anuttarasamyaksambodhi* are rendered in transliteration, they can be distinguished by the contextual clues noted above (the bodhisattva reaches the former, while buddhas attain the latter) and by inquiring into their meaning. *Nirvāṇa* is typically translated into Chinese as *mie*, "extinction." Buddhist thinkers have long debated precisely what becomes extinct in the achieving of *nirvāṇa:* the self? suffering? life itself? What I would urge here is that we consider the scripture as a product of Mahāyāna thought, which, however we decide the connotations of *nirvāṇa*, places a clear priority on a state of enlightenment (. . . *bodhi*) that requires active involvement in the world and bringing salvation to others.

Part Six concludes the text not by a reversal of meaning or a change in register, but by reiterating the usefulness of the perfection of wisdom, the manner in which buddhas and others who understand emptiness can function in the world. Wisdom is neither ineffable nor inactive. Achieved through a process of affirmation and negation, its potency is not restricted to an interior mental realm or a transcendent place. Based on a proper understanding of emptiness, wisdom is, as the scripture says, not "vacuous" (*xu*) but "full" (*shi^d*, also rendered as "real"). As a spell, the perfection of wisdom performs the same function as do buddhas and bodhisattvas: it does away with suffering. What I have translated as "spell" (*zhou;* Skt. *mantra*, cf. the related term *dhāraṇī*) has an intricate and still poorly understood history both within China and all across Asia. Buddhologists are just beginning to appreciate the ramifications of adopting a performative approach to Buddhist language, which contains a wide range of words deemed to be effective for a variety of reasons, because they are conducive to memorization, because of their sound, because they are linked to specific deities, or because they occupy a position in a well developed symbolic system.[26] However the *Heart Sūtra*'s *mantra* be analyzed as a piece of Buddhist language, two facts are clear. Although it is a foreign word transliterated into Chinese sounds, it differs from the other Sanskrit words represented in Chinese sounds discussed so far in that it is not a single technical term. Rather, it is a string of phonemes with semantic value in Sanskrit but not in Chinese. The second, related fact is established conclusively in Fukui Fumimasa's ground-breaking study. It is, to use words quite different than Fukui's, that the *mantra* was synecdochically performative. That is, not only was a small part of the text (the *mantra* at the end) thought to represent the whole, but the entire scripture—and the perfection of wisdom itself—was believed to grant its invoker the power to achieve practical ends. As the anonymous appendix to the copy of the *Heart Sūtra* reproduced in this volume states, "Recite it constantly day and night, and there will be no prayer left ungranted." In fact, the normal way of referring to the text during the Tang dynasty was *Duo xin jing,* which was understood as meaning *The Scripture Containing the Spell "Prajñāpāramitā."* Only during the Ming dynasty did the text's current cognomen, *Xin jing,* interpreted as *Scripture on the Mind* or *Scripture on the Heart of the Perfection of Wisdom,* become popular.[27]

With the above reading entered and marked off as "Buddhological," it is now possible to interrogate the three readings of the *Heart Sūtra* on several disputed issues. The most obvious question, which crops up in the very first line of the text, is what to do with the numerous technical terms. Technical terms include words that represent a foreign (Sanskrit) sound written down in Chinese characters that do not match Chinese vocabulary (e.g., *pusa,* Skt. *bodhisattva*) and words that do have a lexical meaning in classical Chinese

---

26. See, for instance, Luis O. Gómez, "Buddhist Views of Language," in *The Encyclopedia of Religion,* ed. Mircea Eliade, 16 vols. (New York: Macmillan, 1987), 8:446–51; and Donald S. Lopez, Jr., "Inscribing the Bodhisattva's Speech: On the *Heart Sūtra*'s Mantra," *History of Religions* 29, no. 4 (May 1990):351–72.

27. Fukui, *"Hannya shingyō" no rekishiteki kenkyū,* 187–239, 241–321.

(e.g., *wuyun*, Skt. *skandha*, "the five heaps"). What the three readings end up doing with technical terms is largely the same, despite some of their claims to the contrary. Fuller, for instance, begins by reflecting on how to read the first words of the text, "Guanzizai pusa." He notes the word-for-word meaning of each term, compares this translation of the *Heart Sūtra* with other Chinese translations, and concludes that the name, which does make sense in Chinese (as "Observer of the Self-Existent"), should be understood as an alternate form of the Sanskrit name Avalokiteśvara. In translating the word he prefers the Sanskrit proper name, Avalokiteśvara. In his translation of the term (as "the Absolutely Free *bǝk-sat*"), West apparently follows the principle of translating all Chinese words (i.e., words that have an easy lexical meaning in classical Chinese) into English and translating all Sanskrit words (i.e., words that transcribe Sanskrit sounds) into romanized ancient Chinese, a device that conveys to the English reader the same mixture of native and foreign words that a Chinese reader might feel. Teiser's reading examines the lexical meaning of the term Guanzizai and explains it as an alternative way of understanding the Sanskrit analogues. Both Fuller and Teiser note how much more frequently the alternative form of Guanshiyin is used in China.

What these differences amount to, I would claim, is very little. All three readers treat the term as a Chinese translation of a Sanskrit word. They all distinguish between translation by meaning (called *yiyi* in Chinese linguistics) and translation by sound (*yinyi*) and try out both options. They all make reference, implicitly or explicitly, to different versions of the text, including ones in Sanskrit. And they all depend upon commentaries, dictionaries, and other reference works.

The overwhelming similarity in approach and in tools used to read foreign terms is even more striking in light of the claim, made most explicitly by Fuller, that Buddhist texts demand unusual treatment. Consider, for example, what he claims we need to do to understand the four words *ku, ji, mie,* and *dao,* which on first reading appear even less technical than Guanzizai pusa because the meaning of each is overdetermined in classical Chinese. "The only way to know that 'suffering,' 'accumulation,' 'extinguishing,' and 'the Way' are coordinate," says Fuller, "is to read the Sanskrit text or seek clarification elsewhere." But what exactly is involved in "seeking clarification elsewhere," and how does that differ from what we do in trying to make sense of a non-Buddhist text? My suggestion is that the reading of any text is always a matter of "seeking clarification elsewhere." All three readers seek clarification in Sanskrit originals and cognate Chinese texts. In addition, West seeks clarification in drama and the tradition of literary criticism, and Teiser seeks clarification in the cultural history of Chinese Buddhism and trends in the development of Buddhist thought. While relying on similar approaches and methods, each reading places foreign terms against a different, though hardly exclusive, context. There is little here to distinguish the "non-Buddhological" from the "Buddhological" interpretations.

The large number of technical terms in the *Heart Sūtra* raises a broader issue. As all three readings make clear, as a cultural phenomenon Chinese Buddhism is marked by its foreignness. That alterity, never complete, was essential to the tradition: foreign sounds, non-Chinese deities, barbarian customs, unprecedented practices like celibacy were chosen consciously by the proponents of Buddhism and criticized loudly by its detractors. Everything foreign, however, was not the same. In the realm of language, as these readings and other recent scholarship make clear, there was always a broad range of words to choose from. By raising the question of why Xuanzang chose these particular words, Fuller requires us to consider in some detail just what choices were open to Xuanzang and other translators of Buddhist texts.

Scholarship has only just begun to explore in depth the linguistic features of Chinese Buddhist texts. The initial conclusions of that work have important implications for how we read Buddhist texts and interpret the cultural history of Buddhism in China.[28] In the Han dynasty a striking number of vernacularisms began to appear in Chinese translations of Buddhist texts. According to Zürcher, the vernacular elements in those translations include abundant use of binomial expressions (as nouns, verbs, and adverbs), frequent use of verbs of direction, the use of plural suffixes, reduction of pronominal forms, and replacement of the determinative structure A *zhe* B *ye* with the copulative form A *shi* B. The stylistic features typical of Buddhist scriptures include a mixture of transliteration and translation for technical terms; four-character phrasing for most prose sections; paired sentences exhibiting semantic and syntactic parallelism; and alternation of prose and verse (prosimetric form).[29] The work of the Kuchean translator Kumārajīva (350–409) served to enshrine the semivernacular, semiliterary style that had been developing for a few centuries. Kumārajīva's translations quickly became the most popular ones, and other translators elevated his style to that of a Buddhist "church language."

28. The seminal study is by Erik Zürcher, "Late Han Vernacular Elements in the Earliest Buddhist Translations," *Journal of the Chinese Language Teachers Association* 12, no. 3 (October 1977): 177–203. See also: Zhu Qingzhi, *Fodian yu zhonggu hanyu cihui yanjiu*, Dalu diqu boshi lunwen congkan 18 (Taipei: Wenjin chubanshe, 1992); Victor H. Mair, "Buddhism and the Rise of the Written Vernacular in East Asia: The Making of National Languages," *Journal of Asian Studies* 53, no. 3 (August 1994): 707–51; and Erik Zürcher, "A New Look at the Earliest Chinese Buddhist Texts," in *From Benares to Beijing: Essays on Buddhism and Chinese Religion in Honour of Prof. Jan Yün-hua*, ed. Koichi Shinohara and Gregory Schopen (Oakville, Ontario: Mosaic Press, 1991), 277–304.

29. Zürcher, "A New Look at the Earliest Chinese Buddhist Texts."

Among the vast corpus of literature translated from Sanskrit and other Indic languages into Chinese, the texts associated with Xuanzang's name share two characteristics: they are simultaneously precise and unintelligible. Their precision is due to Xuanzang's knowledge of Sanskrit, which was unparalleled among the Chinese-born translators of Buddhist texts, and because he tended to force the Chinese language into Sanskritic patterns. That linguistic twisting accounts for the second quality, the unintelligibility of his translations to a Chinese reader unschooled in Sanskrit.

What emerges from this consideration of the practice of translation in Chinese Buddhism is that Xuanzang's choice of particular words places him at odds with the general attempt to explain Buddhism in terms readily comprehensible to a Chinese audience. The exoticism, esotericism, and insularity that Sinologists typically attribute to Chinese Buddhist texts may well apply to Xuanzang, but not to Buddhism in general. Because it was partly vernacular, Buddhist language (as represented by the most popular translations, not Xuanzang's) was in many ways more comprehensible to the untrained ear than were indigenous texts written in the literary language. Viewed in this context, Xuanzang seems to have taken great care in distancing his translations from the accommodationist norm, making them sound as foreign as possible. While this conclusion differs from the portrayals of Xuanzang by Fuller and West, their interests would hardly exclude the tracing of a nuanced history of translation. Their "Sinological" or "literary" readings share the same interests as the "Buddhological" one offered here.

Up to this point all three readings have presupposed a naive idea of authorship, treating Xuanzang's choice of words in the surviving text as an unproblematic reflection of his singular personality. We need to ask, however, what we know about his writing of the text, and in what sense he can be treated as an author. We should note in the first place that although his name has been attached to the text, the scripture is marked explicitly as "translated by" (*yi^f*) Xuanzang, not "composed by" him.[30] In the guise of translator, he would have faced certain constraints that the author of an original would not. In addition to the limitations of the receptor language, which anyone writing in classical Chinese would face, Xuanzang would also have been limited by the original text and the source language of Sanskrit. In fact, Xuanzang's room for improvisation would have been even smaller than that of the typical translator, because it is most likely that the Xuanzang version of the *Heart Sūtra* came into being because someone took an existing Chinese translation of a Prajñāpāramitā text, modified it slightly, and dubbed

---

30. Several words were used to mark authorship in Chinese Buddhist texts, including *shuo, yu, zhu, zuo, zao,* and *zhi^f*.

it the *Heart Sūtra*. This revisionist understanding of the *Heart Sūtra* is based on Nattier's recent study.[31] If Nattier is correct, then not only was Xuanzang not the primary translator of the text, but the imprint of his individual style is visible in only a few places in the text.[32] Nattier also demonstrates that, unlike the copious documentation for Xuanzang's other translations, we have very little solid evidence tying Xuanzang to the version of the *Heart Sūtra* attributed to him.[33] It is a strong likelihood, then, not only that the Xuanzang version of the *Heart Sūtra* was created by adapting an already existing Chinese (not Sanskrit) version of a Buddhist text, but also that someone else, as yet unknown, was responsible for producing the version of the *Heart Sūtra* that bears Xuanzang's name. These dimensions of authorship are not so much foreign to the traditions of Sinology or Buddhology as they are simply left undetailed in the three readings above.

All three readings make recourse to a distinction between the meaning and the function of the text, or, put differently, between the message and the medium. As for the message, all readings dwell on the dialectical nature of the text. They point out that part of the sūtra's message is that wisdom entails grappling with contradictions like "form is identical to emptiness" and "in emptiness there is no form." Fuller, West, and Teiser also converge in treating the dialectic as having to do, in part, with language. The text is concerned, they claim, not just with wisdom as a psychological or spiritual state, but with the philosophical problems involved in using words to single out discrete things or domains of experience. Given the complexity of the readers' explanations on this point—the extreme contrast between the language of the text and the language of the interpretation—it is worth pausing a moment to consider the grounds of their readings. How, when, and where did it become possible to read Buddhist texts first as constructed in dialectical form, and second as making an argument about the relation between words and reality? In explaining the dialectic as overcoming an opposition between two contradictory statements, the three readers employ a language tied

---

31. See Nattier, "The *Heart Sūtra*." Her analysis is based on grammatical and lexical analysis of the text itself, comparison of the Chinese and Sanskrit versions, and external historical evidence from India, Central Asia, and China.

32. There are only five differences between the version of the *Heart Sūtra* attributed to Xuanzang and the text he is alleged to have adapted, Kumārajīva's translation of *The Large Sūtra on the Perfection of Wisdom* (*Mohe boruo boluomi jing*, Skt. *Pañcaviṃśatisāhasrikā-prajñāpāramitā-sūtra*), T no. 223. All the differences are minor. In one case he transliterates Śāriputra differently than does Kumārajīva (Shelizi rather than Shelifu). In one case he uses a binomial conjunction where Kumārajīva uses a monosyllabic one (*yi fu ru shi* for *yi ru shi*). In three cases he omits the conjunction *yi*[g] at the beginning of a phrase. For a helpful line-by-line comparison, see Nattier, "The *Heart Sūtra*," 159; the divergences I note here occur on lines 1, 4, 15, 16, and 18.

33. Nattier, "The *Heart Sūtra*," 189–94.

loosely to Hegel and post-Hegelian thought. In construing the limitations on knowledge as primarily linguistic in nature, they are exercising an option in the interpretation of Buddhist thought that has become especially popular since the development of analytic philosophy in this century.[34]

The three readers diverge, however, in how they explain the dialectical teaching of the text and in what they consider the dialectic relevant to. West summarizes the import of the text, suggesting that since neither emptiness nor form really exists, the attempt to distinguish essentially between the terms of any binary opposition renders both terms false. While neither Fuller's nor Teiser's readings use the same words, they would not contradict that interpretation. At another point, however, West portrays the meaning of the scripture as "typically Indo-European," by which he means that it is concerned with causation and with the gap between substance and illusion. The focus on substance, claims West, is apparent in the language of the text, which is paratactic, using expressions of substance-identity (A *ji shi* B, A *bu yi* B) and causality (*shi gu, yi . . . gu, yi . . . gu*). West contrasts these constructions—all reified as "Indo-European," despite the fact that they are written in classical Chinese and attested in a variety of Chinese texts, including pre-Buddhist ones—with what he deems to be a uniquely Chinese style of analogical parallels, which utilize a topic-comment structure and offer only a partial description of the topic. While it may be interesting to postulate a general contrast between Indo-European and Chinese modes of thought, West's bifurcation falters from the very beginning. In both Buddhist and non-Buddhist works, Chinese authors prefer to use established Chinese grammatical structures to express something that West regards as essentially un-Chinese, a concern with identity and substance. Faced with a messy situation in which allegedly analogical Chinese authors use manifestly non-analogical structures and have a typically Indo-European fixation on substance, it seems to me that we have a choice. Either we elevate our cultural stereotypes to the level of an unchanging, unlocalized, and unfalsifiable essence, which I believe West has come close to doing, or we admit that Buddhism (or some other expression of Indo-European civilization) was not always separate from Chinese culture, that over the course of a few thousand years both Buddhism and China might have changed.

---

34. For an explicitly Hegelian reading of the concept of emptiness, see T. R. V. Murti, *The Central Philosophy of Buddhism: A Study of the Mādhyamika System*, second ed. (London: George Allen and Unwin, Ltd., 1960), esp. 293–310. For a Wittgensteinian reading of Nāgārjuna, see Chris Gudmunsen, *Wittgenstein and Buddhism* (London: Macmillan Press, Ltd., 1977). For a more detailed analysis of the history of readings of Nāgārjuna, see Andrew P. Tuck, *Comparative Philosophy and the Philosophy of Scholarship: On the Western Interpretation of Nāgārjuna* (New York: Oxford University Press, 1990).

Another avenue West takes in explaining the dialectic of the *Sūtra* is Chinese literary criticism. He also demonstrates how the life of recondite religious texts in China was very much determined by their integration into everyday practice.

Fuller too appreciates the use of thesis and antithesis in the *Heart Sūtra*, finding that, judged by its own principles, the text still leaves us "fixated on the activity of the comparing mind." The presumption of dichotomy, however, emerges in another portion of Fuller's reading. Corresponding to West's need for categories that neatly divide the world into psycho-linguistic halves, Fuller takes refuge in a distinction between "poetry," which unites meanings and contexts into a coherent whole, and "religion," the "otherworldly commitments" which seem to rest on "the radical inadequacy of individuated subjectivity." Ignoring for the moment the question of why as intercultural readers we seem to desire such global categories, these distinctions seem ill-suited to the *Heart Sūtra* and other Prajñāpāramitā literature, which have often been read as describing the achieving of a simultaneous wholeness and emptiness. Perhaps Fuller's bifurcation of poetry and religion has to do with the widespread presumption that "religion" is best defined as referring to a sphere of meaning or a realm of existence distinct from all others. In contrast, however, many contemporary scholars of religion have dispensed with the view that the study of religion, by virtue of the special nature of its subject matter—sacred, personal, transcendent, etc.—is different from other disciplines. Instead, most authorities treat the category as a construction of modern European culture or as an impermanent collection of attributes that varies from one culture to the next.[35]

In Teiser's reading the dialectic is distinctly, though perhaps not uniquely, Buddhist. It is explained in terms of the history of Buddhist thought, and its *telos* is claimed to be the achieving of a nondualistic state of perception, the perfection of wisdom. In the final section of his reading Teiser emphasizes the functioning of that wisdom. He appears to be arguing against unnamed opponents who would construe the result of the dialectic as a mystical merging of subject and object (as in some modern readings of emptiness) or in a celebration of the mythological and the romantic (as in some readings of *Zhuangzi*).

All three readings discuss the function of the *Heart Sūtra*, its performa-

35. Both Geertz and his critics adopt a non-substantialist definition of religion. See Clifford Geertz, "Religion as a Cultural System," in *Anthropological Approaches to the Study of Religion*, A.S.A. Monographs, no. 3, ed. Michael Banton (London: Tavistock Publications, 1966), 1–46, reprinted in Clifford Geertz, *The Interpretation of Cultures* (New York: Basic Books, 1973), 87–125; and Talal Asad, *Genealogies of Religion: Discipline and Reasons of Power in Christianity and Islam* (Baltimore: Johns Hopkins University Press, 1993), esp. 27–54.

tive rather than its propositional value. Above I drew attention to our shared recourse to the idioms of dialectic and of linguistic philosophy in interpreting the text. What is equally remarkable, in my view, is that the essays by Fuller, West, and Teiser all make use of the notion of performance. Whether that shared interest originates in literary criticism, drama studies, speech-act theory, or elsewhere, all three readers attend both to the illocutionary aspects of the text, its ability to bring about change or to do things, and to its locutionary aspects, the stating of propositions. I have referred to the readers' understanding of the propositional content of the text: they regard the "message" of the text as having to do with a dialectic. The performative force of the text crops up especially clearly in the reading of the *mantra* with which the text ends. All three readers recognize that the words work not just because they say something, but because they do something. In Fuller's view what they do is to push the reader to discard words altogether. For West, the *mantra* or the text as a whole is powerful because it is invoked repeatedly. He adds the important detail that at the vernacular level, one word of the *mantra* (*gate*) seems so opaque that it is treated as a god, endowed with the physical features and mysterious powers characteristic of Chinese deities.

On the issue of performatives both Fuller and West move in the right direction, refusing to treat the *mantra* merely as an affront to logic or a failure in meaning. I would differ from them only in trying to close the gap between proposition and performance. An important philosophical point is being made, it seems to me, by including a *mantra* at the end of the *Heart Sūtra*. Using the words of a sūtra performatively has implications for the question of "meaning" and is not simply a matter of "function"—a duality which, we should not forget, I imposed on the discussion in the first place. Put the other way around, the propositional content of the text makes an important point about the illocutionary force of words. In my reading the dialectic of the argument moves toward the view that precisely because words lack a permanent anchor in the nonlinguistic realm, they should be viewed as temporary creations that have limited use—or in short, that words are instrumental. Elite versus vernacular interpretations of the *mantra* (and of the text as a whole) may well diverge neatly into a locutionary as opposed to an illocutionary tendency, respectively, but the two realms ought not to be viewed as everywhere and always distinct.

In conclusion I return to the question with which we began: What is being disowned in the claim, "I am not a Buddhologist"? It is worthwhile counting how many times the readings of the *Mencius* and *Zhuangzi* elsewhere in this volume begin with a self-effacing advertisement that the authors are not specialists in Confucianism and Daoism. The disavowal of Buddhological competence, it seems to me, has less to do with academic training and approaches to interpretation, and more to do with the refusal to accept Buddhism as a Chinese tradition. In discounting their own readings of the *Heart Sūtra*, Fuller and West are simultaneously reflecting their own distance from the academic study of Buddhism and enforcing the alterity of Buddhism to their own image of Chineseness. I am not arguing that Fuller and West are unique in their apprehensiveness about Buddhism. As noted above, the foreign nature of Buddhist language and practice was an essential, if contested, part of the tradition from its inception on Chinese soil, but that otherness was also used to make the tradition "Chinese" in significant ways. Through their disavowal, Fuller and West take a stand on the Chineseness of Buddhism. My claim is not that they are intolerant proponents of Neo-Confucianism intent on extirpating Buddhism, but that past debates over the place of Buddhism in Chinese society are being replayed, wittingly or unwittingly, in our readings of the *Heart Sūtra*. In this respect, Fuller and West take sides with the small minority of people in Chinese history who refused, at least rhetorically, to accept the Sinification of Buddhism. That minority—or rather a confluence of several changing but powerful groups—has exerted the strongest influence on the development of Chinese studies in the West. The dominance of that viewpoint, then and now, means that, as West seems to hint, most modern Sinologists know considerably less about Buddhism than did the educated elite of the Tang—and, I would add, less than the uneducated as well.

In most respects the tools and approaches used by Buddhologist and non-Buddhologist are the same. The differences do not seem to be organized by different methods of interpreting technical terms or by the kabbalization of Buddhist texts by esoteric traditions of scholarship. To me the difficult issue, the real difference between these readings, is: What counts as Chinese? Is Buddhism to be considered a part of the Chinese world? Or, put more academically, what texts do we draw on in interpreting medieval Chinese texts? Are Buddhist texts and traditions relevant or not? My own approach is, to paraphrase Mengzi, why speak of difference (*he bi yue yi*)?

FIVE

Zi jing fu Fengxian yong huai wu bai zi
Du Fu, "Going from the Capital to Fengxian"

TRANSLATION OF "A SONG OF MY CARES
WHEN GOING FROM THE CAPITAL TO FENG-XIAN"

Stephen Owen

A man of Du-ling in commoner's clothes,
the older he grows, the more foolish his fancies.

So naïve in all that he swore to become!—
he secretly likened himself to Hou Ji and Xie.[1]

He proved at last too large to be useful,
white-haired now, and willing to bear privation.

When the coffin closes, all will be settled;
yet these goals ever look for fulfillment.

I worry for our folk to the end of my years,
I sigh, and my guts are in turmoil within.

I earn sneers from old men, once fellow students,
yet I sing out loudly, and with fierce intensity.

I do have aims to live on rivers and lakes,
there to see off my days, aloof and serene.

From *An Anthology of Chinese Literature: Beginnings to 1911*, ed. and trans. Stephen Owen. Copyright 1996 by Stephen Owen and the Council for Cultural Planning and Development of the Executive Yuan of the Republic of China. Reprinted by permission of W. W. Norton and Company, Inc. Notes are from the original.
  1. The significance of the particular two ancient sages to whom Du Fu compares himself is ambiguous. On the one hand, Hou Ji and Xie were important ministers, Hou Ji serving the Sage-King Yao as Master of Farming, and Xie serving Yu as the supervisor of education. But Hou Ji was also the ancestor of the Zhou royal house, while Xie was the ancestor of the Shang.

But I've lived in an age of a Yao or a Shun.[2]
and could not bear to withdraw forever.

Yet now the Halls of State are fully complete,
in the building's structure, no gaps at all.[3]

Like sunflower and pulse, I bend to the sun—
truly hard to rob a thing of its nature.

Then I look around on this ant-breed of men,
who can only go seeking their own little holes.

Why should they aspire to be Leviathan
planning rashly to sprawl in the deeps of the sea?[4]

Hereby I am aware of the pattern of life,
and am ashamed to alone strive for favor.

I have gone on thus stubbornly until now—
I could not bear to just sink to the dust.

But at last I'm chagrined before Chao-fu, Xu You,[5]
men unable to alter their firm resolve.

I drink deeply to banish these thoughts for the while,
then burst into such an unhappy song.

It was year's end, all plants were dying,
and the high hills had cracked in sharp winds.

The royal avenues lay sunken in shadow
as the traveler set forth at midnight.

The frosts were harsh, my coat's belt snapped,
my fingers were stiff, I could not tie it back.

At the break of dawn I passed Mount Li,
the imperial couch on its towering crest.[6]

Ill-omened auroras stuffed a cold sky,
and I tramped along slippery valley slopes.

2. It was conventional politeness to speak of the reigning emperor, in this case Xuan-zong, as a sage-king, like Yao or Shun in high antiquity.

3. That is, there are enough talented men to fill the necessary posts in the government and he, Du Fu, is not needed.

4. In this context, Leviathan, the monstrously large sea creature, seems to be a figure for grand vision and high ambitions.

5. Chao-fu ("Nest-father") and Xu You were exemplary recluses who refused the reins of government when they were offered.

6. This was Hua-qing Palace, the pleasure resort of Xuan-zong and Yang the Prized Consort.

Vapors surged swelling from Jasper Pool,
where the royal guardsmen rub and clack.

There lord and courtiers linger in pleasures,
music stirs, thunders through empty space.

All granted baths there have long hat ribbons,[7]
no short tunics join in their feasts.

Yet silk bolts apportioned in the royal court
came first from the homes of poor women.

Whips were used on their menfolk,
and taxes were gathered to present to the palace.

His Majesty's kindness in baskets for courtiers
is, in fact, to bring life to the principalities.

If the courtiers scorn this ultimate rule,
it is not that Our Lord throws these things away.

Many officers now are filling the court,
it is fitting that kindly men tremble in fear.

Moreover, I've heard golden plate of the Household
is now all in the homes of the Marriage Kin.[8]

In the midst of great halls goddesses dance,
diaphanous film flares from marble flesh.

There are cloaks of sable to warm the guests,
as sad notes of flutes follow harps' clear tones.

Guests are urged to taste camel-hoof soup,
frosty oranges weigh on the sweet tangerines.

Crimson gates reek with meat and wine,
while on the streets, bones of the frozen dead.

Grimness and grandeur, a mere foot apart,
so upsetting I cannot continue to tell.

My northbound cart came where the Jing meets the Wei,
at the official crossing I again changed my track.

Masses of waters came down from the west,
looming high as far as the eye could see.

---

7. The primary attraction of Hua-qing Palace was its hot springs. Those with "long hat ribbons" are, of course, the great officers of the court.

8. The reference here is to the Yangs, the kin of the Prized Consort, who took every opportunity to enrich themselves while the consort enjoyed Xuan-zong's favor.

It seemed as if Kong-tong Mountain had come,
I feared it would knock and break pillars of sky.

We were lucky the bridge had not yet collapsed,
yet the sounds of its crossbeams creaked and groaned.

Travelers reached hands to help each other over,
if the river grew broader, we could not cross.

I had lodged my wife off in a different county,
ten mouths to protect from the winds and snow.

Who could go long without looking to them?
I hoped now to share their hunger and thirst.

When I came in the gate I heard crying out:
my young son had just died of hunger.

I could not suppress a wail of my own
when the whole lane was sobbing.

What troubles me is in being a father
my not getting food caused this infant's death.

I could not have known that before the harvest
such calamity would come to our poverty.

All my life I have been exempt from taxes,
and my name is not registered for conscription.

Considering what bitter things happened to me,
ordinary people must be truly in dire straits.

I brood silent on those who lost livelihoods,
then think of our troops on far campaigns.

Reasons to be troubled are as great as South Mountain,
a chaos that no one can grasp.

WHAT'S IN A TITLE?

"Expressing My Feelings on Going from the Capital to Fengxian Prefecture: Five Hundred Characters" by Du Fu

David R. Knechtges

A title often can provide a guide on how to interpret a poem. First of all, the title may provide specific information that helps us understand the circumstances of composition: on what occasion or for what purpose did the poet write the poem. Second, the title may indicate that the poem belongs to a particular subgenre or theme. This information may be important, for it tells us that the poem may be related to other poems, or a certain tradition of poetry. Du Fu's title, "Expressing My Feelings on Going from the Capital to Fengxian Prefecture: Five Hundred Characters," is one that provides information of both types. First, it tells us something about the circumstances of composition: it is a poem about a journey that Du Fu undertook from the capital to Fengxian (modern Pucheng xian, Shaanxi), about eighty miles northeast of Chang'an. We know that in late 754 Du Fu moved his family to Fengxian to escape the flood and famine that devastated the Chang'an area at that time. According to a note in the *Du Gongbu ji,* Du Fu wrote this poem in the eleventh month of Tianbao 14 (= December 755), which was virtually on the eve of the outbreak of the An Lushan insurrection.[9]

The title also tells us something about the subgenre to which the poem belongs. Du Fu designates his poem *yong huai,* or "Expressing My Feelings." The *yong huai* tradition, which begins with Ruan Ji at the end of the Wei dynasty, was already a venerable one by Du Fu's time. As one can easily determine from its name, the *yong huai* is primarily an expression of feelings that are related to social and political concerns as well as moral values.[10] Another feature of *yong huai* poetry is that rarely is anything said directly—it can involve veiled satires of contemporary events and people, irony, contradictions, and incongruities, all of which lend a certain ambiguity to the work.

The long title of Du Fu's poem tells us that two distinct poetic traditions may be important in this poem: the travel narrative and the *yong huai.* The first section is very much in the *yong huai* mode. From the opening lines we see Du Fu presenting himself in a number of ostensibly contradictory poses: self-effacing then boasting, self-doubting then confident, commiserating with himself then with the plight of the people. Many of his lines are highly ambiguous and subject to varying interpretation. The first ambiguity occurs in the opening lines, in which Du Fu introduces himself in a self-effacing manner:

In Duling there is a commoner clad in homespun,
Growing older, his ideas become more foolish.

Commentators often have argued that Du Fu may not be as self-effacing here as he claims. Self-effacement in fact can often serve an ironical purpose, and this may be the case with these lines. The word *zhuo* is a very interesting one, and has a wide range of meanings, including clumsy, inept, stupid, and foolish. The word is used in the first chapter of *Zhuangzi,* in which Zhuangzi says to Huizi, who found no use for a large gourd: "You are cer-

9. See *Du Gongbu ji* (Hong Kong: Zhonghua shuju, 1972), 1.13b.
10. Donald Holzman, *Poetry and Politics: The Life and Works of Juan Chi (A.D. 210–263)* (Cambridge: Cambridge University Press, 1976), 1.

tainly inept in using the large."[11] The Western Jin poet Pan Yue uses the word
as a key term in his "Xian ju fu," where he equates his "ineptness" with lack
of success in his official career. However, his "ineptness" actually is beneficial,
for it has allowed him to retire into a life of quiet retirement. Some examples from Pan Yue:

> A perspicacious man, He Changyu, once said the following about me: "You
> are certainly 'inept [zhuo] in using your many talents.'" When he refers to
> my "many" talents, how dare I consider myself worthy? But what he says
> about my ineptitude [zhuo] is true and amply demonstrated by the evidence.
> At the present time, when "good and able men are in office," and "all of-
> ficials properly attend to their duties," this inept [zhuo] person should give
> up the idea of gaining favor and honor. Furthermore, my esteemed mother
> still resides with me, and she suffers from maladies of infirmity and old age.
> How could I ignore my duty to remain by her side and care for her with
> cheerful expression merely for the sake of pursuing a petty bushel-and-peck
> office? Thereupon, having seen the measure of knowing enough and know-
> ing where to stop, I hope that my desires may become like drifting clouds.
> I have built a house and planted trees where I may roam and ramble in self-
> contentment. My ponds are sufficient for fishing, and the income from grain
> husking can take the place of tilling the land. I water my garden, sell vegeta-
> bles in order to supply food for my morning and evening meals. I raise sheep
> and sell dairy products in order to anticipate the expenses of the summer
> and winter festivals. Oh, to be filial above all else and to be amicable with
> one's brothers is the way the inept [zhuo] person engages in government.

> I have roamed the long orchards of the canons and scripture,
> Strolled the lofty courses of the ancient sages,
> And thick-skinned as I may be,
> Within I blush before Ning and Qi.
> When the Way prevails I do not serve,
> When the Way does not prevail, I do not feign stupidity.
> How insufficient my shrewdness and guile!
> What a surplus of ineptitude [zhuo] and misfortune!

> In retirement I seek within to examine myself,
> Truly my usefulness is slight and my talents poor.
> I hold to Zhou Ren's fine words—
> But dare I exert myself and join the ranks?
> Barely have I protected my humble self,
> How could I emulate the sage and wise?
> I took up to the "many wonders" and cut off profane thoughts,
> Living carefree, nurturing my ineptness [zhuo] to the end of my days.[12]

---

11. *Zhuangzi, Sbby,* 1.8b.
12. *Wen xuan* (Shanghai: Shanghai guji chubanshe, 1986), 16.697–707.

Du Fu portrays himself as increasingly *zhuo* as he becomes older. In the context of the following lines, *zhuo* takes on an ironical meaning. For example, in the next two lines, Du Fu continues self-disparagement, followed by what some scholars have taken to be outrageous immodesty, the audacious comparison he makes between himself and Shun's ministers of agriculture and education, Ji and Xie:

His hopes how utterly foolish!
He even presumed to compare himself with Ji and Xie.

Du Fu may not be as immodest as he seems, and one could read the second line as an ironical statement. It is reminiscent of a line in Yang Xiong's "Jie chao" (Defense against Ridicule) in which he mocks the pretensions of the ambitious and shallow men of his time: "Everyone considers himself a Ji or Xie, every man deems himself a Gaoyao" (*Han shu* 87B.3568). By his witty recasting of Yang Xiong's line in the syntax of a famous line in the *Lun yu* (*Analects*, 7.1) in which Confucius compares himself to "old Peng," Du Fu seems deliberately to be calling attention to the absurdity of his claims. In other words, perhaps he is inept and foolish because of his impractical ideals—how could anyone in his age possibly think he could emulate the great Ji and Xie. How impractical, how foolish indeed!

Thus, in the next line, Du Fu continues to disparage himself:

As a matter of course, he became unwieldy and useless,
Hair white, he is willing to endure bitter suffering.

In the first line he characterizes himself as *huoluo*[a], which is a variant of *huoluo*[b], the word that occurs in the *Zhuangzi* passage cited above to describe dippers that Huizi tried to make out of a huge "useless" gourd. This word may be related to *kuoluo* and seems to have the meaning of "overly large to be useful." The full *Zhuangzi* passage reads: "Huizi said to Zhuangzi, 'The King of Wei gave me the seed of a large calabash. I planted it, it ripened, and produced a gourd of five bushels. When I filled it with liquid, it was not solid enough to be lifted up. If I split it open to make a dipper, it was so bulky [*huoluo*] it could not hold anything. It was not that it wasn't so astonishingly big, but because it was useless that I broke it into pieces.' Zhuangzi said, 'You, sir, are truly inept in using something large.'"[13] Du Fu seems to be calling himself a useless gourd. However, the uselessness of the gourd, as well as his ineptness and foolishness, are all in the eye of the beholder. In Du Fu's case he is useless because his worth has yet to be recognized. He is the classic example of the "the man of talent who meets an unfavorable

13. *Zhuangzi*, 1.8b.

time" (*huai cai bu yu*). Nevertheless, he will endure hardship in the pursuit of his goals:

> When the coffin closes, the matter ends;
> But until then his ideals he hopes to attain.

What are Du Fu's ideals? He tells us something about them in the next few lines:

> All his years he has worried about the people,
> From sighing his guts are burning inside.
> Laughed at by his venerable old classmates,
> Loudly he sings, ever more fervently.
> This does not mean he had no desire to dwell on river and sea,
> Carefree and detached, to send off days and months,
> But having been born under a ruler like Yao and Shun,
> He could not bear to part from him forever.

In these lines Du Fu seems to declare himself to be a dedicated and loyal servant of the state. Although he is mocked by his contemporaries for his silly worries about the plight of the people, even if he wanted to, he cannot become an eccentric recluse who dwells on "river and sea." He tells us that his age is governed by a sage ruler like Yao and Shun, and thus he cannot morally bring himself to withdraw from the court. However, there may be a qualification to Du Fu's praise for the Xuanzong era. In the next two lines he says:

> The implements of present day court and hall—
> To build an edifice, how are they lacking?

This line resembles the opening couplet of one of the thirty "Za ti" (Miscellaneous Imitations) by Jiang Yan: "A great edifice requires unusual materials; / Ordinary implements will not do for court and hall."[14] The implements of course are men of talent who are in such sufficient supply that a man like Du Fu really has no chance for employment. His sentiments again resemble those of Yang Xiong in his "Jie chao" (Defense against Ridicule):

> The court is like the bank of a river or lake,
> Or an island in the boundless sea.
> A single goose landing there does not make a great increase,
> And a single duck flying away does not make a great loss.[15]

Du Fu continues to declare his loyalty to the emperor by using the metaphor of the mallow plant (*kui*) that reputedly turned itself to face the sun:

---

14. *Wen xuan*, 31.1465.
15. See *Han shu* (Beijing: Zhonghua shuju, 1962), 87B.3568.

The mallow and bean lean toward the sun;
Truly nothing can be deprived of its nature.

Du Fu's line is directly inspired by a passage in a memorial by Cao Zhi in which he requested the emperor to allow imperial relatives to have contact with one another. At the end of his memorial he compares himself to the mallow and bean that constantly lean towards the sun even though the sun does not always return its light to them: "Plants like the sunflower and bean bend their leaves to the sun, even though the sun does not return its light for them. That they always face toward it is because of their devotion. I venture to compare myself with the mallow and bean."[16] Like Cao Zhi, Du Fu declares himself to be an unswerving loyal official whose basic resolve of giving service to the state cannot be altered.

However, Du Fu's view of the court is not as favorable as it first seems. In the next two couplets, which are probably the most ambiguous lines of the entire poem, he introduces the figures of mole cricket and ant, which are contrasted with the giant sea-creature, the whale:

He regards the group of mole-crickets and ants,
Who only seek their own little holes.
Why should they emulate the great whale
Always intent to lie upon the boundless sea?

Conventionally, the whale represents a man of great ambition and integrity who, once he leaves the deep sea and becomes stranded in the shallows, will become victim to such lesser creatures as mole crickets and ants. The locus classicus in Chinese poetry for this theme is the "Diao Qu Yuan" (Lament for Qu Yuan) by the early Han writer Jia Yi (ca. 200–168 B.C.E.):

How can that stagnant eight-or sixteen-foot ditch
Admit a giant boat-swallowing fish?
The sturgeon or whale stranded in a river or lake
Certainly will be controlled by mole-crickets and ants.

Commentators have variously explained the significance of the insects (mole crickets and ants) and the giant whale.[17] Is Du Fu the lowly ant who is so content with his lot he would not wish to emulate the grand aspirations of the whale? Or do the insects represent the petty-minded officials, complaisant in their positions at court, and the whale Du Fu, the man of great ideals and resolve who even aspires to compare himself with the great Ji and Xie? Or does Du Fu portray himself as a lowly ant, who would like to act boldly like the great whale, but is unable to do so because he lacks the power and

16. See Wen xuan, 37.1689.
17. For a summary see Du Fu quanji jiaozhu, 29–30.

position to do so. The reading of the poem does not become much easier as we come near the end of the first section.

> From this he becomes aware of the principle of life,
> And is the only one ashamed to seek favor.
> He suffered torment down to the present;
> How could he bear to sink into the dust?
> At last shamed before Chaofu and Xu You,
> Who were incapable of altering their integrity.

The first line poses several problems. First, we cannot be sure whether Du Fu used *wu*[a] "to be aware of" or *wu*[b] "to be mistaken about." The reading "to be aware of" seems to have more textual support, and also has the virtue of establishing an interesting parallel with the phrase *wu sheng li* that occurs in Xi Kang's "Yang sheng lun" (Discourse on Nurturing Life): "The gentleman knows that the body relies on the spirit in order to stand, and the spirit requires the body in order to exist. He also is aware that the ordering principle of life can easily be lost [*wu sheng li zhi yi shi*] and that one mistake can harm his life."[18] The word *sheng li* in Xi Kang's essay of course applies more strictly to the ways of *yang sheng* or "nurturing life." Du Fu seems not so concerned with nurturing and prolonging life as *sheng ji*, his livelihood or perhaps the course of his life.

What is this course? One path that he seems not to approve of is currying favor and position from men of power and influence. Du Fu even claims he is unique (*du*[b]) among his contemporaries in the mortification that he feels at the prospect of humbling himself before the purveyors of official titles. Yet, as a result presumably of his unwillingness to compromise himself, Du Fu has suffered nothing but failure and frustration (*wuwu*). Because of the ambiguity of the line *ren wei chen ai mo*, which can be taken as interrogative ("how can I bear to sink in the dust and dirt") or indicative ("I shall endure sinking into the dust and dirt"), it is not clear whether Du Fu means he accepts his lot or is complaining about his obscure status.

Another course that Du Fu rejects is reclusion. We have seen above that he claims to have set his mind upon dwelling on "river and sea." In what appears to be an admission of his apostasy, Du Fu says that he is put to shame by the recluses Chaofu and Xu You. Du Fu's lines here can be read in the context of #74 of Ruan Ji's "Yong huai":

> Great were the men of ancient times!
> Indifferent to the world, they were content in poverty.

18. *Wen xuan*, 53.2289.

In later ages the Way has declined and decayed,
Men dash about, stirring up dust and dirt.
He who "perches here and there" is not my type;
He who "wanders about" is not my kind.
Sighing over matters of honor and disgrace,
I go forth to savor the truth of the Way.
Chaofu and Xu You maintained a lofty integrity,
Following this course, they went down to the river bank.

Ruan Ji in these lines condemns those who like Confucius madly dashed about seeking position and influence. He favors the course of recluses such as Chaofu and Xu You who "held high their integrity" (*kang qi jie*). Like Ruan Ji, Du Fu approves of the ideals represented by these two men who withdrew from the world. However, again there is another ambiguity in his statement. Depending on how one understands "*yi qi jie,*" he seems to be saying that either he was "unable to adapt their type of integrity," which was much loftier than his own, or perhaps he was "unable to change his own type of integrity," which meant that he had to continue his quest for favor and position. (The subject of *yi* is not even clear, and another possible reading is as Owen translates, "men unable to alter their firm resolve.") The ambiguity of the statement that we find here and elsewhere perhaps is a reflection of Du Fu's own personal conflict and torment. This sense of doubt and uncertainty is reflected even in the final lines that close this section, in which Du Fu claims to relieve his sorrow with wine and song, yet only becomes ever more afflicted with sorrow:

He drinks deeply to dispel his cares for awhile,
But his hearty song is extremely sad indeed!

The two sections of the poem that follow what one might wish to term the prologue narrate the events of Du Fu's journey. The subgenre of the poetic travel narrative has its origins in the *fu* in such pieces as Liu Xin's "Sui chu fu" (On Fulfilling My Original Resolve), Ban Biao's "Bei zheng fu" (Northward Journey), Cai Yong's "Shu xing fu" (Relating a Journey), and, perhaps most importantly for Du Fu's poem, Pan Yue's "Xi zheng fu" (Westward Journey). The *fu* on travel combines description of the places the poet passes on his journey with moral comments, usually on events and persons associated with historical sites, and sometimes on contemporary events or a personal situation. An example of an event that affects the poet personally is Pan Yue's mention in "Westward Journey" of the death of his infant son:

My infant son died at Xin'an;
We dug a pit by the roadside and buried him.
Though the post station was called Thousand Autumns,

My son had not even a span of seven weeks.
Though I try hard to emulate Yan and Wu,
In truth I am pained by my love.[19]

This incident has a direct parallel in Du Fu's poem, which dramatically recounts Du Fu's sudden shock at hearing the news of the death of his child just as he enters the gate of his house in Fengxian:

Upon entering the gate I hear a loud cry,
My young son has already died of hunger.
Though I wish to hold back lamentation,
The entire lane is already sobbing.

Apart from these two instances, mention of the death of family members, especially children, is virtually unknown in medieval Chinese poetry. Although Du Fu recounts the death of his child differently from Pan Yue, his response to it is similar: like the Western Jin poet, he tries unsuccessfully to suppress his sorrow.

Pan Yue also did not hesitate to condemn rulers who lavished far too much attention on their favorites and who overindulged in sensual pleasures. Consider, for example, these passages in which he refers to the fall of King You of Zhou (Zhou You Wang), who was put to death by the Quan-Rong at the foot of the same Mount Li (Li Shan) described by Du Fu as the site of Xuanzong's revels with Lady Yang:

As I tread the land invaded by the Quan-Rong,
I am angered by the treacherous deceit of Lord You:
He lit false beacons to demoralize the hosts;
Infatuated with his favorite Bao, he indulged her depravity.
His army was defeated above the River Xi;
He himself dies north of Mount Li.
Resplendent and majestic, the Venerable Zhou;
Destroyed, it became a defunct state.[20]

The same Mount Li was the burial place of the First Qin Emperor. As he views the First Emperor's tumulus, Pan Yue comments:

He depleted the empire to give himself lavish burial;
Ever since creation, of such things no one has heard.
To the craftsmen's labors, he gave no thought,
But had them buried alive as recompense for their toil.[21]

19. Trans. David R. Knechtges, *Wen xuan* (Princeton: Princeton University Press, 1987), 2:191.
20. Ibid., 2:207.
21. Ibid.

Du Fu's account of his journey past Mount Li is even more vivid and dramatic than that of Pan Yue. Of course, the main difference is that Du Fu does not reflect on the past of the place, but its present:

> At year's end all the plants are dying,
> And high ridges are rent by fierce winds.
> The thoroughfare of heaven is dark and cold,
> And at midnight a traveler sets forth.
> The frost is harsh, my coat belt snaps.
> My fingers are too stiff to tie it.
> At the break of dawn, I pass Mount Li,
> The imperial coach rests on its tall and towering heights.
> Chiyou clogs the cold sky,
> Where I tramped and tread, valley slopes are slippery.
> At Carnelian Pond vapors thickly swell,
> Where imperial guardsmen rub and bump.
> Lord and vassals linger to enjoy themselves,
> Music sounds forth, thundering into empty vastness.
> Those granted baths are all the "long-capstrings";
> Those joining the feast are not the short-gowned homespun.
> The bolts of silk doled out in the vermilion courtyard
> Originally came from the homes of poor women.
> They whipped and flogged their husbands,
> And collected taxes to present to the imperial palace.
> The sage emperor bestows baskets of kindly favor,
> For he wishes the state and country to thrive.
> If vassals ignore this supreme principle,
> How can our ruler throw these things away?
> Many officers fill the court;
> It is fitting that good-hearted men quake in fear.
> Further, I have heard that the golden plates of the inner palace,
> Are all in the homes of the Wei and Huo.
> Within the halls dance divine sylphs,
> Misty gossamer envelops their jade flesh.
> For warming the guests there are sable furs,
> Mournful pipes follow upon pure-toned harps.
> They urge the guests to eat camel-hoof stew,
> Frosty oranges weigh upon fragrant tangerines.
> Vermilion gates reek with meat and ale,
> While on the roads there are bones of frozen dead.
> Grandeur and decay are just eight inches or a foot apart;
> Overcome with grief, I cannot continue my tale.

These lines cited above more or less speak for themselves, and unlike in the prologue, when he is talking mainly about his goals and aspirations, Du

Fu seems much clearer when speaking of corruption and abuses, even those associated with the imperial house.

In the final section of the poem, Du Fu continues his travel narrative. As long as Du Fu is relating his travels, his account is clear and relatively free of ambiguity and problematical lines. Some of the description is almost *fu*-like, especially the hyperbolic portrayal of the flood waters (massed ice)[22] that he encounters as he reaches the confluence of the Jing and Wei rivers. He describes the rising waters as *zuwu*, a binome that is usually reserved for describing tall and precipitous peaks. The line *yi shi Kongtong lai* is ambiguous. Are the waters so high they resemble the Kongtong Mountains from which the Jing and Wei Rivers take their source? Or does Du Fu imagine the great cumulative force of the waters as they gather speed and force on their flow from their western source in the Kongtong peaks?

> My northbound cart approaches the Jing and Wei juncture,
> At the official ford I again change my track.
> Massed waters come down from the west,
> Jutting upward, high as the eye can see.
> It seems as if the Kongtong Mountains had come,
> And I fear they will bump heaven's pillar, breaking it.
> Fortunately the bridge has not yet broken,
> Yet the sounds of its cross-supports groan and moan.
> Travelers join hands to help each other over,
> The stream is so broad, they cannot cross.

As Du Fu comes to the end of his difficult and dangerous journey, and arrives at the prefecture of Fengxian where his wife and children had taken refuge, instead of obtaining relief and joy from the family reunion, he finds even more grief and sorrow as he hears of the death of his son:

> My old wife I lodged in a different prefecture,
> Ten months separated from me by wind-blown snow.
> Who could keep them uncared for so long?
> I hoped to go there and share their hunger and thirst.
> Upon entering the gate I hear a loud cry,
> My young son has already died of hunger.
> Though I wish to hold back lamentation,
> The entire lane is already sobbing.

Although he laments his personal tragedy, Du Fu assumes the persona of the public-minded official that he claimed to be in the prologue ("All his

---

22. Or, following the variant reading of *qun bing* for *qun shui*: "Massed ice comes down from the west."

years he has worried about the people"), and expresses his indignation at the plight of those less fortunate than he, who is able to avoid taxes and military conscription:

> What shames me in being a father
> Is that in not getting food his life was cut short.
> I could not have known before the autumn harvest
> In our poverty there would be sudden calamity.
> Throughout my life I have been excused from taxes,
> And my name has never been registered for military campaigns.
> Considering what has happened to me, which was hard and bitter enough,
> Ordinary people must be tormented indeed!
> Silently I ponder those who lost their livelihoods,
> And think about soldiers far away on campaigns.

Du Fu concludes his poem with another hyperbole. His sorrow and worries are so great, they overtop the crest of the lofty Zhongnan Mountains of the capital area.

> The causes of my worries rise high as the Zhongnan Mountains;
> Vast and boundless, they cannot be cleared away.

Du Fu uses the binomial descriptive *hongdong* ("vast and boundless", which usually describes a vast, shapeless, boundless expanse). The word applies not only to the extent of his sorrows and cares, but also conveys the boundless depth of his despair and hopelessness. This type of expression is uniquely Du Fu, and clearly sets him apart from the *fu* poets who may have inspired his travel narrative.

DU FU, "SONG OF MY CARES EN ROUTE FROM THE CAPITAL TO FENGXIAN"

Lynn Struve

This poem, in large part the narration of an actual journey, begins at the end in terms of the author's emotional movement. It then contemplates what we read in the center and constrains that contemplation with the beginning. By this I mean that Du Fu, overcome by grief and remorse at his son's death (lines 81–100), seems impelled to write a poem of condemnation and lament for the times (lines 33–80) but fears lapsing into self-righteousness and self-pity. So he devotes the first part (lines 1–32) to reminding himself, and telling us, how ambivalently subject he has been to the vanities and self-delusions of men in his social class.[23] The result, in my eyes, is two juxtaposed medi-

---

23. In this, my interpretation differs from that of Susan Cherniack, who suggests a movement of spiritual growth from the first one-third of the poem (which she terms a prologue)

tations: one on the question of "to-serve-or-not-to-serve" the state in the first third of the poem; the other on relations between the sociopolitically privileged and the unprivileged in the latter two-thirds (subdividable at lines 80–81). Both of these meditations show Confucian dispositions characteristic of the pre–neo-Confucian era.

On the question of to-serve-or-not, Wolfgang Bauer has shown that certain influential pre-Qin texts (principally the *Changes, Analects,* and *Zhuangzi*), irrespective of their associations with Confucianism or Daoism, internally or mutually approved nonservice either as (1) permanent getting-away from the world of affairs, or (2) temporary withdrawal to await more propitious circumstances.[24] Subsequently, not only during the Era of Division, when Buddhism and Daoism gained predominant influence, but even during the Han dynasty, the first emphasis (on irrevocably fleeing or hiding, whether for personal autonomy or for self-preservation) seems to have held greatest favor. Those who tried to have it both ways—such as "hermits at court" (*chaoyin*), "hermits in town" (*shiyin*), and men who withdrew to await more advantageous political circumstances—seem to have been vulnerable to suspicion and derision, or at least to have been regarded as poseurs who simply wished to better enjoy a certain kind of elite lifestyle.[25]

Particularly in lines 13–14 of this poem, where he acknowledges a one-time attraction to living by the "rivers and seas," and in lines 29–30 where he expresses admiration for the uncompromising ancient hermits Chaofu and Xu You, Du Fu conforms with the Han-through-Tang emphasis. He frames his choice as one between continuing to pin his hopes on the court and getting away entirely, once and for all. Du Fu spent the rest of his life essentially as we see him here: struggling to protect himself and his family from the armed disruptions of the age, and troubled at heart by his own ambivalence between dedication to dynasty and country and attraction to a reclusive existence (often couched in Buddho-Daoist terms).[26]

This way of posing the question of whether to serve or not became less

---

into and through the latter two-thirds. "Three Great Poems by Du Fu" (Ph.D. diss., Yale University, 1988), esp. 111.

24. Wolfgang Bauer, "The Hidden Hero: Creation and Disintegration of the Ideal of Eremitism," in *Individualism and Holism: Studies in Confucian and Taoist Values,* ed. Donald Munro (Ann Arbor: Center for Chinese Studies of the University of Michigan, 1985), 161–64. Bauer makes several other insightful distinctions of elements within Chinese eremitism, besides the ones that I mention here. See also Aat Vervoorn, *Men of the Cliffs and Caves: The Development of the Chinese Eremitic Traditions to the End of the Han Dynasty* (Hong Kong: The Chinese University Press, 1990).

25. Bauer, "The Hidden Hero," 167–70.

26. See, for instance, William Hung, *Tu Fu: China's Greatest Poet* (Cambridge, Mass.: Harvard University Press, 1952), 264–66.

common among Confucians from the Song Dynasty through the early Qing.
Then, temporary withdrawal as a mode of protest aimed at reforming political conditions became prevalent—as a means of preserving personal autonomy until bad conditions might change for the better, or in the form
of "compulsorily eremitic" loyalism vis-à-vis a ruined culture or a fallen dynasty.[27] During that era, the Neo-Confucian stress on commitment to reform, and to loyalty toward state and ruler, made withdrawal always temporary in principle. Improvement in the political atmosphere, or the
return of a legitimate dynastic house and cultural order, always were seen
as possibilities—no matter how remote—for which the "superior man"
(*junzi*) needed to be prepared.

A telling moment in the shift from Tang to Song emphases has been
identified by Tze-ki Hon, who cogently explains the significance of Hu Yuan's
(993–1059) departure from the previously standard Kong Yingda (574–648)
interpretation of the "Hidden Dragon" (*qianlong*) line attached to the
"Qian" hexagram in the *Changes*. Kong simply had read the line as rein-
forcement of Confucius's injunction to hide oneself when the Way does not
prevail under Heaven[28] (which could be seen as just about any time after the
sagely era). Hu Yuan, however, emphatically distinguished between "hiding
one's body," which might be permissible under certain circumstances, and
"forsaking one's mission" to advance the common good, which never could
be condoned.[29] In refuting the earlier view of the sage as someone who frees
himself from captivity in human affairs to unite in freedom with nature or
the universe, Hu Yuan heralds Neo-Confucianism's closer bonding of the
superior man to social and political service *in principle*. This occurred precisely as any given elite gentleman's statistical chances of actually holding
public office began to decline because of the increases in population, high
literacy, and the competitiveness of the civil service examinations that characterized later imperial China. The consequent willingness to approve withdrawal only if it were somehow a lying in wait for honorable opportunities
to serve perhaps is epitomized by the early-Qing classic of dissident statecraft,
the *Mingyi daifang lu* of Huang Zongxi.[30]

27. See Frederick Mote, "Confucian Eremitism in the Yuan Period," in *The Confucian Per-
suasion*, ed. Arthur Wright (Stanford, Calif.: Stanford University Press, 1960), 202–40; and Tu
Wei-ming's article, "Towards an Understanding of Liu Yin's Confucian Eremitism," in *Yuan
Thought: Chinese Thought and Religion under the Mongols*, ed. Hok-lam Chan and W.T. de Bary
(New York: Columbia University Press, 1982), 233–77.

28. *Analects*, 8.13.

29. Tze-ki Hon, "Northern Song *Yijing* Exegesis and the Formation of Neo-Confucianism,"
(Ph.D. diss., University of Chicago, 1992), chap. 3, 80–91.

30. The meaning of *mingyi* as "a phase in the cosmic cycle during which the forces of darkness prevail but the virtuous preserve their integrity," and the controversy over Huang's inten-

The latter two-thirds of Du Fu's poem again shows another sort of pre-Neo-Confucian sensibility in the way a man of the elite looks upon the common people and his relation to them. His view is essentially Mencian in that (1) he "values the people" (*yi min wei gui*) as the fundament of the state and bemoans the tendency of those in privileged positions to forget (and thus abuse) the source of their wherewithal to indulge in luxury and warfare (lines 49–52 and 67–70); and (2) the wrong and right ways for governments to treat the people are seen mainly as matters of imposing heavy, untimely demands on them or maximally letting them be. Mencius's thoughts about benefiting the people had emphasized *relieving* them of onerous obligations and *not interfering* with their pursuit of livelihoods.[31] This strain in Confucian thought seems to have assumed that the will of Heaven to propagate life would naturally be fulfilled through the daily efforts of ordinary people unless hindered by the human perversities that attend powerholding: greed, ostentation, vainglory, et cetera. Hence the emphases in the *Mencius,* and in this poem by Du Fu, on the need to *alleviate*—taxes, the draft, other impositions—and on *leaving* more for the people to live and grow on, rather than concentrating resources wastefully at court or destructively in military campaigns (note lines 93–98).

Emotively, this pre-Neo-Confucian view of relations between *shi^e* and *min* entailed a certain kind of empathy—a reaching of the "heart that cannot bear" (*bu ren xin*) to see the sufferings of others across a class line that was clear and unquestioned (relative to the situation in later centuries). This sort of compassion, however profound, was simple in the sense of being unburdened by abstruse ethico-philosophical theories. It stands in contrast to the greater engagement of government and sociopolitical leaders with the populace, and to the more active approaches to benefiting the people that began to be advocated in Northern Song times.[32] The latter, a new call among Confucians for *positive intervention* in commoners' lives, predictably gave rise to countless debates (at least through late Ming). Central to those debates was whether presumably Confucian-guided policies were violating the dis-

---

tions in writing and titling this work, are discussed in W. T. de Bary's Introduction to *Waiting for the Dawn: A Plan for the Prince—Huang Tsung-hsi's Ming-i-tai-fang lu,* trans. de Bary (New York: Columbia University Press, 1993), 5–8.

31. See Xiao Gongquan, *Zhongguo zhengzhi sixiang shi,* 4th ed. (Taipei: Zhongguo wenhua chuban shiye weiyuan hui, 1965), 1:87–90 (trans. F. W. Mote, *A History of Chinese Political Thought* [Princeton: Princeton University Press, 1979], 1:150–53).

32. Ouyang Xiu's (1007–1072) "Essay on Fundamentals" (*Ben lun*) and Cheng Hao's (1032–85) "Ten Matters Calling for Reform" (*Chen zhi fa shi shi*) come easily to mind. For translations, see W. T. de Bary et al., comps., *Sources of Chinese Tradition* (New York: Columbia University Press, 1965), vol. 1: esp. 388–89, 399–403.

tinction, now less distinct than ever, between promoting the interests of the people and legalistically promoting the interests of the state.

The class line between *shi^e* and *min* also was becoming less distinct, as "new" Confucians spoke increasingly in terms of engagement with the people. Again predictably, the mode and tenor of that engagement became highly controversial in the Neo-Confucian era. Quintessential in those controversies—laden with implications—was the difference in judgment between the so-called Cheng-Zhu and Lu-Wang schools over whether the characters *qin min* in the third phrase of the *Greater Learning* (*Da xue*) should be read *xinmin*, "renew the people," connoting the presentation of inspiring, virtuous models for them to emulate, or *qinmin*, "love the people," connoting intimacy, personal identification, and more direct, involved forms of caring.[33]

It may seem ironic that, in this discussion of Du Fu's attitude toward the common people, the *pre*-Neo-Confucian orientation is characterized as Mencian, since we usually associate the Confucian revival of the late Tang and Northern Song with "the rise of the Mencius."[34] This irony is instructive. Du Fu's Mencian sentiments at the particular time when he conceived the "Song of My Cares" underscore the importance of the An Lushan Rebellion as a catalyst in the change from earlier Tang, when the *Mencius* was looked to merely for practical information on ritual, social, and institutional questions,[35] and later Tang, when the moral-ethical dimensions of that work began to receive emphasis. However, that movement in the sphere of Confucian classical studies, especially during the Northern Song, often had very specific political motivations.[36] It should be distinguished from more diffuse movements in Confucian culture—that is, in people's general outlook on life—to which Du Fu's poem gives memorable voice.

33. For English translations of Zhu Xi's (1130–1200) and Wang Shouren's (1472–1529) respective comments on that particular phrase, see Daniel K. Gardner, *Chu Hsi and the* Ta-hsueh: *Neo-Confucian Reflection on the Confucian Canon* (Cambridge, Mass.: Harvard University Council on East Asian Studies, 1986), 89–90; and Wing-tsit Chan, trans. and comp., *A Source Book in Chinese Philosophy* (Princeton: Princeton University Press, 1963), 660–61. See also Sano Kōji, "Shushi igo ni okeru 'Daigaku' kan no hensen," *Setsurin* (Aichi Kenritsu Daigaku) 34 (Feb. 1986): 54–55; and Sakai Tadao, "Ōgaku no shominsei ni kansuru shakai teki rekishi teki igi," *Ryūkoku shidan* 56–57 (1966): 193–203.

34. Huang Chun-chieh, "The Rise of the *Mencius:* Historical Interpretations of Mencian Morality, ca. A.D. 200–1200," Ph.D. diss. (University of Washington, 1980), esp. chap. 3.

35. See David McMullen, *State and Scholars in T'ang China* (Cambridge: Cambridge University Press, 1988), 81–82, 110–11.

36. See Zhu Weizheng, "Zhongguo jingxue yu Zhongguo wenhua," *Fudan xuebao* (Shehui kexue) (1986, no. 2): 16–27.

THE CRISIS OF WITNESSING IN DU FU'S
"A SONG OF MY THOUGHTS WHEN GOING FROM
THE CAPITAL TO FENGXIAN: FIVE HUNDRED WORDS"
Wai-yee Li

Du Fu tells of his thoughts at his journey's end. As is expected of the *yonghuai* mode, he dwells on the moral and sociopolitical implications of what he witnessed for his self-definition and for the fate of the country. Du Fu recreates the chronology of his experiences: the sense of foreboding from the beginning, indignation at the court's corruption, compassion for the suffering of the people, fear and melancholy as he confronts the hazards of the journey, suspense and expectation as he draws close to home, the final shock of discovering his young son's death upon his return. The sequential and logical progression here is reflected in a narrative of control and resolution: the poet states his aspiration, writes as witness to and judge of the ills of his times, and transmutes personal grief into broad compassion for the people. The idea here of poetry functioning as witness to history is what earns Du Fu the epithet "poet-historian" (*shishi*). However, we have to imagine the poet remembering his journey with the tragic knowledge that he discloses only at the very end of the poem. This final traumatic moment casts uncertain light on his journey and sustains a parallel narrative of skepticism, despair, and loss of control. The tensions between the chronology of witnessing and the chronology of composition, between the poet's self-perception and his understanding of history, define new dimensions for the idea of "poet-historian."

The poet's profession of faith at the beginning of the poem combines self-deprecation and fierce pride, self-doubt and stubborn conviction. Du Fu brackets his declaration with self-observation: he is merely "a commoner of Duling," becoming, contrary to what one may expect (*zhuan*), more and more naïve and obtuse (*zhuo*) as he advances in years; in his folly (*yu*[a]) he secretly (*qie*) aspires to be likened to Ji and Xie (lines 1–4) who feel empathy and compassion for all.[37] The irony here is no more than stating the opposite of

---

37. See *Mencius*, 4B.29: "When Yu thinks of the people drowning in the world, it is as if he himself is drowning. When Ji thinks of the hungry people in the world, it is as if he himself is hungry," cited in *Du Fu shi xuanzhu*, ed. Xiao Difei (Beijing: Renmin wenxue, 1979), 57–58. See also Wang Youzhong's *Du Yi*, quoted in *Du shi xiangzhu*, comp. Qiu Zhao'ao (reprint, Taipei: Wenshizhe chubanshe, 1985), 4.235. Both Ji and Xie are ministers of the sage king Shun. Ji is the ancestor of Zhou, who taught the people agriculture; Xie is the ancestor of Shang, a culture hero who spread civilization and education. Du Fu alludes to Ji and Xie also in "*Fu* on the Sacrifice at the Southern Suburb": "For after the emperor's ascension, everybody considers

what is meant, a function of the gap between the poet's grand vision and the uncomprehending, unsympathetic world. In these first twelve lines potentially negative words such as *zhuo* and *yu*[a] only underline the theme of integrity and great aspirations unrecognized, even as the "great useless thing" (*huoluo*[a], l. 5) in the *Zhuangzi* may prove useful once a new context is defined. Du Fu's lofty vision seems incongruous only because of his humble position.[38] Du Fu is not really apologetic about his immodest and impractical aspiration. He proclaims the steadfastness of his will (*zhi*) that defies hardship, old age and death (lines 6–8). His burning compassion for the suffering of the people may earn him the sneers of his fellow-students, but in response his song only becomes more intense and passionate (lines 9–12).

The tone of the poem becomes more troubled as of line 13. The reality of seeking office causes much greater anguish than the grand vision of becoming Ji and Xie. The poet first considers the choice of disengagement: "I am not without desire for lakes and seas, / there to send off, free and aloof, the days and months" (lines 13–14). The idea of withdrawal from the world has already been suggested previously in the mention of the "great useless thing" (*huoluo*[a]). We recall that in the *Zhuangzi* the great useless gourd may find its proper use when being turned into a boat and put to lakes and rivers. The decorum of the subsequent counterargument for service (lines 15–16; 19–20) does not make it more compelling and convincing: the poet's avowed reluctance to leave the service of a sage-king comparable to Yao and Shun is obviously merely conventional (lines 15–16). Even as the sunflower cannot but turn to the sun, the poet cannot go against his nature and give up the desire to serve (lines 19–20), although he modestly claims his superfluity in an era when there are many talented men in government: "the Halls of State are now fully complete, / Of this structure [of polity] how can one say there is any lack?" (lines 17–18). This assertion about good government is another polite lie, and might have been included to heighten the poet's sense of displacement and confusion with respect to seeking and keeping office. Du Fu then proceeds to consider his inability to choose disen-

---

themselves living the times of the sage kings Tang and Yu. / For forty years, every family considers themselves Ji and Xie" (*Du shi xiangzhu*, 24.1219). For a more critical view of the immodesty of this comparison, see Ke Changzhi's *Yunyu yangqiu*, quoted in *Du shi xiangzhu*, 4.240. For other examples in Du Fu's poetry where he seems to speak in the imperative voice of Ji and Xie, see Su Shi's comment, included in *Tang Song shi juyao*, ed. Gao Buying (Taipei: Hongye shuju, 1987), 51.

38. The irony of this comparison lies in the fact that while "the great useless thing" in *Zhuangzi* can become useful only in the realm of Daoist freedom, where worldly criteria of usefulness are set aside, "the great useless thing" here is still hoping for worldly recognition. The idea of Daoist freedom is considered and rejected in the next section of the poem.

gagement in the context of an extended metaphor. He asks us to consider ants which should look for their own little holes instead of aspiring to become leviathans coursing in the ocean's depths (lines 21–24). Is Du Fu here comparing himself or his contemporaries to the undiscerning ants (the latter judgment may imply the poet's self-representation as the freely roaming leviathans)?[39] The former comparison seems to me more compelling, because otherwise we would have to account for a sudden shift of focus from the poet to his antlike, small-minded contemporaries.

The process of self-definition in this section of the poem (lines 13–32) is much more tortuous: the poet changes his stance every two lines. Each position is defined only to be questioned or demolished. He is ashamed to court favor (line 26); yet he cannot bear to perish in oblivion, "sinking with the dust" (line 28). While he feels the beckoning call of "the lakes and the seas" (line 13), he is nevertheless ashamed in front of the ancient recluses, Chaofu and Xu You, for he cannot change his principles to follow their alternative of withdrawing from the world (lines 29–30). The classic dilemma of choosing between engagement and disengagement (*jintui chuchu*) in the Chinese tradition undergoes here ironic turns, for neither engagement nor disengagement is for the poet a viable choice. His hope for service has been constantly thwarted, a situation which he describes politely, but without real conviction, as the consequence of his superfluity in a government replete with talents (lines 17–18). The minor appointment he finally secured in the fall of 755, shortly before his journey from the capital to Fengxian, was to become quite meaningless with the outbreak of the An Lushan Rebellion a month later. Indeed, the impending war and chaos render both engagement and disengagement impossible. (Although commonly assumed to have been written on the eve of the Rebellion, the poem could also have been written or revised after its outbreak. In other words, the questioning of both service and withdrawal can be based on what Du Fu describes in the rest of the poem, or it can be reinforced by actual knowledge of the cataclysmic events that transpired.) When the poet breaks into song again, it is no longer the passionate song of conviction (line 12) but the plaintive song of extreme sorrow (line 32). The poet's changing self-definitions are thus reflected in two opposite conceptions of his art: as powerful, redemptive voice tantamount to a mode of action; and as release of his own pent-up emotions that carry little tangible consequences for the world.[40]

39. Susan Cherniack summarizes these two views and suggests that Du Fu is deliberately ambiguous. See her Ph.D. dissertation on "Three Great Poems by Tu Fu" (Yale University, 1988), 118–19, 134–35.

40. These different views of his own art are often articulated in close, ironic juxtaposition. See, for example, "This many-colored brush once made a difference in the cosmic order, / Now

One-third of the way into the poem, Du Fu turns to the actual journey. The long middle section devoted to the journey (lines 33–80) alternates between two modes of seeing or imagining, which are in turn associated with the modulations of self-perception in the first third of the poem. First, Du Fu writes with the moral authority of a witness as he juxtaposes the splendor and decadence of the court with the misery and deprivation of the common people. "Just before daybreak I passed Mount Li, / The imperial couch rests among its towering peaks" (lines 39–40). Du Fu could not have seen the "imperial couch," but the mere fact of passing by Mount Li gives his ruminations urgency.[41] Even as he moves from perception to imagination, his imagination moves from the general to the particular, from outside to inside. What he might have seen in his journey, "Ominous warclouds filling the cold sky, / Cliffs and valleys slippery from tramping feet" (lines 41–42), leads him to imagine dense vapors arising from Jasper Pool and imperial guards with their halberds touching each other (lines 43–44), and emperors and ministers enjoying hot baths in Huaqing Palace (lines 45–48). The dense vapors (line 43) suggest enveloping enclosure, and music reaching high heavens (line 46) evokes reckless abandon. The world inside the palace is thus defined by a false sense of self-containment and an ungrounded confidence of power, both are implicitly challenged and undermined by the encroaching "ominous warclouds" (line 41).

The description of the Mount Li palaces is immediately followed by the famous lines from the middle of the poem, which use the plight of the commoner producing cloth and silk for taxes to indict the corrupt forces at court (lines 49–52). This is the moral conclusion the poet draws from his account of imperial and aristocratic pleasures in the Mt. Li palaces. (The references to "long hat-strings" and "short hempen coat" [lines 47–48] as kenning for privileged inmates of the palace and humbly dressed commoners[42] are metonymically linked to "Cloth and silk distributed at the vermilion court, /

---

my white head sinks in sorrow as I chant my song and gaze afar" (last two lines of the eighth poem in "Autumn Meditations: Eight Poems" [Qiuxing bashou], *Du shi xiangzhu*, 17.873–74); "Is it true then that my writings have so stirred those within the four seas, / That without reason carriage and horse should be troubled to stop by the riverside?" ("A Guest Arrived," [Bin zhi], *Du shi xiangzhu*, 9.480); "Aware only that my loud song moves gods and spirits, / How would I know about death by starvation and bodies filling ditches and valleys?" ("Drunken Song" [Zuishi ge], *Du shi xiangzhu*, 3.187).

41. Susan Cherniack discusses Du Fu's route from Changan to Fengxian in "Three Great Poems by Tu Fu," 151–53. According to the hypothetical route she reconstructs, Du Fu would have passed Mount Li on the right at a distance of nine miles (152).

42. In "Drunken Song," Du Fu refers to himself as "The uncouth guest from Duling, even more scorned by others, / Wears a short and tight hempen coat, his hair silken white" (*Du shi xiangzhu*, 3.187).

Come from the homes of poor humble women" [lines 49–50].) The same shift from splendor to misery is repeated in the description of the luxuries enjoyed by the Yang clan (lines 59–67), which is starkly juxtaposed with "by the wayside, the frozen dead" (line 68). This line, which is the second half of a couplet (the first half reads: "Within the crimson gates, the stench of wine and meat" [line 67]), has all the visual force of a scene that Du Fu might well have encountered on his journey. The jarring juxtaposition of abundance and deprivation robs the poet of words (lines 69–70), but actually this whole section (lines 39–70) is marked by clarity of purpose and confidence of enunciation. The moral equation is so clearly defined that, even as the poet balances and contrasts the oppressors and the oppressed, he finds room to defend the emperor and blames the injustices he is describing on evil ministers (lines 53–58). This, then, is the first kind of seeing and imagining: the scenes described here have clear contours, they illustrate the poet's moral purpose, and they are premised on the poet's moral authority as one who is witness to history and who aspires to be likened to Ji and Xie in his broad compassion.

There is a second kind of seeing related to the more immediate experience of the journey, the account of the poet's bewilderment and the hardships he suffers which brackets the moral vision developed between lines 39 to 70. He is travelling in the season of decay and melancholy, high winds, dark heavens, uncertain light, and bitter cold (lines 33–38). Images of doom and destruction assume mythic, apocalyptic proportions: Chunks of ice tumbling from extreme height, apparently from Hongtong Mountain, threaten to knock against the pillar of heaven and bring about, once again, the deluge (lines 73–76). Passage is difficult, the roads are being changed (line 72), the bridges are precariously supported and groaning (lines 77–78), the river is so broad that it may not be crossed (line 80). The poet is no longer judging and pondering, the ominous images here are not contained by moral schemes: instead they seem to herald a general collapse and disintegration. We have here an echo of the powerless Du Fu, who compares himself to ants whose aspiration to be whales seems all too preposterous, whose engagement has little tangible consequence, and whose song merely releases pent-up feelings.

The poet goes home, but the dialectic of the two self-images is not over. Du Fu longs to share the hunger and thirst of his family (line 84)—we recall that Ji feels hungry when there are hungry people in the world—and returns to finds his infant son dead from starvation. Is the grand claim of universal empathy and compassion thereby undermined? Have bitterness and irony finally overcome the sense of moral purpose? For a moment this seems to be the case, as Du Fu feels the shame of a father who fails to feed his son (lines 89–90). We are returned to the image of the frustrated poet mocking his own grand aspirations. However, the other Du Fu reasserts himself: he links his personal grief to universal grief, to the misery of those worse off than himself (lines 93–98). The concluding image is a comparison of the "reasons for sorrow" (*youduan*) with the magnitude of Zhongnan Mountain, so limitless that it cannot be grasped (line 100). This is an image of loss of control, but its raison d'être is the misery of the people with which he empathizes better because of personal anguish. The poet submerges his own sorrow in the suffering of the multitude: this is his way of mediating between two self-images and reconciling grand vision with personal helplessness.

PERSPECTIVE ON READINGS OF DU FU, *ZI JING FU FENGXIAN YONG HUAI WU BAI ZI*

Stephen Owen

There is a wonderful complementary symmetry in the readings of Knechtges, the scholar of pre-Tang literature, and Struve, the intellectual historian of the Ming and Qing. Knechtges finds two earlier genres, the *yonghuai* and the travel narrative; Struve finds "two juxtaposed meditations," one on the question of service versus withdrawal and the other on "relations between the sociopolitically privileged and the underprivileged." The intellectual historian sees the issue of service and withdrawal, which is to undergo an important transformation in the next few centuries; the literary scholar sees a specialized discourse, the *yonghuai* genre, which shapes the formulation of the issue of service and withdrawal through the mediation of past texts and gives the poet a unique means to address it in his own case. Struve sees a pre-Neo-Confucian attitude toward the proper role of government vis-à-vis the people; Knechtges finds established discursive occasions when the question might arise. Knechtges reads from Du Fu back to earlier texts that inform the poem and help us understand the resonance of certain utterances; Struve's Du Fu looks forward, reading Du Fu's commitments in relation to things to come. This variance of disposition can even be seen on the structural level of reading: Knechtges's Du Fu builds forward to the death of his child, while Struve's Du Fu tells his story already framed by the knowledge of what was to come.

Struve reads backward in a fascinating way, beginning with the premise of Du Fu's "grief and remorse at his son's death," which leads to the middle section of "condemnation and lament for the times," but prefaced with the strange meditation of the first third to avoid lapsing into self-righteousness in his attack on the age. Wai-yee Li also stresses the retrospective nature of the poem, that the representation is shaped by knowledge of its concluding tragedy; but she offers a very persuasive account of the order of the poem as a "narrative of resolution and control," in which the poet passes through inner conflicts, followed by experience as a witness of history, to a final stance of certainty from which he can offer judgment as the "poet-historian." In contrast to Struve's isolation of key issues and Knechtges's linear reading, Li's is an integrative reading, built around oppositions between witnessing and composition, private experience and a public voice that speaks for the social whole. Moreover, she sees this process as a movement from the former to the latter (at the close of her reading she calls this mediation between the two, but Du Fu is quite explicit about the subordination of the private to the public, and it seems that the private act of witnessing, compelling because of its closeness and particularity, is the means to move to the public).

One area that invites reflection is how the three readers handle the long passage of apparently contradictory positions and assertions that make up the beginning of the poem. Struve looks through the morass and singles out the question of service and withdrawal, leaving it as a question. Knechtges, the committed linear reader, articulates the apparent claim of the text and then negates it, either revealing the possibility of irony or a subsequent qualification ("Commentators have long argued that Du Fu may not be as self-effacing here as he claims"; "Du Fu may not be as immodest as he seems . . . "; "However, Du Fu's view of the court is not as favorable as it first seems"). Li begins her discussion of the passage by pointing out that it is comprised of contradictory impulses and traces the countermoves and ironies. There is, however, one point of contradiction at which she balks: she consistently describes passages in which Du Fu speaks well of court officers and the emperor as mere politeness, statements "without real conviction." This raises interesting questions about "meaning what one says" and conventional declarations of political faith. One possibility is that Du Fu does indeed mean what he says, that he cannot, for profound ideological reasons, hold the emperor responsible, and that he does not blame much of the civil bureaucracy— only the Yangs. An interesting variation on this would question the relation between polite, conventional utterance (but not "merely polite"), with historical and ideological underpinnings, and conviction. Often in such circumstances people "mean what they say" precisely because they need not question the utterance and measure it against their convictions. An alternative possibility is that this is sarcasm, radically negative irony. But each of these possibilities is more interesting than "mere politeness."

Another interesting question is when the poem was composed. Knechtges cites the *Du Gongbu ji* that the poem was composed in the eleventh month of Tianbao 14 (Dec. 755–Jan. 756), right before the outbreak of the An Lushan Rebellion. Such dating is based on the uncritical assumption that poems were composed immediately after the events in them transpired. Waiyee Li acknowledges that the poem might well have been composed or revised later, after the Rebellion broke out. Here is a fine issue: composed before the Rebellion, it gives the dark temper of the times, its foreboding;

composed later, the poem's stark immediacy is actually an interpretation based on knowledge of the consequences.

Ultimately Struve's is the most immediate and psychological reading of the poem, and it is the terms of Du Fu's reflection that stand out in their historical context. Knechtges offers the most purely literary reading, in which experience is represented through the mediation of past texts (and as a result Knechtges's reading more easily permits the possibility that Wai-yee Li raises, that the work might have actually been composed or radically revised well after the events represented). Wai-yee Li's reading does not quite combine these two, very distinct positions; but her reading offers, within representation, a dramatization of the movement from experience to representation.

SIX

Yingying zhuan
Yuan Zhen, "Biography of Yingying"

TRANSLATION OF YUAN ZHEN (779–831), "YING-YING'S STORY"

Stephen Owen

In the Zhen-yuan Reign (785–804) there was a certain man named Zhang, of a gentle nature and handsome appearance. He held steadfastly to his personal principles and refused to become involved in anything improper. Sometimes a group of friends would go off to a party and behave riotously. While the others tried to outdo one another in wanton and unbridled recklessness, Zhang would remain utterly composed, and they could never get him to act in an intemperate manner. At this time he was twenty-three and had never been intimate with a woman. When a close friend questioned him about this, Zhang excused himself, saying, "The famous lecher of antiquity, Deng Tu-zi, was not a man of passionate desire; his were the actions of a brute. I am someone who is truly capable of passionate desire, but simply have not encountered it. How can I say this? Things of the most bewitching beauty never fail to leave a lasting impression on my heart, and this tells me that I am not one of those free of passion." And the one who had questioned him acknowledged this in him.

Not long afterward, Zhang visited Pu-zhou. About a dozen leagues east of the city there was a residence for monks known as the Temple of Universal Salvation, where Zhang took up lodgings. It happened that a widow, one Madam Cui, was on her way to Chang-an; and since her journey took her through Pu-zhou, she too stopped over at this temple. Madam Cui had been born a Zheng and Zhang's mother had also been a Zheng. When they traced the family connection, it turned out that she was his maternal aunt at several removes.

That year Hun Zhen, the Military Governor, passed away in Pu-zhou, and Ding Wen-ya, the court officer left in charge, was not liked by the troops. After the funeral, they rioted and pillaged widely in Pu-zhou. Madam Cui had a great wealth of household goods as well as many servants. The hostel was frantic with alarm, and they did not know where to turn for help. Zhang had earlier developed friendly relations with the circle around the commandant of Pu-zhou, and he asked for guards to protect Madam Cui. As a result, no harm came to her. About a dozen days later, the Investigator Du Que arrived with an imperial commission to take charge of the troops, and he issued commands to the army, after which the disturbance ceased.

Madam Cui was exceedingly grateful for Zhang's kindness, so she had a feast prepared in his honor. As they dined in the central hall, she said to Zhang, "Your widowed aunt lives on, carrying her young children with her. I have had the misfortune of a close call with a major outbreak of violence among the troops, and I truly could not have protected these children's lives. Thus it is as if my young son and daughter owe their lives to you. What you have done for us cannot be compared to an ordinary kindness. I would now insist that they greet you with all the courtesies due to an elder brother, in the hope that this might be a way to repay your kindness." Then she gave this order to her son. His name was Huang-lang, a gentle and handsome boy somewhat over ten years old. Next she gave the order to her daughter: "Come out and pay your respects to your elder brother; you are alive because of him." A long time passed, and then the girl declined on the excuse that she wasn't feeling well. Madam Cui said angrily, "Mr. Zhang protected your life. Otherwise you would have been taken captive. How can you still keep such a wary distance from him!" After another long wait, the daughter came in. She wore everyday clothes and had a disheveled appearance, without having dressed up specially for the occasion. Tresses from the coils of her hair hung down to her eyebrows and her two cheeks were suffused with rosy color. Her complexion was rare and alluring, with a glow that stirred a man. Zhang was startled as she paid him the proper courtesies. Then she sat down beside her mother. Since her mother had forced her to meet Zhang, she stared fixedly away in intense resentment, as if she couldn't bear it. When he asked her age, Madam Cui said, "From September 784, the first year of the emperor's reign, until the present year, 800, makes her seventeen years old." Zhang tried to draw her into conversation, but she wouldn't answer him.

Finally the party ended. Zhang was, of course, infatuated with her, and he wanted to express his feelings but had no way. The Cuis had a maidservant named Hong-niang. Zhang greeted her courteously a number of times and then seized an opportunity to tell her what he felt. The maid was scandalized and fled in embarrassment, at which Zhang regretted what he had said. When the maid came the next day, Zhang was abashed and apologized, saying nothing more about what he wanted. But then the maid said to Zhang, "What you said is something you should not have dared to say and something you should not dare allow to get out. However, you know the kinship ties of the Cuis in some detail. Given the gratitude Madam Cui feels toward you, why don't you ask for her hand in marriage?"

Zhang replied, "Ever since I was a child I have by nature avoided unseemly associations. When I have been around women, I would never even give them suggestive glances. I never would have thought that a time would come when I found myself so overwhelmed by desire. The other day at the party, I could scarcely control myself. For the past few days I walk without knowing where I am going and eat without thinking of whether I am full or not. I'm afraid I won't last another day. If I had to employ a matchmaker to ask for her hand [in] marriage, with the sending of betrothal tokens and formal inquiries about names, it would be another three months, and I would be a fish so long out of the water that you would have to look for me in a dried fish store. What do you think I should do?" The maid replied, "Miss Cui is virtuous and guards herself scrupulously. Even someone she held in the highest regard could not lead her into misconduct by improper words; plans laid by lesser folk will be even harder to carry through. She does, however, like to compose poems and is always mulling over passages, spending a long time on pieces of wronged love and admiration. You should try to seduce her by composing poems that express your love indirectly. Otherwise there will be no way."

Zhang was overjoyed and immediately composed two "Spring Verses" to give to her. That evening Hong-niang came again and handed over a piece of colored notepaper to Zhang, saying, "Miss Cui has instructed me to give you this." The piece was entitled "The Bright Moon of the Fifteenth." It went:

> I await the moon on the western porch,
> my door half ajar, facing the breeze.
> Flower shadows stir, brushing the wall—
> I wonder if this is my lover coming.

Zhang understood the subtle message implied. That night was April 14. There was an apricot tree on the eastern side of her apartments, and by climbing it, he could get into her quarters. On the following evening, the fifteenth, when the moon was full, Zhang climbed the tree and got into her quarters. When he reached the western porch, the door was indeed half ajar. Hong-niang was lying there asleep in her bed, and Zhang roused her. Hong-niang was startled: "How did you get in here?" Zhang lied to her, "Ying-ying's note summoned me. Now go tell her that I'm here." Soon afterward Hong-niang returned, saying over and over again, "She's here! She's here!" Zhang was overjoyed and surprised, certain that he would succeed in this enterprise.

But when Ying-ying did arrive, she was in proper attire with a stern expression on her face. She proceeded to take Zhang to task item by item: "By your kindness you saved our family, and that was indeed generous. For this reason my sweet mother entrusted you with the care of her young son and daughter. But how could you use this wicked maid to deliver such wanton verses to me? I first understood your saving us from molestation as virtue, but now you have taken advantage of that to make your own demands. How much difference is there between one form of molestation and the other? I had truly wanted to simply ignore your verses, but it would not have been right to condone such lecherousness in a person. I would have revealed them to my mother, but it would have been unlucky to so turn one's back on a person's kindness. I was going to have my maid give you a message, but I was afraid she would not correctly convey how I truly feel. Then I planned to use a short letter to set this out before you, but I was afraid you would take it ill. So I used those frivolous and coy verses to make you come here. Can you avoid feeling shame at such improper actions? I want most of all that you conduct yourself properly and not sink to the point where you molest people!" When she finished her speech, she whirled about and went off. Zhang stood there in a daze for a long time. Then he went back out the way he had come in, by that point having lost all hope.

A few nights later, Zhang was sleeping alone by the balcony when all of a sudden someone woke him up. He rose in a flash, startled, and found that it was Hong-niang, who had come carrying bedding and a pillow. She patted Zhang, saying, "She's here! She's here! What are you doing sleeping!" Then she put the pillow and bedding beside his and left. Zhang rubbed his eyes and sat up straight for a long time, wondering whether he might not still be dreaming. Nevertheless, he assumed a respectful manner and waited for her. In a little while Hong-niang reappeared, helping Ying-ying along. When she came in, she was charming in her shyness and melting with desire, not strong enough even to move her limbs. There was no more of the prim severity she had shown previously. The evening was the eighteenth of the month, and the crystalline rays of the moon slanting past his chamber cast a pale glow over half the bed. Zhang's head was spinning, and he wondered if she might not be one of those goddesses or fairy princesses, for he could not believe that she came from this mortal world. After a while the temple bell rang and day was about to break. Hong-niang urged her to leave, but Ying-ying wept sweetly and clung to him until Hong-niang again helped her away. She had not said a word the entire night.

Zhang got up as the daylight first brought colors to the scene, and he wondered to himself, "Could that have been a dream?" In the light there was nothing left but the sight of some make-up on his arm, her scent on his clothes, and the sparkles of her teardrops still glistening on the bedding. A dozen or so days later it seemed so remote that he was no longer sure. Zhang was composing a poem called "Meeting the Holy One" in sixty lines. He had not quite finished when Hong-niang happened to come by. He then handed it to her to present to Ying-ying.

From that point on, she allowed him to come to her. He would go out secretly at dawn and enter secretly in the evening. For almost a month they shared happiness in what had earlier been referred to as the "western porch." Zhang constantly asked about how Madame Zheng felt, and she would say, "I can't do anything about it." And she wanted him to proceed to regularize the relationship. Not long afterward Zhang was to go off to Chang-an, and before he went he consoled her by telling her of his love. Ying-ying seemed to raise no complaints, but the sad expression of reproach on her face was very moving. Two evenings before he was to travel, she refused to see him again.

Zhang subsequently went west to Chang-an. After several months he again visited Pu-zhou, and this time his meetings with Ying-ying lasted a series of months. Ying-ying was quite skilled at letterwriting and a fine stylist. He repeatedly asked to see things she had written, but she would never show him anything. Even when Zhang repeatedly tried to prompt her by giving her things he himself had written, he still hardly ever got to look over anything of hers. In general, whenever Ying-ying did show something to someone else, it was always the height of grace and polish; but she appeared unaware of it. Her speech was intelligent and well reasoned, yet she seldom wrote answering pieces in response to what he sent her. Although she treated Zhang with the greatest kindness, she still never picked up his verses in a poetic exchange. There were times when her melancholy voluptuousness took on a remoteness and abstraction, yet she continually seemed not to recognize this. At such times, expressions of either joy or misery seldom showed on her face. On another occasion she was alone at night playing the harp, a melancholy and despairing melody. Zhang listened to her surreptitiously, for had he asked her to play, she would not have played any more. With this Zhang became even more infatuated with her.

Soon afterward Zhang had to again go west to Chang-an, to be there in time for the literary examination. This time, on the evening before he was to leave, he said nothing of his feelings, but instead sighed sadly by Ying-ying's side. Ying-ying had already guessed that this was to be farewell. With a dignified expression and a calm voice, she said gently to Zhang, "It is quite proper that when a man seduces a woman, he finally abandons her. I don't dare protest. It was inevitable that having seduced me, you would end it— all this is by your grace. And with this, our lifelong vows are indeed ended. Why be deeply troubled by this journey? Nevertheless, you have become unhappy, and there is no way I can ease your heart. You have always claimed that I am good at playing the harp, but I have always been so shy that I couldn't bring myself to play for you. Now that you are going to leave, I will fulfill this heartfelt wish of yours." Thereupon she brushed her fingers over the harp, playing the prelude to "Coats of Feathers, Rainbow Skirts." But after only a few notes, the sad notes became so unsettled by bitter pain that the melody could no longer be recognized. All present were sobbing, and Ying-ying abruptly stopped and threw down the harp, tears streaming down her face. She hurried back to her mother's house and did not come back.

The next morning at dawn, Zhang set out. The following year, not having been successful in the literary competition, Zhang stayed in the capital. He then sent a letter to Ying-ying to set her mind to rest. The lines Ying-ying sent in reply are roughly recorded here:

> I received what you sent, asking after me. The comforting love you show is all too deep. In the feelings between man and woman, joys and sorrows mingled. You were also kind to send the box of flower cutouts and the five-inch stick of lip rouge—ornaments that will make my hair resplendent and my lips shine. But though I receive such exceptional fondness from you, for whom will I now make myself beautiful? Catching sight of these things increases my cares, and nothing but sad sighs well within me. From your letter I am given to understand that you are occupied by the pursuit of your studies in the capital. The path to progress in studies does indeed depend on not being disturbed. Yet I feel some resentment that I, a person of so small account, have been left behind forever in a far place. Such is fate. What more is there to say?
>
> Since last autumn I have been in a daze as though I did not know where I was. In the chatter of merry gatherings I sometimes make myself laugh and join in the conversation, but when I am alone in the still of night, tears never fail to fall. And when I come to dream, my thoughts usually are of the misery of separation, which stirs me until I am choked with sobbing. When we are twined together, absorbed in our passion, for a brief while it is as it once used to be; but then, before our secret encounter comes to its culmination, the soul is startled awake and finds itself sundered from you. Although half of the covers seem warm, yet my thoughts are on someone far, far away.
>
> Just yesterday you said goodbye, and now in but an instant the old year has been left behind. Chang-an is a place of many amusements, which can catch a man's fancy and draw his feelings. How fortunate I am that you have not forgotten me, negligible and secluded as I am, and that you were not too weary of me to let me occupy your thoughts for at least a moment. My humble intentions have no means to repay this. But when it comes to my vow to love you forever, that is steadfast and unwavering.
>
> Long ago, connected to you as a cousin, I happened to be together with you at a banquet. Having inveigled my maidservant, you consequently expressed your private feelings. Young people are unable to maintain a firmness of heart. You, sir, stirred me as Si-ma Xiang-ru stirred Zhuo Wen-

jun, by playing the harp. Yet I did not resist, as did Xie Kun's neighbor by throwing her shuttle when he approached her. When I brought my bedding to your side, your love and honor were deep. In the folly of my passion I thought that I would remain in your care forever. How could I have foreseen that, "once having seen my lord," it would be impossible to plight our troth? Since I suffer the shame of having offered myself to you, I may no longer serve you openly as a wife. This will be a source of bitter regret that will last until my dying day. I repress my sighs, for what more can be said? If by chance in the goodness of your heart you would condescend to fulfill my secret hope, then even if it were on the day of my death, it would be for me like being reborn. But, perchance, the successful scholar holds love to be but of little account and sets it aside as a lesser thing in order to pursue things of greater importance, considering his previous mating to have been a vile action, his having taken enforced vows as something one may well betray. If this be so, then my form will melt away and my bones will dissolve. Yet my glowing faith will not perish. My petals, borne by the wind and trailing in the dew, will still entrust themselves to the pure dust beneath your feet. Of my sincerity unto death, what words can say is all said here. I sob over this paper and cannot fully express my love. Please, please take care of yourself.

This jade ring is a thing that I had about me since I was an infant. I send it to you to wear among the ornaments that hang at your waist. From the jade is to be drawn the lesson of what is firm and lustrous, thus unsullied. From the ring is to be drawn the lesson of what continues on forever, never breaking. Also I send a single strand of tangled silken floss and a tea grinder of speckled bamboo. These several things are not valuable in themselves. My message is that I would have you, sir, be as pure as the jade, that my own poor aspirations are as unbroken as the ring, that my tearstains are on the bamboo, and that my melancholy sentiments are like this twisting and tangled thread. Through these things I convey what I feel, and will love you always. The heart is close, though our bodies are far. There is no time set for us to meet. Yet when secret ardor accumulates, spirits can join even across a thousand leagues. Please take care of yourself. The spring breeze is often sharp, and it would be a good idea to force yourself to eat more. Be careful of what you say and guard yourself. And do not long for me too intensely.

Zhang showed her letter to his friends, and as a result many people at the time heard of the affair. One good friend, Yang Ju-yuan, was fond of composing verses and wrote a quatrain entitled "Miss Cui":

Pure luster of this young Pan Yue—

    even the jade cannot compare;
sweet clover grows in courtyard

    as snows first melt away.
The amorous young talent

is filled with spring desires—
poor Miss Xiao, her broken heart

in a letter of just one page.

I, Yuan Zhen of He-nan, completed Zhang's "Meeting the Holy One" in sixty lines.

Pale moonlight breaks in above curtains,
fireflies flash through the sapphire air.
The distant skies begin to grow dim,
and below, trees have grown leafy and full.
Past the yard's bamboo come notes of dragon flutes,
the well-side beech is brushed by phoenix song.

Her filmy gauze hangs like a thin haze,
soft breezes resound with her waist-hung rings.
Crimson standards follow the Goddess of the West,
the heart of clouds proffers the Lad of Jade.
As night's hours deepen, people grow still,
or meeting at dawn in the drizzling rain.
Pearl-glow lights up her patterned shoes,
blooms' brilliance hidden by embroidered dragon.
Jade hairpin, its colored phoenix in motion,
gauze cape that covers red rainbows.
He says that from this Jasper Flower Beach
he must go to dawn court at Green Jade Palace.

By his roaming north of the city of Luo
he chanced on Song Yu's eastern neighbor.
When he flirted, at first she gently refused,
but in secret soft passions already conveyed.
From her lowered coils the tresses' shadows stirred,
her circling steps obscured in jade white dust.
Face turned, glances flowed like flowers and snow,
she mounted the bed, bunched satins borne in arms.
Mated ducks, their necks twined in dance,
kingfishers encaged in passion's embrace.
Her black brows knit in modesty,
her carmine lips, warming, grew softer.
Breath pure as the fragrance of orchids,
her skin glossy, her marble flesh full.
Worn out, too tired to move her wrist,
so charming, she loved to curl up.
Her sweat flowed in beads, drop by drop,
her tangled tresses thick and black.

No sooner made glad by this millennial meeting,
she suddenly heard night's hours end.

At that moment resentful, she lingered on,
clinging with passion, desire unspent.
A sad expression on languid cheeks,
in sweet lines she vowed the depths of love.
Her ring-gift revealed a union fated,
a love-knot left showed hearts were the same.
Cheeks' powder in tears flowed on night's mirror,
lamp's last flickering, insects far in the dark.
As the sparkling rays still dwindled away,
the sun at dawn grew gradually bright.

She rode her cygnet back to the Luo;
he played his pipes as he climbed Mount Song.
Her musk still imbued the scent of his clothes,
his pillow oily, still flecked with her rouge.

Thick grow the grasses beside the pool,
wind-tossed, the tumbleweed longs for the isle.
Her pale harp rings with the crane's lament,
she looks toward the stars for the swan's return.

The sea is so vast, truly hard to cross;
and the sky is high, not easy to reach.
Goddess moving in cloud, nowhere now to be found;
and Xiao-shi is there in his high chamber.

Every one of Zhang's friends who heard of the affair was stirred to amazement. Nevertheless, Zhang had already made up his mind. I was on particularly good terms with Zhang and asked him to explain. Zhang then said, "All such creatures ordained by Heaven to possess bewitching beauty will inevitably cast a curse on others if they don't do the same to themselves. Had Cui Ying-ying made a match with someone of wealth and power, she would have taken advantage of those charms that win favor from a man, and if she were not the clouds and the rain of sexual pleasure, then she would have been a serpent or a fierce dragon—I do not know what she would have transformed into. Long ago King Shou-xin of Yin and King You of Zhou controlled domains that mustered a million chariots, and their power was very great. Nevertheless, in both cases a woman destroyed them. Their hosts were scattered, they themselves were slain, and even today their ignominy has made them laughingstocks for all the world. My own virtue is inadequate to triumph over such cursed wickedness, and for this reason I hardened my heart against her." At the time all those present were deeply moved.

Somewhat more than a year later, Ying-ying married another, and Zhang too took a wife. He happened to pass through the place where she was living and asked her husband to speak to her, wanting to see her as a maternal cousin. Her husband did speak to her, but Ying-ying refused to come out.

The fact of Zhang's pain at such a rebuff showed on his face. Ying-ying found out about this and secretly composed a piece whose verses went:

> Ever since I have wasted to gauntness
>
> > and the glow of my face has gone,
> I toss and turn thousands of times,
>
> > too weary to get out of bed.
> Not because of him at my side
>
> > that I am ashamed to rise—
> grown haggard on your account, I'd be
>
> > ashamed in front of you.

And she never did see him. A few days later, Zhang was ready to go and she composed another poem to say a final farewell.

> Rejected, what more can be said?—
> yet you were my love back then.
> Take what you felt in times gone by
> and love well the person before your eyes.

From that point on, he knew nothing further of her.

People at the time generally accepted that Zhang was someone who knew how to amend his errors. At parties, I have often brought up this notion. One would have those who know not do such things, but those that have done such things should not become carried away by them.

In a November in the Zhen-yuan Reign, my good friend Li Shen was staying over with me in the Jing-an Quarter. Our conversations touched on this affair, and Li Shen made particular comment on how remarkable it was. He consequently composed "Ying-ying's Song" to make it more widely known. Cui's childhood name was Ying-ying, and he used this in the title.

THE STORY OF YINGYING

Pauline Yu

Yingying zhuan tells us the story of young Zhang, about whom opinions among contemporary readers are likely to vary widely. I have taught this *chuanqi* several times in courses on Chinese literature in translation and have always found it interesting to see how students respond to the narrative. Discussions tend to center on a core group of questions: why does Zhang do what he does; why does Yingying do what she does; why is this called the story of Yingying if it is told from Zhang's perspective; is Zhang's behavior sensible; what does the narrator think of Zhang; and what should we think of him.

While there are occasionally some demurrers, by and large the view of the women in the class will be both predictable and prevailing, and Zhang will be judged as a hypocritical and self-interested cad. Doubts will linger, however, concerning the attitude of the narrator at the end and on the degree of irony—if any at all—in the apparently positive judgment on the part of his cronies on the success with which Zhang was able to correct his mistakes.

Students rarely find the possible autobiographical dimension of the story of any great interest. Whether or not Yuan Zhen was writing about events of his own experience, the awkwardness and embarrassment of which might have led to the peculiarities and lapses in the account, does not seem to them to be a question that offers much explanatory power, although it has of course consumed the attention of critics for centuries. And so we set that issue aside, as an obsession characteristic of certain interpretive traditions.

What inevitably becomes central, then, is the question of motivation. We want to read the characters as behaving in ways that make sense by the terms of human behavior that would be familiar, if not to us, then—to the extent we can know or imagine it—in the context of mid-Tang China. We read the story mimetically. And why not? There are all sorts of markers that steer us in that direction: the reign period mentioned at the very beginning of the piece, the details of event and place, the specific names of figures surrounding the narrative itself. And there are ingrained habits of reading fictional narrative. Moreover, the issues of sexual inexperience, attraction, entrancement, engagement, and abandonment are all familiar to us, as are the social and cultural conventions within which they are situated.

We can then explain the story, possibly, as a movement from order, sustained by ritual/propriety (*li*), whose imminent threat by the charms of the bewitching female (*wu zhi youzhe*) is signaled at the very beginning. Through the consequent infatuation or delusion (*huo*) that occurs, disorder (*luan*— a word that appears close to a dozen times in the text) prevails, until separation and self-interest manage to restore order and return characters to their proper social roles. Nonetheless, certain actions remain difficult to explain. If Zhang, for example, was such a proper gentleman (*fei li bu ko ru*), then why does he refuse to do the right thing with respect to Yingying? If Yingying understands so well the proper separation of the sexes, then why does she show up at his bedside with pillow and coverlet in hand? Responses to such concerns will typically refer to cultural conventions about alluring, dangerously changeable, and kingdom-toppling women or more universal assumptions about the sexual drives and mores of young adults. We also note that Yingying virtually never utters a word, although a letter from her occupies a disproportionate amount of space in the narrative as a whole. Zhang, on the other hand, doesn't seem to write very much (his first poem gets the job done, to be sure, but is utterly conventional, and his second poetic composition has to be brought to completion by his friend Yuan Zhen), whereas he can't seem to stop talking, spilling details of his affairs indiscreetly and sharing Yingying's letter with his companions in the capital (who, for their part, demonstrate an appalling lack of judgment in applauding Zhang for his ability to mend the faults of his past). This leads us to wonder, finally, whether the author might be intending to induce us as readers to pass critical judgment at once on the protagonist, his narrator, and his audience.

We can spend a lot of time in this way on *Yingying zhuan:* there is enough in the story that seems recognizable, appealing, and poignant to engage this sort of attention, and enough that seems perplexing to elicit discussion. But such an approach is never adequately satisfying, and I think it has to do with the problems created by our impulses to read a story like Yingying's as in some way mimetic of human behavior and/or as a document of Chinese culture. Whether it is read as critical or accepting of those norms is ultimately irrelevant.

As a narrative, *Yingying zhuan* is alternately fat and thin: there just isn't enough to hang onto in the places where you would like to find it. In this context it is important to recall that even though it deviates in some respects from some of the more familiar types of *chuanqi*, it retains enough of the genre's conventions to remind us of its literary type, most notably in the rhetorical display of the letter and poems and recourse to the coincidental and the supernatural. Virtuosity, however fragmentary, prevails over verisimilitude. *Yingying* is, indeed, a consummate writerly text, one that seems to be talking self-referentially as much about what it is doing as text as about what it as text contains.

Quite apart from what to me are the inadequacies of mimetic, psychological, or sociocultural readings, the following aspects of *Yingying zhuan* are worth noting. The first is the sheer quantity of the text that is itself other texts—letter, poems, and the like. The second is the degree of agency ascribed to these texts, each of which, quite typically, is further laden with layers of other texts; the poems and letter initiate, continue, or bring closure to the relationship between Zhang and Yingying. Not only are the text's texts performative, moreover, but they are performed, read aloud to appreciative audiences within and outside the text itself. Such acts of performance cannot but call attention to the fact that their medium itself is a site of performance.

Yingying zhuan engages us in a consideration of what writing can do, then, and it also addresses self-consciously the special powers of narrative. It has been argued that fiction in China was recognized as dangerous because it violated Confucian norms, but I think this misses a more important point. *Any* telling of a story was inherently destabilizing because—in its very telling—it could put into question the givenness of norms, behavior, and all assumptions about human action. By opening the door onto discursive variations on the immanence of things as they existed, narrative enabled consideration of the possible discursiveness of what would otherwise be taken for granted (such as social norms). In other words, what made fiction both so alluring and so threatening was not that it might undermine specific sets of codes, but that it called attention to their very constructedness.

What is particularly interesting about *Yingying zhuan* in this context is the way in which its consideration of ritual propriety, entrancement, delusion, and disorder in the realm of sexual relations (mentioned above) speaks with equal cogency to this foregrounding of the agency of the text as text. Just as the characters move from order to its disruption and final restoration, so the text as fictional narrative makes us acutely aware of its very textuality— its manipulation of words whose allure and danger lie precisely in their ability to put into question the givenness of things as we take them to be. In this view it does not matter, finally, if behavioral motivations appear obscure or gaps remain unexplained in the narrative, for the very failure of the text to approach adequacy of explanation brings to the fore the arbitrariness of what it is doing. And it is this very arbitrariness of writing that is destabilizing (*luan*); order can triumph, therefore, only when the story finds its name and literally comes to an end.

MIXTURE OF GENRES AND MOTIVES FOR FICTION IN "YINGYING'S STORY"

Wai-yee Li

For the modern reader the most intriguing part of "Yingying's Story" is probably Zhang's explanation of why he abandons Yingying: those endowed with supreme beauty (*youwu*) would bring calamities upon themselves and others associated with them; in order to protect himself from Yingying's unpredictable and pernicious transformations Zhang has to "brave violence to his feelings" (*renqing*). Chen Yinke suggests that this strange piece of reasoning constitutes the discursive dimension expected of *chuanqi* fiction.[1] He cites Zhao Yanwei (ca. 13th cent.), who claims that *chuanqi* fiction "combines various forms and genres, it can demonstrate talent for historical writings [*shicai*], poetic flair [*shibi*], and discursive power [*yilun*]." The process of submitting *chuanqi* stories to those in positions of power as a means to seek office and patronage is known as "warming scrolls" (*wenjuan*).[2] Without accepting

1. Chen Yinke, *Yuan Bai shijian zhenggao* (Shanghai: Shanghai guji chubanshe, 1980), 16.
2. Zhao Yanwei, *Yunlu manchao* (Shanghai: Zhonghua shuju, 1958), 8.111.

Zhao's historical explanation of the sociopolitical functions of *chuanqi*,[3] we can yet find the idea of mixture of forms and genres suggestive. Such a view of *chuanqi* implies an ideal of inclusiveness, wherein the mixture of styles, moods, and voices is intrinsic to the genre.[4] One way of reading *chuanqi* is thus to unravel different generic strands and show how they support different interpretations.

Let us begin with the idea of discursive dimension. In "Yingying's Story," it refers specifically to Zhang's rhetorical connection with his milieu. Zhang's self-justification at the end of the story echoes the self-understanding he proclaims at the beginning, when he is questioned about his abstinence from amorous exploits and responds by declaring himself "not one who has forgotten passions" (*fei wangqing zhe*): "as for those supremely beautiful among women [*wu zhi you zhe*], they do not fail to linger on in my thoughts." Unlike the indiscriminate Master Dengtu, he is "one truly enamored of beauty" (*zhen haose zhe*) who just has not happened upon a worthy object of desire.[5] In both instances Zhang's self-defense is followed by the approbation and sympathy of his interlocutor and audience. They apparently admire his initial restraint, which indicates true discrimination, and approve of his final abandonment of Yingying, which like his abstinence shows self-control and sound judgment. Such public approbation assumes general acceptance of the idea that beautiful women, insofar as they inspire desire and passion, undermine the order of the polity and equilibrium of the self and should therefore be shunned. Zhang's references to *youwu* at the beginning and the end of the story ring with echoes of the femme fatale in history and fiction. His position thus draws upon the authority of historical writings condemning the *youwu*.[6]

Passion is on public display in this story. The public in question presumably includes the author himself. Zhang shows Yingying's letter to his friends,

3. Victor Mair suggests that the evidence for such a practice is scant and unconvincing, and that Zhao Yanwei's remarks refer more to poetry than to prose. See Victor Mair, "Scroll Presentation in the T'ang Dynasty," in *Harvard Journal of Asiatic Studies* 38, no. 1 (1978): 35–60.

4. Such an ideal seems to inform the mixture of levels of style and the principle of juxtaposition and alternation in the structure of both *chuanqi* drama and full-length narrative fiction (*zhanghui xiaoshuo*). The mixture of and tensions between genres are often invoked in European theories of the novel. See, for example, M. M. Bakhtin, *The Dialogic Imagination: Four Essays*, trans. C. Emerson and M. Holquist (Austin: University of Texas Press, 1981).

5. An allusion to "*Fu* on Master Dengtu Enamored of Beauty" (*Dengtu zi haose fu*) attributed to Song Yu. In this *fu* (rhyme-prose or prose-poem) Song Yu accuses Master Dengtu of undiscerning lust and defends himself against the charge of being amorous and susceptible by describing how, in his supercilious discrimination, he successfully resists temptation.

6. The locus classicus of the term is found in the *Zuo zhuan*, when the mother of Shuxiang, minister of Jin, warns him against marriage with the daughter of the infamous Xia Ji, who "killed three husbands, one ruler, one son, destroyed one country and two ministers." Shuxiang's mother cites an ancient proverb: "Extreme beauty must have [in it] extreme evil," and supports her ar-

thereby eliciting poetic responses from Yang Juyuan and Yuan Zhen. Neither Yang Juyuan's quatrain nor Yuan Zhen's long poem address the rancor and bitterness in Yingying's letter. Yang uses it to celebrate Zhang's role as "talented scholar of amorous sensibility" (*fengliu caizi*), and Yuan Zhen offers an ornate and sensual poetic account of a sexual union with a seductive and compliant goddesslike woman. Yuan Zhen, who is on especially good terms with Zhang, asks Zhang why he ends the affair with Yingying. The question prompts Zhang's speech of self-justification referred to earlier. If we accept the autobiographical theory of the story, which Chen Yinke convincingly argues,[7] then the presence of Yuan Zhen as friend, interlocutor, and interpreter in the story dramatizes the sense of the author as his own public. However, any potential self-division in such a rhetorical set-up is suppressed, since Yuan Zhen, Zhang, and his friends agree that Zhang acts judiciously: "Among Zhang's contemporaries many commended him for skillfully repairing his errors." Yuan purports to tell the story as warning against wayward passions, so that "those who know about it will not act in the same way; and those who act in the same way will not be confounded." In these rhetorical contexts, including that of storytelling, the renunciation of passion is concomitant with social integration. The discursive dimension of the story is thus metafictional:

---

gument with numerous historical examples. She concludes, "Also the fall of the Three Dynasties and the demotion of Gongzi [Shensheng, crown prince of Jin], were all due to such a creature [*wu*]. Why would you do this [i.e., marry such a *youwu*]? For there are those endowed with supreme beauty, enough to move a person [i.e., make him deviate from the right path]. When someone without virtue and righteousness [marries such a beauty], calamities are bound to follow." See Yang Bojun ed., *Chunqiu Zuo zhuan zhu* (Beijing: Zhonghua shuju, 1981), Zhao 28.2. On another occasion, Shuxiang's mother predicts disaster for the clan because of the beauty of one of her husband's secondary wives: "Deep mountains and great swamps produce dragons and snakes. She is beautiful, and I am afraid she will produce dragons and snakes to bring calamities upon you" (*Zuo zhuan*, Xiang 21.5). In "Yingying's Story," Zhang also maintains that "[his] virtue is insufficient to overcome evil," hence he must "brave violence to his feelings."

The *Zuo zhuan* contains numerous examples of beautiful women who bring calamities on themselves, their clans, their countries, and the men with whom they associate. Besides Xia Ji, notable examples include Duke Zhuang of Zheng's mother (*Zuo zhuan*, Yin 1.4); Ji Zhong's daughter (Huan 15.2); Wen Jiang, consort of Duke Huan of Lu (Huan 18.1); Lian Cheng's sister (Zhuang 8.3); Lady Li, consort of Duke Xian of Jin (Zhuang 28.2, Xi 4.6); Ai Jiang (Min 2.3); Duke Huan of Qi's consorts (Xi 17.5); Mu Jiang (Cheng 16.5, Xiang 9.3), Sheng Mengzi of Qi (Cheng 16.11, 17.6); Tang Jiang (Xiang 25.2); Shuhu's mother (Xiang 21.5); Qi (Xiang 26.8); Duke Ping of Jin's consorts (Zhao 1.12); Nanzi (Ding 14.8). "Great indeed is the ancestral Zhou house, / Baosi destroyed it" ("Zhengyue," in "Xiaoya"): these lines from the *Classic of Poetry* (*Shi jing*, quoted in *Zuo zhuan*, Zhao 1.3) imply that Baosi embodies the decadent excesses that bring down the Zhou royal house.

7. See Chen Yinke, *Yuan Bai shijian zhenggao*, 81–116.

it is a proleptic reply to the reader's response as well as the representation of the reception of the story.

At the other end of the public justification of renunciation are the poetic passages celebrating passion. It is interesting to note that none of these are penned by Zhang. We are told that he addresses to Yingying two poems on spring, the unfinished "Poem on Meeting the Divine One, thirty couplets," and a letter declaring his love. But none of these are recorded in the story. Instead an extended account is given in Yuan Zhen's sequel to Zhang's "Poem on Meeting the Divine One." The composite Zhang-Yuan voice (Yuan Zhen gives the most elaborate poetic description of the affair and also poses the question that gives Zhang the opportunity to justify himself) gives credence to the autobiographical theory by establishing both the inside and the outside perspectives on passion. Yuan's poem is replete with echoes of the goddesses celebrated in the erotic tradition in Chinese poetry, including examples from the *fu* tradition, whose imagery is in turn incorporated in later love poems such as those anthologized in *New Songs from the Jade Terrace* (*Yutai xinyong*). References to celestial precincts ("Saying that she comes from the Jade Flower Pool, / And is about to pay her respects at the Green Jade Palace" [lines 17–18]) establish Yingying's goddesslike aura. Allusions to Song Yu's poetic expositions ("*Fu* on Gaotang" [*Gaotang fu*], "*Fu* on the Goddess" [*Shennü fu*], "*Fu* on Master Dengtu Enamored of Beauty" [*Dengtu zi haose fu*]) abound in Yuan's sequel to Zhang's "Poem on Meeting the Divine One": "morning meetings in the drizzling rain" (line 12), "Wandering cloud, without fixed abode" (line 59), "By chance I turned to Song Yu's eastern neighbor" (line 20). The line "riding her cygnet she returned to the River Luo" (line 49) and the gift of ring and avowal of eternal love and devotion (lines 41–44) allude to Cao Zhi's "*Fu* on the Goddess of the River Luo" (*Luoshen fu*).[8]

Unlike the goddess in the *fu* of Song Yu and Cao Zhi, whose unpredictable transformations and movements leave the poet pining and melancholy, the "Divine One" in Yuan Zhen's poem is compliant and tender. As with the depiction of woman in "palace-style poetry" (*gongti shi*), refusal is coy and playful, a secret affirmation of love ("Gently rejecting playful seduction at first; / she yet secretly transmits tender feelings," lines 21–22). The diction of Yuan's poem is ornate and heavily sensual, which indicates that it cannot be written for one's cousin or, for that matter, any respectable, marriageable woman. The sensual diction echoes Zhang Wencheng's "Wandering in the Caves of the Immortals" (*Youxian ku*), which also celebrates the blissful en-

---

8. "*Fu* on Gaotang" begins with an account of how the goddess of Mount Wu offers herself to the king of Chu in his dream. She leaves with these words: "I am on the sunlit side of Mount Wu, where the high hills are precipitous—at dawn as morning clouds, in the evening as passing rain, mornings and evenings, beneath the sunlit terrace." Upon waking the king sets up a

counter with a divine woman: indeed, the matching surnames of the protagonists, Zhang and Cui, in the two stories may not be accidental.[9] The separation from the Divine One is presented as the inevitable consequence of
the passage from night to day: "Just as we rejoice over the millennial meeting, / All of a sudden we hear the night watch's end" (lines 47–48). Abandonment and betrayal are no longer the issue, the goddess and her lover
have to go different ways: riding her cygnet she returns to the River Luo,
while he must go up Mount Song (lines 49–50); she is like the wandering
cloud, with no fixed abode, while he stays in his high chamber (lines 59–60).
The very epithet of "Divine One"[10] marks inevitable separation: the status
of the lady is both too high and too low. As fairy immortal her sojourn in
the human world must need be brief; as secular charmer of dubious social
station—probably a courtesan—her liaison with her ambitious lover cannot
end in marriage.

The motif of "meeting the Divine One" celebrates the intensity of passion.
On the night of their union, "Zhang was elated. He even thought that she
must have come from the ranks of goddesses and fairy immortals, and not
from the world of mortals." The experience is so unexpected and intense
that he awaits it and looks back on it in a state of dreamlike trance. The image of Yingying as goddess also gives her the aura of mystery and uncertainty.
She is both alluring and forbidding. In her first meeting with Zhang, she is
petulant and uncommunicative. She then summons Zhang with a poem, only
to speak as moralist and take him to task for his designs to gain access to her.
The reversal in this instance is so drastic and unexpected that the reader may
legitimately wonder whether Yingying is acting according to plan or merely
to cover up her own confusion. When she finally comes to Zhang, it is again
entirely on her own initiative and takes Zhang totally by surprise. The image
of the ambivalent goddess thus turns Yingying into obscure object of desire
who controls and manipulates Zhang's emotions. Ironically, although Zhang
eventually abandons Yingying, in the first half of the story Zhang is at her

---

shrine for her and calls it "Morning Cloud." Hence the metaphoric and metonymic identification
of the goddess with cloud and rain. In *"Fu* on Master Dengtu," Song Yu describes how his beautiful eastern neighbor climbs over the wall, gazing at him silently and soulfully for three years.
In *"Fu* on the Goddess of the River Luo," the goddess offers her jade pendant in return for the
poet's gift of girdle jade and proposes an assignation in the depths of the river. When the poet
hesitates and then rejects the goddess (also claiming caution and fear of being deceived by a
being of intractable transformations), she professes eternal love and devotion and returns to
the River Luo.

9. Chen Yinke makes the same point in *Yuan Bai shijian zhenggao,* 109.

10. "Divine One" (*zhen*) or "fairy-immortal" (*xianren*) often refers to Daoist priestesses, courtesans, or other varieties of profane charmers.

mercy, thus allowing him to present himself in the end as fearful victim of Yingying's capricious transformations. Zhang is introduced as someone who "held fast to his principles, and would not act against rules of propriety." For such a paragon of restraint to lose control, so the author seems to imply, the responsibility must lie with Yingying's seductive charms. To present Yingying as goddess of ambiguous aspect and to emphasize her control over the situation is thus to justify Zhang's termination of the affair.

As obscure object of desire Yingying does not have a voice, even as ambivalent goddesses in the literary tradition do not speak. She hides her talents and her emotions: her reticence is part of her aura of mystery. Only when the affair draws to its close does she find a voice, and she adopts the dominant feminine voice available to her from the literary tradition: the plaintive voice of the abandoned woman. The authority of this voice is derived from Yingying's capacity to explain the story. Yingying's skillful use of the word *luan* to refer to disorder in the public realm, sexual transgression, and her own confusion and sorrow (as symbolized by the tangled skeins of silk [*luansi^a*], one of her gifts to Zhang and a standard pun for "confused thoughts" [*luansi^b*]) defines the logic of the plot as equilibrium imperiled and reestablished. She declares that it is fitting that what begins as transgression should end as abandonment. Her letter combines acceptance of rejection, suppressed rancor, and vague hopes of regaining Zhang's love. Her last two poems addressed to Zhang profess lingering love and longing, and urge Zhang to love his new wife with whatever feelings he felt for her. This, then, is the other lyrical mode in the story. It undermines the topos of the intractable goddess. Yingying's voice here is plaintive, the opposite of the divine woman toying with the emotions of her lovers. There are then three images of Yingying in the story: first, as pathetic abandoned woman, an image premised on her own poems and letter; second, as would-be femme fatale, an image constructed by the protagonist-narrator; third, as seductive, unpredictable goddess, an image presented by Yuan Zhen and the protagonist. These images define different ways of reading the story. Zhang emerges from these interpretations as being either callous or prudent.

Whereas the discursive dimension of the story assumes reflection and control (Zhang's self-control and his attempt to control the reader's response), the lyrical moments purport to be rhetorically uncensored. Yuan's sequel to Zhang's "Poem on Meeting the Divine One" and Yingying's letter and poems draw on the dominant modes of representing women in the Chinese poetic tradition: as ambivalent, elusive divine woman and as abandoned woman, respectively. Both images are defined by a rhetoric of excess and noncontrol: while Yuan's poem celebrates passion and ecstasy, Yingying's writings evoke intense pathos.

Why and how does the author bring all these disparate elements together?

What are the motives for fiction? How does the autobiographical theory affect our reading? These questions devolve on the narrative flow, what Zhao Yanwei designates as "talent for historical writings," which I understand as the art of reticence, nuances, and complexity in narrative prose. If we think back on the historical writings of Sima Qian, for instance, we can also appreciate a comparable mixture of lyrical moments and dispassionate accounts, theoretically "objective" presentation and subjective interpretation, emphasis on subtlety and nuances, and the juxtaposition of disparate, sometimes conflicting interpretations which lies at the basis of the historian's impartiality. Admittedly "talent for historical writings" is more often traditionally understood as the mastery of precise and concise prose with a clearly articulated moral vision. However, historical writings represent one of the earliest contexts for considering the discrepancy between surface and meaning, even though the irony is presumably stable and governed by a subtle moral intention. As such they may be fruitfully compared with more radical modes of ambivalence and indeterminacy in other genres.

Yuan Zhen apparently wants the reader to accept Zhang's self-justification and Yuan's poem as definitive accounts, yet by quoting Yingying at length he also undermines them and exposes their artificiality. Why is so much space devoted to Yingying's own version of the story? Is it because Yingying's words answer the male protagonist-author's desire to be desired? Do they perhaps define the author's elegiac mood toward love lost and betrayed? Or is it because such are the words of the historical "Yingying," as the autobiographical theory would have us believe? Chen Yinke maintains that Yuan Zhen is writing his own story and presents Zhang's (i.e., his own) behavior as justifiable because the Tang sociohistorical context did countenance the abandonment of a woman of dubious social station (probably a courtesan) in the interest of a more advantageous marriage. The logic of Chen's argument implies that Yingying's "real position" is encoded in the story, most obviously in Yuan's sequel to "Poem on Meeting the Divine One." In other words, Chen's autobiographical theory discounts any possible irony. Irony, however, can and often does coexist with the autobiographical impulse. While there is little evidence of self-conscious irony undermining the position of the narrator-protagonist, we can see that "Yingying's Story" expresses the need to tell different stories, which is quite plausible if we consider autobiography as a motive for fiction. The story presents contradictory attitudes toward desire: awareness of the dangers of passion and self-congratulation on the mastery of passion in the interest of sociopolitical integration, celebration of a passion intensified by an elusive object of desire, melancholy mood mourning love lost and betrayed. Whether we equate Yuan Zhen with Zhang is immaterial, although if we make the connection the contradictions are more interesting. The narrative that weaves together different strands, moods, and modes is remarkably sparse, filled with lacunae and silence. The form of the *chuanqi* allows the author to modulate different stories in one story, to explore the liminal space between fact and fiction, to be both authoritative and evasive, both lying and telling the truth. In this sense the mixture of genres in *chuanqi* defines the motives for fiction.

ON *YINGYING ZHUAN,* BY YUAN ZHEN

Katherine Carlitz

Yuan Zhen might well have been amazed to learn that in *Yingying zhuan* he had created not just a tale but an icon. For centuries, the title alone has conjured up a whole realm of sexual adventure. This may not have been exactly what Yuan Zhen intended, for it seems to me that Yuan was writing a story about the elusiveness of passion rather than the satisfaction of passion. In any case, audiences apparently found Yuan's version of the tale unsettling, and Yuan eventually lost ownership of his own story. From the twelfth-century *zhu gong diao* (medley) version on through the *zaju* and *chuanqi* dramas of the Yuan and Ming, passion is rewarded with marriage. In the process, public perception of *Yingying zhuan* itself changed, as it became difficult to remember the protagonists of the Tang tale without reference to the far less arduous satisfactions of the drama.

We can examine this shift in perception by looking not only at the oral performing tradition, but also at a little-studied fifteenth-century classical language novella *Zhong qing li ji* (An Elegant Compendium of Sentiments Conjoined),[11] which openly reads and comments on *Yingying zhuan*. The novella subjects Yuan Zhen's subtle tale of renunciation to reversals that make it simpler and sexier, and ultimately take the problem of passion in a different direction. This new solution to the problem of passion derives not just from the Ming text's having had more time to come up with an answer, but from a change in problematic, as we will see. Language takes off in a different direction as well: both texts are in "classical Chinese," but the Ming language is very different from that of the Tang.

Yingying zhuan is calibrated as carefully as a poem, moving from the straight prose of description to the more stylized prose of Yingying's letter, which by *evoking* the actions previously described actually makes us aware of our distance from them, and finally to the poems that tell us how to understand the action, poems written by and for those outside the action altogether. The opening sentences of the tale efficiently suggest the passion to come,

11. For information on dating and authorship, see Chu Hung-lam, "The Authorship of the Story *Zhong qing li ji,*" *Asia Major,* 3d ser., vol. 1, no. 1 (January 1988): 71–82.

but that passion is acted out in such a void of silence ("She had not said a word the entire night") that it induces anxiety rather than satisfaction. (What *is* her response? Why *is* she there?) The culmination of *Yingying zhuan* is not in the satisfaction of desire, but in the realization that the desire and its object are both ultimately elusive. This realization is expressed in Yuan Zhen's poem "Meeting with the Holy One," which draws on the imagery of *fu*, the poetic genre invented to evoke that which eludes our grasp.

The opening lines of *Yingying zhuan* create Zhang as such an improbable virgin that we sense the passion waiting for him on the next page: *wei chang jin nü se*, he had *not yet* (*wei*) experienced (*jin*, drawn near to, been exposed to) the attractions of women. Hongniang the maid describes Yingying as just another such virgin, who guards herself (*zi bao*) so impregnably that she can neither be violated (*fan*) nor entered (*ru*^a^). But just as the virgin Zhang knows himself to be a man of *qing* or passion, so Hongniang, by telling us what Yingying reads, tells us of Yingying's own reservoir of *qing*.

Madame Cui unwittingly sets trouble in motion by bringing these two susceptible young people together, a role that would be played up in the dramatic versions of the story. But all this trouble takes place in the side wing of a liminal place, locating passion somewhere outside of real life and its responsibilities. When Zhang and Yingying go back to their respective homes, they return to real life and marry other people. The second half of *Yingying zhuan* is devoted to the evocation of the dreamlike events in that liminal place: Yingying's letter (a letter of evocation, of nostalgia, of sorrow) moves Zhang's friends to try to encapsulate it in verse. The experience itself was ambiguous and elusive, which means that all we can have, ultimately, are these epistolary and poetic evocations. Writing replaces the experience (Yingying never lets Zhang see her writing until they are *separated*).

Such distancing never occurs in *Zhong qing li ji* at all. The hero and heroine of *Zhong qing li ji* not only read *Yingying zhuan*, they take it to bed with them and evaluate Yingying's experience in light of their own. For these young people, it is only lived experience that can bring stories of love to life (thus we are reading about the limits of literary experience). And their experience is totally satisfactory to them: everyone's sexual and literary needs are met in this story. But as we will see, this story about the easy satisfaction of passion is really a story about the *uses* of passion; it does not have the *problem* of passion at its core, as *Yingying zhuan* did.

Formally, *Zhong qing li ji* is a typical *caizi jiaren* (scholar and beauty) romance, a rather perfunctory prose narrative that acts as a showcase for verse. Its plot draws not only on *Yingying zhuan* but also on *Jiao Hong ji* (The Tale of Jiao and Hong), another account of young cousins who take their romantic destiny into their own hands, with tragic results. (This Yuan dynasty classical-language tale, like *Yingying zhuan*, was transformed into *zaju* and *chuanqi* during the Ming.)[12] The hero, Gu Lu, a young man of good family from Qiongzhou in Guangdong, is sent to convey his family's congratulations to the family of an uncle who has just been appointed to office. (The two families are related through an elderly aunt, a kinship tie reminiscent of *Yingying zhuan.*) When he catches sight of his cousin Yuniang he falls in love with her at once, but initially restrains himself because he *"zhi qi ci,"* or "knows his place" (in the family hierarchy). (The word "west" is everywhere here: Gu is housed in the West Wing, and is made a tutor, *xi bin* or "western guest," to Yuniang's younger brother.) The aged aunt instructs Yuniang to see that Gu Lu is taken care of ("Give him everything he asks for"), and when Yuniang responds to Gu Lu's request for some betel by wrapping the nuts in leaves and inscribing them with a poem, his desire is enflamed and he throws caution to the winds. As in *Yingying zhuan,* he writes a suggestive poem in response to what he thinks is an invitation, and Yuniang repulses him with Confucian indignation. But soon she is standing beneath *his* window responding in verse to the poems he intones, and rifling through *his* papers when he is out of his room (she wants to see if he has written anything about her). After several false starts ("Just as they were about to *he huan* [join their pleasure], they heard the maid coming," or her parents returning, etc.) he hits on a plan to make assignations possible. He feigns illness in order to have himself moved from the West Wing to the East Wing and from the East Wing to the main hall, where the two will be able to find each other at night. Yuniang tells Gu that she has long read *Yingying zhuan* and *Jiao Hong ji,* and despaired of experiencing anything so dramatic herself! Gu assures her that given her own daring, her story is in no way inferior to Yingying's. The author has obviously read both *Yingying zhuan* and its *zaju* transformation: the first time Gu Lu finds Yuniang after he has had himself moved into the house, she is in the garden burning incense and praying to the moon, just as when Zhang plays his lute for Yingying to overhear in Part II, Act One of the *zaju.*

As in *Yingying zhuan,* Gu Lu returns home but manages to return and carry on the relationship. But in a major difference from the Tang tale, Gu Lu when at home visits the courtesan who had initiated him into the arts of love. She and her "colleagues" (*tong ban*) not only accept his new relationship but sagely evaluate Yuniang for him and give them their blessing.[13] What was hidden and secret in *Yingying zhuan* here has a cheering section of experts!

As disclosure looms and the two face the apparent impossibility of marriage (Gu Lu adduces three reasons: they are cousins, he dares not disobey his parents, and he dares not *tell* his parents), the old aunt sweeps the difficul-

12. For a late Ming chuanqi version, see *Jiao Hong ji,* ed. Ouyang Guang (Shanghai: Gu ji chu ban she, 1988).
13. This also takes place in the late Ming chuanqi *Jiao Hong ji.*

ties away and persuades both sets of parents of the suitability of the match. Gu Lu passes the examinations and the two are married.

Zhong qing li ji leaves very little to the imagination. We know just enough about Yingying's fondness for "tales of love and sorrow" to appreciate the depth of her *qing*, but in *Zhong qing li ji* we learn exactly what Yuniang reads and what she expects from it. Zhang in *Yingying zhuan* is a model of propriety though a man of *qing*, while Gu Lu, more explicitly described, is sensually attractive (*feng zi*) and an old hand with the ladies. Madame Cui's ultimate responsibility for Zhang's and Yingying's romance is quietly suggested in the Tang tale, but here in *Zhong qing li ji* the aged aunt positively throws the two together ("Give him anything he wants!"). Yuniang is a virgin (more on this below), but only in physical terms: in her actions she is as assertive as any hot-blooded young man. And whereas Zhang has to wait out the one moment of retardation in *Yingying zhuan,* namely Yingying's apparent invitation followed by temporary repudiation, the retardations in *Zhong qing li ji* amount more or less to pornography. (All this foreplay is of course as much in the service of writing as of sex: every interruptus is followed by one or two commemorative poems!)

But most striking is the way recapitulation is handled in the two stories. In *Yingying zhuan,* it is Yingying's mournful letter that retells the tale in the context of bitter loss, and it is that sense of loss that moves Zhang's associates to poetry. In *Zhong qing li ji,* the affair is retold in Gu Lu's long poem to the courtesan Weixiang, with every expectation that desires will be met.

Zhong qing li ji is of more historical than literary interest, but even so it shows us how "classical Chinese" need not be the terse, elliptical, evocative instrument of *Yingying zhuan,* but can instead be expansive and denotative, rather in the manner we associate with the vernacular of Ming fiction. The material world is evoked with vigor here: when Gu Lu has to leave Yuniang the first time, she sends him home with "ten *liang* of white gold, four bolts of blue silk, twenty handkerchiefs, and twenty pairs of belt-pendants." When he leaves the second time, she sends presents for his courtesan friends: bracelets, skirts, belts. And the language is used to describe the physical world with a specificity that foreshadows *Hong lou meng:* the halls, pavilions, hedges, and paths where the couple meet are all named.

As might be expected, the "classical Chinese" of *Yingying zhuan* and *Zhong qing li ji* deals with sex much differently. Yuan Zhen's technique in *Yingying zhuan* weights each word. In the opening description of Zhang, the phrase "he had not *yet* experienced the attractions of women" tells us that he is *soon* to experience them. The fact that Yingying's defenses are so impregnable that no one can enter tells us that he *will* enter. And there is wonderful playing with meanings of the word *zhi*[e] all through the progress toward their first night together: Zhang wants to *zhi qing* (take passion to its utmost, *zhi*[e]) as soon as he sees Yingying, and she (emphasizing the seductive power of poetry) writes a poem *yi qiu qi bi zhi,* "so as to insure that he would arrive [*zhiᵉ*]," ostensibly to receive a reproof, but actually to further the real inevitability (*bi*) of *zhiᵉ* here, which is to *zhi qing.* Both senses of the word are evoked by the excitement in Hongniang's voice when she ushers Zhang sheng into the bedchamber, exclaiming "*zhi yiᵃ! zhi yiᵃ!* He has arrived!"

In *Zhong qing li ji,* sex is suggested through endless jocular double entendre, and the relation of writing to sex is handled in a much more matter-of-fact way than in *Yingying zhuan.* It is when he receives the betel and sees Yuniang's poem that Gu Lu realizes that she *shi zi,* understands characters, which tells him that a "West Wing affair" (*xi xiang zhi shi*) is possible. In praising her daring he compares Yuniang to Zhuo Wenjun, a standard figure for uniting sex and writing outside of approved channels. (Zhuo ran off with the Han dynasty poet Sima Xiangru after a literary courtship.) And when Gu Lu and Yuniang carry out their "West Wing affair" and take *Yingying zhuan* to bed with them, they evaluate the Tang tale's use of language in terms of their own experience. On the one hand, Gu Lu points out to Yuniang that the real fame of Yuan Zhen's story rests on his poem "Meeting the Holy One," and he praises Yingying's final poems of renunciation, "Ever since I have wasted to gauntness . . . " and "Rejected, what more can be said?" as worthy of Bo Juyi and Du Mu. But when the conversation turns to the other book they have brought to bed with them, *Jiao Hong ji,* Gu Lu and Yuniang are more severe: criticizing a line that speaks of the sorrows in meeting and the joys of parting, they reject such subtlety as nonsense.

But this would deny the pleasure they themselves took in Yingying's poems of parting, and the sorrow they felt upon reading Yuan Zhen's "Meeting the Holy One." In *Zhong qing li ji* none of these paradoxes is relevant; there is no *problem* of passion. This is because *Zhong qing li ji* is less interested in passion itself than in fitting passion into the repertoire of the *shiᵉ,* the gentleman socialized to govern. Unlike *Yingying zhuan,* which is set so unquestionably within the world of high culture that no signposts to its social level are necessary, *Zhong qing li ji* lets us know repeatedly that we are reading about the *shidafu* (scholar-gentry) world. Gu Lu "knows his place" in the hierarchy (this was the kind of thinking that identified a *shiᵉ* as a *shiᵉ*), while Yuniang in her turn insists that she will marry a *shiᵉ* and not a "vulgar" (*su*) husband. The very geography of the story emphasizes its social locus: far from the liminal realm of the temple, the action in *Zhong qing li ji* takes place in a gentry home described with loving specificity, and Gu Lu manages to have himself and his love affair moved from the periphery to the center! And the way loss of virginity is treated in *Zhong qing li ji* further signposts the Ming *shidafu* social level, with all its anxious need to specify itself. In *Yingying zhuan,* loss of virginity is conclusive proof of the grandeur of passion, as we know from all the emphasis on virginity (the impregnable defenses, etc.) at the beginning of the tale. Yingying speaks of herself as "sullied" after Zhang leaves her, but the structure of *Yingying zhuan* makes us understand this as an almost pro forma bow to the conventions. The real reason Zhang leaves is *so that he can have the experience of having left,* since leaving Yingying proves that he has experienced a passion too grand for quotidian marriage. In *Zhong qing li ji,* however, loss of virginity is proof of something else. "As they roll to and fro" on their first night together, a spot of blood appears on Gu's robe. Yuniang instantly snips out the bit of cloth and tells Gu Lu to save and treasure it.[14] Gu Lu celebrates the spot of blood again when he describes the affair in his long poem to Weixiang the courtesan. This celebration is all about the way Yuniang has been shown to be a good *shidafu* girl worthy of our hero, despite her pro forma lament that Gu Lu will have to leave her now that she is defiled. (No such thought crosses his mind: quite to the contrary, he assures her, she has now proven that she equals the heroines of *Yingying zhuan* and *Jiao Hong ji.*) And having proven her worthiness (or to speak the very material language of this Ming text, having acquired the attribute of passion), she begins to speak in the canonical language of *shi[e]* self-presentation, announcing that nothing will sway her resolve (*zhi*), and thanking Gu Lu's courtesan friends for the "trustworthy loyalty" (*zhong hou*) of their poems to her. And these very courtesans (*zhi qing ren,* or "those who know passion," as Gu Lu calls them) enrich Gu's *shi[e]* persona by the *qing* they bestow on him. Whereas the virginity of hero *and* heroine in *Yingying zhuan* underscores the explosive danger of *qing,* and leads to a resolution where *qing* has to be distanced, *qing* in *Zhong qing li ji* is comfortably presented as the necessary experience of the *shi[e].*

The *zhu gong diao, zaju,* and *chuanqi* transformations of *Yingying zhuan* chose a different set of implications to pursue. In all of these versions, the drama is adversarial, as *qing* (the lovers) triumphs over ill-advised power (Madame Cui). The Korean *Chun hyang ka* (*Chun xiang ge* in Chinese, or "Song of Spring Fragrance")[15] takes this implication even further, as the Yingying-style heroine resists the lustful governor, rather than her mother, before the hero can return to reclaim her. *Zhong qing li ji* never achieved the same level of popularity as any of these other versions, but it shows us how a beloved story could be reinterpreted to meet a new set of social needs.

14. This is also found in the late Ming *Jiao Hong ji.*
15. See the translation in Richard Rutt and Kim Chon-un, trans., *Virtuous Women: Three Masterpieces of Traditional Korean Fiction* (Seoul: National Commission for UNESCO, 1974), 237–333.

PERSPECTIVE ON READINGS OF *YINGYING ZHUAN*

Peter Bol

Katherine Carlitz, Wai-yee Li, and Pauline Yu have composed a set of essays on *Yingying zhuan* that are so compatible that I am inclined simply to note how these explorations of dissonance in and around *Yingying zhuan* are in harmony. Carlitz, Li and Yu create a single picture, I think, because the authors have thought a great deal about how the voices and values we find in texts are literary or, more generally, cultural constructions. These are literary studies by literary scholars.[16] They persuade me that *Yingying zhuan* should be read as a literary work whose problematic lies in containing conflicting voices and contradictory values and whose appeal for us stems from its inability to contain that conflict successfully. And yet their accomplishment, perhaps because it is accompanied by an ofttimes dazzling sensitivity to the artfulness of the story, draws attention away from the ways in which the story is no fiction. It obscures the ways in which a literary work is that most rare of historical facts: the kind we can see and touch directly, so to speak, a millennium after it came into being. It is an historical fact directly accessible to us, one free of all mediation but for that which we impose ourselves. It is a window through which we can gaze on a part of social reality directly because the window is that reality.

Yuan Zhen's "Biography of Yingying" is about conflict. There are conflicts within the story—between the social expectations and passions of Zhang and Yingying, for example—and with the story. Li's commentary deftly unravels discursive, lyrical, and historical narrative styles and the contrasting images of Yingying: abandoned woman, would-be femme fatale, and unpredictable goddess. These multiple narrative lines open the way for divergent interpretations and judgments. This in turns leads readers into conflict with the story. Carlitz points out that the story did not fit the sensibilities of many later readers, who not only rewrote it in different genres but also changed it to suit themselves. In the fifteenth-century novella "An Elegant Compendium of Sentiments Conjoined," the latter-day Yingying and Zhang end up happily married! That, of course, resolves the problem of how we should judge Zhang's abandonment of Yingying. Contemporary readers find themselves at odds with the story as well; as one of my students put it, it is "not good on women." Yu's notes on the mimetic, self-centered reading of *Yingying zhuan*

---

16. This was due to a mistake in programming. A fourth essay by Stephen Owen has appeared separately in his book *The End of the Chinese "Middle Ages": Essays in Mid-Tang Literary Culture* (Stanford: Stanford University Press, 1996). Readers of that work, "Conflicting Interpretations: 'Yingying's Story'" (149–73), will see that his essay is entirely compatible with the essays we include here.

describe the approach most students initially choose when asked to "think about" a text in the humanities. But it is also true that this story begs the reader to make judgments and that "our" judgment as readers—our judgment as embodiments of our personal projections of a moral society—is a central issue in the story in itself. Yingying thrives on conflict and contradiction.

The second point of agreement in these essays is their focus on the story as a literary construction. Yu argues convincingly that *Yingying zhuan* is the "consummate writerly text." It is a text about the performance of texts, where texts have agency, and where texts—vehicles for inculcating the social norms necessary to good order—undermine propriety by exposing it as a literary construct, by exposing its literary foundation. Carlitz shows how the story is commented upon, transposed into different genres, and rewritten. Li's essay illustrates that *Yingying zhuan*'s narrative lines and characters are visible to well-texted readers in part because they are embedded in literary history and make use of the texts and language of the past.

Can we read this work historically? Or at least is there an alternative way of reading *Yingying zhuan*? As Stephen Owen has observed, we can see it as a naïve work and conclude that the author reveals more than he ought to; we can read as an ironic work and admire the author for his critique of his own class. We can suppose the characters to be "real" and ask for whom and why such behavior was justifiable in the early ninth century, as Chen Yinke does in denying that the story is problematic. The challenge for historians is to avoid the pitfall of creating correspondences between the story in the text and the social world we associate with the author and instead look for ways to make historical sense of these essays' conclusions: this is a tale of conflict and it is very much a literary work.

Yuan Zhen (775–831) lived in a world where leading intellectual figures—people who thought and wrote about values—were literary figures. The men we think of as his contemporaries—Han Yu (768–824), Lü Wen (772–811), Li Ao (774–836), Liu Yuxi (772–842), Bo Juyi (772–846), Liu Zongyuan (773–819), Zhang Ji (766–829), et cetera—witness this. The price of admission to Tang intellectual culture in the early ninth century was literary accomplishment. It had to be, for this was still the dominant way of addressing the connections that scholars were supposed to be able to make between the past and politics, morality, and personality in the present. Moreover, precisely at this moment Yuan's generation was writing about how responsible scholars ought to engage in *wen* (literature/culture) and *xue* (learning). We do not have to argue that Yuan is addressing the issue of how one ought to write to conclude that he is showing that he can write well, something that locates him in the mainstream rather than on the margins.

What might historians make of the conflicts in Yuan's story? This was an era when scholars were aware that the conflicts between civil and military interests, centralizing policies and provincial localism, and state and church had devastating consequences. These conflicts provide context for the events in the story and, at least in terms of their personal histories, both Zhang and Yuan reflect a desire for the primacy of civil, centralizing, and state interests in restoring order. I would suggest, however, that the text as a whole reveals a particular understanding of the sources of conflict and disorder on a more fundamental level.

It seems to me that Yuan Zhen connects the conflict between different perspectives—or different values—to the problematic relationship between "self" and "things" (*wo* and *wu*). Emotional responses (*qing*) come into being out of this relationship—between a perceiving self and the others or "things" perceived. Emotions are responses to things that impinge upon the self; they are of the self but are orchestrated, so to speak, by the thing. As Li points out, Yingying is a "thing," albeit the most excellent example of her category (she is a *youwu*), but she can try to stir Zhang. The reverse is true as well. They are simultaneously responsive selves and things to be responded to. What the story explores is the fact that when "things" gain the ability to stir us, they rouse passions (*qing*). Passions create conflicts of perspective, because two agencies have come into play and there is no longer a self-centered hierarchy of authority.

This text has a vision of people as empty, unintending, and unselfconscious until roused. And yet the arousal of emotions is also the very moment at which people realize their ability to be substantial, conscious, intending creators of culture (and literature). And culture—in this story it is the literary composition—can be a force for order and disorder because it consists of things with the very human power of seducing and guiding the emotional responses of the observer and reader. This, I submit, is the territory Yuan Zhen traverses in *Yingying zhuan*.

What Yuan has not done is to pursue the possibility of a self that can construct its own internal substance, so that it can have spontaneous yet socially responsible emotional responses without becoming entangled and enslaved by the things that stimulate it. He is no Han Yu or Liu Zongyuan. He has treated the problems of his age in terms of actual human behavior, he has made us aware of the roots of disorder in the world, and he has shown us that when the human and the cultural are linked by emotions they gain real power. But he has not—and in this he strikes me as being much like his friend Bo Juyi—shown us that there is anything we can do about it. Not only that, he has shown us that he was incapable of trying to do anything about it. The end of his tale is a return to decent society and a rejection of his emotional history as a mistake. It is, I suspect, the perspective that made Buddhism so persuasive, for its solution to the problem of being moral was to take the rejection of *qing* to the extreme by holding out the promise of true emptiness.

But at least some contemporary literary intellectuals reached a very different conclusion. They believed that being capable of responding emotionally and acting responsibly required not an acceptance of social norms but a self-conscious commitment to being different from the times. The celebration of being different—of being in tension with dominant values—was most forcefully articulated by Han Yu.

Yingying zhuan is a document from a moment when elite culture was changing profoundly. Yuan Zhen is caught in those changes, but he is a relatively hopeless, cowardly voice, unwilling to put himself and his future at risk. It is appropriate that our volume closes in this era, before the new world has taken such clear form that it is available to conservative voices to echo. Carlitz's discussion of the fifteenth-century reworking of the tale gives us a glimpse of that new world. That, she tells us, was to be a world where people were more inclined to think about how to make use of passion for social harmony than about the problem of the passions. It was to be also a world where literature would matter less, where experience would test the authority of writing rather than writing defining the meaning of experience. But Yuan Zhen was part of a different world, one which the writings this book treats belonged to, where intellectual life was a cultural event and the line between the literary and intellectual was not so easy to draw. We can read *Yingying zhuan* as a romantic fiction that thwarts being romanticized, and we can read it as evidence of the cultural and moral crisis that would bring that world to an end.

SEVEN

Bi fa ji
Jing Hao, "Notes on the Method for the Brush"

A RECORD OF THE METHODS OF THE BRUSH

A Personal Reading (The Codger and the Painter Wannabe)

Stephen H. West

In Taihang Mountains is a broad valley, and within it are several hectares of land—these I ordinarily plow in order to live.[1] One day I ascended Spirit Bell Mountain to gaze about, and tracing my way back, I entered a grand portal of cliffs. Moss-grown trails watered with dew, strange-shaped rocks wreathed in auspicious mists—I quickly entered into the place, which was filled with ancient pines.

> Broad Valley (*hong gu*) is also a place name in Henan. Here, however, I believe he is simply using it in its sense as a wide valley. The same with Spirit Bell Mountain (*Shen zheng shan*). The notes to the Peking annotations remark that the named Spirit Bell Mountain is quite a distance from Broad Valley and cannot be the same mountain, etc., etc. I think we should assume that the author is using the idea of "spirit bells" as a simple metaphor of rocks that ring out when struck (well attested, for instance, in *Shanhai jing*), thereby implying some sense of otherworldly nature. The text is giving a spiritual, not an actual geography. He enters a hidden, utopian realm, "squeezing through an opening to another world" (a common literary trope) in the same manner as Tao Yuanming's famous Peach Blossom Spring. It is deserted, but full of preternatural power—trails overgrown with moss, decked with auspicious dews, strange rocks, mists.

Translation copyright 2000 by Stephen H. West.

1. I am using Jing Hao, *Bi fa ji*, annotated by Wang Bomin, *Zhongguo hualun congshu* (Beijing: Renmin meishu chubanshe, 1963), as the base text; this has previously been translated by Susan Bush and Hsio-yen Shih as "The Significance of Old Pines," in *Early Chinese Texts on Painting* (Cambridge, Mass: Harvard-Yenching Institute/Harvard University Press, 1985), 145–71.

In the center was a lone tree, arm-spans around, its skin old and grizzled with lichen, its flying scales mounting the void with coiling kracken force, about to plunge into the Cloudy Han.

> To translate this description of the twisting tall pine as a simile as earlier works have done (i.e., "as if it were a coiling dragon") misses the point. This tree is a dragon poised to plunge back into its watery depths, the celestial counterpart of the Han River (our Milky Way). A truly supernal creature whose imminent form graces the hidden valley.

Those [others] that formed groves doubled their splendor in cool ethers; those incapable of it humbled themselves, embracing their own integrity. Some turned their roots backward out of the earth, some bent down to cut across the main current. They hung from the banks, coiled in the creek, were cloaked in moss, split apart boulders.

> The term *jie⁴*, which I have translated here as "integrity," can also mean "joints" or "segments" of bamboo, etc. Its use here opens up the possibility now of imbuing the pines not only with a supernatural power but with ethical value as well. This creates a needed opening for allegory: the trees of the grove, happy in like company, the stunted trees content to maintain their own integrity—people.

Consequently I was taken back by their unusualness, and I made a circuit to enjoy them. The next day I took my brush and went back to sketch them. I had to do thousands of trees before any of them looked like an authentic representation.

> This introduces the idea of "authenticity" or "genuineness." This term is difficult to control. It may mean anything from the untouched representation of phenomena in nature—both as outward appearance and as inner power—to authenticity of feeling, to honesty, depending on how it is contextualized. Here he opens by using it in the context of the authentic appearance of the tree. One textual variant, *fang zhi qi zhen* instead of *fang ru qi zhen*, would result in a somewhat more profound rendering: "I had to do thousands of trees before I came to know the authentic [nature of trees]." His apparent inability to see into the inner nature of objects militates against accepting the variant.

The next spring, when I came back to these stone-drum cliffs I met an old codger who asked me what I was doing here, and I answered him by explaining all the reasons that I had come. The codger said, "Do you know the method of the brush, sir?"

I said, "Codger, your visage is that of an uncultivated man. Can you possibly know anything about the rules of the brush?"

> He reveals his limitations, his inability to see below the surface of things.

The codger said: "How, sir, can you know what I may hold inside?" I heard him and was shamed and surprised. The codger said: "If you are fond of learning when young, then in the end you can succeed. Now, there are six essentials to painting: One is called 'vital energy,' two is called 'resonance,' three is called 'thought,' four is called 'scene,' five is called 'brush,' and six is called 'ink.'"

I said, "Painting is pattern. If one simply values likeness one gets the authentic representation. Can it really be so complicated?"

> The reply in Chinese is *ɣwai tsia ɣwa ia*. The term literally means flower, but can be used to mean pattern or ornamental adornment. Wannabe suggests likeness (*si*) is the same as authentic representation (*zhen*).

The codger said, "It is not so. Painting is to etch lines. One sizes up the image of a thing and from that seizes upon what is authentic in it. If it is the visible pattern of a thing—seize its visible pattern; if it is the essential substance of a thing—seize its essential substance. One cannot seize on visible pattern and make it essential substance. If one does not know this technique one can perhaps squeeze out a likeness, but the representation of authenticity can never be attained."

> "Painting to etch lines" in Chinese is *ɣwai tsia ɣwai ia*. What I have called the representation of authenticity is more precisely rendered as "to map out authenticity"—not only its likeness, but all of its hidden ramifications as well.

I said, "What do you take to be likeness? What do you take to be authenticity?"

The codger said, "Likeness gets the shape, but drops out the vital energy. Authenticity is when vital energy and essence are both abundant. As a general rule, if vital energy is passed only through external pattern and is dropped out of the image, then image dies."

> Codger has now drawn some important distinctions, which I take to be as follows: Image (*xiang*) is construed to be the total perceivable representation of a thing; it is composed of external pattern (*hua^a*) or shape (*xing^a*), vital energy (*qi*), and the physical essence of an object (*zhi^g*). Authenticity is a product of both essence and vital energy, which are internal.

I thanked him and said, "I have long known that calligraphy and painting are the study of noted worthy men. This plowboy knows that it is not my place to practice them. I merely play with the pen, picking it up, setting it down. So, in the end I have not been successful. I am ashamed to be favored with receiving your instruction on these essentials, for it is certain that I am incapable of true painting."

The codger said, "Fetishes and desires are the thieves of life. Noted worthies set their pleasure free in the lute and calligraphy, in sketching and painting. By this they replace and expel random desires. Once you have made painting dear to you, simply set a schedule for the progress of your study and do not vary from it."

> He draws a parallel between the perfection of ethical knowledge through sustained moral action and the perfection of artistic style by tenacious practice and devotion.

"As for the essentials of sketching and painting, I will explain them to you in detail. Vital energy—one's heartmind follows it and the brush moves in accord with it, seizing the image without confusion. Resonance—one must conceal any traces [of the artist's brush] yet establish the shape [of the object], and completely fulfill the formal elements without slipping into common vulgarity."

> I wonder if the relationship between vital energy and resonance is that between a sense of immediate power within the painting itself and an affective power that lingers after the act of perception? In poetic terminology, resonance often means a kind of lingering sensation or flavor that stays with the reader as a kind of aesthetic recall.

"Thought—pare down to and appropriate the essential gist; concentrate your imaginative thinking to give shape to the object. Scene—give proper sequence to the movement of the seasons, seek out the subtle to create the authentic. Brush—although you rely on rules and regulations, let it move, turn, change, and penetrate. Stick to neither essence nor shape, let it fly, let it move. Ink—high, low, thick or thin, evaluate the depth of each object. Let the pattern and shading be completely natural as though it had not come from the pen."

> This passage draws a nice parallel between an imaginative, active mind and flexibility of technique. The freedom of the brush—it is adaptive, nimble, as active as flying—is a product of calculation on the part of the painter, who must conceal, establish, seize upon, concentrate, and evaluate. True unfettered expression is the product of careful observation, thought, and selection.

He spoke again: "Spirit, subtlety, originality, cleverness. Spirit—all marks of activity [on the part of the artist] disappear and images take shape spontaneously from the nimble movement of the brush. Subtlety—one's thought traverses heaven and earth, provides categories of affinity in ten thousand different ways for all of the nature and character [of things therein], so that outward design and inner structural pattern accord with [the objects'] demeanor. Thus 'the multiple things flow' from the pen.

Spirit is the ineffable, demonic power of a good work of art, that element that we recognize but cannot describe that sets art apart from craft; here clearly expressed as that part of the painting that appears with a natural force apparently unmediated by the artist. I am using "subtle" here to stand for both subtle and subtile—both in the sense of clarifying and drawing fine distinctions and being keenly responsive to those differences. The last line is a variation of a line from the *Book of Changes* (*Yijing*), under the *qian* hexagram: *yun xing yu shi pin wu liu xing*, "Clouds move, rain spreads: the many different things flow into shape." This is a particularly apt quote, since it is meant to demonstrate how the *qian* force, which is essentially a heavenly agent, creates shape and form in the world of *kun*, or earth, through the nurturing power of rain. The change in the last character of this four-character phrase is not meant to be an adjunct to the *Yijing* quote, as it has been translated ("[as it is stated in the *Book of Changes*] 'all the objects are [appropriately] settled into [their forms]' by the brush."). The substitution is intended and effectively replaces the agent of the cosmos with the painter, who, like that agent, performs the same creative act in an equally spontaneous and natural manner.

"Originality—traces of an untrammeled [brush] are unanticipated, perhaps contrary or different from the authentic scene, or pursuing the principle of a thing only in a one-sided manner. Works attained through this may be called 'full of the brush but without thought.' Cleverness—to whittle or stitch together little seductions and falsely bring them on par with affairs of major importance. One forces the sketching of sections of outward design and makes the vital energy and image ever more vague. This is called 'a paucity of fruit and plethora of flower.'"

I see both of these negative factors as an intrusion of personality into painting. If the lines before this passage are meant to represent the finest of painting, then we perhaps should understand that process as one in which the painter becomes a mediator of nature. The strong verbs of action that were used before to describe activity on the part of the painter—seizing, taking, evaluating, etc.—probably ought to be seen as a process of entering into nature, of tapping into its inner energy, of restructuring it rather than structuring it on the silk. This is an interesting point of convergence and divergence between painting and writing. They are both involved with relaying images, in one case visually on the page, in the other as reconstructed mental image. In both cases, the ideal is for the poet or the painter to disappear from the poem or the painting and present an illusion of unmediated reflection of the world outside. Painting, it seems to me, has an edge here because it can visually reproduce the world as a tangible image. Poetry, especially if chanted, can only recreate a mental replica based on words. While I realize that both poetry and painting are stamped by a kind of idiolect, a visual image can be reflected in a mirror, a lake, even a mirage, so other things in nature can approximate the representation of the painter. Words are solely a human creation (although this begs the question posed by poets like Ouyang Xiu, who see the world filled with a zoological variety of languages); are they therefore tied more strongly to personality than style is to a painter? Is it the analytical and classificatory nature of language that is an impediment to creating this illusion of unmediated phenomena? (I am reminded of the last couplet of Tao Qian's famous poem: "There is authentic meaning in all this, / Desire to discriminate it and already the words are lost" [*ci zhong you zhen yi, yu bian yi wang yan*].)

"Generally there are four forces in the brush: they are called muscle, flesh, bone, and breath. When the pen ceases but the [meaning is not] broken it is called ligature; gaining substance through thickening and thinning is called flesh; strength and straightness that [determines whether a work] is dead or alive is called bone; delineating the painting without quailing is called breath. Therefore it can be known that ink that is thick and plain loses the body [of the painting] and that which is too slight in form destroys the correct breath. Those where the ligatures are dead have no flesh, those where the brush stops have no ligature, those that squeeze out a seductive beauty have no bone."

> I have chosen breath rather than vigor as a translation for *qi* here because of the metaphor of the body, although the two are actually one. As is well known, Chinese aesthetic and philosophical concepts are related—the world is conceived of as an evolving organism—and share the sense of a dynamic process of evolving of being in a constant state of motion or flux. I presume this is also one reason why a good deal of the vocabulary of this piece is drawn from the *Book of Changes*. The structural integrity of the work and its animating power are also expressed in the metaphor of a living body.

"There are also two kinds of defects: the first is called nonform, the second is called form. Defects of form: flowers and trees out of season, the building small, the person too large. Or perhaps the trees are taller than the mountain or the bridge does not reach far enough up the bank. These are categories that can be construed from form. As for defects of this order—one cannot alter the layout. Defects of nonform: when vital energy and resonance both have disappeared, when the image of the thing is completely perverse. Even though brush and ink have been applied, its categories are that of dead objects. Because this is a problem of artless style, one cannot either trim it away or rework it."

> One text suggests a variant for the line "one cannot alter the layout" (*bu ke gai tu*) as "one can still alter the layout" (*shang ke gai tu*). The logic of this change is that problems of perspective or of actual lines can be fixed,

but the inability to "see" nature is not a technical problem. This is appealing, since it makes the distinction between the kind of regimen required to shape the mental and ethical field of creativity and the technical elements of layout. However, if we read it as I have translated it above, then it makes the inner person the seat of both aspects. Perhaps reminiscent of the relationship between inner nature and outward form found between *ren* and *li*? This would make sense in binding technical practice and mental regimen in an inseparable unity as inner experience.

"Since you like to draw clouds, forests, mountains, and streams it is necessary that you understand the sources of objects and their images. Now a tree's birth and growth are in accord with the nature that it receives. The pine grows bent but is not crooked. It can be thick or sparse, neither dark green nor light green. From the time it is a tiny sapling it is naturally upright and the mind it has as a sprout is never brought low. Once its tendent force is toward independence and loftiness, its branches grow low, bend downward, or even hang straight down without touching the ground and are divided into layers as though clssked in the forest. They are like the wind of a gentleman's virtue."

> The language used in this description is that of ethics. For instance, the phrase "grows bent but is not crooked" can also mean "has been wronged but will not bend" in a context of injustice and response to that injustice. The play on the word nature (*xing*[b]) and life (*sheng*) is clearly drawn from *Mencius* 6A and his famous debate with Gaozi on human nature. The bond between ethics and symbology of the pine tree is sealed with the last line, lifted from a quote in the Confucian *Analects* (12.19): "The innate virtue of the gentleman [*junzi*] is as wind; that of the small person, as grass. When the grass meets the wind, it inevitably bends." This is typically Confucian in the fact that it does not imply force—rather a certain transforming power to which another thing is receptive. Thus, the pine holds dominion not by force but by the virtue of its innate power, to which all other trees and plants are receptive.

"Some are painted as flying dragons or coiling krackens, with wildly placed branches and leaves—but this is not the vital energy or resonance of the pine."

> Cf. Wannabe's description of the pine in the opening passage, in which he describes it as a dragon. Was he simply overwhelmed by the outward appearance of the tree, but did not see the authentic nature of the pine, which holds the same ethical force as a *junzi*? Or is the codger, in fact, only a moralist who is incapable of seeing that the pine may also hold the same relationship to living creatures as it does to plants—a noble dragon arching over lesser beasts.

"The growth of the arbor vitae: it is active with many twists, it is luxuriant but does not flower, there are clear distinctions in its segmented [branches], its outward design turns to follow the sun. Its leaves are like knotted thread and its branches [are wide-weaved] like hempen clothes. Some are painted [in clean undulations] like a snake or like undyed [smooth] silk, or have an empty center or [its outward design] is turned the wrong ways. This is also false.

"That the shape and substance are different in each case for the catalpa, the paulownia, the cedrela, the oak, the elm, the willow, the mulberry, and the sophora is something that even distant thinkers agree on, something that is clearly discernible in each and every case.

"The image of mountains and streams is produced by both vital energy and tendent force. Therefore those pointed on top are called peaks [*feng*ª], those flat on top are called flattops [*ding*], those with round tops are called roundtops [*luan*ª], those that are linked together are called ranges [*ling*], those with caves are called caverned [*xiu*], those with steep sides are called scarps [*ya*ª], the middle and lower parts of the scarps are called cliffs [*yan*ª]; where a road penetrates into a mountain is called a valley [*gu*ª]; those without roads are called canyons [*yu*ᵇ]. The stream in a canyon is called a brook [*xi*], one lined by mountains a creek [*jian*ª]. Although roundtops and peaks may be different at the summit, the ridges and ranges and bottom connect together, now hiding, now revealing forests and springs, indistinct as it moves from far to near. Painting a landscape without these images is wrong."

> The poverty of nonscientific vocabulary in English for shapes and sizes of mountains and streams of water, and the regionalized (or even national) nature of that vocabulary, is quite stunning.

"Some who paint flowing water go wild as soon as they apply the brush—the outward design is like broken thread, there are no rising or falling sections of waves. This is also wrong. Now, as for fog, clouds, mists, and vapors, there is an appropriate season for them to be light or heavy; their tendent force is dependent on the wind. In every case their image cannot be fixed. One must do away with any complicated representation of them and select their general features. Only after one can deduce right and wrong in this manner can one receive instruction in the methods of the brush."

I said, "Who among those who were learned in the past had fulfilled [these six essentials]?"

Codger said, "Those who actually got it were few. Xie He classified Lu Tanwei as the very best, but now it is hard to find any traces of Lu's own hand. Paintings left by Zhang Sengyou are extremely deficient in basic principles. Now, as for 'applying color by kind': there have been capable artists since antiquity. But as for the practice of graded washes of watered ink, that began in our Tang dynasty. The trees and rocks of former Second Secretary

Zhang Zao are replete in both vital energy and resonance and are extremely fine in brush and ink. His authenticity and thought were surpassing and he did not value the five colors—he is a man unprecedented in the past and unsurpassed in the present."

> Xie He (early sixth century) was an early critic of painting. He ranked the works of Lu Tanwei as the best of the best. His classification scheme is similar to that of Zhong Rong in the *Shipin*. Zhang Sengyou was most noted for the wall paintings commissioned for temples by Liang Wudi. Zhang Zao was an early Tang painter noted for his landscapes, especially trees and rocks. In his short history and critique of landscape painting here, Jing Hao is applying his criteria. So we should read terms like "brush," "ink," "authenticity," "vital ether," "resonance," etc., in light of his earlier definitions and understand this to be not just a history of the development of landscape painting but a judicious selection of good and bad examples of application of *his* principles.

"Qu Ting and the Exalted Master of the White Clouds—their vital energy and images are abstruse and subtle, and in all cases have captured the hidden secrets [of painting]. Their movements transcended the ordinary and reached a depth that is unfathomable."

> Nothing is known about Qu Ting, but the Exalted Master of the White Clouds is the famous scholar and Daoist Sima Chengzhen (647–735). The lexicon used to describe their works is adapted from Daoist discourse: "hidden" (*you^c*), "subtle" (*miao*), "mysterious" (*yuan* = *xuan*), all terms commonly used to describe the ineffable Dao.

"Assistant Director of the Right, Wang Wei (701–61)—his brush and ink are lithesome and radiantly beautiful, his vital energy and resonance are lofty and pure. Images are brought to completion with clever drawing, and these are animated by authenticity and thought. General Li Sixun (651–718)— profound in principle and far-reaching in thought. The traces of his brush are extremely fine. Although clever and outwardly patterned, they are greatly deficient in colors (= grades) of ink. The hermit Xiang Rong's (late eighth–early ninth century) trees and rocks are blunt and rough, with sharp corners but without [protuberance/swelling?]."

> The word (*chui?*) appears in no dictionary; but if allied to other words in this phonetic family, it can possibly mean "swelling," "protuberance," "knob," etc.

"In his use of the ink he has gotten the 'gates of mystery' but in his application of the brush he lacks any of its bones. Be it so, in his abandonment he has not lost either vital energy or image of the authentic primordial [state],

and he was, from the beginning, able to greatly reduce cleverness and seductive beauty."

> Cf. above: "Those where the ligatures are dead have no flesh, those
> where the brush stops have no ligatures, those that squeeze out a
> seductive beauty have no bone."

Wu Daozi (eighth century)—his brush excelled in image, and his bone and
vital energy were naturally loft. . . . But it is also a pity he had no ink."

> In another essay, Jing Hao remarked, "Wu Daozi, in painting landscapes,
> has brush but no ink; Xiang Rong has ink, but no brush." The meaning
> of the phrase following "naturally lofty" (*shu bu yan tu*) is not clear to me.
> Bush and Shih have translated it as "he achieved painting which made
> rival artists speechless." It could possibly mean that, if we take *shu . . . tu* as
> verb-object, and understand *shu* as "to set up" or "establish" and, by exten-
> sion, "to create." This seems to me a weak reading. I would suggest reading
> it as "when establishing [images], he did not speak of (= had no need of)
> mapping them out first." At any rate, its meaning is opaque to me.

"Supernumerary Chen Tan, the monk Dao Pin, and those below them in
skill are roughly of the ordinary kind. Their contrivances have no originality, and in the actualization of brush and ink there are plenty of places where
one can see their own marks. Now I have shown you this path, but I cannot
completely explain it all."

Subsequently I took out the "Painting of the Extraordinary Pine" that I
had drawn previously and showed it to him. Codger said, "Flesh and brush
have no method to them, the ligatures and bones do not turn together. How
can you apply these to such an extraordinary pine? Since I have now taught
you, sir, the proper brush method . . . "

> This last line appears to be incomplete—there is either a dropped line in
> the text, or the second part of the line remains unspoken.

Only then did he bring several pieces of raw silk and ordered me to draw on
them in front of him. Codger said, "'Your hand, my heart!' I have heard it
said, 'Examine his words and know his moral actions.' Can you eulogize this
[pine?] with words?"

> An interesting passage that sites the text in the middle of the ethical
> values of literature. It has long been an aphorism that one can know
> a person through his or her writing (*jian qi wen zhi qi ren*). Moreover,
> the phrase *zi neng yu wo yan yong zhi hu* has a pronoun as an object, the
> antecedent of which is somewhat unclear. Does "it" refer to the pine on
> the silk, or the pine itself? The underlying question, of course, is, "Can
> language reproduce the qualities of the pine as well as this painting has?"

I thanked him, saying, "Only now do I know that moral development through instruction is the duty of the sage and the worthy. They cannot leave off, no matter if they live long or die early, for they are moved by and respond to what they see as traces of goodness or repugnance [? or: I am moved and respond to the revealed traces of good and evil?]. Having been led [to the right path] and advanced [by you] in such a manner as this, dare I not fulfill your command?"

Consequently I composed "Encomium for the Ancient Pine," which reads,

> Neither dropping its leaves "nor putting on airs"—
> That staunch pine alone.
> Tendent force lofty and precipitous,
> It can still forfeit its integrity to show respect.
> Leaves long, a canopy of jade-green,
> Branches coiled, dragons of red.
> Below are tendrilling grasses,
> Deep in the shade, thick and luxuriant.
> This is how it attained its growth,
> Tendent force drawing near the cloudy peaks.
> Raise the eyes up along its soaring trunk [rising above all others],
> Supporting thousands of canopied limbs,
> Soaring and majestic in the middle of the brook—
> A jade-green luminescence covered by mist.
> Strange branches hang downward,
> Restless, shifting, adaptive.
> When it joins ordinary trees below,
> "It brings them to harmony but does not accommodate itself to them."
> This is why it was valued and written of in poems—
> It possessed the moral air of the Superior Man.
> This breeze is fresh and unceasing,
> And its faint murmur crystallizes in the void.

The pine, first encountered as a supernal object, full of a nearly mythic power, is finally tamed as a cultural and ethical symbol. The lexicon of description is indebted to Confucianism; two phrases are drawn directly from the *Analects,* one ascribing to the pine the attributes of a Superior Man (*he er bu tong*—following Yang Bojun's interpretation in his *Lunyu yi zhu*) and the other of the master, Confucius himself (*ju bu rong*). Some nice parallels are developed by framing a discussion of painting and technique by the pine: it dominates landscape painting as an object of power and force, and its qualities, construed in an ethical world, dominate the life of a person. Its symbology provides an interesting bridge between art and ethics and between painting and literature. Wannabe's initial reaction of being overwhelmed by the power of the pine and his inability to draw it—before receiving an essentially moral instruction on painting—is an interesting comment on the need to refine through

ethical action a fertile inner ground of receptivity to external stimulus.
That is, although the discussion is about techniques of landscape
painting, the educational process is one of moral (hence, aesthetic)
cultivation. And of course, it answers the implicit question above:
literature can portray the same values.

Codger sighed in approval over its extraordinary quality for a long time, then
said, "I hope that you will stay hard at it; then you can forget brush and ink
and possess the authentic scene. The place I live is amid the stone drum cliffs,
and I am styled the Master of the Stone Drum Cliff."

I said, "I want to put myself in your service."

Codger said, "This is not the inevitable outcome [of our meeting]." Consequently, I quickly bid goodbye and departed. On another day I sought him
out, but he had disappeared. Later on I practiced his techniques of the brush,
and having valued what I had received as instruction, I now edit and collect
them to provide a standard set of rules for painting [that later generations
can follow].

BI FA JI
Stephen Owen

This treatise is built around pedagogic *fa* ("method") material of a Late Tang
flavor, mixing "theory" with categorical taxonomies. This formally conventional material is set in an anecdote, a "scene of instruction."[2] Though such
scenes of instruction have their conventional aspects, both their norms and
particular variations are significant, situating the introduction of the pedagogic material. On the conventional side of the frame story, the anonymous
old man, clearly a Daoist type, suggests esoteric knowledge received by a
chance encounter and outside of the established social structures of education (though our anonymous old man demonstrates a remarkable connoisseurship of Tang painting, which could come only from moving in elite circles). Surprise and accident here govern the transmission of knowledge. Such
knowledge derives from an encounter that is accidental, of limited duration
(the teacher must be removed from the stage after the lesson is given), and
thus not generally accessible. The reader is implicitly told that he cannot go
find the old man and get instruction in his school—he must rely on this text.
Thus the text divulges esoteric knowledge (knowledge properly transmitted

2. For convenience I use the term "Tang" here to include the Five Dynasties; Jing Hao himself refers to *wu Tang dai*, though we do not know the situation from which Jing Hao makes this
reference. Although the *Bunkyō hifuron* shows the existence of *fa* pedagogy in the eighth century, the handling of the lesson here shares many features with texts of literary pedagogy from
the ninth and tenth centuries.

through the personal relation of master and disciple), as in Daoist and some Buddhist religious texts.

The particular deviation from normative "scenes of instruction" in the anecdotal frame does deserve some reflection. The narrator begins with a mysterious encounter with numinous pines and returns to depict them on his own. There is a process of learning from encounter, observation, and practice that approaches success: "when he had done several tens of thousands, they [his sketches] were like the genuine ones." This is interesting because such immediacy of representational study is given here only to be superseded by the esoteric instruction of the old man. The implied message is clear and characteristic of the Tang: the authority of esoteric learning supersedes what one can learn on one's own. The autodidact painter only prepares himself for higher learning from the authority. The *Bi fa ji* inserts itself in the position of the esoteric human authority as a secondary textual representation of such authority; it textually represents the old man's learning and is its counterpart—otherwise one could learn painting on one's own, simply by observation and practice, without the essay.

The old man begins with the staple of Tang pedagogy: a taxonomy of essentials, arranged hierarchically from the most general to the most immediate. The young man proposes a definitional error ("painting [marking] is the flower[y]," *huazhe hua ye [a]*), an error compounded by an equally problematic elaboration: "Valuing similitude achieves the genuine" (*gui si de zhen*). Within established values, such primacy given to externals begs correction.[3]

The old man's correction draws authority from the form of the tautological gloss (*hua zhe hua ye [b]*), which appeals to other senses of a word which, in the given context, would be understood in a more limited way (for example, *Feng feng ye* in the "Preface" to the *Mao shi*). The *hua*[b] of "marking out" is thus linked to "measurement" or "estimation," with the object being not the thing itself but its "image," *xiang*. I will not attempt my own history of this loaded word *xiang;* in a context like this, I doubt such a history is warranted. It is used unreflectively in the Tang as "appearance" or "semblance" and here seems to be the positive alternative to merely external "similitude," *si*. In the context of the technical terms that surround it, this *xiang* is "appearance" in a deeper sense than *si*, a mode of "appearance" that leads the deliberative painter to grasp the "substance" (fruit, *shi*[d]) as well as the "flower," *hua*[a].

At this point the writer is merely offering handles for the old man's exposition and the frame ceases to be important. The old man's answer is, how-

---

3. *Si* is an interesting term. By itself as an "unmarked term," as given here, it is presumed to be purely external. To be salvaged for the primacy of the interior in representations, it must be made a "marked term," such as *shensi*, "spirit resemblance."

ever, interesting. The privileging of *qi* as the interior term is expected; its presence guarantees authenticity, *zhen*. What is not expected from similar texts is the elaboration: "Whenever the *qi* is transmitted in the flower and omitted in the semblance [*xiang*], it is the death of the semblance." Both *hua*ᵃ and *xiang* are external terms; we are reminded that we are dealing with a treatise on painting that *must* valorize external appearance (as a treatise of poetry need not). Instead of the familiar "outside bad/inside good," here we have a bad outside (*hua*ᵃ) and a good outside (*xiang*); what differentiates them is the immanence of *qi*. We should also here point out that *hua*ᵃ usually suggests engrossing intricacy and detail ("flowery" as well as "flower"), while *xiang* represents something more schematic, some legible integrity of the representational whole.

The next exchange between the old man and the writer is remarkable, even though it is merely preparatory for what is explicitly the next stage of the lesson. Painting, calligraphy, and other genteel arts such as *qin* playing are explained as substitutes for destructive passions and desires. Poetry and writing are not included. In the ninth century poetry is commonly referred to as an obsession, *pi*, as these other aesthetic activities would also be. In "Chanting Alone in the Mountains," Bai Juyi had linked poetry with karmic attachments:

> Each person has some one addiction,
> my addiction is to writing:
> All worldly attachments have melted away,
> I am left with this sole affliction.

There would, I think, have been no problem in inserting painting, calligraphy, or *qin*-playing here in place of literary pursuits in this passage. This is the beginning of the transformation of poetry to a place as one aesthetic activity among others in *wenren* culture. I suspect that the exclusion of poetry and writing from the list of aesthetic alternatives to dangerous desire in the *Bi fa ji* is due to the fact that writing, with its link to social qualification procedures, is still considered something "serious," as opposed to the aesthetic activities, which are pastimes.

The development of the notion of aesthetic pastimes as *pi*, "obsession," lies behind the remarkable defense of painting and other aesthetic activities here. Such activities are substitutes, *dai*, for baser passions and thus approved.

The dialogue interrupts but does not thwart Tang pedagogic rhetoric. When the old man tells the writer that he should continue his study to the end, the expert reader knows that the initial taxonomy of six terms will next be elaborated ("going further" is not following a linear argument but going into detail regarding preestablished terms). I hope I will be forgiven the suspicion that the form of exposition (and thus of the kind of knowledge promised) is more significant than the particular formulations of elaboration. Consider, for example, the amplification of the term *qi*: "mind follows the process of the brush, and one seizes the semblance [*xiang*] without error [uncertainty]." Such stress on the immediacy of doing (*qi* here belonging to the painter rather than the thing represented) is one of the attributes commonly associated with *qi*. However, I suspect that Jing Hao could have said a hundred other things here without changing our sense of the lesson. There is a great deal in this work that is a variable reaffirmation of shared values. (Imagine if he had written: "Always hesitate and be doubtful in your representation of something; don't just let your brush move freely, but take care to catch the exact proportions of each component of the whole." At this point any student of Chinese aesthetics would gasp.) Whenever we see a value expressed whose alternative is unimaginable at that historical moment, we should not take it simply as an intellectual proposition. Rather we should look at its function within the discourse as a whole or see if there is something of interest in the particular terms of its reformulation.

Although there are various points of interest in the amplification of the Six Essentials, one revealing (though not, I think, anomalous) particular formulation is in Scene (*jing*): "set as your standard the contingencies of the moment [season]." The temporal circumstantiality of "scene" reminds us what this word means in Chinese. There were already categorical "scenes" ("spring scenes," etc.), but scene is radically localized, and primarily localized in time. Thus we do not use *jing* in the same way that we might say in English "the scene of the Grand Canyon." *Jing* is determined not as some essentialized object of contemplation, but through a temporally and spatially localized perceiver.

Next the old man offers four more categories, amplifies them, then four categories of "force," *shi*[b], in handling the brush, amplifying them in the alternative form in which the terse qualification precedes the term (*weizhi* X). The first set of four categories (spirit, fineness, marvel, and artfulness) were relatively "spiritual"; the second set (sinew, flesh, bone, *qi* [breath]) are somatic. At this point we know, by the customs of such pedagogic expositions, that "faults," *bing*, will soon appear.

When we leave the faults, we come again to material of interest, not so much because it represents something "original" or profound, but because it elaborates something rarely elaborated: *xing*[b], which I understand as "categorical nature." *Xing*[b] is not the particular nature of a thing per se, and it is the abstract "given nature [of any thing]" only by generalizing from its primary sense as "categorical nature." The issue here is not nature as a whole, nor is it the nature of the particular thing in itself, but the categorical nature of a pine as opposed to that of a cypress. In the Western theoretical tradition we would say that the stress on the object of representation is here typological: if the painter does a particular pine, it is a particular pine as a typical pine. Before unpacking the implications of this in regard to the frame narrative and the first part of the essay, let me stress that through the term *xing*[b] the "typical" is given an ontological grounding (an Aristotelian *tupos* would give us much the same thing, but much history has passed since we could use the term "typical" with quite the same force): the described properties of the pine that the painter should represent determine its identity, what it "is."

This does, however, bear a close relation to the beginning of the essay. In the opening the writer went out and drew what he observed, external appearances; the old man advised him to look deeper—to interior terms such as "substance," *shi*[d], "material," *zhi*[g], and *qi*, and to the privileged exterior manifestation of "semblance," *xiang*. Here we see that the normative Gestalt that organizes interior terms and which we see through *xiang* is the categorical term *xing*[b]. Something like: "to see the Pine in the tree that you see before you," to see all the particulars of the percept in relation to the categorical "pine." If a pine, by circumstantial determinations, looks like a cypress [realizing that I have given away the idea of categorical norm in this formulation], one sees it in representation not as some hypothetical pure percept (the "like the genuine ones" of the beginning of the essay), but precisely as deviation from a categorical norm. We might—without intending disrespect—see the relation between such a theory of representation and a botanical handbook that would permit the user to "recognize" a pine in its variety.

The "Nature and Normative Form" (*Tixing*) chapter of *Wenxin diaolong* is a similar treatment of genres, grounded in some norm that unfolds in the particular. While this is not surprising, there are large cultural and political implications in this mode of "estimating," *du*[a], particular phenomena in regard to their embodiment of categorical norm.

The passage that follows ("the images of mountains and waters," *shanshui zhi xiang*) animates categorical norm in descending and increasingly fluid variation. As suggested above, the painter is the one who does not paint appearances rashly, *kuang*, but paints them with awareness of the underlying order in their variation. A century after Jing Hao we will use the term that Jing Hao does not use: *li*[b]. Though he does not use the term, Jing Hao's argument, such as it is, has a vested interest in finding such a term with the weight it was to acquire.

Let me gloss over the "character appraisal," *pinti renwu*, section that follows. One should measure the comments made here against those made elsewhere, look at the historical story being told in the attributes and selection. The appraisal of various historical figures is a subcategory in the technical pedagogic treatise (*fa*), sometimes separate, and sometimes following the taxonomy of essentials, as here (Tang calligraphic treatises are excellent examples).

The last section of the essay has an unexpected twist that makes this text more than one more *fa.* Although the writer proclaims himself to be a "plowman," there is no question (as in his first response to the old man) that he is a member of the literary elite. The wisdom of the painter is a kind of understanding that is outside the system of literary learning. But once the literary man has mastered this technique that makes possible some translinguistic identification ("your hand [brushwork] is my mind"), the old man asks for the verbal representation as a complement. The literary text produced becomes both the counterpart of the visual representation and the elite repayment for the lesson which transcends elite status. The imperatives of the frame narrative overcome the imperatives of *fa* contained within the frame narrative.

Thus we have the "Verse on Old Pines." Unlike the initial, naïve representation of percepts, this is a normative representation (*zan*, the genre, unlike *shi*, promises a purely normative representation). The process of pedagogy in the essay, devaluing the immediacy of the percept in favor of the reflective discovery of sensuous norm within the percept, points toward this kind of counterpart in verbal representation. The "elevation" of painting, precisely the pedagogic process implicated in the whole essay, moves toward such an elite verbal representation. Class forces are at work in the ideology of representation; and despite the hierarchical inversion of the frame story ("Old fellow, your deportment and frame are those of a rustic—how could you understand the *fa* of the brush?"), the underclassed values of painting are making a claim on the highest values of elite culture. After doing so, their representative, the old man, asks for a verse to "second" (*zan*) them.

Before commenting on the *zan*, let me return to the formulation: "your hand is my mind." This is obviously an appeal to one of the highest elite values, that of the "one who knows the tone," the *zhiyin*. In the *Liezi* version of the Bo Ya and Zhongzi Qi story, Bo Ya praises Zhongzi Qi's ability to listen and give words to what he hears: "the images you envision are like [what was in] my heart." In the case of Bo Ya and Zhongzi Qi, we have a unique friendship of long standing, with each friend using a different expressive medium: for Bo Ya music and for Zhongzi Qi words that comment on his experience of the music. In the *Bi fa ji*, however, we have a chance encounter between the writer and the old man; and the ground of the version of communication here is not in individual feeling, but in the representation of normative *xiang* grounded in nature. Thus the implicit claim here is that *anyone* would feel the "rightness" of representations by our newly enlightened painter. They would look and say: "Ah! Now *that's* a pine tree."

It may be the stress on the visual norm of *xiang* that permits the figurative implications that come through so clearly in the *zan; xiang* is also strongly associated with figural meaning. The pine tree embodies "the quality of a superior man." By leaving the mimesis of sensuous surfaces (what the speaker had achieved on his own before meeting the old man) and learning to represent the norm within the visual particular, painting is able to have conceptual content embodied in "images," *xiang,* as poetry does.

Finally the essay ends as we know it must, with the old man offering his Daoist toponym, Guyanzi, and, as he must, disappearing without a trace, leaving the present writer as the sole possessor and transmitter of the esoteric knowledge the old man has provided.

His last words of advice before identifying himself and departing are: "Brushwork and ink may be forgotten, yet you may [still] have a genuine scene." It troubles no one accustomed to such texts that "brushwork," *bi^d,* and "ink," *mo,* were two of the Six Essentials that were the heart of the old man's instruction. What was previously "essential" (*yao*) now becomes something that "may be forgotten" (*kewang*). The rejection of the technical in favor of the intuitive reaffirms general values; however, in pedagogic taxonomies of literary composition like the old man's "Essentials," the technical aspects or externals are usually given at the end of a list. My intention in pointing this out is to reiterate what I said earlier: the "meaning" of such statements is in their appeal to shared values and discursive norms. The text is not an "argument" in a strict sense but a formulation [and application to painting] of what readers were already disposed to believe. It would be overinterpretation to say that at the end the old man means: "And *now,* having seen evidence of your enlightened expertise in painting, you can disregard the last two of my Six Essentials, brushwork and ink."

What drives the old man's final bit of advice is the most basic pattern of learning, and hence of pedagogy: to begin with technique (Six Essentials) or some other version of reflective study and to end by asserting the values of prereflective performance, when technique becomes "second nature."

HOW TO READ A CHINESE PAINTING

Jing Hao's Bi fa ji

Martin Powers

It was William Carlos Williams who said "no ideas but in things." The sentiment is well-suited to Jing Hao's essay on painting. Consider the following lines:

> Since you like to paint clouds and trees, mountains and streams, it is
> necessary to understand the origins of each object [*wu*] and its expressive
> figure [*xiang*]. When a tree grows, it does so according to its received

nature. A pine tree in growing may curve but will never become crooked or perverse . . . From the time it is a sapling onward it is naturally upright, its developing heart/core will not bend/bow. Its stature is thus solitary/independent and tall/noble.[4]

Up to this point Jing Hao has said nothing that is not literally true of the object "pine tree."[5] The core does grow upright; pines are tall and may grow in isolation. The native reader (or the sinologist), however, knows that *xin* is not just "core" but also "heart"; *du*[b] is not just "solitary" but also "independent"; *gao* is not just "tall" but also "noble." The idea of independence is inherent in the condition of spatial isolation. The idea of nobility is inherent in the condition of height. Each objective feature of the natural object is significant for a human observer.

At this stage in the text these two sets of meanings hover about in indeterminacy like a quantum wave/particle. But the author drives home their significance very shortly when he says that "in the forest, the horizontal layers of its branches appear to be piled one upon the other. Thus [appearing as a breeze blowing gently over the swaying grasses], they are like the breeze of a virtuous gentleman [which inspires the people to lead virtuous lives]."[6] The writer has simply described the objective features of pine trees. His language, however, enables him simultaneously to highlight matters of human significance.

Throughout this essay I will be assuming that texts about painting were not written as abstract exercises, but refer in all cases to concrete painting techniques familiar to the author. Thus no one ever writes of a "landscape" in neutral terms, as if there were such a thing. The concept "landscape" presupposes the notion that a natural "view" involves an aesthetic experience which is in dialogue with paintings of such views. For this reason the language a writer of painting theory adopts can tell us much about concepts of representation underlying his essay. Taking the example of the passage just cited, it can hardly be fortuitous that the human significance of the pine is expressed in gestural configurations: bending, uprightness, crookedness, solitariness. For this reason I have not interpreted *wu xiang* as a compound mean-

4. Compare Susan Bush and Hsio-yen Shih, *Early Chinese Texts on Painting* (Cambridge, Mass.: Harvard University Press, 1985), 146–47.

5. See Stephen Owen's discussion of the factual, object-oriented nature of Chinese poetic imagery in Stephen Owen, *Traditional Chinese Poetry and Poetics: Omen of the World* (Madison: University of Wisconsin Press, 1985), 13–15. A similar point is explored at length in Pauline Yu, *The Reading of Imagery in the Chinese Poetic Tradition* (Princeton, N.J.: Princeton University Press, 1987), ch. 5.

6. Here I have relied heavily on Susan Bush's insightful translation. See Bush and Shih, *Texts,* 147.

ing "object." In keeping with Williams's sentiments, one might treat *wu* as the thing and *xiang* as the idea expressed in the thing's structure, configuration or disposition. Since such expressive shapes can be reproduced in a painting, much of Jing Hao's essay is dedicated to convincing the budding painter that his representation of *wu* must be such as to reveal its *xiang*.

If this view is correct, then it implies a mode of pictorial expression based upon structural configurations. Such an approach would contrast sharply with the European tradition, where allegory and attribute are the normal vehicles for abstract ideas. The notion that mood and character could be revealed in bodily motion was not unknown in the European tradition.[7] In China, however, unlike Europe, art critics appear to have transferred this mode of expression directly to landscape when the latter became an important genre.

This thesis finds immediate application in Jing Hao's essay, for he concludes his remarks on the pine tree by referring to its *qiyun:* "Sometimes a pine tree is painted like a coiling dragon in flight, its branches and leaves growing in wild disarray. This does not represent the *qiyun* of pine trees."[8]

To translate *qiyun* here as "spirit resonance" contributes little to our understanding of the passage. I have argued that the critical term *qiyun* originally described the manner or character detectable in a person's posture, motions and gestures. This interpretation parallels Chen Zhaoxiu's argument that *qi*, in Liu Xie's sixth-century literary theory, corresponds roughly to the modern *qizhi*, or "character."[9] The term *qiyun* was applied to painting during the Six Dynasties period because figure painting was the dominant mode of expression at that time. Human character was a major issue for the ruling elites of this period, so critics developed concepts to describe the ways in which character and manner could be expressed visually.[10] If we apply this understanding of *qiyun* to the Jing Hao essay one can make better sense of the last line, translating as follows: "[Such configurations] contradict the character of pine trees." In this rendition Jing Hao's final point grows naturally out of the preceding text. Jing Hao had established earlier that the pine's human significance was expressed in its straight, independent and unbending postures. Though it may bend, it never becomes "crooked." Naturally, the twisted structure of coiling dragons expresses a character markedly different from this. If

7. Michael Baxandall, *Painting and Experience in Fifteenth Century Italy* (Oxford: Oxford University Press, 1972), 60–81.

8. Translation based upon Bush and Shih, *Texts,* 147.

9. Chen Zhaoxiu, *Wenxin diaolong shuyu tanzhe* (An Investigation into Critical Terms in Liu Xie's *Wenxin diaolong*) (Taipei: Wenshizhe Publishing Co., 1986), 120–24.

10. Martin J. Powers, "Character (Ch'i) and Gesture (Shih) in Early Chinese Art and Criticism," in *International Colloquium on Chinese Art History,* 1991, 4 vols., (Taipei: National Palace Museum, 1992), 2:909–31.

this interpretation is correct, it suggests that the expressive element in the figure (*xiang*) was derived from the sense of motion implied in the shape.

In reference to human figures, a gestural theory of pictorial expression does not require special ontological or epistemological assumptions; many traditions of painting worldwide seem to have adopted one or another version of the idea. Applied to landscape, however, it does. Landscape, unlike human figures, is not animate in any obvious sense. Jing Hao's theory seems to imply, moreover, that what is most significant about natural objects is their motion, explicit or implicit. Such a view is clearly at odds with the Greco-Roman tradition, in which substances or essences are regarded as truly real, while movement, like color, or other attributes, are classed as "accidents."

Jing Hao's concern with the expressive potential of the movement suggested by structure might strike one as odd had not scholars in other areas also stressed the role of dynamic models in Chinese traditions of thought. In calling attention to the nominalist character of ancient Chinese thought, A. C. Graham and Chad Hansen have cast doubt upon any attempt to impose essentialist modes of reasoning on Chinese sources.[11] Abandoning essentialism requires turning to more dynamic spatial models, and Graham has been articulate in favoring this view for early China: "Chinese philosophy, as much as Western, is a quest for the eternal behind the transient; but the West has sought it through the subject, through substance (for example, Platonic forms), China through the directive, as Way. For the verb-centered consciousness everything is process, and there can be constancy only in the paths of the changing."[12]

I am not certain about the "eternal behind the transient," but attention to the term "verb-centered consciousness" might help to illuminate large chunks of Chinese painting theory. There are those who maintain that thought itself—or at least the logic of thought—is inescapably spatial in character. Such concepts as "possession" or even consciousness, it has been argued, seem to presuppose a figure/ground model, as it were, in the "wiring" of our minds.[13] Even if one remains cool to such theories, an epistemology founded on the inviolable discreteness of identities would have to find pictorial expression in a style stressing figure/ground distinctions.

11. See, for example, A. C. Graham, "Relating Categories to Question Forms in Pre-Han Chinese Thought," reprinted in A. C. Graham, *Studies in Chinese Philosophy and Philosophical Literature* (New York: Institute of East Asian Philosophies, 1986), 360–411; Chad Hansen, *Language and Logic in Ancient China* (Ann Arbor: University of Michigan Press, 1983), especially 141 ff.

12. Graham, "Categories," 403.

13. Ronald W. Langacker has argued that certain fundamental cognitive operations are based upon figure/ground distinctions. See "Reference-point Constructions," *Cognitive Linguistics* 4, no. 1 (1993): 1–38. For more on the spatial character of cognition, see also George

Depending upon the degree to which it is stressed, the distinction between figure and ground corresponds to the assertion that the most essential information about an object's identity is contained within itself. The more thoroughly an object is integrated with its pictorial surroundings, the more complex and contingent its identity becomes. Figure/ground distinctions are important in narrative and descriptive pictures because, within a story, discrete agents may assume cause-and-effect relations with respect to one another. One agent issues commands, another obeys; one desires, another resists, but for the point of the story to remain clear, the identities of the agents must remain distinct. It is not surprising, then, that "clarity of form" tends to be stressed in the Classical tradition of painting in Europe.[14]

The point here is certainly *not* that Chinese art is based on motion and Western art on substance. The histories of China and Europe are too varied and complex for such grand generalizations. Figure/ground distinctions are sometimes favored in Chinese art, for example, in the engravings of Later Han Shandong. In such works, delineating the identities of individual figures was clearly a major concern of both draftsman and audience.[15] Much of Chinese figure painting, in fact, sets the figure off against a blank or simple ground. The motion-centered model suggested by Graham could hardly apply to all of Chinese history, but it does suggest the availability of a motion-oriented epistemology in the tradition. I am suggesting that Jing Hao made use of that availability.

The linguistic philosophers are not the only ones to have noticed a distinctive approach to the problem of substances and identities in some Chinese writings. A resonant—if not strictly parallel—line of thinking can be found in the field of Chinese literature. Stephen Owen's account of the Chinese concept of *wen* (pattern) and its implications for Chinese poetry is consistent with Graham in that it eschews an essentialist reading of Chinese thought:

> The history of Western literary thought develops in a melancholy competition between determining representation and a determining but hidden "original" content . . . But if literature [*wen*] is the entelechy of a previously

---

Lakoff and Mark Johnson, "Conceptual Metaphor in Everyday Language," *The Journal of Philosophy* 77, no. 8 (1980): 453–86; Hoyt Alverson, "Metaphor and Experience: Looking Over the Notion of Image Schema," in *Beyond Metaphor: The Theory of Tropes in Anthropology*, ed. James W. Fernandez (Stanford, Calif.: Stanford University Press, 1991), 94–117.

14. For the moral overtones of clean pictorial distinctions in the classical tradition see Michael Greenhalgh, *The Classical Tradition in Art* (New York: Harper & Row, 1978), 200–204.

15. For one view of the rhetorical implications of this style see Martin J. Powers, *Art and Political Expression in Early China* (New Haven, Conn.: Yale University Press, 1991), 171–187.

unrealized pattern, and if the written word [wen] is not a sign but a schematization, then there can be no competition for dominance. Each level of wen, that of the world and that of the poem, is valid only in its own correlative realm; and the poem, the final outward form, is a stage of fullness.[16]

Of course the "original" content in much European thought is that subject, that essence, which our languages encourage us to identify with the real. Unless I misunderstand Owen, the interdependence of identities implied in his scheme is in no way essentialist, and the fact that this world cannot be separated from the human interpretation of it is consistent with nominalism. It seems to me also that, when he speaks of "correlative" realms, Owen does not have in mind anything like sympathetic magic, for this would require that discrete identities "influence" one another across space by means of some mystical force (an essentialist account). Rather, when speaking of "categorical association," he says that "each thing and event of the world is the fragment of a coherent whole, and knowledge of the whole unfolds out of the fragment."[17] In this reading, the identities of individual objects are ultimately interdependent.

If one were to schematize this view of the world in visual form, I would be inclined to adopt a fractal pattern, in which the same structures realize themselves in similar ways at different places and at different scales. In such a schema no causation is involved because the little spiral at one corner of the design is simply one individual expression of a pattern manifesting itself more largely and in slightly different form elsewhere.[18]

Fractal-like dispositions do occur in the history of Chinese pictorial art. They are most obvious in early Han depictions of the circulating qi and the living creatures who quite literally grow out of its path of circulation. In such compositions a small vocabulary of shapes appears again and again in variations at different scales. In a micro-view one variant will turn out to be a dragon; another, a goat or a vegetable form. In such a pictorial scheme, the virtual absence of figure/ground distinctions hampers the delineation of discrete identities, although differences will emerge upon close inspection. However, the identities of "different" objects not only share a common "flow" from which they all emerge—they may even be seen as individual expressions of a small set of "patterns." Insofar as such a picture makes assertions about the nature of Nature, it must have been informed by an epistemology

16. Stephen Owen, Omen, 21.
17. Ibid., 23.
18. I am assuming that the popularization of fractals has evolved to the point that all readers will be familiar with them. Those who are not may consult Nina Hall, ed., The New Scientist Guide to Chaos (London: Reed Business Information, Ltd., 1992). The trendy appeal of fractals should not blind the sinologist to their potential for modeling some features of Chinese thought.

in which the identities of the objects depicted were understood to be, in some sense, shared. Artist and viewer alike had to subscribe to this epistemology.

Fractal-like patterns also occur in Chinese landscape. In fact, the major traditions, such as the Dong-Ju tradition, the Guo Xi tradition, or the Li Cheng tradition, can all be distinguished according to the kinds of "patterns" (painterly gestures) that serve at different scales to represent mountains, hills, rocks, clouds and even trees. It would not be too extreme to see in such structures diagrams of the notion that "each thing and event of the world is the fragment of a coherent whole, and knowledge of the whole unfolds out of the fragment." Indeed, one wonders if the li^b which Chinese writers so often "see" in natural scenery does not refer to concrete dispositions of fractal patterns such as river systems or the branching of mountain ranges, but that is a subject for another essay.

Whether we speak of *xiang, qi* or li^b, the key concept is "identity." The basic work of pictorial artists consists in delineating the identities of objects, and each mode of representation necessarily adopts an epistemological orientation. The special value of art critical texts lies in the fact that the author will unwittingly help to highlight this epistemology through the terms used to describe relationships between the depiction and the depicted. This brings us back to Jing Hao, for his is the earliest text to systematically apply the traditional discourse of figural expression to landscape.[19] His use of *qi,* shi^b and *xiang* all presuppose that what is significant and authentic in natural objects is not their substance but their configuration.

In the following examples, shi^b always implies a gesture, disposition or stance expressive of personal qualities:

Pan jiu zhi shi, yu fu yunhan.

"[The pine's] gestures were like those of a writing dragon about to ascend the milky way."[20]

Shi ji du gao.

"Its stature is thus solitary/independent and tall/noble."

---

19. Gu Kaizhi used some of the same terms to describe landscape, but of course he did not provide a systematic theory of landscape painting. See William Acker, trans., *Some T'ang and Pre-T'ang Texts on Chinese Painting,* 3 vols. (Leiden: E. J. Brill, 1954 and 1974), 2:73, 3:71.

20. The personal quality here is the character of a man of startling talent. The metaphor goes back at least as far as Warring States times, but is stated explicitly in *Yantielun.* The court officers in the salt and iron debates maintain that, when men of accomplishment acquire positions of stature, "they are like dragons plunging into water or soaring serpents disporting on the clouds." Huan Kuan, *Yantielun* (Shanghai: Shanghai Renmin Publishing Co., 1974), 10.23. Translation based upon Esson M. Gale, trans., *Discourses on Salt and Iron,* reprint ed. (Taipei: Chengwen Publishing Co., 1973), 63–64. Earlier references occur in *Zhuangzi* and *Yanzi chunqiu.*

Shi gao er xian, qu jie yi gong.

"Its stature is high/noble and inaccessible/aloof, yet deferential [bending] in respect [to others]."

Qu jie of course means to be deferential, but the idea is expressed in part through reference to the gesture of bending, or yielding, to others. Again, it is obvious that human beings can express themselves in such ways and earlier art critics were aware of this.[21] Here, however, Jing Hao is applying this idea to natural objects and by extension to landscape painting. Once we understand this, the close relationship of *qi* and *shi*[b] in Jing Hao's scheme becomes intelligible:

Shan shui zhi xiang, qi shi xiang sheng.

"In the expressive figures of the landscape, the characters and gestures of things give rise to one another."

The thesis I am proposing here enables one to render these lines as a coherent statement of theory. Character *qi* is what is expressed, but it is expressed by means of gesture *shi*[b]. The gesture, however, being a motion, cannot actually be seen on silk within the fictive space of the painting (literati painting, with its emphasis on brush stroke as a record of a gesture, had not yet been invented); the gesture is only implicit in a form, the expressive figure of the tree, rock or hill. Jing Hao's theory has a special term for this expressive figure, namely, a *xiang*.

There is no need to suppose that Jing Hao invented this use of *xiang*. Comparable usages can be found in the *Zhou yi*. In the *Xici* one can find sentences in which the configurational nature of *xiang* manifests itself:

Fen wei er yi xiang liang.

"They are divided into two in order to express/represent [the idea of] pairedness."

She zhi yi si, yi xiang sishi.

"They are counted through by fours, in order to express/represent [the idea of] the four seasons."[22]

"Two" relates to "pairedness" as the pine's solitariness (*du*[b]) relates to its independence. The first term is a structure displayed in a thing (*wu*); the second term is the same structure regarded as expressing something humanly

---

21. Powers, "Character and Gesture," 914.
22. *Zhou yi jijie zhi buzheng*, ed. Yang Chia-luo (Taipei: Shijie Books, 1975), 8.393–394.

significant, a *xiang*. When *xiang* is used as a verb, "express" conveys something of its sense. However, when it is used as a noun, the emphasis changes. Sometimes it appears as if that something expressed, the *xiang*, may be a *consequence* of some other activity, and in this manner, by metonymy, becomes a sign for that activity. For example:

> *Shigu jixiong zhe, shide zhi xiang ye.*[23]

> "For this reason [*shigu*], fortune and misfortune [*jixiong*] are [*ye*] the expression/sign [*xiang*] of [*zh^h*] gain and loss [*shide*]."

Note that the proposition is not put the other way around. It may not be that bad luck brings about losses. Rather, the word order suggests that our sense of misfortune may be both a consequence and an expression of having suffered some loss.

> *Bianhua zhe, jintui zhi xiang ye.*[24]

> "Transformation is the expression/sign of alternating changes."

This reading takes *jintui* as a compound, much like *fangyuan*, where the latter is best translated as "shape," not "the round and the square." Transformation is a value-laden consequence which we recognize after change has taken place. The engine of change is understood as the process of alternating conditions, "advancement and retreat."

> "The sages had the means with which to survey the origins of [phenomena] in the world and to draft their forms and appearances. [Their drafts] expressed [*xiang*] the [significance of the] objects appropriately. Therefore, we call them 'expressions' [*xiang*]."[25]

In this reading the verbal and nominal uses of *xiang* acquire their separate senses naturally. Of course we refer to the hexagrams as "expressions," because they "express" the dynamic structure of all phenomena. In each case, the significant element is a structure or configuration in which some kind of action is implicit.

I would not claim that *xiang* always carries this sense in Chinese writings. China's culture is rich and multistranded. Not all pictorial strategies are fractal in nature, and not all discourses are built upon verb-oriented thinking. It may even be that the "verb-centered" reading of *xiang* is less appropriate

---

23. *Zhou yi*, 8.369.
24. Ibid., 8.370.
25. Ibid., 8.383. Compare also Yu, *Imagery*, 39.

for the *Book of Changes*. I list these examples to show that Jing Hao could have derived the notion of *xiang*-as-figure from one reading of the *Book of Changes*. On the more positive side, my reading is consistent with two points Pauline Yu has made in her more extensive study of the term. First, Yu argues that *xiang* does not correspond to "representation" in the European sense. The concept of mimesis is lacking. She shows, for instance, that *xiang* is much more integrally related to its object than "representation" implies. In my reading, Jing Hao's *xiang* is naturally close to its object because the "expression," as interpreted by the observer, is a consequence of the object's structure. Secondly, like Owen, Yu sees categorical correspondences as intrinsically dynamic in nature.[26] My reading of Jing Hao would tend to conform to this thesis also.

Quite possibly Jing Hao's most revealing use of *xiang* occurs in the following passage:

> In the expressive configurations of the landscape, the characters and
> gestures of things give rise to one another. Therefore [in mountains],
> pointed forms are called "peaks," flat ones are called "plateaus." . . . Al-
> though the peaks and hilltops are distinct, the hills and ranges beneath
> them are connected, first hiding then revealing forests and streams, [creat-
> ing an effect] similar to that of distance. To paint landscapes lacking this
> expressive configuration is also contrary [to nature].

The "therefore" at the outset of this passage indicates that the examples provided of mountain forms are meant to illustrate the meaning of "in the expressive configurations of the landscape, the characters and gestures of things give rise to one another." In keeping with everything said about *xiang* above, some of these forms are solitary, some connected, some are steep, some slope gently and so on. Each of these configurations harbors a distinct expressive figure which is implicitly dynamic. Shape and action are fused as when a bent tree which, to the European eye, looks static, is interpreted as "bending" deferentially. All shapes express some kind of gesture, even if that gesture is the act of being solitary.

A comparably dynamic understanding of form may underlie Jing Hao's explanation of the representation and perception of distance. As he views the *xiang* of the landscape, he realizes that, while peaks appear to be separate, they ultimately connect at their root. There is significance in this; it is an expression of a fundamental unity underlying apparently distinct units. By virtue of their shape, the peaks can be seen as individuating themselves from a mass of connected earthy excrescences. He realizes further that the same structure/process of (fractal-like) individuation out of union can be

26. Yu, *Imagery*, 39–43.

seen in the configurations of forests and the streams. They all share in this process of individuation and in this sense can be said to share some portion of their identity; they are of the same "kind." But since individuation is a process or path, it has a direction; it proceeds from "there" to "here." It is the arrow of this reticulate process of development that gives rise to the sense of distance in landscape, both "real" and painted. It follows that a painting in which such a configuration is absent will be contrary to nature. It is contrary to nature not because it looks "unrealistic," but because it does not adequately reproduce in its manufacture or appearance the structure of natural processes.

One example of how this technique might have worked in practice can be seen in a painting which could, arguably, date to this period (fig. 7.1). In this work, which bears Jing Hao's sobriquet hidden among the rocks, the artist quite literally conveys a sense of distance by increasing or decreasing both size and levels of individuation in a zigzag path from top to bottom (or vice versa). Whether this painting is of the tenth century, as some believe, or simply a very good early copy, the techniques adopted for describing recession in space are common to many surviving copies of works from the tenth century.[27] Possibly Jing's text harbors a subtle rationale for that technique.

It will be obvious that this reading of Jing Hao contradicts most previous interpretations chiefly in the absence of essentialist suppositions. This distinction will become more obvious still in the interpretation of the term *zhen* (real, authentic). Because it is often confused with "Truth," *zhen* lends itself very easily to an essentialist reading of the text. Consider the following lines, which Shio Sakanishi translates as follows:

> Painting is delimitation. By weighing the appearance of objects, one grasps their reality. Present outward form as outward form, and inner reality as inner reality. . . . Resemblance reproduces the formal aspects of objects, but neglects their spirit; truth shows the spirit and substance in like perfection. He who tries to transmit the spirit by means of formal aspect and ends by merely obtaining the outward appearance, will produce a dead thing.[28]

This is a difficult passage which perhaps cannot be satisfactorily rendered into English without commentary. Nonetheless, one feels that Plato would have found this reading attractive. The contrast between outward form and inner "reality," or the eternal battle between falsehood and truth, matter and spirit, implies a world of discrete identities in which the essence of each is

27. See Lawrence Sickman's entry on this work in Lawrence Sickman et al., *Eight Dynasties of Chinese Painting* (Cleveland: Cleveland Museum of Art/Indiana University Press, 1980), 11–12.

28. Shio Sakanishi, trans., *The Spirit of the Brush*, second ed. (London: John Murray, 1948), 87.

Figure 7.1. Jing Hao (ca. 870–98 – ca. 935–40), *Travelers in Snow-Covered Mountains*. Five Dynasties (907–960). Hanging scroll with ink, white pigment and slight color on silk. The Nelson-Atkins Museum of Art, Kansas City, Missouri (Purchase: Nelson Trust).

Figure 7.2. Detail of fig. 7.1.

obscured by the "accidents" of external form. The Oriental artist, however, endowed with mystical insight, sees through the phenomenological clutter to capture the "true" reality. It is understandable that such an interpretation should appeal to readers accustomed to the essentialist orientation of European thought. If, more recently, students of Chinese culture have begun to leave essentialism behind, it is perhaps because it is only in the late twentieth century that intellectuals in the humanities have begun to feel more comfortable with the lessons of Gödel, Heisenberg, Wittgenstein and Zhuangzi. Under these circumstances, it may be possible to venture an alternate reading. According to the interpretation offered above, the expressive structure of a tree is not an inner essence obscured by outer form. It is there all over the tree for all to see. There is nowhere it is not. This does not guarantee, however, that any artist will recognize what is significant in the structure, any more than the presence of two sticks requires that one see in them an expression of pairedness. One suspects that, for Jing Hao, the significance, the expressive figure, is "there" in the tree, whether we see it or not, but in order for it to enter the painting, the artist has to see it first.[29] One might echo Stephen Owen, saying that "each level of *wen*, that of the world and that of the [art work], is valid only in its own correlative realm." Nonetheless the two realms are interdependent. The world is not an illusion, but neither is it available to us free of interpretation as a *Ding an sich*.

A translation consistent with this interpretive stance might look something like this:

> To paint is to plan [i.e., lay out configurations]. One grades the objects and their expressive figures, selecting what is genuine. [If you want to paint] an object's decorative details, select [the object's] details. [If you want to paint] an object's actual [figure], select its actual [figure]. One cannot establish the actual [disposition of an object] by selecting its decorative details.

This passage is packed with significant terms. The importance of "select" (*quᵃ*) in this and other early texts (such as Guo Xi's primer on landscape painting) implicitly recognizes some degree of relativity in the act of representation. The limitations of representation force the artist to "choose" from among a range of qualities, all of which might be "there" to varying degrees. Thus the artist cannot depict everything he sees as it "really" is. If he could, there would be no need to emphasize the need for choice. This contrasts with an attitude common in European writings as late as the time of Sir Joshua Reynolds (early nineteenth century), namely, that the artist really can depict the "Truth." Thirty years ago this disparity might have been touted as evidence

29. This would help to explain why the concept of "meeting," (*hui* or *yuᶜ*) is so important in Chinese art theory, but that is a topic appropriate to another essay.

for a lack of "scientific" thinking in China, but in a post-Foucauldian era such a claim would no longer hold. Indeed, now it is Reynolds who appears naïve, while art historians routinely recognize that all pictorial styles require choice. There is no such thing as a neutral style.

Another important term is du^a. Even in early texts the term du^a can simply mean "to measure." However, I suspect that Jing Hao gives to it here an overtone closer to its pre-Han usage. Within the ceremonial grading system of ancient times, du^a often referred to the measurement of human worth, i.e., the "grade" of rank expressed in differential levels of material quality and ornamentation in ceremony. Thus it meant to differentiate grades of importance.[30] According to Jing Hao's text, the artist must select from among the wealth of natural detail those forms and configurations that he feels are most significant.

As students of China know, hua^a is also rich in associations. Since Warring States times it often carried a negative connotation, suggesting some object encrusted with wasteful, laborious details. By late Warring States and early Han times it was associated with courtly opulence in contrast to the scholar's virtuous economy.[31] This particular dichotomy is clearly a live issue for Jing Hao, who consistently stresses the value of modest substance in contrast to empty display. Previously I have tried to associate such views in texts on art with emerging non-aristocratic discourses during the Five Dynasties and Northern Song periods. This view, in my mind, is consistent with many of the insights Peter Bol offers in his recent book on the political and social implications of Song cultural discourses.[32] Whether or not one agrees with Bol's thesis or mine, the two studies present sufficient material to suggest that the showy-opulence-versus-substance theme had become both a cultural and a

30. E.g.: "All this is so that they may provide [suitable] clothing for sacrifices in the temple and insignia for the flags, so as to distinguish the various ranks according to their different degrees/grades [du^a]." *Liji jijie*, ed. Sun Xidan (Beijing: Zhonghua Publishing Co., 1989), 16.458–459. See also passages in *Zuozhuan hui jian*, comm. Takezoe Shin'ichiro (Taipei: n.p., 1961), 2:10–16; *Xunzi jishi*, ed. Li Disheng (Taipei: Xuesheng shuju, 1991), 7.119–121.

31. See Martin J. Powers, "Artistic Taste, the Economy and the Social Order in Former Han China," *Art History* 9, no. 3 (September 1986), 285–305.

32. I first delivered the argument for nonaristocratic discourses in tenth-century painting theory in a lecture for the Mellon series entitled "The Art of Interpreting," sponsored by the History of Art department at Penn State, 1989. After reading Peter Bol's book in 1993 I made amendments to the essay so as to make use of his insights and evidence. That article, "Discourses of Representation in Tenth and Eleventh Century China," was published in Susan C. Scott, ed., *The Art of Interpreting: Papers in Art History from Pennsylvania State University* 9 (University Park: Pennsylvania State University Press, 1995), 89–125. For a more comprehensive discussion of the interplay between cultural discourse and society during the Tang-Song transition, see Peter Bol, *"This Culture of Ours": Intellectual Transitions in T'ang and Sung China* (Stanford, Calif.: Stanford University Press, 1992).

social issue among intellectuals by the tenth century. For this reason we must not read Jing Hao's essay naïvely; it is in his interests to establish a theory of painting in which content takes priority over ornate detail. It is also to his benefit to authorize the painter's work by appeal to the natural order rather than to opulent display.

Having said this, we are left with the question of which formal features in a painting might correspond to "decorative detail." The text does not allow a definitive answer, but my best guess is that Jing Hao is referring to details of form and texture through which an artist may exhibit his technical virtuosity and tickle the sensibilities of connoisseurs who equate rich detail with artistic skill. Because such virtuosity is most readily displayed in details of texture or minor features of form, it naturally detracts from the structural coherence required for rendering the "figure" or *xiang*. This explains why one cannot establish the object's "actual" (figure) by means of decorative detail. From the standpoint of visual perception, the two are at odds with one another. One cannot focus on a wealth of surface detail and to the same degree comprehend an object's *Gestalt*.

This reading is also consistent with what follows:

> [If a painting stresses] resemblance, one captures the form [*xing*[a]] but loses [the object's] character [*qi*]. [If a painting attains] what is authentic [*zhen*], then character [*qi*] and substance [*zhi*[g]] are equally present. Whenever [one tries to] convey character through surface beauty [*hua*[a]], one loses the significant figure [*xiang*]. This is the death of the figure [*xiang*].

From early times onward *xing*[a] (form) tends to refer to material, palpable bodies. In *Zhuangzi* it sometimes simply means "corpse." Thus the choice of this term is appropriate for contrasting "dead" forms with those in which motion is implicit. By focusing on surface texture and details of form, an artist may indeed convey a strong sense of the object's substantial presence—its weight, volume and so on. This would be especially so of Five Dynasties and Northern Song painting, where volume is described by surface texture rather than chiaroscuro. However, because the perception of surface detail competes with the perception of a form's structure, clearly an overemphasis on surface detail leads to the death of the "figure," the *xiang*. On the other hand, character (*qi*) is expressed through the gesture (*shi*[b]) implicit in a shape. Since the structure of such a figure is its source of expression—its *xiang*—it follows that losing *qi* implies the loss of *xiang*.

What about *zhen*? Depicting the expressive structure of an object enables an artist to convey its character, its significance and even its volume or "substance." Indeed, from Han times onward certain schools of painting relied almost exclusively on the portrayal of motion to convey a sense of volume. By the tenth century, texture also would contribute to a sense of volume.

Jing Hao does not proscribe the use of texture; he simply warns against a reliance on excessive detail. For this reason, character (implicit motion) and substance (accuracy of shape, volume and texture) can be equally present. This condition is what Jing Hao calls "genuine."

Defining *zhen* in this way is not a dispassionate observation but an intelligent rhetorical ploy. In both China and Europe, *zhen* and Truth served as effective devices for establishing social priorities. *Zhen* is not Truth because the rhetorical power of Truth derives from its claim to be independent of human interests. If Calvinism is not simply my preferred mode of worship, but is in fact the Truth, then I am justified in persecuting anyone who worships otherwise, for Truth is Good. The persecution, moreover, is not a partial, self-serving act on my part, but a necessary consequence of a Truth that is independent of myself. At least, this is what we are supposed to believe.

As is clear from Jing Hao's essay, *zhen* is not independent of human presence. The expressive figures the artist selects are those genuinely present in nature—among others—but recognizing what is "genuine" (most significant) requires the exercise of judgment by a human being. The artist chooses from among many phenomena those most significant for people. The most significant ones are the genuine ones. Texture may be present in a pine, all right, but it is not significant. It is the pine's independence (du^b) that is most significant. This is why ornate detail is contrasted with the object's "actual" figure. Jing Hao is claiming that an object's movement, or character, is more "actual"—more important to its identity—than its texture, but he is not saying that texture is not "there." The artist makes an interpretive "selection," not an ontological claim.

Of course, *zhen* is no less rhetorically effective for all that. *Zhen* is the opposite of falsehood—it carries authority. In this essay Jing Hao has identified the "genuine" with those dynamic structures in nature expressing significant things. One of the significant things they express is the actuality (shi^d) of simple integrity and the superficiality of ornate beauty. When Jing Hao calls this "genuine," he offers it as a claim against other, implied claims. He makes no appeal either to God or to scripture (a feature, incidentally, associated by European historians with "modernity"). Nonetheless, his scheme appeals to the authority of "nature" in contrast to opulence and he hopes to convince others of the coherence of his view. He is not arguing for the Truth; he is arguing for an alternative discourse.

One should be cautious not to infer too much from Jing Hao's essay. Although some features of his argument are widespread in Chinese traditions (the non-essentialist framework, for instance), others are peculiar to tenth- and eleventh-century discourses. His understanding of the nature and origins of our sense of distance, for instance, corresponds well to strategies for representing distance in the tenth and early eleventh centuries. By the time

Guo Xi's text appeared in the late eleventh century, a new understanding of distance had replaced that which we find in Jing Hao's text. Likewise, the idea that dynamic shapes are inherently expressive remains important in Chinese art theory, but evolves in radical ways. Shortly after the time of Su Shi (1037–1101), the expressive power of shapes could be understood to convey not the "actual" character of a natural object, but the *subjective* character of the artist: "When he painted withered trees, the dried-up branches would twist like dragons leaving no clue [as to their origins]. The texture strokes on his rocks were also original and weird, just like the pent-up twistings in his heart."[33]

It follows that, in literati theory, the meaning of *zhen* also changes drastically. It no longer refers to a match between the expressive figures of the painting and those of natural objects. Now it refers rather to a match between the expressive figures in the painter's mind and those that appear in his or her work.[34] In either case, it would appear worthwhile to pursue the implications of "verb-centered" consciousness for investigating both the theory and the practice of Song Dynasty painting.

PERSPECTIVE ON READINGS OF "THE RECORD OF THE METHOD OF THE BRUSH"

Willard Peterson

For more than four hundred years the brief text known as "The Record of [My Instruction in] the Method of the Brush" has been regarded as an important statement on the aesthetic of landscape painting. The framing story is simple; the problem it sets out for us is intractable. The narrator of the story tells us he found an out-of-the-way place in the mountains with old pine trees. Standing alone was a massive pine, a veritable dragon. (I agree with West's emphatic point that we should not read a simile here; this tree is not merely *like* a dragon.) The other trees were clumped in groves or otherwise disposed around the terrain. The narrator admired them all and the entire strange scene. The next day he returned there with a brush to sketch/draw/paint it; the verb he used, *xie*, is ambiguous but at the very least involved use of his brush. The object of the verb, a pronoun, is commonly read as a plural referring to the pine trees, but I propose we might consider the pronoun as singular, referring to the lone, massive pine, the one that stood out from the rest. After nearly innumerable tries, the narrator succeeded in pro-

33. Deng Chun, *Hua ji* (dated 1167), *Zhongguo meishu lunzhu congkan* series, ed. Huang Miaozi (Beijing: Renmin meishu, 1963), 3.16.

34. For a fuller exposition of this problem, see my article on "Discourses of Representation in Tenth and Eleventh Century China," op. cit.

ducing what he deemed to be a genuine rendering—of the singular old pine in my reading, but of pine trees of that place or even in general for other readers. Was the product of his brush genuine? How does one determine what is genuine? How does a genuine depiction come into being? The framing story implies that these are questions to which the body of the text is to respond, but only the first one is immediately and directly answered—with a no. I propose to consider readings of the text from the perspective of these questions.

The scholarly consensus is that "The Record of the Method of the Brush" was authored by Jing Hao in the tenth century. The version of the text we have today is based on one printed in the 1590s as part of a compilation ascribed to the great literary figure, Wang Shizhen (1526–1590). The compilation, entitled *Wang shi hua yuan*, included many important texts on the art of painting, and since its inclusion "The Record of the Method of the Brush" has been part of the established corpus of theories on landscape painting. In the twentieth century the text has been analyzed and translated numerous times. The edited text, extensive annotation, and a modern translation (except for the poem) were prepared by Wang Bomin in the series *Zhongguo hualun congshu* (Beijing: Renmin meishu, 1963). This is the version of the text used by our three readers. It apparently was not seen by Kiyohiko Munakata, whose authoritative study and translation in English was published in 1974 as *Ching Hao's Pi-fa-chi: A Note on the Art of Brush* (Ascona, Switzerland: Artibus Asiae, 1974). Munakata reviewed the problems of authorship and transmission of the text, acknowledged previous translations (by Waley, Siren, Sakanishi, Lin Yutang, and Aoki and Okamura), prepared an account of the extant biographical materials related to Jing Hao, and sought to situate the text in the larger context of intellectual traditions and the history of landscape painting before and after the tenth century. Munakata's translation was reprinted in Susan Bush and Hsio-yen Shih's compilation *Early Chinese Texts on Painting* (Cambridge, Mass.: Harvard University Press, 1985), but without his wide-ranging annotation, and with the suggestion to move the date of the *Bi fa ji* to the eleventh century (367).

Munakata asserted that the artistic beliefs expressed in "The Record of the Method of the Brush" unify Confucian moral values and what he called Daoist mysticism under Jing Hao's notion of Reality (which is Munakata's rendering of the word *zhen*). The purpose of the "Record" is to provide a theory of how to harmonize brushwork and ink-wash to create that Reality. "And the Reality of Nature was, to him, a manifestation of Cosmos, the harmonious structure based upon Confucian moral virtues, which was at his time a counterpart to the reality of human society characterized by, at least temporarily, chaos and injustice" (8).

Our three readers—West, Owen, and Powers—adopt different approaches to "The Record of the Method of the Brush," but they all, like Munakata, bump against what I regard as the problem of what is genuine. What should it mean, for the narrator of the "Record," to depict a pine tree? I take that to be a reduced or perhaps overly simplified statement of the aesthetic dilemma we as readers are being asked to confront by the author. "The Method of the Brush" is, I presume, an attempt to teach us how to deal with the dilemma of "genuine representation." (This verbal formulation, it should be noticed, may be construed as paradoxical or even self-contradictory.)

West's self-styled "personal reading" is presented in the format of his own translation with interspersed comments. He comes to what I call the dilemma in his comment on the passage near the end, when the old man he calls Codger asks our narrator if he is able to eulogize "it" with words. West asks, "Does 'it' refer to the pine on the silk, or the pine itself?" (Notice that from the context, reference is now being made to a singular "extraordinary pine" which the author earlier had made the subject of his efforts with his brush.) Since the old man has just denounced as inadequate the narrator's previous effort, the "Painting of the Extraordinary Pine," we may infer that the pronoun does not refer to any previous painting. The old man has just presented some lengths of silk and ordered the narrator to sketch/draw/paint "it," but there is no indication that the narrator has done so before the old man's exclamation, "Your hand, my heart," and his request for an encomium. We as readers may infer (and many do, hence West's question) that there is a painting on which the eulogy is to be written. If there is a new painting of the ancient pine tree, then the direct answer to West's question is that the words of praise to "it" could be referring both to the pine tree newly rendered on the gift silk (although it seems strange to me that the painter would write an encomium about his own production) and to the old extraordinary pine tree itself. The words of the encomium preserve this ambiguity by not mentioning anything about painting.

In spite of raising this ambiguity, West presumes there is a painting which satisfies Codger's methodological criteria. West's answer to what I call the dilemma is that the new painting succeeds as a "genuine representation" of the pine tree and thus we may proceed to ask, as he does, "Can language reproduce the qualities of the pine as well as this painting has?" In answering his question, West identifies three distinct realms or strata at play in the "Record of the Method of the Brush": (Confucian) ethics, painting, and literature. By implication, there is a fourth realm or stratum, the physical world of the pine tree as a living entity. In West's phrase, "the pine, first encountered as a supernal object, full of nearly mythic power, is finally tamed as a cultural and ethical symbol." Thus he answers his own question: words, language, literature—the encomium perhaps—"can portray the same values" as the painting can as a "genuine representing" of the values attached to the pine tree. Presumably either medium (poetry or painting) conveying these "same values" involves the pine tree as "a cultural and ethical symbol," to use West's term.

From a different tack, Owen in his reading makes an interpretive point similar to West's in connecting poetry and painting with (Confucian) moral values. "The pine tree embodies 'the quality of a superior man.' By leaving the mimesis of sensuous surfaces . . . and learning to represent the norm within the visual particular, painting is able to have conceptual content embodied in 'images,' *xiang*, as poetry does." This seems to privilege what Owen calls "elite verbal expression." He seems to reverse West's question to make it, Can painting reproduce the qualities of the pine as well as the poem has? Owen reads "The Record of the Method of the Brush" as a whole as implying "the 'elevation' of painting" away from "naive representation of percepts" (as in the beginning of the framing story) toward "the reflective discovery of sensuous norm within the percept." The pivotal term in Owen's interpretation is *xiang*, which he translates as "images," "semblance," and "'appearance' in a deeper sense" than similitude; he refers to it with such glosses as "sensuous norm," "visual norm," "some legible integrity of the representational whole," and "associated with figural meaning." (I should point out that at the beginning of his essay Owen acknowledges that *xiang* is a "loaded word," but implies it is not problematic here.) Most importantly, Owen reads *xiang* as the means or medium through which we see (*sic;* he probably means nonsensory apprehension, not visual perception here) the nature (*xing*^{b}), or, more accurately in his view, the "categorical nature" of a thing, such as a pine tree. The *xiang* (appearance) enables you "to see the Pine in the tree that you see before you." (This rather makes *xing*^{b} into a Platonic Form, but I leave that issue aside here.) The method being taught in this text, in Owen's reading, involves "the representation of normative *xiang* grounded in nature. [The categorical nature or natures of the things being painted? Or Nature, the realm of heaven-and-earth?] Thus the implicit claim here is that *anyone* would feel the 'rightness' of representations by our newly enlightened painter. They [*sic*] would look and say: 'Ah! Now *that's* a pine tree.'" I think the author of "The Record of the Method of the Brush" did not intend that "anyone" or everyone would be able to look at the painting of the pine tree and perceive it as a "genuine representation," any more than the narrator was able to do so before he had imbibed the teaching in "The Method of the Brush." The viewer, it would seem, needs to be as "enlightened" as the painter. To educate viewers is as necessary a function of "The Method" as educating painters.

Owen has provided answers to the questions implied in the framing story. How does one determine what is a genuine representation? By apprehending that it is one that represents the normative *xiang* (image?) by which one apprehends the categorical nature of the thing. How does a genuine representation come into being? By the creative efforts of someone who through learning the techniques of "The Method" achieves "prereflective performance" of his art.

Powers extends his reading of the method in Jing Hao's text to become his own proposed method of reading a Chinese landscape painting. In order to do this, Powers chooses to read some key terms in an unusual fashion. Beginning with the interesting claim that critical vocabulary was applied to persons and to figure painting and later applied to landscape painting by Jing Hao, and further claiming that such terms should be understood in a dynamic and processual rather than static or substantive (or what he calls "essentialist") sense, Powers proposes that qi (which West renders as "vital energy" and Munakata as "spirit") should be read as "character" (which is "detectable in a person's posture, motions and gestures") and shi^b ("force" in the translations of Munakata, West, and Owen) as "gesture." I believe many readers will be able to grasp what Powers seems to have in mind when he says that a mountain range as well as a pine tree may be perceived to have "character" and to be making a "gesture" in a landscape painting and, presumably, among what he calls "natural objects" and "natural scenery." Powers takes $xiang$ as "expressive figure" and "configuration," and as a verb meaning "to express." (Given his emphasis on what he calls "verb-oriented thinking," Powers might have done better to render $xiang$ as figuring, configuring, and expressing, but we shall see why he cannot.)

Consider the sentence "*Shan shui zhi xiang, qi shi xiang sheng.*" Munakata's version is, "The different formations [*xiang*] of mountains and streams are formulated by the combinations of life force [*qi*] and formal force [*shi^b*]." By his use of the verb "formulated," Munakata takes the sentence to refer to activity on the plane surface of a painting. West has, "The image of mountains and streams is produced by both vital energy and tendent force," which takes the sentence and its context as referring to "phenomena in nature." I think Powers may be taking the sentence to be about landscape painting when he renders it as, "In the expressive figures [or configurations] of the landscape, the characters [*qi*] and gestures [*shi^b*] of things give rise to one another." (Notice that this interpretation is quite different from Owen's view that *xiang* are the means by which one may apprehend "categorical natures" [*xing^b*] of things.) For Powers, this sentence contains "a coherent statement of theory"; he seems to be referring to both Jing Hao's and his own method of seeing a landscape painting. I infer this because Powers says "character" (*qi*) can be "expressed only by means of gesture" (*shi^b*), and gesture, "being a motion, cannot actually be executed on silk; the gesture is only implicit in the expressive figure of the tree, rock or hill." This explanation seems to put the *xiang* on the silk as a product of the painter's skill. My inference is strengthened when Powers goes on to cite the "Great Commentary" of the *Book of Changes* to explicate *xiang*. In his unusual reading, a *xiang* is a "consequence or result of some other activity." (The usual reading is to take the prognostications of "well-fortuned" and "ill-fortuned" as figures occurring prior to the predicted "gain" and "loss.") Powers thinks "our subjective sense of misfortune [i.e., the divination text's forecast, in the usual reading] is both a consequence and an expression of having suffered some loss." Thus for Powers *xiang* seem to be products, expressions of dynamic structure "in which some kind of action is implicit." (He does not say latent or potential.) Powers makes his point explicitly: "In my reading Jing Hao's *xiang* is naturally close to its object [but, I add, here not apparently 'of' the object] because the 'expression,' as interpreted by the observer, is a consequence of the object's structure." This is an innovative reading, and it has the merit of showing how we might see a landscape painting as paralleling a painting of a human which captures the vitality of the subject's character in a dynamic moment for the viewers to apprehend the "genuine" person or mountain scene. However, Powers undermines this reading by adding another meaning to *xiang*. Perhaps because he is "comfortable with the lessons of Gödel, Heisenberg, Wittgenstein, and Zhuangzi," Powers undoes his own interpretation of *xiang* by relocating it from the silk of the landscape painting to the "natural scenery." In this added sense, the *xiang* is not just "there all over the tree for all to see," which implies that *xiang* is an aspect of appearance and perception. It is also, for Powers, an attribute of the tree. As he puts it, "One suspects that, for Jing Hao, the significance, the expressive figure [i.e., the *xiang*], is 'there' in the tree, whether we see it or not, but in order for it to enter the painting, the artist has to see it first. . . . " In this sentence, *xiang* cannot be a "consequent or result of some other activity;" it is there prior to, and regardless of, anyone's perception or depiction of it. Defining "the basic work of pictorial artists" as "delineating the identities of objects," with identity apparently intended to mean the particular character of the human depicted in a portrait or the scene depicted in a landscape painting, Powers asserts that art theory texts usefully expose "the [epistemological?] relationships between the depiction and the depicted," and that Jing Hao's "use of *qi* [character], *shi*[b] [gesture] and *xiang* [figural expression?] all presuppose that which is significant and authentic [or genuine?] in natural objects is not their substance but their configuration [*xiang*]." In this manner Powers must come to the dilemma of "genuine representation."

In Powers's terms, the condition "Jing Hao calls 'genuine'" involves depicting *xiang* that are in the "natural scenery." "Depicting the expressive structure of an object enables an artist to convey its character [*qi*], its significance and even its volume or 'substance.'" "In the reinterpretation, it is "the genuine" that is "expressed" [*xiang*?] on the silk. According to Powers, "As is clear from Jing Hao's essay, *zhen* [genuine] is not independent of human presence. The expressive figures [*xiang*] the artist conveys are regarded as those genuinely present in nature, but recognizing what is genuine requires a human presence. . . . Those [recognitions?] that are most significant are the genuine ones." Of course this undermines the theory of *xiang* being results conveying characters and gestures in the picture plane, and creates the new problem of how to determine or recognize significance. Powers seems to think he has finessed this problem when he writes, apparently with Jing Hao of the tenth century in mind, that "the meaning of *zhen* [genuine] . . . refers to a match between the expressive figures [*xiang*] of the painting and those [*xiang*] of natural objects." If I am correct in inferring that "identity" is not like "match," the question is begged, How is a "match" achieved? The framing story implies it is not an easy matter of achieving similitude.

I propose we look again at the text of "The Record of [My Instruction in] the Method of the Brush." Conventional as it may be in genre and content, it is intended to tell us readers something. What do we read? One day the narrator went into a mountainous area and saw some old pine trees, of which one large pine stood alone. The next day, he returned with his brush, and after many tries (although we are not told how long a period elapsed), the narrator had one or more (products of his brush) which to him were as if genuine (*zhen*). Not knowing any better at this stage of the narrative, we readers interpret "genuine" here to mean an apparently genuine (or authentic or truthful or real) pictorial rendering of a pine tree or pine trees. The next spring (which clearly conveys the idea that some time has elapsed), the narrator was in a mountainous place with stone-drum cliffs when he met an old man. Later the old man tells the narrator that he lives in this place and is styled Master of Stone-Drum Cliff. We also read that he appears to be a rustic. He turns out to have well-formed judgments on the famous learned painters of the past. And of course he provides the narrator with a set of oral teachings on the method of the brush. It seems that we as readers cannot know more than these bits and pieces which are part of the narration. But we can make suppositions, and I suppose the grand old lone pine tree which appears in anthropomorphized form to the narrator. (Remember Powers's point about starting with figure painting?)

Old Pine Tree, if I may call him that, asks the narrator what's up. The narrator tells him what he has told us: that after many tries he succeeded in producing a genuine pictorial rendering of—Old Pine Tree. My guess is that anyone who is told that his or her picture has been painted wants to see it and have an opinion about its "authenticity." We all tend to do it with photographs. Why not Old Pine Tree? At first dubious about Old Pine Tree's having an opinion worth considering, the narrator-painter submits to hearing a list of the Six Essentials of painting (*hua*[b]). Then he interrupts to complain that there is no need for such complication; he gives what all art historians take to be a naïve artist's explanation of painting: painting (as process and product) is flowering (as process and product). The meaning of "flowering" is usually taken in the direction of ornamented, decorative, superficial, and so on, but I think the statement will stand as conveying a sentiment still to be heard today: a (good) painting is a pretty or attractive one. The narrator also gives a naïve statement of method: aiming to achieve a genuine depiction of one's subject, one simply values likeness. At this point in the narration Old Pine Tree has not been shown the narrator's portrait of him, but no matter, he dismisses the narrator's statements about painting as not so.

Instead, Old Pine Tree offers a substitute explanation of painting which seems like a tautology and compels commentators to gloss ingeniously: painting (as process and product) is painting (as process and product). In response to the narrator's (and perhaps anticipating commentators') attempts to explain or define painting as this or that, Old Pine Tree makes what I take to be an insightful point: painting is not some other process or product (such as flowering or duplicating or measuring); painting is what it is. Think of Magritte's well-known painting of a pipe with the legend, "Ceci n'est pas une pipe." Of course a pipe in a painting is not a pipe (to be used in smoking), and a pine tree in a portrait is not a pine tree, but our ordinary language lends itself to omission or suppression of the distinction. Lest the narrator (and the reader) infer that Old Pine Tree is just being simple-minded, he overwhelms the narrator with philosophical juggling about *zhen* (genuine or authentic). This is all too erudite for the narrator, who despairs he cannot succeed to such painting. Not to worry, Old Pine Tree assures him, I shall tell you about it. Thus we have exposition of Six Essentials, Four Critical Assessments applied to painting, Four Forces in using one's brush, and Two Types of Defects commonly encountered in painting. In each of these categorical expositions, we have explicit mention of brush and ink. The lesson on the figures (*xiang*) of things is illustrated (so to speak) by way of the example of a pine tree—a pine tree in the mountains, not a painted one.

As Munakata, West and Powers each point out, the descriptive language deployed here for the pine tree has implications of moral values. Old Pine Tree is explicit that the branching of the pine tree is like (*ru*, as if) the powerful, transforming wind of the moral exemplar (*junzi*). Old Pine Tree also reminds the narrator that painting goes wrong by mistaking the figure (*xiang*) of particular species of trees. Similarly, mountains and streams and atmospheres have differing figures (*xiang*) which the painter needs to get right. To show the narrator and us readers that Old Pine Tree knows what he is talking about, we have a review of his judgments on learned painters from the past.

The instruction on painting is all words. Old Pine Tree has not shown the narrator how to do anything, nor even asked him to look at anything. It is at this juncture that the narrator brings out the product of his brush done prior to this spring encounter. It is a depiction of the extraordinary pine. A portrait of Old Pine Tree? As it was done before the instruction on the method of the brush, it will not do, and Old Pine Tree says so. He gives the narrator some lengths of silk to try again, but whether a painting is immediately produced shall remain moot. What is not in doubt is that the narrator accedes to the request for an encomium in words, an "Encomium for Old Pine Tree." The poem depicts (if I may use that word) with his brush the figure (*xiang*) of the extraordinary pine tree the narrator earlier had tried to draw/sketch/paint with his brush. The figure of Old Pine Tree presented to us by the words clearly has moral implications; we are told explicitly in the poem that it also has literary implications.

What we as readers have here is the figure (*xiang*), whatever that might exactly mean, of Old Pine Tree in the words of the encomium, and the figure of the extraordinary pine tree in the words of Old Pine Tree (and also, perhaps, at the beginning of the narrative, in the descriptive words of the narrator), and (at least potentially) the figure of the extraordinary pine tree as produced by brush and ink on silk, and by inference the figure of an extraordinary pine tree out in the mountains in northwest China in the tenth century. These figures (*xiang*) are not identical. I would go further than West and claim that we should not think of one as an image or representation of another. Remember painting is painting. Music is music. The rocks, plants and water in a garden are, in the first instance, things (*wu*) and figures (*xiang*) themselves, even when certain viewers may choose to see them as images or resemblances of something else. The figures of Old Pine Tree in the several media are each conveying moral qualities—as in the transforming wind of the moral exemplar—and if the moral qualities are "genuine," then the figure (*xiang*) in any particular medium is genuine. The author of "The Record of [My Instruction in] the Method of the Brush" is making a moral as much as an aesthetic claim.

GLOSSARY

A *bu yi* B	A 不異 B
A *ji shi* B	A 即是 B
A *shi* B	A 是 B
A *zhe* B *ye*	A 者 B 也
An Lushan	安祿山
anju	安居
ba	霸
Ban Biao	班彪
bao	苞
bao[a]	暴
"Bei zheng fu"	北征賦
"Ben lun"	本論
bense	本色
bi	彼
bi[a]	辟
bi[b]	芘
bi[c]	庇
bi[d]	筆
Bi fa ji	《筆法記》
"Bi gong"	閟宮
bian[a]	辨
bian[b]	辯
bianhua zhe, jintui zhi xiang ye	變化者, 進退之象也
bing	病
Bo Yi	伯夷
boluomiduo	波羅蜜多
boruo	般若
Boruo boluomiduo xin jing	般若波羅蜜多心經

Boruo boluomiduo xin jing lüeshu	般若波羅蜜多心經略疏
Boruo boluomiduo xin jing youzan	般若波羅蜜多心經幽贊
Boruo boluomiduo xin jing zan	般若波羅蜜多心經贊
bu dong xin	不動心
bu ke gai tu	不可改圖
bu ren xin	不忍心
bu tian	補天
buding	不定
bushi	布施
Cai Yong	蔡邕
caizi jiaren	才子佳人
Cao Zhi	曹植
Chaofu	巢父
chaoyin	朝隱
Chen Mengjia	陳夢家
Chen Qiaocong	陳喬樅
"Chen zhi fa shi shi"	陳治法十事
Cheng Hao	程顥
cheng ti	成體
Cheng Xuanying	成玄英
Cheng Yaotian	程瑤田
cheng zhang	成章
Cheng-Zhu	程・朱
chengxin	成心
ch'i	氣
chongyan	重言
chuanqi	傳奇
Chūgoku kodai shahon shikigo shūroku	《中國古代寫本識語集錄》
chui	踹
ci zhong you zhenyi, yu bian yi wang yan	此中有眞意, 欲辯已忘言
Cui	崔
da	大
da[a]	達
da[b]	牽
Da Mao gong	大毛公
Da xue	大學
dai	代
dajue	大覺
Dao / dao	道
Datang xiyu ji	《大唐西域記》
Daoshu	道樞
"Daya"	大雅
de	德
"Dengtuzi haose fu"	登徒子好色賦

Di / di[a]	帝
di[b]	禘
Di Ku	帝嚳
"Diao Qu Yuan"	弔屈原
diaogui	吊詭
dilai	地籟
ding	頂
Ding Fubao	丁福保
dizi	弟子
du[a]	度
du[b]	獨
Du Fu	杜甫
Du Gongbu ji	《杜工部集》
Dunhuang baozang	《敦煌寶藏》
Dunhuang	敦煌
Duo xin jing	多心經
er	而
Erya	《爾雅》
Erya yishu	《爾雅義疏》
fa	法
Facheng	法成
fan	犯
fang	方
fang ru qi zhen	方如其眞
fang zhi qi zhen	方知其眞
fangyuan	方圓
Fanyi mingyi ji	《翻譯名義集》
Fayue	法月
Fayun	法雲
Fazang	法藏
fei	非
fei[a]	腓
fei bi wu wo, fei wo wu suo qu	非彼無我, 非我無所取
fei li bu ko ru	非禮不可入
fei wangqing zhe	非忘情者
feizi zhi	腓字之
fen wei er yi xiang liang	分爲二以象雨
feng	風
feng[a]	峰
Feng feng ye	風風也
Feng Menglong	馮夢龍
feng zi	風姿
fengliu caizi	風流才子
Fengxian	奉先

Fodian yu zhongguo hanyu cihui yanjiu	《佛典與中國漢語詞彙研究》
fu	賦
fuᵃ	弗
fuᵇ	祓
Fu Sinian	傅斯年
Fudan xuebao (Shehui kexue)	《復旦學報（社會科學）》
Fukui Fumimasu	福井文雅
"Futian"	甫田
"Fuyang Hanjian Shijing jianlun"	阜陽漢簡《詩經》簡論
gan wen	敢問
gao	高
Gao Heng	高亨
Gao mei	高禖
"Gao mei jiao she zu miao kao"	高禖郊社祖廟考
"Gaotang fu"	高唐賦
"Gaotang shennü chuanshuo zhi fenxi"	高唐神女傳說之分析
Gaoxin	高辛
Gaozi	告子
Gongsun Chou	公孫丑
gongti shi	宮體詩
gu	故
guᵃ	谷
Gu Lu	辜輅
Gu wuyi yu liushi kao	《古巫醫與六詩考》
guan	觀
Guan shi yin	觀世音
Guan Zhong	管仲
Guanyin	觀音
Guanzi	《管子》
Guanzizai	觀自在
Guanzizai pusa	觀自在菩薩
gui si de zhen	貴似得眞
Guo Xiang	郭象
"Guofeng"	國風
Han Feizi	韓非子
Han shu	《漢書》
Han Ziqiang	韓自強
"Hannya shingyō" no rekishiteki kenkyū	《般若心經の歷史的研究》
hao	好
Hao	滈
haoran zhi qi	浩然之氣
he er bu tong	和而不同
he huan	合歡
hebi yue yi	何必曰異

heju	何居
hong gu	洪谷
Hong lou meng	《紅樓夢》
hongdong	鴻洞
Hongniang	紅娘
Hou Ji	后稷
"Hou Ji shenhua tanyuan"	后稷神話探源
Hu Pingsheng	胡平生
Hu Yuan	胡瑗
Hu Zhu'an	胡竹安
Hu Zi	胡仔
hua	化
hua[a]	華
hua[b]	畫
huaicai buyu	懷才不遇
Huainanzi	《淮南子》
Huang Qing jingjie xubian	《皇清經解續編》
Huang Yongwu	黃永武
Huang Zongxi	黃宗羲
huazhe hua ye [a]	畫者華也
huazhe hua ye [b]	畫者畫也
hui	會
Huihong	惠洪
Huizhong	惠忠
hun	魂
huo	惑
huoluo[a]	濩落
huoluo[b]	瓠落
Ikeda On	池田溫
"Ji"	紀
Ji / ji[b]	稷
ji	集
ji[a]	疾
ji jian ji hao	既堅既好
Jia Yi	賈誼
jian	堅
jian[a]	澗
jian qi wen zhi qi ren	見其文知其人
Jiang	姜
jiang	降
Jiang Shaoyu	蔣紹愚
Jiang Yan	江淹
Jiang Yuan	姜嫄
"Jiang Yuan lü daren ji kao"	姜嫄履大人跡考

Jiao mei	郊禖
Jiao Hong ji	《嬌紅記》
jie	介
jie[a]	節
"Jie chao"	解嘲
jie qi zhigao	解其桎梏
jiesi	潔祀
jieti	解體
jin	今
Jin'gang	金剛
jing	景
Jing Hao	荊浩
jintuichuchu	進退出處
jiu	舊
Jiumoluoshi	鳩摩羅什
ju	居
ju bu rong	居不容
junzi	君子
kang qi jie	抗其節
ke	克
ke qi ke yi	克崎克両
kewang	可忘
"Kōbai kō"	高禖考
Kobayashi Taichirō	小林太市郎
kong	空
Kong Fanli	孔凡禮
Kong Yingda	孔穎達
Kongzi	孔子
ku	苦
kuang	狂
kui	葵
Kuiji	規基
kuoluo	廓落
Li ji	《禮記》
li	禮
li[a]	栗
li[b]	理
Li Shan	驪山
Li Shaoyong	李少雍
Li Zhi	李贄
liang	兩
liangxing	兩行
Liao Deming	廖得明
Lin Qingzhang	林慶彰

ling	岭
Liu Xin	劉歆
Liu Yuxi	劉禹錫
Lu	魯
lü di wu min	履帝武敏
Lu-Wang	陸・王
luan	亂
luan[a]	孿
luansi[a]	亂絲
luansi[b]	亂思
lun[a]	論
lun[b]	綸
Lunyu yizhu	《論語譯注》
Luo Guanzhong	羅貫中
"Luoshen fu"	洛神賦
Lüshi chunqiu	《呂氏春秋》
Ma Ruichen	馬瑞辰
manyan	曼衍
Mao Chang	毛萇
Mao Heng	毛亨
Mao shi	《毛詩》
Mao shi zhuan jian	《毛詩傳箋》
Meng Bin	孟賁
menglang zhi yan	孟浪之言
Mengzi	孟子
miao	妙
mie	滅
min	民
min[a]	敏
ming	明
Mingyi daifang lu	《明夷待訪錄》
mo	墨
Mohe boruo boluomi damingzhou jing	摩訶般若波羅蜜大明咒經
mu[a]	拇
mu[b]	栂
nai	乃
Nanguo Ziqi	南郭子綦
ngjugx	寓
ngugx[a]	耦
ngugx[b]	偶
Ning Xiyuan	寧希元
"Ōgaku no shominsei ni kansuru shakai teki rekishi teki igi"	王學の庶民性に關する社會的歷史的意義

Ono Gemmyō	小野玄妙
Ouyang Xiu	歐陽修
Pan Yue	潘岳
panqiu zhi shi, yu fu yunhan	蟠虬之勢, 欲附雲漢
pi	癖
ping	平
pinti renwu	品題人物
po	魄
posuomosuo	婆娑沒索
Pubian zhizang boruo boluomiduo xin jing	普遍智藏般若波羅蜜多心經
Pucheng	蒲城
pufu	匍匐
pusa	菩薩
Qi	棄
Qi[a]	齊
qi	氣
qi[a]	崎
qi[b]	跂
qi[c]	企
qi[d]	岐
qi[e]	愒
Qi wu lun	齊物論
Qian	乾
qianlong	潛龍
qie	竊
qiliuqulü	乞留曲律
qing	情
qinmin	親民
Qiongzhou	瓊州
qiyi	崎嶷
qiyun	氣韻
qizhi	氣質
qu	去
qu[a]	取
Qu Wanli	屈萬里
Quan-Rong	犬戎
qun bing	群冰
qun shui	群水
ren	仁
ren wei chen ai mo	忍爲塵埃沒
renlai	人籟
renqing	忍情
renzhe ai ren	仁者愛人

renzhe bi you yong	仁者必有勇
renzhe bu you	仁者不憂
renzhe jing	仁者靜
renzhe le shan	仁者樂山
renzhe ren ye	仁者人也
renzhe wu bu ai	仁者無不愛
renzhe wu di	仁者無敵
renzhe yi qi suo ai ji qi suo buai	仁者以其所愛及其所不愛
rjɔg	似
ru	如
ru[a]	入
ru qi zhen	如其眞
Ruan Ji	阮籍
rushi	如是
Ryūkoku shidan	《龍谷史壇》
Sakai Tadao	酒井忠夫
sangwo	喪我
Sanjia shi yishuo kao	《三家詩遺說考》
Sanjia shi	三家詩
Sano Kōji	佐野公治
se	色
se bu yi kong, kong bu yi se. se ji shi kong, kong ji shi se.	色不異空，空不異色。色即是空，空即是色。
Setsurin	《說林》
shang	上
shang ke gai tu	尙可改圖
shangdi	上帝
Shanhai jing	《山海經》
shanshui zhi xiang	山水之象
shanshui zhi xiang, qi shi xiang sheng	山水之象, 氣勢相生
she zhi yi si yi xiang si shi	揲之以四以象四時
Shelifu	舍利弗
Shelizi	舍利子
shen	深
shen[a]	神
shen[b]	身
shen zheng shan	神鉦山
sheng	生
sheng[a]	聲
sheng ji	生計
"Sheng min"	生民
sheng min ru he	生民如何
Shengfomu boruo boluomiduo jing	圣佛母般若波羅蜜多經
Shenglei	《聲類》
Shenhua yu shi	《神話與詩》

"Shennü fu"	神女賦
shenshi	神尸
shensi	神思
Shenzi	申子
shexi	舍息
shi	識
shi[a]	是
shi[b]	勢
shi[c]	使
shi[d]	實
shi[e]	士
shi[f]	詩
Shi	《詩》
shi gao er xian, qujie yi gong	勢高而險，屈節以恭
Shi ji	《史記》
shi ji du gao	勢既獨高
shi jian shi hao	實堅實好
Shi jing	《詩經》
Shi jing jinzhu	《詩經今注》
Shi jing tongshi	《詩經通釋》
Shi jing xuanzhu	《詩經選注》
Shi jing yanjiu lunji	《詩經研究論集》
Shi jing yi yi	《詩經義譯》
Shi jing yundu	《詩經韻讀》
Shi Junbao	石君寶
Shi Nai'an	施耐庵
Shi sanjia yi jishu	《詩三家義集疏》
shi zi	識字
Shiben	《世本》
shibi	詩筆
shicai	史才
shidafu	士大夫
shifei	是非
shigu	是故
shigu jixiong zhe, shide zhi xiang ye	是故吉凶者，失得之象也
Shihu	施護
Shipin	《詩品》
shishi	詩史
Shisi jing xinshu	《十四經新疏》
shiyin	市隱
shou	受
shu bu yan tu	樹不言圖
"Shu xing fu"	述行賦
shuangsheng dieyun	雙聲疊韻
shuiju	誰居
shuo	說

Shuo ya	《說雅》
Shuowen	《說文》
Shuowen jiezi	《說文解字》
Shuowen jiezi gulin	《說文解字詁林》
"Shushi igo ni okeru 'Daigaku' kan no hensen"	朱子以後における『大學』觀の變遷
si	似
si[a]	祀
Si wen Hou Ji	思文后稷
Sima Biao	司馬彪
Sima Xiangru	司馬相如
su	俗
Su Shi	蘇軾
"Sui chu fu"	遂初賦
suiran	雖然
Sun Zuoyun	孫作雲
Taishō shinshū daizōkyō	《大正新修大藏經》
Takakusu Junjirō	高楠順次郎
Tang	唐
Tang fan fandui ziyin boruo boluomiduo xin jing	唐梵翻對字音般若波羅蜜多心經
Tian	天
tianfu	天府
tianjun	天鈞
tianlai	天籟
tianni	天倪
tixing	體性
tjiagx	者
tong ban	同伴
tzu-fan [zifan]	自反
wang	忘
Wang Bomin	王伯敏
Wang Li	王力
Wang shi hua yuan	《王氏畫苑》
Wang Shizhen	王世貞
Wang Shouren	王守仁
Wang Wengao	王文誥
Wang Xianqian	王先謙
Watanabe Kaigyoku	渡辺海旭
Wei	魏
wei chang jin nü se	未嘗近女色
weizhi X	謂之 X
wen	文
Wen Yiduo	聞一多

wenjuan	溫卷
wenren	文人
Wenxin diaolong	《文心雕龍》
wo	我
wo si ru he	我祀如何
wu[a]	悟
wu[b]	誤
wu	物
wu ku ji mie dao	無苦集滅道
wu sheng li	悟生理
wu Tang dai	吾唐代
wu wu ming yi wu wu ming jin	無無明亦無無明盡
wu xiang	物象
wu yun	五蘊
wu yun liu gen	五蘊六根
wu zhi youzhe	物之尤者
wuhua	物化
wuwei	無爲
wuwu	兀兀
wuxing	無形
xi	溪
xi bin	西賓
Xi Kang	嵇康
xi xiang zhi shi	西廂之事
"Xi zheng fu"	西征賦
xia	夏
"Xian ju fu"	閒居賦
xian sheng ru da	先生如達
xiang[a]	相
xiang[b]	想
xiang	象
xianren	仙人
Xiao Gongquan	蕭公權
Xiao Mao gong	小毛公
Xici	《繫辭》
Xie	契
xin[a]	歆
xin	心
Xin jing	心經
Xinbian zhuzi jicheng	《新編諸子集成》
xing[a]	形
xing[b]	性
xing[c]	行
xing dao	行道
xinmin	新民

xinzhai	心齋
xiu[a]	秀
xiu	岫
xu[a]	嘘
xu	虛
Xu You	許由
xuan	玄
xuan zhi you xuan	玄之又玄
xuanjie	縣解
Xuanzang	玄奘
xue	學
xun	循
"Ya" / ya	雅
ya[a]	崖
yan	言
yan[a]	岩
Yan Dunyi	嚴敦頤
Yang Bojun	楊伯峻
Yang Naien	楊耐恩
"Yang sheng lun"	養生論
Yang Xiong	揚雄
Yanzi	《晏子》
yao	要
yi[a]	嶷
yi[b]	嚘
yi[c]	仡
yi[d]	以
yi[e]	議
yi[f]	譯
yi[g]	亦
yi	易
yi fu rushi	亦復如是
yǐ gu	以故
yī gu	依故
yi min wei gui	以民爲貴
yi qi jie	易其節
yi qiu qi bi zhi	以求其必至
yi rushi	亦如是
yi shi	以是
yi shi Kongtong lai	疑是崆峒來
Yi Yin	伊尹
Yijing	《易經》
yilun	議論
yin	因
yin[a]	禋

ying	穎
Yingying zhuan	《鶯鶯傳》
yinshi	因是
yinyi	音譯
yiyi	義譯
yiyi qi da	驛驛其達
yong huai	詠懷
you[a]	攸
you[b]	褎
you[c]	幽
you	遊
you jie you zhi	攸介攸止
youduan	憂端
youwu	尤物
Youxian ku	《遊仙窟》
yu	語
yu[a]	愚
yu[b]	峪
yu[c]	遇
yu fa ru ci zhongzhong	余髮如此種種
Yu Guanying	余冠英
Yu Yue	俞樾
yuan	元
Yuan Zhen	元稹
Yuance	圓測
yue chu xu	樂出虛
"Yue ling"	月令
Yueming heshang du liucui	月明和尚度柳翠
yun xing yu shi pin wu liu xing	雲行雨施品物流形
Yuniang	瑜娘
Yutai xinyong	《玉臺新詠》
yuyan	寓言
ywai tsia ywa ia	畫者華也
ywai tsia ywai ia	畫者畫也
Za ti	雜體
"Zaishan"	載芟
zaju	雜劇
zan	贊
zao	造
Zengzi	曾子
zhang	章
Zhang	張
Zhang sheng	張生
zhege jiushi nage	這個就是那個
zhen[a]	震

zhen	眞
zhen haose zhe	眞好色者
Zheng Xuan	鄭玄
zheng	正
zhenjun	眞君
zhenzai	眞宰
zhi	志
zhi[a]	止
zhi[b]	祉
zhi[c]	知
zhi[d]	智
zhi[e]	至
zhi[f]	製
zhi[g]	質
zhi[h]	之
zhi qi ci	知其次
zhi qing ren	至情人
zhi yan	知言
zhi yi	知意
zhi yi[a]	至矣
zhihui	智慧
Zhihuilun	智慧輪
zhiren	至人
zhiren wuji	至人無己
zhiyan	卮言
zhiyin	知音
zhong[a]	種
zhong[b]	腫
zhong hou	忠厚
Zhong qing li ji	《鍾情麗集》
Zhongguo hualun congshu	《中國畫論叢書》
"Zhongguo jingxue yu zhongguo wenhua"	中國經學與中國文化
Zhongguo zhengzhi sixiang shi	《中國政治思想史》
zhou	咒
"Zhou benji"	周本記
"Zhou song"	周頌
"Zhou song shuo"	周頌說
Zhou yi	《周易》
Zhou You Wang	周幽王
zhu	著
zhu gong diao	諸宮調
Zhu Qingzhi	朱慶之
Zhu Weizheng	朱維錚
Zhu Xi	朱熹
zhuan	轉
Zhuang Zhou	莊周

Zhuangzi	莊子
Zhuangzi jishi	《莊子集釋》
Zhuangzi zuanjian	《莊子纂箋》
zhufa	諸法
zhuo	拙
Zhuo Wenjun	卓文君
zi	自
zi[a]	字
zi bao	自保
zi neng yu wo yan yong zhi hu	子能與我言詠之乎
zi wo guan zhi	自我觀之
zifan	自反
ziji	自己
Ziqi	子綦
ziqu	自取
Ziran (ziran)	自然
zixing	自性
Ziyou	子游
zizai pusa	自在菩薩
zuo	作
zuo you	左右
Zuo zhuan	《左傳》
zuwu	崒兀

《詩經》

生民之什

245. 生民　八章四章章十句四章章八句

①厥初生民。時維姜嫄。生民如何。克禋克祀。以弗無子。履帝武敏歆。攸介攸止。載震載夙。載生載育。時維后稷。　②誕彌厥月。先生如達。不拆[1]不副。無菑無害。以赫厥靈。上帝不寧。不康禋祀。居然生子。　③誕寘之隘巷。牛羊腓字之。誕寘之平林。會伐平林。誕寘之寒冰。鳥覆翼之。鳥乃去矣。后稷呱矣。　④實覃實訏。厥聲載路。誕實匍匐。克岐克嶷。以就口食。蓺之荏菽。荏菽旆旆。禾役穟穟。麻麥幪幪。瓜瓞唪唪。　⑤誕后稷之穡。有相之道。茀厥豐草。種之黃茂。實方實苞。實種實襃。實發實秀。實堅實好。實穎實栗。即有邰家室。　⑥誕降嘉種。維秬維秠。維穈維芑。恒[2]之秬秠。是穫是畝。恒之穈芑。是任是負。以歸肇[3]祀。　⑦誕我祀如何。或舂或揄。或簸或蹂。釋之叟叟。烝之浮浮。載謀載惟。取蕭祭脂。取羝以軷。載燔載烈。以興嗣歲。　⑧卬盛于豆。于豆于登[4]。其香[5]始升。上帝居歆。胡臭亶時。后稷肇祀。庶無罪悔。以迄于今。

　1. 拆一作坼　　2. 恒一作亙　　3. 肇一作肇　　4. 登一作豋　　5. 香一作馨

Reprinted from William Hung, et al., *A Concordance to Shih Ching* 毛詩引得. *Sinological Index Series*, suppl. no. 9 (Peip'ing: Harvard-Yenching Institute 哈佛燕京學社, 1934).

《孟子》

公孫丑上 2

公孫丑問曰。夫子加齊之卿相。得行道焉。雖由此霸王不異矣。如此則動心否乎。孟子曰。否。我四十不動心。曰。若是、則夫子過孟賁遠矣。曰。是不難。告子先我不動心。曰。不動心有道乎。曰。有。北宮黝之養勇也。不膚橈【橈一作撓】。不目逃。思以一豪【豪一作毫】挫於人、若撻之於市朝。不受於褐寬博。亦不受於萬乘之君。視刺萬乘之君若刺褐夫。無嚴諸侯。惡聲至必反之。孟施舍之所養勇也。曰。視不勝猶勝也。量敵而後進。慮勝而後會。是畏三軍者也。舍豈能為必勝哉。能無懼而已矣。孟施舍似曾子。北宮黝似子夏。夫二子之勇、未知其孰賢。然而孟施舍守約也。昔者曾子謂子襄曰。子好勇乎。吾嘗聞大勇於夫子矣。自反而不縮。雖褐寬博、吾不惴【惴一作遄】焉。自反而縮。雖千萬人、吾往矣。孟施舍之守氣又不如曾子之守約也。曰。敢問夫子之不動心與告子之不動心、可得聞與。告子曰。不得於言勿求於心。不得於心勿求於氣。不得於心勿求於氣、可。不得於言勿求於心、不可。夫志、氣之帥【帥一作師】也。氣、體之充也。夫志至焉。氣次焉。故曰。持其志勿暴其氣。既曰。志至焉。氣次焉。又曰持其志勿暴其氣者何也。曰。志一則動氣。氣一則動志也。今夫蹶者趨者、是氣也。而反動其心。敢問夫子惡乎長。曰。我知言。我善養吾浩然之氣。敢問何謂浩然之氣。曰。難言也。其為氣也、至大至剛。以直養而無害。則塞於天地之間。其為氣也、配義與道。無是餒矣。是集義所生者。非義襲而取之也。行有不慊於心、則餒矣。我故曰。告子未嘗知義。以其外之也。必有事焉而勿正。心勿忘。勿助長也。無若宋人然。宋人有閔其苗之不長而揠之者。芒芒然歸。謂其人曰。今日病矣。予助苗長矣。其子趨而往視之。苗則槁矣。天下之不助苗長者寡矣。以為無益而舍之者、不耘苗者也。助之長者、揠苗者也。非徒無益而又害之。何謂知言。曰。詖辭知其所蔽。淫辭知其所陷。邪辭知其所離。遁辭知其所窮。生於其心。害於其政。發於其政。害於其事。聖人復起必從吾言矣。宰我、子貢善為說辭。冉牛、閔子、顏淵善言德行。孔子兼之。曰。我於辭命則不能也。然則夫子既聖矣乎【一無乎字】。曰。是何言也。昔者子貢問於孔子曰。夫子聖矣乎。孔子曰。聖則吾不能。我學不厭教不倦也。子貢曰。學不厭、智也。教不倦、仁也。仁且智。夫子既聖矣乎。夫聖、孔子不居。是何言也。昔者竊聞之。子夏、子游、子張皆有聖人之一體。冉牛、閔子、顏淵則具體而微。敢問所安。曰。姑舍是。曰。伯夷、伊尹【一無伊尹二字】何如。曰。不同道。非其君不事。非其民不使。治則進。亂則退。伯夷也。何事非君。何使非民。治亦進。亂亦進。伊尹也。可以治則治可以止則止。可以久則久。可以速則速。

孔子也。皆古聖人也。吾未能有行焉。乃所願、則學孔子也。伯夷、伊尹於
孔子。若是班乎。曰。否。自有生民以來未有孔子也。曰。然則有同矣。
曰。有。得百里之地而君之。皆能以朝諸侯有天下。行一不義。殺一不辜。
而得天下。皆不爲也。是則同。曰。敢問其所以異。曰。宰我、子貢、有若
智足以知聖人。汙不至阿其所好。宰我曰。以予觀於夫子。賢於堯舜遠矣。
子貢曰。見其禮而知其政。聞其樂而知其德。由百世之後。等百世之王。莫
之能違也。自生民以來未有夫子也。有若曰。豈惟民哉。麒麟之於走獸。鳳
凰之於飛鳥。泰【泰一作太】山之於土垤。河海之於行潦。類也。聖人之於
民、亦類也。出於其類。拔乎其萃。自生民以來未有盛於孔子也【也上一衍
者字】。

Reprinted from William Hung et al., *A Concordance to Mencius* 孟子引得. *Sinological Index Series* (Peip'ing: Harvard-Yenching Institute 哈佛燕京學社, 1931–47).

《莊子・內篇》

二 齊物論

南郭子綦隱机【机一作几】而坐。仰天而噓。荅【荅一作嗒】焉似喪其耦【耦一作偶】。顏成子游立侍乎前。曰。何居乎。形固可使如槁木。而心固可使如死灰乎。今之隱机者非昔之隱机者也。子綦曰、偃不亦善乎而問之也。今者吾喪我。汝知之乎？女【女一作汝】聞人籟而未聞地籟。女聞地籟而未聞天籟夫。子游曰。敢問其方。子綦曰。夫大塊噫氣。其名為風。是唯無作。作則萬竅怒呺。而獨不聞之寥寥【寥寥一作飂飂】乎。山林之畏【畏一作煨】佳【佳一作隹】。大木百圍之竅【竅一作窽】穴。似鼻。似口。似耳。似枅。似圈。似臼。似洼者。似汙者。激者。謞者。叱者。吸者。叫者。譹者。宎者。咬者。前者于而隨者唱喁。泠風則小和。飄風則大和。厲風濟則眾竅為虛。而獨不見之調調之刁刁乎。子游曰。地籟則眾竅是已。人籟則比竹是已。敢問天籟。子綦曰。夫吹萬不同。而使其自已也。咸其自取。怒者其誰邪。大知閑閑。小知閒閒。大言炎炎【炎一作淡】。小言詹詹【詹一作閻】。其寐也魂交。其覺也形開。與接為搆。日以心鬬。縵者。窖者。密者。小恐惴惴。大恐縵縵。其發若機括。其司是非之謂也。其留如詛盟。其守勝之謂也。其殺若秋冬。以言其日消也。其溺之所為之不可使復之也。其厭也如緘。以言其老洫【洫一作溢】也。近死之心莫使復陽也。喜怒哀樂慮嘆變慹姚佚啟態。樂出虛。蒸成菌。日夜相代乎前而莫知其所萌。已乎已乎。旦暮【暮一作莫】得此。其所由以生乎。非彼無我。非我無所取。是亦近矣。而不知其所為使。若有真宰。而特不得其眹。可行已信。而不見其形。有情而無形。百骸九竅六臟。賅而存焉。吾誰與為親。汝皆說【說一作悅，後倣此】之乎。其有私焉。如是皆有為臣妾乎。其臣妾不足以相治乎。其遞相為君臣乎。其有真君存焉。如求得其情與不得。無益損乎其真。一受其成形。不忘以待盡。與物相刃相靡。其行盡如馳。而莫之能止。不亦悲乎。終身役役而不見其成功。苶【苶一作薾】然疲役而不知其所歸。可不哀邪。人謂之不死奚益。其形化。其心與之然。可不謂大哀乎。人之生也。固若是芒乎。其我獨芒。而人亦有不芒者乎。夫隨其成心而師之。誰獨且無師乎。奚必知代而心自取者有之。愚者與有焉。未成乎心而有是非。是今日適越而昔至也。是以無有為有。無有為有。雖有神禹。且不能知。吾獨且奈何哉。夫言非吹也。言者有言。其所言者。特未定也。果有言邪。其未嘗有言邪。其以為異於鷇音。亦有辯乎。其無辯乎。道惡乎隱而有真偽。言惡乎隱而有是非。道惡乎往而不存。言惡乎存而不可。道隱於小成。言隱於榮華。故有儒墨之是非。以是其所非。而非其所是。欲是其所非。而非其所是。則莫若以明。物無非彼。物無非是。自彼則不見。自知則知之。故曰。彼出於是。是亦因彼。彼是。方生之說也。雖然。方生方死。方死方生。方可方不可。方不可方可。因是因非。因非因是。是以聖人不由。而照之於天。亦因是也。是亦彼也。彼亦是也。彼亦一是非。此亦一是非。果且有彼是乎哉。彼是莫得其偶。謂之道樞。樞始得其環中。以應無窮。是亦一無窮。非亦一無窮也。故曰。莫若以明。以指喻指之非指。不若以非指喻指之非指也。以馬喻馬之非馬。不若以非馬喻馬之非馬也。天地一指也。萬物一馬也。可乎可。不可乎不可。道行之而成。物謂之而然。惡乎然。然於然。惡乎不然。不然於不然。物固有所然。物固有所可。無物不然。無物不可【一本可下有：可於可而不可於不可，不可於不可而可於可也，二句】。故為是舉莛與楹。厲與西施。恢【恢一作弔】恑憰怪。道通為一。其分也成也。其成也毀也。凡物無成與毀。復通為一。為是不用而寓諸庸。庸也者用也。用也者通也。通也者得也。適得而幾矣。因是已。已而不知其然謂之道。勞神明為一。而不知其同也。謂之朝三。何謂朝三。狙公賦芧。曰。朝三而暮四。眾狙皆怒。曰。然則朝四而暮三。眾狙皆悅。名實未虧。而喜怒為用。亦因是也。是以聖人和之以是非。而休乎天鈞【鈞一作均】。是之謂兩行。古之人其知有所至矣。惡乎至。有以為未始有物者。至矣盡矣。不可以加矣。其次以為有物矣。而未始有封也。其次以為有封焉。而未始有是非也。是非之彰也。道之所以虧也。道之所以虧。愛之所以成。果且有成與虧乎哉。果且無成與虧乎哉。有成與虧。故昭氏之鼓琴也。無成與虧。故昭氏之不鼓琴也。昭文之鼓琴也。師曠之枝策也。惠子之據梧也。三子之知幾乎。皆其盛者也。故載之末年。唯其好之也。以異於彼。其好之也。欲以明之。彼非所明而明之。故以堅白之昧終。而其子又以文之綸終。終身無成。若是而可謂成乎。雖我亦成也。若是而不可謂成乎。物與我無成也。是故滑疑之耀。聖人之所圖也。為是不用而寓諸庸。此之謂以明。今且有言於此。不知其與是類乎。其與是不類乎。類與不類。相與為類。則與彼無以異矣。雖然。請嘗言之。有始也者。有未始有始也者。有未始有夫未始有始也者。有有也者。有無也者。有未始有無也者。有未始有夫未始有無也者。俄而有無矣。而未知有無之果孰有孰無也。今我則已有謂矣。而未知吾所謂之其果有謂乎。其果無謂乎。天下莫大於秋豪之末。而大山為小。莫壽於殤子。而彭祖為夭。天地與我並生。而萬物與我為一。既已為一矣。且得有言乎。既已謂之一矣。且得無言乎。一與言為二。二與一為三。自此以往。巧歷不能得。而況其凡乎。故自無適有以至於三。而況自有適有乎。無適焉。因是已。夫道未始有封。言未始有常。為是而有畛也。請言其畛。有左有右。有倫【倫一作論】有義【義一作議】。有分有辯。有競有爭。此之謂八德。六合之外。聖人存而不論。六合之內。聖人論而不議。春秋經世先王之志。聖人議而不辯。故分也者有不分也。辯也者有不辯也。曰。何也。聖人懷之。眾人辯之。以相

示也。故曰。辯也者有不見也。夫大道不稱。大辯不言。大仁不仁。大廉不
嗛。大勇不忮。道昭而不道。言辯而不及。仁常而不成。廉清而不信。勇忮
而不成。五者园而幾向【向一作嚮，下倣此】方矣。故知止其所不知。至
矣。孰知不言之辯。不道之道。若有能知。此之謂天府。注焉而不滿。酌焉
而不竭。而不知其所由來。此之謂葆光。故昔者堯問於舜曰。我欲伐宗膾胥
敖。南面而不釋然。其故何也。舜曰。夫三子也。猶存乎蓬艾之間。若不釋
然何哉。昔者十日並出。萬物皆照。而況德之進乎日者乎。齧缺問乎王倪
曰。子知物之所同是乎。曰。吾惡乎知之。子知子之所不知邪。曰。吾惡乎
知之。然則物無知邪。曰。吾惡乎知之。雖然。嘗試言之。庸詎【詎一作
巨】知吾所謂知之非不知邪。庸詎知吾所謂不知之非知邪。且吾嘗試問乎
女。民濕寢則腰疾偏死。鰌然乎哉。木處則惴慄恂懼。猨猴然乎哉。三者孰
知正處。民食芻豢。麋鹿食薦。蝍蛆甘【甘一作且】帶。鴟鴉【鴉一作鵶】
耆【耆一作嗜】鼠。四者孰知正味。猨。猵狙以爲雌。麋與鹿交。鰌與魚
游。毛嬙麗姬【麗姬一作西施】。人之所美也。魚見之深入。鳥見之高飛。
麋鹿見之決驟。四者孰知天下之正色哉。自我觀之。仁義之端。是非之涂。
樊然殽【殽一作散】亂。吾惡能知其辯。齧缺曰。子不知利害。則至人固不
知利害乎。王倪曰。至人神矣。大澤焚而不能熱。河漢沍而不能寒。疾雷破
山風振海而不能驚。若然者。乘雲氣。騎日月。而遊乎四海之外。死生無變
於己。而況利害之端乎。瞿鵲子問乎長梧子曰。吾聞諸夫子。聖人不從事於
務。不就利。不違害。不喜求。不緣道。無謂有謂。有謂無謂。而遊【遊一
作施】乎塵垢之外。夫子以爲孟浪之言。而我以爲妙道之行也。吾子以爲奚
若。長梧子曰。是皇【皇一作黃】帝之所聽熒【聽熒一作灑榮，熒一作瑩】
也。而丘也何足以知之。且女亦大早計。見卵而求時夜。見彈而求鴞炙。予
嘗爲女妄言之。女以妄聽之矣。旁【旁一作謗】日月。挾【挾一作扶】宇
宙。爲其脗【脗一作㳷】合。置其滑【滑一作汩】涽【涽一作潘】。以隸相
尊。衆人役役。聖人愚芚。參萬歲而一成純。萬物盡然。而以是相蘊【蘊一
作緼】。予惡乎知說生之非惑邪。予惡乎知惡死之非弱喪而不知歸者邪。麗
之姬。艾封人之子也。晉國之始得之也。涕泣沾襟。及其至於王所。與王同
筐【筐一作匡】床。食芻豢。而後悔其泣也。予惡乎知夫死者不悔其始之蘄
生乎。夢飲酒者。旦而哭泣。夢哭泣者。旦而田獵。方其夢也。不知其夢
也。夢之中又占其夢焉。覺而後知其夢也。且有大覺而後知此其大夢也。而
愚者自以爲覺。竊竊然知之。君乎牧乎。固哉。丘也與女皆夢也。予謂女夢
亦夢也。是其言也。其名爲弔詭。萬世之後。而一遇大聖知其解者。是旦暮
遇之也。既使我與若辯矣。若勝我。我不若勝。若果是也。我果非也邪。我
勝若。若不吾勝。我果是也。而果非也邪。其或是也。其或非也邪。其俱是
也。其俱非也邪。我與若不能相知也。則人固受其黮闇。吾誰使正之。使同

乎若者正之。既與若同矣。惡能正之。使同乎我者正之。既同乎我矣。惡能
正之。使異乎我與若者正之。既異乎我與若矣。惡能正之。使同乎我與若者
正之。既同乎我與若矣。惡能正之。然則我與若與人俱不能相知也。而待彼
也邪。何謂和之以天倪【倪一作霓】。曰。是不是。然不然。是若果是也。
則是之異乎不是也亦無辯。然若果然也。則然之異乎不然也亦無辯。化聲之
相待。若其不相待。和之以天倪。因之以曼衍。所以窮年也。忘年忘義。振
於無竟【竟一作境】。故寓諸無竟。罔兩【兩一作浪】問景【景一作影】
曰。曩子行。今子止。曩子坐。今子起。何其無特【特一作持】操與。景
曰。吾有待而然者邪。吾所待又有待而然者邪。吾待蛇蚹蜩翼邪。惡識所以
然。惡識所以不然。昔者莊周夢爲胡蝶。栩栩【栩一作翩】然胡蝶也。自喻
適志與。不知周也。俄然覺。則蘧蘧【蘧蘧一作據據】然周也。不知周之夢
爲胡蝶與。胡蝶之夢爲周與。周與胡蝶則必有分矣。此之謂物化。

Reprinted from William Hung et al., *A Concordance to Chuang Tzŭ* 莊子引得. *Sinological Index Series*, suppl. no. 20 (Peip'ing: Harvard-Yenching Institute 哈佛燕京學社, 1931–47)

般若波羅蜜多心經[1]

唐[2] 三藏法師玄奘[3] 譯

觀自在菩薩。行深般若波羅蜜多時。照見五蘊皆空。度一切苦厄。舍利子。
色不異空。空不異色。色即是空。空即是色。受想行識亦復如此。舍利子。
是諸法空相。不生不滅。不垢不淨。不增不減。是故空中。無色。無受想行
識。無眼耳鼻舌身意。無色聲香味觸法。無眼界。乃至無意識界。無無明。
亦無無明盡。乃至無老死。亦無老死盡。無苦集滅道。無智亦無得。以無所
得故。菩提薩埵。依般若波羅蜜多故。心無罣礙。無罣礙故。無有恐怖。遠
離顛倒夢想。究竟涅槃。三世諸佛。依般若波羅蜜多故。得阿耨多羅三藐三
菩提。故知般若波羅蜜多。是大神咒。是大明咒是無上咒。是無等等咒。能
除一切苦。眞實不虛故。說般若波羅蜜多咒。即說咒曰

[4] 揭帝[5] 揭帝[5]　　般f羅揭帝[5]　　般[6]羅僧揭帝[5] 菩提僧莎[7] 訶
般若波羅蜜多心經

1. Prajñāpāramitā hṛudaya　2. 一作〔唐〕　3. 奘下一有（奉詔）4. 咒文 Gate gate
pāragate pārasamgate bodhi Svāhā.　　5. 帝一作諦　　6. 般一作波　　7. 僧莎一作薩婆

Reprinted from Takakusu Junjirō 高楠順次郎, Watanabe Kaigyoku 渡辺海旭, and Ono Gemmyō
小野玄妙, eds., *Taishō shinshū daizōkyō* 大正新修大藏經, 100 vols. (Tokyo: Taishō issaikyō kankōkai,
1924–35), vol. 8, no. 251, p. 848.

自京赴奉先縣詠懷五百字

【唐】 杜 甫
（天寶十四載十一月初作）

杜陵有布衣老大意轉拙許身一何愚【樊作過】竊比稷與契居然成濩落白首甘【一云苦】契闊蓋棺事則已此志常覬豁窮年憂黎元嘆息腸【一作腹】內熱取笑同學翁浩歌彌激烈非無江海志蕭洒送【一作迭】日月生逢堯舜君【一云堯為君】不忍便永訣當今廊廟具構廈豈云缺葵藿傾太陽物性固莫【一作難】奪顧惟螻蟻輩但自求其穴胡為慕大鯨輒擬偃溟渤以茲悟生理獨恥事干謁兀兀遂至今忍為塵埃沒終愧巢與由未能易其節沉飲聊自適【一作遣】放歌頗愁絕歲暮百草零疾風高岡裂天衢陰崢嶸客子中夜發霜嚴衣帶斷指直不得【一作能】結凌晨過驪山御榻在嵽嵲蚩尤塞寒空蹴踏崖谷滑瑤池氣鬱律羽林相摩戛君臣【一云聖君】留懽娛樂動殷膠葛【荊作膠葛 一作蠐螬 一作福崱嵲 一作湯嶍】賜浴皆長纓與宴【一作謀】非短褐彤庭所分帛本自寒女出鞭撻【一作箠】其夫家聚斂貢城闕聖人筐篚恩實欲【一作願】邦國活臣如忽至理君豈棄此物多士盈朝廷仁者宜戰慄況聞內金盤盡在衛霍室中堂舞【一作有】神仙煙霧散【一作蒙】玉質煖客【一云蒙】貂鼠裘悲管逐清瑟勸客駝蹄羹霜橙壓香橘朱門酒肉【一作禽】臭路有凍死骨榮枯咫尺異惆悵難再述北轅就涇渭官渡又改轍群冰【一作水】從西下極目高崒兀疑是崆峒來恐觸天杜折河梁宰牟坼枝橰聲窸窣行旅相攀援川廣不【一作且】可越老妻寄異縣十口隔風雪誰能久不顧庶往共飢渴入門聞號咷幼子飢【一作餓】已卒吾寧舍一哀里巷亦【陳作猶】嗚咽所愧為人父無食致夭折豈知秋未【一作禾】登貧窶有倉卒生常免租稅名不隸征伐撫迹猶【一作獨】酸辛平人固騷屑默思失業徒因念遠戍卒憂端齊【一作際】終南澒洞不可掇

Reprinted from Du Fu 杜甫, *Du Gongbu ji* 杜工部集 (Hong Kong: Zhonghua shuju 中華書局, 1972).

鶯鶯傳（又名會眞記）
《太平廣記》

【唐】　元　稹

　　貞元中，有張生者，性溫茂，美丰容。內秉堅孤，非禮不可入。或朋從游宴，擾雜其間，他人皆洶洶拳拳，若將不及，張生容順而已，終不能亂。以是年二十三，未嘗近女色。知者詰之。謝而言曰：“登徒子非好色者，是有淫行。余眞好色者，而適不我值。何以言之？大凡物之尤者，未嘗不流連於心，是知非忘情者也。”詰者哂之。

　　亡幾何，張生游於蒲。蒲之東十餘里，有僧舍曰普救寺，張生寓焉。適有崔氏孀婦，將歸長安，路出于蒲，亦止茲寺。崔氏婦，鄭女也。張出于鄭，緒其親，乃異派之從母。是歲，渾瑊薨於蒲。有中人丁文雅，不善於軍，軍人因喪而擾，大掠蒲人。崔氏之家，財產甚厚，多奴僕，旅寓惶駭，不知所托。先是，張與蒲將之黨友善，請吏護之，遂不及於難。十餘日，廉使杜確將天子命以統戎節，令於軍，軍由是戢。鄭厚張之德甚，因飾饌以命張，中堂宴之。復謂張曰：“姨之孤嫠未亡，提攜幼稚。不幸屬師徒大潰，實不保其身。弱子幼女，猶君之生也，豈可比常恩哉！今俾以仁兄禮奉見，冀所以報恩也。”命其子，曰歡郎。可十餘歲，容甚溫美。次命女：“出拜爾兄，爾兄活爾。”久之，辭疾。鄭怒曰：“張兄保爾之命。不然，爾且擄矣。能復遠嫌乎？”久之，乃至。常服悴容，不加新飾，垂鬟接黛，雙臉銷紅而已。顏色艷異，光輝動人。張驚，爲之禮。因坐鄭旁。以鄭之抑而見也，凝睇怨絕，若不勝其體者。問其年紀，鄭曰：“今天子甲子歲之七月，終今貞元庚辰，生十七年矣。”張生稍以詞導之，不對。終席而罷。張自是惑之，願致其情，無由得也。

　　崔之婢曰紅娘。生私爲之禮者數四，乘間遂道其衷。婢果驚沮，腆然而奔。張生悔之。翌日，婢復至。張生乃羞而謝之，不復云所求矣。婢因謂張曰：“郎之言，所不敢言，亦不敢泄。然而崔之族姻，君所詳也。何不因其德而求娶焉？”張曰：“予始自孩提，性不苟合。或時紈綺閒居，曾莫流盼。不爲當年，終有所蔽、昨日一席間，幾不自持。數日來行忘止，食忘飽，恐不能逾旦暮，若因媒氏而娶，納采問名，則三數月間，索我於枯魚之肆矣。爾其謂我何？”婢曰：“崔之貞慎自保，雖所尊不可以非語犯之；下人之謀，故難入矣。然而善屬文，往往沉吟章句，怨慕者久之。君試爲喻情詩以亂之。不然，則無由也。”張大喜，立綴“春詞”二首以投之。是夕，紅娘復至，持綵箋以授張，曰：“崔所命也。”題其篇曰：“明月三五夜”。其詞曰：

待月西廂下，迎風戶半開。拂牆花影動，疑是玉人來。

張亦微喻其旨。是夕歲二月旬有四日矣。

崔之東有杏花一樹，攀援可踰。既望之夕，張因梯其樹而踰焉。達於西廂，則戶半開矣。紅娘寢於床，生因驚之。紅娘駭曰：“郎何以至？”張因紿之曰：“崔氏之箋召我也，爾爲我告之。”無幾，紅娘復來，連曰：“至矣至矣！”張生且喜且駭，必謂獲濟。及崔至，則端服嚴容，大數張曰：“兄之恩，活我之家厚矣。是以慈母以弱子幼女見托。奈何因不令之婢，致淫逸之詞？始以護人之亂爲義，而終掠亂以求之；是以亂易亂，其去幾何？誠欲寢其詞，則保人之姦，不義。明之於母，則背人之惠，不祥。將寄於婢僕，又懼不得發其眞誠，是用託短章，願白陳啓。猶懼兄之見難，是用鄙靡之詞，以求其必。至非禮之動，能不愧心。特願以禮自持，無及於亂！”言畢，翻然而逝。張自失者久之，復踰而出。於是絕望。

數夕，張生臨軒獨寢，忽有人覺之。驚駭而起，則紅娘斂衾攜枕而至，撫張曰：“至矣，至矣！睡何爲哉！”並枕重衾而去。張生拭目危坐久之，猶疑夢寐，然而修謹以俟。俄而紅娘捧崔氏而至。至則嬌羞融冶，力不能運支體，曩時端壯，不復同矣。是夕，旬有八日也。斜月晶瑩，幽輝半床。張生飄飄然，且疑神仙之徒，不謂從人間至矣。有頃，寺鐘鳴，天將曉。紅娘促去，崔氏嬌啼宛轉，紅娘又捧之而去，終夕無一言。張生辨色而興，自疑曰：“豈其夢邪？”及明，睹粧在臂香在衣，淚光熒熒然猶瑩於茵席而已。是後十餘日，杳不復至。張生賦“會眞詩”三十韻，未畢，而紅娘適至，因授之，以貽崔氏。自是復容之。朝隱而出，暮隱而入，同安於曩所謂西廂者，幾一月矣。張生常詰鄭氏之情，則曰：“知不可奈何矣。”因欲就成之。

亡何，張生將之長安，先以情諭之。崔氏宛無難詞，然而愁怨之容動人矣。將行之夕，不復可見，而張生遂西下。

數月，復遊於蒲，舍於崔氏者，又累月。崔氏甚工刀札，善屬文。求索再三，終不可見。往往張生自以文挑之，亦不甚觀覽。大略崔氏之出人者，藝必窮極，而貌若不知；言則敏辯，而寡於酬對。待張之意甚厚，然未嘗以詞繼之。時愁艷幽遠，恒若不識，喜慍之容，亦罕形見。異時獨夜操琴，愁弄悽惻。張竊聽之。求之，則終不復鼓矣，以是愈惑之。

張生俄以文調及期，又當西去。當去之夕，不復自言其情，愁嘆於崔氏之側。崔已陰知將訣矣，恭貌怡聲，徐謂張曰：“始亂之，終棄之，固其宜矣。愚不敢恨。必也君亂之，君終之，君之惠也。則沒身之誓，其有終矣。又何必深感於此行？然而君既不懌，無以奉寧。君常謂我善鼓琴，向時羞顏，所不能及。今且往矣，既君此誠。”因命拂琴，鼓“霓裳羽衣序”。不數聲，哀音怨亂，不復知其是曲也。左右皆歔欷。崔亦遽止之，投琴，泣下流漣，趨歸鄭所，遂不復至。明旦而張行。

　明年，文戰不勝，遂止於京。因貽書於崔，以廣其意。崔氏緘報之詞，粗載於此，云：

　　捧覽來問，撫愛過深。兒女之情，悲喜交集。兼惠花勝一合，口脂五寸，致燿首膏脣之飾。雖荷殊恩，誰復爲容？睹物增懷，但積悲嘆耳！伏承示於京中就業，進修之道，固在便安。但恨僻陋之人，永以遐棄。命也如此，知復何言！自去秋已來，常忽忽如有所失。於諠譁之下，或勉爲語笑，閑宵自處，無不淚零。乃至夢寐之間，亦多感咽離憂之思。綢繆繾綣，暫若尋常。幽會未終，驚魂已斷。雖半衾如煖，而思之甚遙。一昨拜辭，倏逾舊歲。長安行樂之地，觸緒牽情。何幸不忘幽微，眷念無斁。鄙薄之志，無以奉酬。至於終始之盟，則固不忒。憶昔中表相因，或同宴處。婢僕見誘，遂致私誠。兒女之心，不能自固。君子有援琴之挑，鄙人無投梭之拒。及薦寢席，義盛意深。愚陋之情，永謂終託。豈期既見君子，而不能定情；致有自獻之羞，不復明侍巾櫛。沒身永恨，含嘆何言！倘仁人用心，俯遂幽眇，雖死之日，猶生之年。如或達士略情，舍小從大，以先配爲醜行，以要盟爲可欺，則當骨化形銷，丹誠不泯，因風委露，猶託清塵。存沒之誠，言盡於此。臨紙嗚咽，情不能申。千萬珍重，珍重千萬！玉環一枚，是兒嬰年所弄，寄充君子下體所佩。玉取其堅潤不渝；環取其始終不絕。兼亂絲一絇，文竹茶碾子一枚。此數物不足見珍，意者欲君子如玉之眞，俾志如環不解。淚痕在竹，愁緒縈絲。因物達成，永以爲好耳。心邇身遐，拜會無期。幽憤所鍾，千里神合。千萬珍重！春風多厲，彊飯爲佳。慎言自保，無以鄙爲深念！

　張生發其書於所知，由是時人多聞之。所善楊巨源好屬詞，因爲賦“崔孃詩”一絕云：

　　清潤潘郎玉不如，中庭蕙草雪銷初。風流才子多春思，腸斷蕭孃一紙書。

河南元稹亦續生“會眞詩”三十韻，詩曰：

　　微月透簾櫳，螢光度碧空。
　　遙天初縹緲，低樹漸蔥蘢。
　　龍吹過庭竹，鸞歌拂井桐。
　　羅綃垂薄露，環珮響輕風。
　　絳節隨金母，雲心捧玉童。
　　更深人悄悄，晨會雨濛濛。
　　珠瑩光文履，花明隱繡龍。
　　瑤釵行彩鳳，羅帔掩丹虹。
　　言自瑤華浦，將朝碧玉宮。
　　因游洛城北，偶向宋家東。
　　戲調初微拒，柔情已暗通。

　　低環蟬影動，迴步玉塵蒙。
　　轉面流花雪，登床抱綺叢。
　　鴛鴦交頸舞，翡翠合歡籠。
　　眉黛羞偏聚，唇朱暖更融。
　　氣清蘭蕊馥，膚潤玉肌豐。
　　無力慵移腕，多嬌愛斂躬。
　　汗流珠點點，髮亂綠蔥蔥。
　　方喜千年會，俄聞五夜窮。
　　留連時有限，繾綣意難終。
　　慢臉含愁態，芳詞誓素衷。
　　贈環明運合，留結表心同。
　　啼粉流宵鏡，殘燈遠闇蟲。
　　華光猶苒苒，旭日漸瞳瞳。
　　乘鶩還歸洛，吹簫亦上嵩。
　　衣香猶染麝，枕膩尚殘紅。
　　冪冪臨塘草，飄飄思渚蓬。
　　素琴鳴怨鶴，清漢望歸鴻。
　　海闊誠難度，天高不易衝。
　　行雲無處所，蕭史在樓中。

　　張之友聞之者，莫不聳異之，然而張亦志絕矣。稹特與張厚，因徵其詞。張曰：“大凡天之所命尤物也，不妖其身，必妖於人。使崔氏子遇合富貴，乘寵嬌，不爲雲爲雨，則爲蛟爲螭，吾不知其所變化矣。昔殷之辛，周之幽，據百萬之國，其勢甚厚。然而一女子敗之，潰其眾，屠其身，至今爲天下僇笑。余之德不足以勝妖孽，是用忍情。”於時坐者皆爲深嘆。

　　後歲餘，崔已委身於人，張亦有所娶。適經所居，乃因其夫言於崔，求以外兄見。夫語之，而崔終不爲出。張怨念之誠，動於顏色。崔知之，潛賦一章，詞曰：

　　　　自從別後減容光，萬轉千迴懶下床。不爲旁人羞不起，爲郎憔悴
　　卻羞郎。

　　竟不之見。後數日，張生將行，又賦一章，以謝絕云：

　　　　棄置今何道，當時且自親。還將舊來意，憐取眼前人。

　　自是，絕不復知矣。

　　時人多許張爲善補過者。予嘗於朋會之中，往往及此意者，使夫知者不爲，爲之者不惑。貞元歲九月，執事李公垂宿於予靖安里第，語及於是。公垂卓然稱異，遂爲“鶯鶯歌”以傳之。崔氏小名鶯鶯，公垂以命篇。

Reprinted from Bu Wen 卜文, ed., *Zhongguo lidai duanpian xiaoshuo xuan* 中國歷代短篇小說選, *Zhongguo gudian wenxue congshu* 中國古典文學叢書 (Hong Kong: The Shanghai Book Co., 1968).

筆法記

【五代】荆浩　撰

太行山有洪谷，其間數畝之田，吾常耕而食之。有日，登神鉦山，四望迴跡，入大嚴扉，苔徑露水，怪石祥煙，疾進其處，皆古松也。中獨圍大者，皮老蒼蘚，翔麟乘空，蟠虬之勢，欲附雲漢。成林者，爽氣重榮；不能者，抱節自屈。或迴根出土，或偃截巨流，掛岸盤溪，披苔裂石。因驚其異，遍而賞之。明日，攜筆復寫之，凡數萬本，方如其眞。明年春，來於石鼓岩間遇一叟，因問，具以其來所由而答之。

叟曰："子知筆法乎？"曰："叟，儀形野人也，豈知筆法耶？"叟曰："子豈知吾所懷耶？"聞而慚駭。

叟曰："少年好學，終可成也。夫畫有六要：一曰氣；二曰韻；三曰思；四曰景；五曰筆；六曰墨。"

曰："畫者，華也。但貴似得眞，豈此撓矣！"

叟曰："不然，畫者，畫也。度物象而取其眞。物之華，取其華。物之實，取其實，不可執華爲實。若不知術，苟似可也，圖眞不可及也。"

曰："何以爲似？何以爲眞？"

叟曰："似者，得其形遺其氣，眞者，氣質俱盛。凡氣傳於華，遺於象，象之死也。"

謝曰："故知書畫者，名賢之所學也。耕生知其非本，玩筆取與，終無所成，慙惠受要，定畫不能。"

叟曰："嗜慾者，生之賊也。名賢縱樂琴書，圖畫代去雜慾。子既親善，但期始終所學，勿爲進退。圖畫之要，與子備言：氣者，心隨筆運，取象不惑；韻者，隱跡立形，備儀不俗；思者，刪撥大要，凝想形物；景者，制度時因，搜妙創眞；筆者，雖依法則，運轉變通，不質不形，如飛如動；墨者，高低暈淡，品物淺深，文采自然，似非因筆。"

（叟）復曰："神、妙、奇、巧，神者，亡有所爲，任運成象；妙者，思經天地，萬類性情，文理合儀，品物流筆；奇者，蕩跡不測，與眞景或乖異，致其理偏，得此者，亦爲有筆無思；巧者，雕綴小媚，假合大經，強寫文章，增邈氣象，此謂實不足而華有余。

"凡筆有四勢：謂筋、肉、骨、氣。筆絕而斷謂之筋，起伏成實謂之肉，生死剛正謂之骨，跡畫不敗謂之氣。故知墨大質者失其體；色微者敗正氣，筋死者無肉，跡斷者無筋；苟媚者無骨。

"夫病有二：一曰無形，二曰有形。有形病者，花木不時，屋小人大，或樹高於山，橋不登於岸，可度形之類也。是如此之病，不可改圖。無形之病，氣韻俱泯，物象全乖，筆墨雖行，類同死物，以斯格拙，不可刪修。

"子既好寫雲林山水，須明物象之源。夫木之生，爲受其性。松之生也，枉而不曲遇，如密如竦，匪青匪翠，從微自直，萌心不低。勢既獨高，枝低復偃，倒掛未墜於地下，分層似疊於林間，如君子之德風也。有畫如飛龍蟠虯，狂生枝葉者，非松之氣韻也。柏之生也，動而多屈，繁而不華，捧節有章，文轉隨日，葉如結線，枝似衣麻。有畫如蛇如素，心虛逆轉，亦非也。其有楸、桐、椿、櫟、榆、柳、桑、槐，形質皆異，其如遠思即合，一一分明也。

　　"山水之象，氣勢相生。故尖曰峰，平曰頂，圓曰巒，相連曰嶺，有穴曰岫，峻壁曰崖，崖間崖下曰岩，路通山中曰谷，不通曰峪，峪中有水曰溪，山夾水曰澗。其上峰巒雖異，其下岡嶺相連，掩映林泉，依稀遠近。夫畫山水無此象亦非也。有畫流水，下筆多狂，文如斷線，無片浪高低者，亦非也。夫霧雲煙靄，輕重有時，勢或因風，象皆不定。須去其繁章，采其大要。先能知此是非，然後受其筆法。"

　　曰："自古學人，孰爲備矣？"

　　叟曰："得之者少。謝赫品陸之爲勝今已難遇親蹤；張僧繇所遺之圖，甚虧其理。夫雖類賦彩，自古有能，如水暈墨章，興吾唐代。故張璪員外樹石，氣韻俱盛，筆墨積微。眞思卓然，不貴五彩，曠古絕今，未之有也。麹庭與白雲尊師，氣象微妙，俱得其元，動用逸常，深不可測。王右丞筆墨宛麗，氣韻高清，巧寫象成，亦動眞思。李將軍理深思遠，筆跡甚精，雖巧而華，大虧墨彩。項容山人樹石頑澀，稜角無　　，用墨獨得玄門，用筆全無其骨。然於放逸，不失眞元氣象，元大　　巧媚。吳道子筆勝於象，骨氣自高，樹不言圖，亦恨無墨。陳員外及僧道芬以下，粗昇凡格，作用無奇，筆墨之行，甚有行跡。今示子之徑，不能備詞。"

　　遂取前寫者《異松圖》呈之。叟曰："肉筆無法，筋骨皆不相轉，異松何之能用。我既教子筆法。"乃齎素數幅，令對而寫之。叟曰："爾之手，我之心。吾聞察其言而知其行，子能與我言詠之乎？"謝曰："乃知敎化，聖賢之職也，祿與不祿，而不能去，善惡之跡，感而應之。誘進若此，敢不恭命。"因成《古松贊》曰：

　　"不凋不容，惟彼貞松。勢高而險，屈節以恭。葉張翠蓋，枝盤赤龍。下有蔓草，幽陰蒙茸。如何得生，勢近雲峰。仰其擢幹，偃擧千重。巍巍溪中，翠暈煙籠。奇枝倒掛，徘徊變通。下接凡木，和而不同。以貴詩賦，君子之風。風清匪歇，幽音凝空。"

　　叟嗟異久之，曰："願子勤之，可忘筆墨，而有眞景，吾之所居，即石鼓岩間，所字即石鼓岩子也。"曰："願從侍之。"叟曰："不必然也。"遂亟辭而去。別日訪之而無蹤。後習其筆術，嘗重所傳，今遂修集以爲圖畫之軌轍耳。

Reprinted from Wang Bomin 王伯敏, ed., *Zhongguo hualun congshu* 中國畫論叢書 (Beijing: Renmin meishu chubanshe 人民美術出版社, 1963).

CONTRIBUTORS

Peter K. Bol is Professor of Chinese History and Chair of the Department of East Asian Languages and Civilizations at Harvard University.

Katherine Carlitz is affiliated with the Department of East Asian Languages and Literatures at the University of Pittsburgh. She is the author of *The Rhetoric of Chin P'ing Mei,* and has published articles on Ming dynasty fiction and drama and on the Ming dynasty cult of women's virtue. Currently she is writing a book about a sixteenth-century exemplar of that cult, and doing research on late Ming literati drama publishing.

Michael Fuller is Associate Professor of Chinese Literature in the Department of East Asian Languages and Literatures of the University of California, Irvine. He is the author of *The Road to Eastslope: The Development of Su Shi's Poetic Voice* (1990) and *An Introduction to Literary Chinese* (1999), as well as a chapter, "Sung Dynasty Shih Poetry," in the *Columbia History of Traditional Chinese Literature* (forthcoming).

David R. Knechtges is Professor of Chinese in the Department of Asian Languages and Literature at the University of Washington. He is the author of *Two Studies on the Han Fu* (1968), *The Han Rhapsody: A Study of the Fu of Yang Xiong* (1976), *The Han Shu Biography of Yang Xiong* (1982), and numerous articles. Three volumes of his projected eight-volume translation of the *Wen xuan* have been published by Princeton University Press.

Wai-yee Li teaches Chinese literature at Harvard University. She is the author of *Enchantment and Disenchantment: Love and Illusion in Chinese Literature* (1993). She is now at work on a book entitled *The Readability of the Past in Early Chinese Historiography.*

Stephen Owen is James Bryant Conant University Professor and teaches in the Departments of East Asian Languages and Civilizations and Comparative Literature at Harvard University.

Willard Peterson is Professor of East Asian Studies and History at Princeton University.

Martin Powers is Sally Michelson-Davidson Professor of Chinese Arts and Cultures at the University of Michigan. In 1991 his *Art and Political Expression in Early China* received the Joseph Levenson Prize for the best book in pre-twentieth-century Chinese studies. He is completing a book tracing the ideological uses of ornament during China's transition from feudalism to a bureaucratic state in classical times, entitled *Graphic Paradigms of Self*.

Lynn Struve, Professor of History and of East Asian Languages and Cultures at Indiana University, was trained as an undergraduate in Chinese language and literature at the University of Washington and as a graduate student in Chinese area studies and in premodern Chinese history at the University of Michigan. Her research focuses on the political and intellectual history of seventeenth-century China, particularly the dynastic transition from Ming to Qing and the scholarship of Huang Zongxi.

Stephen F. Teiser is Professor in the Department of Religion at Princeton University. He is the author of *The Ghost Festival in Medieval China* (1988) and *"The Scripture on the Ten Kings" and the Making of Purgatory in Medieval Chinese Buddhism* (1994).

Stephen H. West is Professor of Chinese Literature in the Department of East Asian Languages at the University of California, Berkeley.

Pauline Yu is Professor of Chinese Literature in the Department of East Asian Languages and Cultures and Dean of Humanities in the College of Letters and Science at UCLA.

INDEX

Analects, 3, 125, 152, 161; cited, 4, 208, 212.
    See also Confucius
Ānanda, 132
Aristotle, 81
authenticity, 234–35, 236, 237; vs. likeness,
    204; in representation, 203–4, 232,
    239–40; 214; vs. Truth, 229, 235
Avalokiteśvara (Guanyin), 119, 132, 133,
    134, 136, 138

Bailey, Sir H. W., 126
Ban Biao, 156
Ban Gu, 3
Bauer, Wolfgang, 161
Baxter, William R., 15, 16
"Bei zheng fu" (Northward Journey), 156
Bi fa ji (Notes on the Method for the Brush):
    scene of instruction in, 213–14; Tang
    pedagogic mode in, 214, 215
Biography of Yingying. See *Yingying zhuan*
Bo Juyi, 196, 200, 215
Bo Ya, 218
Bo Yi, 47, 53
Bol, Peter, 233
bu dong xin (unmoved or unstirred heart),
    41, 49
Buddhism: Indian, 133; Mahāyāna, 133,
    135, 136

Cai Yong, 156
Cao Zhi, 154, 188

"Chanting Alone in the Mountains," 215
Chaofu, 155, 156, 161, 167
Chen Xuanying, 74, 75, 76, 96
Chen Yinke, 185, 187, 191
Chen Zhaoxiu, 221
Cheng Yaotian, 23, 24
Chow Tse-tsung, 20
chuanqi genre, 184, 185–86, 192
classic (*jing*), concept of, 26
Confucius (Kongzi): cited, 4, 86, 99; por-
    trayed as sage, 44, 53–54, 56. See also
    Analects

Da xue (*Great Learning*), 164
dao: as a Daoist concept, 96, 102; early
    concept of, 30
Daya, 29, 30
"Dengtu zi haose fu" (*Fu* on Master Dengtu
    Enamored of Beauty), 188
dialogue: in *Mencius*, 54, 55, 56; in *Zhuangzi*,
    98–99, 100
"Diao Qu Yuan" (Lament for Qu Yuan), 154
dragons, representations of, 82–87, 108–9
Du Fu, 150; attitude toward commoners,
    163–64; as historian-poet, 165, 169,
    170–71; as influenced by Mencius, 163–
    64; lamentation of personal tragedy
    vs. public misery, 159–60, 169–70;
    self-characterized as *huoluo* (unwieldy
    and useless) gourd, 152, 166; self-
    comparison to Ji and Xie, 152, 165;

Du Fu (*continued*)
   self–image as whale or ant, 154, 167,
      169; self-portrayal as loyal subject, 153–
      54; view of reclusion, 155–56, 161. See
      also *Zi jing fu Fengxian yong huai wu bai zi*
Du gongbu ji, 150, 171
Du Mu, 196
Duan Yucai, 23

Early Chinese Texts on Painting, 237
emptiness, 133–34, 136; vs. appearance
      (or form), 124, 127, 141
Erya, 18

fiction, dangers of, 184–85
figure and ground distinctions, 80, 81,
      82–83, 223, 224
flood-like *qi*. See *Mencius*
Frede, Michael, 106, 112
fu on travel, 156
Fu Sinian, 16
Fukui, Fumimasa, 137
Fung Yu-lan, 3

Gao Heng, 18, 31, 32
"Gaotang fu" (*Fu* on Gaotang), 188
gesture, 225–26, 228, 240
"Going from the Capital to Fengxian." See
      Zi jing fu Fengxian yong huai wu bai zi
Graham, A. C., 72, 76, 79, 92, 98, 222, 223
Guanzi, 87
Guo Shaoyu, 3
Guo Xi, 236
Guo Xiang, 73, 75
Guofeng, 28
Guoyu, 87

Halperin, Richard, 28
Han Feizi, 7, 85, 89, 90, 91
Han Yu, 200, 201
Hanfei. See *Han Feizi*
Hansen, Chad, 79, 80, 92, 222
Heart Sūtra. See *Xin jing*
hermeneutics, 34
History of the Han Dynasty, 3
Homer, 29
Hon, Tze-ki, 162
Hong lou meng, 195
Hu Yuan, 162

Huainanzi, 87, 91
Huang Tingjian, 127, 128
Huang Zongxi, 162
Huayan jing, 128
Huizi, 150
Huizhong, 120
Huo Cunfu, 88

identity of things, 80, 81–84, 223–25
image. See *xiang*

Jia Yi, 154
Jiang Yan, 153
Jiao Hong ji, 194, 196, 197
"Jie chao" (Defense against Ridicule), 152,
      153
Jingfa, 87, 88, 89, 91
Jingshi tongyan, 129
Journey to the West, 127

Karlgren, Bernhard, 17, 18, 19, 21, 22, 23,
      27, 32
Kong Yingda, 21, 162
Kumarajīva, 139

Laozi, 7; compared to a dragon, 86–87
Li Fang-kuei, 22
Li ji, 20
Li Zhi, 124, 127
Liezi, 218
Liu Xie, 221
Liu Xin, 16, 156
Liu Zongyuan, 200
Lord, Albert B., 26
Lu Tanwei, 210
"Luoshen fu" (*Fu* on the Goddess of the
      River Luo), 188
Lüshi chunqiu, 20, 87

Ma Ruichen, 19, 23, 24
Mao Chang, 15
Mao Commentary, 15, 17, 18, 19, 21, 22,
      23, 24
Mao Heng, 15, 20
Mao shi, 14, 15. See also *Shijing*
Mao shi zhuan jian, 15, 16
Mencius, 125, 163, 164, 208; comparison
      among Confucius's, Bo Yi's, and Yi Yin's
      sagely ways, 44, 47, 53; discussion of *bu*

dong xin (unmoved or unstirred heart) in, 41, 49; discussion of "flood-like *qi*" in, 42, 46, 51, 52; moral righteousness, 51; relation between *qi* and heart, 42, 50–51; relation between the will and *qi*, 42, 46; verbal transmission of the past, 56; *zhi yan* ("know words" or insight into words), 43, 47, 52, 53, 57

Mencius (Mengzi): having an unmoved heart, 45; as a sage, 55

Mingyi daifang lu, 162

Munakata, Kiyohiko, 237, 238, 240, 243

Nattier, Jan, 141

nirvāna, 136

"Notes on the Method for the Brush." See *Bi fa ji*

oral transmission, 26

Outlines of Pyrrhonism, 103, 104, 105, 106

Ouyang Xiu, 207

Owen, Stephen, 199, 223, 224, 228

painting: as an aesthetic pastime, 215; landscape elements of, 209; *qi* in, 215, 216; representation of distance in, 228–29; six essentials of, 204, 205, 209–10, 216, 219; spirit in, 205

Pan Yue, 151, 156, 157, 158

Parry, Milman, 26

passions, problems of, 192, 196, 200, 201

Peerenboom, R. P., 88, 89

perfection of wisdom, 133, 136–37, 143

performative texts, 6

pine: as cultural and ethical symbol, 212–13, 219, 220, 239, 243; as supernal object, 203, 238

Qi wu lun (Seeing Things as Equal): concept of *ziran* (self-so), 81–82; formal structure of, 77–78; impossibility of knowledge, 99–100, 102, 107; instability of reference, 95–96; loss of self, 93–94; notion of language, 96–97, 101; notion of prime mover, 80–81; perspective, 79–80, 81, 86; on the relation between body and spirit, 74; relation between "other" and "me," 79, 80; on speech act, 76–77

qiyun (spirit resonance), 221

Qu Wanli, 19, 31, 38

Qu Yuan, 5

Reynolds, Sir Joshua, 232, 233

Ruan Ji, 150, 155, 156

Sanjia shi, 15

Śāriputra, 133, 136

scholar and beauty romance, 193

"Seeing Things as Equal." See *Qi wu lun*

Serruys, Paul L-M, 18

service vs. withdrawal, 161–62, 166

Sextus Empiricus, 103, 104, 105, 109, 112

Shanhai jing, 202

Sheng min (*Mao* 245): agrarian aristocracy, 28; Hou Ji as both plant and human, 28, 29; itemization of things, 29, 30, 38; lineage of Hou Ji, 19; naming phases of reproduction, 28; notion of *min*, 26–27, 33; performance of ritual in, 39; as a ritual poem, 19–20, 26, 30, 32–34, 37, 38, 39; working with natural process, 30

Shenglei, 73

"Shennü fu" (*Fu* on the Goddess), 188

Shi ji (Records of the Historian), 26, 27, 29

Shi jing yi yi, 31

Shi Yuanzhi, 128

Shijing: compilation into a collection, 14, 16; Mao text of, 14, 15; oral transmission of, 16, 26; phonological studies of, 15–16; Zheng Xuan's use of variant interpretations, 15, 35

—odes cited or discussed: "Fu tian" (*Mao* 211) 18; "Da tian" (*Mao* 212), 24; "Si wen Hou Ji" (*Mao* 275), 34; "Zaishan" (*Mao* 290), 29, 31; "Bi gong" (*Mao* 300), 34. See also *Sheng min*

Shipin, 210

Shu jing, 87

"Shu xing fu" (Relating a Journey), 156

Shuihu zhuan, 129

Shun, King, 48, 53, 56, 153, 166

Shuowen jiezi, 15, 22, 23, 73

Sima Biao, 74

Sima Chengzhen, 210

Sima Qian, 191

skandha (Five Aggregates or Heaps), 123, 133–34

skepticism, 104–6, 109–11
Song Yu, 188
Ssu Hsiu-wu, 89
Su Shi, 127, 128, 236
"Sui chu fu" (On Fulfilling My Original Resolve), 156

Tang intellectual culture, 199–200, 201
Tao Yuanming, 202, 207
Turner, Karen, 88

Waley, Arthur, 23, 32
Wang, C. H., 18, 26
Wang, Wengao, 128
Wang, Xiaobo, 88
Wang Bomin, 237
Wang Li, 17
Wang shi hua yuan, 237
Wang Shizhen, 237
Wang Wei, 210
Warring States, 82; visual culture in, 82–86, 92
Wen, King, 33, 48
Wen Yiduo, 21
Wenxin diaolong, "Tixing" chapter (Nature and Normative Form), 217
Wu, King, 33
Wu Daozi, 211
wuwei (non-interference), 89

Xi Kang, 155
"Xi zheng fu" (Westward Journey), 156
"Xian ju fu," 151
xiang (image), 217, 218–19, 234; definitions of, 214, 226–28, 239–42; relation to object, 219–21
Xiang Rong, 210, 211
Xie He, 209, 210
Xin jing (Heart Sūtra): anomalies of Xuanzang's version of, 132; authorship of Xuanzang's version of, 140–41; dialectic of, 141–44; influence on Chinese poetry and poetic criticism, 127–28; as mantra (spell), 126–27, 129, 137, 144; skandha (Five Aggregates or Heaps), 123, 133–34; syntax of compared to Confucian Classics, 124–25; Xuanzang's translation of, 140
Xu You, 155, 156, 161, 167

Xuanzang, 119, 120, 132, 140, 141
Xuanzong, Emperor, 157

Yang Bojun, 212
"Yang sheng lun" (Discourse on Nurturing Life), 155
Yang Xiong, 152, 153
Yanzi, 85
Yao, King, 48, 53, 56, 153, 166
Yi Yin, 47, 53
Yijing (Zhou yi or Book of Changes), 84, 87, 161, 162, 206, 207, 226, 228, 241
Yingying zhuan (Biography of Yingying): conception of beautiful women in, 181, 183, 186; dramatic adaptations of, 197; motif of abandoned woman in, 190; narrative adaptation of, 193–97; portrayal of Yingying as a goddess in, 188–90; texts within the text of, 184; as a writerly text, 184, 199; as Yuan Zhen's autobiography, 183, 187–88, 191
"Yong huai," 155
yonghuai genre, 150, 165
"Youxian ku" (Wandering in the Caves of the Immortals), 188
Yu Guanying, 19
Yu, Pauline, 228
Yu Yue, 74
Yuan Zhen, 199. See also Yingying zhuan
Yutai xinyong (New Songs from the Jade Terrace), 188

"Za ti" (Miscellaneous Imitations), 153
Zhang Wencheng, 188
Zhang Zao, 210
Zhao Yanwei, 185, 191
Zheng Xuan, 15, 18, 20, 21, 22, 24, 29, 35
zhi yan. See Mencius
Zhong qing li ji (An Elegant Compendium of Sentiments Conjoined), 192, 193, 195, 196, 197, 198
Zhong Rong, 210
Zhongguo hualun congshu, 237
Zhongzi Qi, 218
Zhou, Duke of, 33
Zhou Song, 29, 30
Zhuangzi, 4, 72, 85, 101, 129, 143, 150, 152, 161, 166, 234; literary style of, 79. See also Qi wu lun

—passages of chapters cited or discussed: "All Under Heaven," 7, 95–96; "Free and Easy Wandering," 93, 150–51, 152; "The Great Ancestral Teacher," 94, 102

Zi jing fu Fengxian yong huai wu bai zi (Going from the Capital to Fengxian): contradic-tory positions or assertions in, 150, 152, 154, 160–61, 165–67, 171; date of composition, 150, 167, 171

zifan (self-reflection), 56

Zuo zhuan, 23, 87, 125

Zürcher, Erik, 139